1300mN
01

THE ECONOMIC DEVELOPMENT OF *Spain*

Report of a Mission Organized by the
International Bank for Reconstruction and Development
at the Request of
the Government of Spain

THE ECONOMIC DEVELOPMENT

OF SPAIN

PUBLISHED FOR The International Bank for Reconstruction and Development
BY The Johns Hopkins Press, Baltimore

THE MISSION

Sir Hugh Ellis-Rees, K.C.M.G., C.B., Mission Chief

Benjamin B. King,	Chief Economist
Warren C. Baum,	Economist
Kenneth A. Bohr,	Industrial Economist
P. Caralp,	Adviser on Railways
Eric Carlson,	Adviser on Urban Development
Alberto Castagnola,	Industrial Economist
Howard J. Craven,	Public Finance Economist
Duncan S. Ferguson,	Adviser on Irrigation
Kurt Krapf,	Adviser on Tourism
Karlheinz Mentzner,	Adviser on Highways
Ralph E. Rechel,	Transport Economist
Franco Rotondi,	Adviser on Agricultural Production
Lorne T. Sonley,	Agricultural Economist
Giuseppe Tardini,	Adviser on Electric Power
B. Samuel van Deinse,	Adviser on Maritime Shipping and Ports
H. David Davis,	Editor

PREFACE

This is the report of an economic survey mission to Spain which was organized by the International Bank for Reconstruction and Development at the request of the Government of Spain. The basic objective of the mission, as agreed by the Government and the Bank, was to assist the Spanish Administration in the preparation of a long-term development program designed to expand and modernize the Spanish economy and thereby to raise the standard of living of the Spanish people while, at the same time, maintaining financial stability.

The mission consisted of seventeen members from seven countries. After a briefing session in Washington, the mission arrived in Spain in March 1961 and remained there until mid-June. After leaving Spain, the mission reassembled in Washington to prepare its report. Mr. Lee Austin, who served as Adviser on Industry while the mission was in Spain, subsequently resigned. In late May 1962, the Mission Chief and several other members of the mission returned to Spain for further consultations.

The mission is grateful for the cooperation it received from the Spanish Government. The Mission Chief had the honor of being received by the Head of State. Ministers and their staffs were available for discussions which were most helpful to the mission's work. Discussions were also held with the leading officials of various autonomous public organizations, with representatives of many regional and local agencies, with private industrial, agricultural, commercial and banking interests, with chambers of commerce, with officials of many syndicates and with a large number of private individuals.

The mission worked in close collaboration with Mr. Louis Armand and Mr. Xavier Dorsch, who served as consultants to the Spanish Government on matters of organization and operation of the railroads and highways respectively, as well as with members of their staffs. The mission also gratefully acknowledges the assistance it received, in the form of consulting advice and special studies, from Professor Pasquale Saraceno of the Instituto Per La Recostruzione Industriale (IRI) of Rome and from officials of the Associazione Per Lo Sviluppo Dell' Industria Nel Mezzogiorno (SVIMEZ), also of Rome.

While in Spain, the mission members traveled extensively throughout the country, visiting a large number of development projects and viewing a wide range of economic activities.

This report is divided into six sections: the first and second offer comments on public policies for development and the ways in which the Government can in general guide the economy, while the remaining four sections deal respectively with transportation, agriculture, industry and power and other sectors. However, the various sections of this report—like the various sectors of the Spanish economy—should be regarded as an interrelated whole. The later sections should be considered against the background of the earlier ones and in relation one to the other. The principal points of these six sections are set forth in the summary which precedes the report.

In transmitting the report to the Government of Spain, the President of the Bank noted that, since the Executive Directors and the management customarily do not review the recommendations of economic survey missions in detail, the report as transmitted represents the views of the mission rather than those of the Bank. The President added, however, that he believed that the findings of the report deserved the most careful consideration and discussion.

CONTENTS

ix

SECTION III. TRANSPORTATION

SECTION IV. AGRICULTURE

SECTION V. INDUSTRY AND POWER

SECTION VI. OTHER SECTORS

LIST OF MAPS

SUMMARY

SUMMARY

The following Summary is designed to provide a brief account of the general lines of the report and its principal recommendations. By its nature it cannot cover all the recommendations, nor can it explain adequately the reasoning behind them. Its purpose, therefore, is not in any way to replace the full text, without which the mission's proposals cannot be properly understood or used as a guide in formulating policies and carrying them out.

Section I

DEVELOPMENT POLICY

ECONOMIC GROWTH AND OBJECTIVES

1. The Spanish economy has in recent years been expanding at a good pace and moving steadily in the direction of greater economic interdependence with the rest of the world and, more specifically, closer integration with the European economy. The most significant step in this direction was the stabilization program of 1959. Following the success of this program, the Government's economic policy has been increasingly directed toward the long-range development of the economy. It was against this background that the Spanish Government asked the International Bank for Reconstruction and Development to appoint a mission to make recommendations which would assist it in preparing a development program.

2. The report of the mission sent to Spain by the International Bank for Reconstruction and Development is based on the view that the most appropriate type of planning at this juncture in Spain is "indicative" planning. Under this kind of planning, the Government does not attempt to order every aspect of economic life. Its role is rather:

a. to propose a rate of growth for the economy as a whole and work out the implications of that proposal for the principal economic magnitudes and for the growth of the principal sectors;

b. to state the actions it proposes as a consequence, to take in respect to its economic policies toward both the public and

3

private sectors and to those investments for which it is responsible in order to achieve and sustain the indicated rate of growth.

3. The report of the mission is intended to serve as a step in the process of planning of this kind. Such planning must be viewed as a continuous process through which programs and policies are regularly reviewed and evolved on the basis of subsequent developments and as more information becomes available.

4. The development program must, of course, be prepared and reviewed continuously in the light of the general objectives of the Government. There may be some occasions when different economic and social objectives may appear to be inconsistent with each other. It is necessary, therefore, to weigh carefully the consequences of different courses of action. A particular case is the relief of either rural or regional poverty, which are often identical problems, in contrast to the stimulation of the economy as a whole. The inconsistency is, however, more apparent than real, except possibly in the very short run.

5. It is only by a policy of stimulating the growth of the economy as a whole that a general solution can be found to the problems caused by disequilibrium in employment, income and regional development. A high rate of growth, reinforced by measures to assist the free mobility of men and capital, is the most positive means of raising living standards and relieving the hardships of rural poverty. Some of the measures which appear to be more direct are apt to be costly and may tend to slow down the rate at which income and production as a whole can be raised.

6. The prospects for the growth of the Spanish economy are very favorable and, with suitable policies and the requisite public and private investment effort, an annual growth rate of 5 percent per capita should be possible over an extended period. This would make it possible to raise the level of income in the industrial and service sectors twofold within a decade; income would also grow in the agricultural sector, but necessarily at a slower rate. Total employment could increase by about one million persons over the decade; at the same time, there should be a large shift of manpower out of agriculture, especially from the more traditional pursuits. With this movement of manpower, which the Government should actively encourage, it should be possible for per capita incomes of those who remain in rural areas to rise at much the same rate as those in the rest of the economy and, subsequently, for the level of agricultural incomes to approach more closely those elsewhere in the economy.

POLICIES FOR ECONOMIC GROWTH

7. Spain has the physical and human resources with which to achieve and maintain a high rate of economic growth. The greatest opportunity for doing so lies, in present circumstances, in the more economical use of the savings of the economy that are available for public and private investment. This will call for greater awareness of economic costs in both the market and non-market sectors of the economy.

The Market Economy

8. Cost consciousness in the market economy can be promoted through the discipline of the price mechanism. This discipline should be applied to public and private enterprises alike and the former should set an example in their financial accounting.

9. Distortions that prevent the price mechanism from functioning properly should be eliminated as far as possible, in particular through:

a. removal of price controls, either immediately or, where absolutely necessary, in stages;

b. abolition of subsidies taking the form of special prices between state enterprises;

c. avoidance of subsidization through concessionary interest rates which tend to promote unsound investments and to reduce the opportunities for employment;

d. limitation of the use of special incentives to fields where there is a clear and present need. In such cases, discrimination in their application should be avoided.

10. The forces of competition should be encouraged by removing, wherever possible, controls or administrative procedures which hamper initiative. Progressive exposure to foreign competition should be the principal weapon against monopolistic practices. Capital from abroad, though necessarily subject to some regulation, should be stimulated by positive action to help and encourage the foreign investor.

11. The Government can do much to encourage initiative in the market economy by clarifying its intentions and simplifying its regulations, especially in the fields of tariffs and taxation.

The Non-Market Economy

12. In the non-market economy, the Government should delegate the responsibility for initial review of expenditure proposals to the ministries and other organisms, which should establish the requisite units to review them. Proposals would be subject to further scrutiny by a comparable unit in the Ministry of Finance and by the Planning Commission in order to ensure that expenditures are as low as possible for the purpose in hand and that the purpose is in line with the Government's economic policy.

13. To ensure that public investment funds make their maximum contribution to economic development, investment proposals should be closely scrutinized in the following respects:

a. to limit the number of projects under construction to those that can be carried forward to completion at a normal rate;

b. to ensure adequate maintenance as against new construction;

c. to ensure coordination of the various elements of a project that are the responsibility of different organizations;

d. to weigh alternative ways of meeting a particular objective in order to arrive at the solution with the lowest cost;

e. to study market prospects in order to avoid overinvestment;

f. to ensure that social expenditures are not unduly costly for the purpose to be accomplished and that they reach as many recipients as possible.

DEVELOPMENT ORGANIZATION

14. The task of carrying out an economic development program is very complex and demands careful organization at the center. It also requires a determination in all sections of the administration to work together in the interests of the program.

15. The Government has taken steps to facilitate this organization by establishing an office of Planning Commissioner in the Presidency to be the focal point below the Delegate Committee for Economic Affairs for ensuring coordination among ministries, syndicates and private interests, and for centralizing consideration of the problems of economic development.

The Role of the Planning Commission

16. One of the tasks of the Planning Commission, and its advisory bodies, should be to undertake the prognosis of the nature and pace of change in the structure of the economy in the long term, in order to provide a common basis for planning in the public and private sectors. The Commission should also ensure that the various sector programs are commensurate with available resources and consistent with the projected rate of development. The results of these investigations could form the basis for a development plan. If the Government prepares such a plan, it should not attempt too much; it is not necessary, for example, to estimate public expenditures in great detail. What is needed is a framework in which the annual budget can be cast; it will have to be revised from time to time, since policies must be flexible to meet changing conditions. In fact, more important than the planning document is the planning process in which government departments and the private sector, under the guidance of the Planning Commission, interchange views and establish a consistent perspective against which to formulate and review development policies.

17. The Planning Commission will have an important role in undertaking the staff work needed by ministries for the formulation of economic policy. The Commission should ensure that investment proposals are consistent with the objectives of the development program and should coordinate the policies of the administration in implementing that program. There will also be important studies to provide a foundation for future investment decisions, undertaken under the auspices of the Planning Commission.

The Role of Other Government Bodies

18. Effective coordination between the Planning Commission and the various ministries is of first importance, but any formal system for facilitating interdepartmental consultation should be simple and, where possible, the Commission might usefully rely on *ad hoc* arrangements.

19. Equally important is coordination within each ministry concerned with the development program. A central unit within the ministry, which is in contact with the Planning Commission, should have this responsibility. Moreover, the work of autonomous public bodies and public enterprises attached to each ministry should be adapted to enable them to carry out a coordinated policy in the field.

20. One method of ensuring that investment proposals conform to the objectives of the long-term program is for each ministry concerned to submit an annual economic report to the Delegate Committee, through the Planning Commission, containing a view of the long-term prospects in the sector and an explanation of the investment proposals.

Remuneration of the Civil Service

21. Since the development program must determine the shape of the administration, and not the reverse, it is important to have an efficient and flexible organization. This responsibility will fall largely on the civil service whose competence and qualifications are unquestionable, but, if it is to be carried out efficiently, the Government should give its early consideration to the question of civil service pay.

22. The system for supplementing the basic salaries of civil servants by payments from funds accumulated by individual ministries in the course of their operations (e.g., by surcharging investment expenditure) may become incompatible with the policies for economic development. Decisions on public expenditure will have to be governed by the needs of the program and should not at the same time be capable of adversely affecting staff salaries. It would be better to break the link between these two questions. To this end, the establishment of a centrally administered system is strongly recommended. Under this system, civil servants are remunerated on a uniform basis and on a scale appropriate to their status and conducive to their following a full-time career in the public service, thus relating their emoluments to their service to the State and not to the operations of their ministry. Such a change would remove anomalies between ministries, give a greater sense of security and redound to the efficiency and objectivity of the public service as a whole. The adequacy of pensions and the link between an official's basic pay and his position within the official corps to which he belongs are also recommended for study.

Statistics

23. There has been some official recognition of the need for good statistical information both in long-range planning and in shorter-run guidance of the economy. While this recognition has led to outstanding improvements in the statistical field, in certain respects, much remains to be done.

24. There needs to be more coordination in this field both to ensure that the various agencies employ the same classification, and that the extent of coverage is made clear.

25. There is often a multiplicity of effort with various agencies collecting similar information and often not distributing it. The Instituto Nacional de Estadistica (INE) should act as the centralized agency in this field and it should be accorded the staff, machines and money required to carry out this function. In particular, the development of macroeconomic statistics, such as national accounts, should be centered in the Instituto Nacional de Estadistica.

BUDGETARY IMPLICATIONS OF DEVELOPMENT EXPENDITURE BY THE CENTRAL ADMINISTRATION

26. The financial implications of the various recommendations contained in the report should be viewed in the light of the expected overall growth of public revenues and of the expenditure needs for purposes other than development. It should be borne in mind, however, that many of the proposed investment figures are illustrative, either because detailed information on costs was not available or because specific estimates could not be provided until new studies were undertaken.

27. Taking the rate of growth of national income proposed above and assuming the same relationship between the growth of income and of fiscal receipts that has existed in the past, the increase in public revenues that can be forecast would make it possible, without borrowing or external aid, to carry out over the next five years the development proposals in the report and also to finance an increase of two-thirds in expenditures for purposes other than those specified. Some of the expenditures in the latter category will undoubtedly require less than this kind of increase. One of the first priority claims on additional expenditure would be an increase in pay and pensions for the civil service; such an increase would be substantial and still leave a sizable sum for increases for other purposes.

28. It appears therefore that the proposed expenditures for development are reasonably within the financial capabilities of the Government. This underlines the point that rapid economic development is dependent less on an increase in the resources available for investment (or on the share of the public sector in these resources) than on a more effective use of resources.

Section II

GENERAL GUIDANCE OF THE ECONOMY

THE INTERDEPENDENCE OF PUBLIC POLICIES

29. In planning the future expansion of the economy as a whole, it will be important to keep constantly in view the interrelationship between monetary and financial movements and the external payments position.

30. There should be unified and effective control of monetary, fiscal and foreign economic policies. It will also be important to have in readiness the instruments for controlling, or influencing, the economy. Adequate statistical information will be required for this purpose and, although such information may emanate from various sources, it should nevertheless be in a form in which the interconnection between the different sectors is readily apparent.

31. If governmental actions need to be applied to the allocation of resources, care should be taken that such actions, whether direct or indirect, do not place restrictions on those activities which are promoting the growth of the economy. Furthermore, a careful balance must be established between the public and private sectors and within each sector on the basis of the functions to be performed.

FISCAL MANAGEMENT

The Public Accounts

32. The budget is a vital step in the planning process. It must therefore be clear in its intentions. Furthermore, the public accounts should be a comprehensive, consistent, timely body of information, both in retrospect and as to forecasts.

33. The public accounts should, in particular, be:

   a. clear as to definition;
   b. capable of consolidation with respect to the whole public sector or parts of it;
   c. amenable to analysis so that income and expenditure can be usefully categorized;
   d. capable of being identified for purposes of control.

34. There are some 1,600 autonomous organizations in the Spanish public sector which are responsible for the greater part of public investment and a sizable part of national investment. These organizations have a great variety of functions and many have special sources of income of their own. This complicates the task of public accounting, which is never easy.

35. For this and other reasons, the public accounts do not adequately meet the criteria referred to above, although a new system of classification of public accounts which represented a great advance was introduced by the Ministry of Finance in 1957. This new classification should serve as the basis for further reforms, which are all the more necessary since the absence of adequate information on the finances of the public sector deprives the Government of an essential tool for economic planning.

36. The Ministry of Finance should be in a position to ensure that:

a. a consistent classification of public bodies is established according to the nature of their activities;

b. within each category of public bodies a uniform system of accounting is constantly used;

c. all public bodies present their budgets and final accounts at least as quickly as the General Administration;

d. published financial summaries avoid the inclusion of different categories of income and expenditure under a single heading;

e. published summaries of expenditure are in a form more closely approaching a breakdown by function;

f. all relevant information is published in relatively few documents and is also available in a suitably consolidated form.

37. There is a particular need to reclassify autonomous organizations. Some have a commercial function; others have a financial function; and others are engaged in more typically governmental activities. As much as possible, public enterprises in the market economy should be conducted on commercial lines and keep their accounts accordingly; thus, when their decisions are based on noneconomic considerations— as sometimes they must be—it will be possible to determine the costs involved, and decide how they should be covered. In the case of autonomous organizations of a noncommercial character, an effort should be made to integrate many of them and their accounts into the Government itself. At the same time, the system of central administration

should be modified to allow for the flexibility which such organizations often need.

Control of Expenditure

38. For unified, effective control of the public sector, there should be one central unit within the Ministry of Finance responsible for advising the Minister on the kinds of information required, for seeing that it is collected, for analyzing the impact of taxation, borrowing and expenditure on the economy and for making recommendations on the basis of the analysis. It should also ensure that expenditure proposals are presented in coherent programs and that the Government is getting adequate value for the expenditure of public money.

39. The economical and judicious use of public funds should begin with the ministries which spend the money and, accordingly, all the more important ministries should establish and provide adequate staff for special project and program review units where these do not now exist. With respect to investment projects, these units would forecast demand, compare costs with benefits, review alternatives and forecast financial requirements.

40. In order to exercise more detailed control over expenditure, all investment projects costing more than, say, 10 million pts should be listed separately showing, in addition to the expenditure allocation for the year, total estimated cost, remaining cost and time required for completion. A start should be made at including the larger autonomous organizations.

Tax Policy

41. The proposed central unit would also act as a clearing house for economic information to be derived from tax returns, including the necessary forecast of revenue.

42. The tax system, while necessarily drawing an increasing volume of revenue from the more dynamic sectors of the economy, should not destroy incentives. Nor should there be arbitrary discrimination either between firms in the same industry or between different industries, except for well-defined purposes. The tax system should be sensitive to economic growth and fluctuations.

43. Indirect taxes should be carefully examined to see to what extent they produce economic distortions, particularly in the case of taxes on intermediate goods. Furthermore, much could be achieved by a simplification of small taxes and a reduction in their number. Finally, the

system of earmarked taxes levied by autonomous organizations should be reviewed.

44. Individuals and corporations are liable for a range of direct taxes on income and property according to source and also to a complementary tax on income as a whole. Collection of direct taxes has presented difficult administrative problems. In order to increase receipts, a system of global assessments has been introduced for some of the taxes, whereby the total is assessed for a whole group and then shared among those in it. Although successful in uncovering new taxpayers, in increasing receipts and making tax liabilities more equitable, the system still has some disadvantages. The original intention of evolving it away from a number of taxes with variable schedules toward a coordinated tax on income as a whole should be maintained.

MONETARY MANAGEMENT

45. For successful prosecution of future development, Spain requires a fluid, sensitive market for long- and short-term capital, in which there is free transfer of savings between institutions to satisfy evolving needs. Some new institutions may be necessary for specialized needs. Control over this market should be unified and effective. The Government has taken two important measures to this end: the law of December 26, 1958, on medium- and long-term credit institutions and the bank reform law of April 1962.

The Central Bank

46. One feature of the bank reform law is the nationalization of the Bank of Spain and its transformation into a full central bank, including the integration of internal and external monetary affairs through the absorption of various functions of the Foreign Exchange Institute. This is a most desirable step. While the Government has the last word on matters of national finance, it should conduct its own operations in such a way as to avoid undermining the authority of the Bank, the agency to which it has delegated responsibility for monetary control. The Bank should have at its command adequate instruments for this control.

47. In order that the central bank can advise the Government on the techniques of monetary control arising from the latter's fiscal policies, automatic recourse of public agencies to the central bank, outside the purview of the general operations of the Treasury, should be reduced to the absolute minimum. In this way, the net financial position of the

public finances could be dealt with on an aggregate basis rather than allowing it to emerge from the independent actions of a multiplicity of government agencies.

48. Movements in the government's balance with the Bank of Spain should be financed, not only by payments into or overdrafts on its current account with the Bank, but also by market operations, including those in short-term securities. Short-term securities would also add a useful liquidity instrument to the money market.

Private Banks

49. The bank reform law envisages that the Bank of Spain will have a regulatory influence on money through rules on rediscount operations and the deposits of the private banks in the Bank of Spain, through open market operations and through other instruments of monetary control. It will also be responsible for inspection of private banks. The Bank of Spain is equipped to exercise these powers, which it clearly should have. However, the private banks have hitherto possessed the privilege of automatic pledgeability of the long-term public debt, in the form of long-term securities, and this is a serious impediment to the control of liquidity. Because of the very large amounts of this form of debt outstanding, its influence can be formidable. A reasonable solution would be for the Government and the banking community to negotiate a series of conversion operations.

50. The Government is rightly moving in the direction of more competition and greater specialization in the private banking field. It will establish a legal basis for investment banks and will limit the equity participations of the present private banks. An important step in opening up alternative sources of finance and creating greater competition will be achieved by relaxing the prohibition on the establishment of new banking institutions.

Savings Banks

51. The savings banks have enjoyed a rapid growth of deposits. They are now a potent source of savings and it is important to ensure the necessary flexibility in their use. The time has come to modify the fixed percentage rules, whereby they are obliged to put 65 percent of the increase of their deposits into government securities (in practice, largely the Instituto Nacional de Industria (INI) and its enterprises). This regulation prevents the savings banks from sharing adequately

in the financing of the private sector and hampers the transferability of savings in the economy.

52. The savings banks are well suited, by virtue of their local character, to extend greatly their lending activities in agriculture, industry and housing. They have a particular role to play in fostering small enterprises but need not be limited to them. Furthermore, they could combine in groups for the long-term financing of regional development in medium-size industry and agriculture.

53. The fiduciary position of the savings banks could be protected by regular portfolio inspection by the Credit Institute of the Savings Banks which might also consider the establishment of a deposit insurance scheme. The Institute could facilitate the transfer of funds from surplus to deficit areas.

Official Credit Institutions

54. Under the 1958 law, six official medium- and long-term credit institutions were made dependent for their funds on the Ministry of Finance and a Committee on Medium- and Long-Term Credit was established with powers to authorize capital issues and grant special credits. The latter is now to be transformed into an Institute with over-all responsibility for official credit institutions and for advising the Government on medium- and long-term credit.

55. There is a great need for long-term credit in a number of sectors and the official credit institutions should concentrate on this need. The institutions should be alive to the necessity for a continuous review of evolving needs, and aim at turning over some forms of financing to other institutions and taking up new ones. This process will be facilitated if interest rates are, generally speaking, kept close to market rates. Special incentives may be necessary in certain cases, but should as far as possible be in the form of direct subsidies.

56. To fulfill their purpose, the institutions should take a more liberal view of risk and sometimes invest without collateral security where there is evidence of personal initiative and the prospect of good returns. They also should, where necessary, consider the opening of branch offices.

57. Annual allocations should be based on the best estimate that can be made in advance of the sums that can be prudently lent at market rates. There should be flexibility in adjusting allocations during the year and in reducing or increasing borrowing on the market, directly or indirectly through the Treasury. Adjustment of allocations should

naturally be subject to the conjunctural needs of the economy, but official credit institutions should not be singled out for the purpose.
58. The Credit Institute is concerned with the over-all supply of medium- and long-term credit in both the public and the private sectors. In the public sector, consideration should be given to the extension of the Institute's supervision to all public lending. In the private banking sector, supervision should be confined, as far as possible, to general policy guidance, with technical implementation under the supervision of the central bank. This would make for a more unified control over the private financial sector.

FOREIGN ECONOMIC POLICY

59. The stabilization plan, adopted in July 1959, has had many beneficial effects. Foreign exchange receipts have risen, imports are taking place more freely and on more advantageous terms, and capital is being attracted from abroad. Moreover, inflation has been halted and internal and external equilibrium restored.
60. It cannot be emphasized too strongly that a continuation of this stability is an essential condition for any long-term growth of the economy. Within this framework, the aim of foreign economic policy should be to bring about a major expansion of the external sector, since Spain has neither the resources nor the market with which to develop its economy in isolation. The objectives of this policy should be twofold:

    a. to facilitate increased imports of goods and services necessary for development, and to procure them at the lowest cost and under the most advantageous conditions consistent with a minimum protection of domestic producers;

    b. to expand earnings from exports, tourism and other invisibles, and to attract the foreign capital necessary to finance increased imports.

Import Controls

61. The Government has correctly fixed as its goal the removal of all quantitative restrictions on imports and has made good progress in this direction. The present payment position makes it possible to extend the liberalization program rapidly. The Government should establish, and make known, a schedule for the removal of quotas so that

producers will have the necessary planning information. For the future development of Spanish industry, liberalization should be extended to cover more capital equipment. While quotas remain in effect, efforts should be made further to simplify administrative procedures.
62. One limitation to free imports is constituted by state trading on a bilateral basis. The Government has recently transferred a number of products to private channels, and this process should continue.

Tariff Policy

63. Tariff policy should be considered primarily in the context of its effect on economic development and on the possibility of integrating the Spanish economy into Western Europe.
64. Viewed in this light, it is evident that the Government should proceed to a systematic reduction in the level of duties in the 1960 tariff, which is relatively high, particularly in the case of capital goods needed for development. This will require that administrative procedures be adjusted to provide greater speed and flexibility. Lowering tariffs would contribute to economic development in several ways:

a. it would help reduce production costs for industries that have to use imported goods;

b. it would direct scarce funds for new investment into more productive channels;

c. it would discourage high-cost, inefficient enterprises and thereby improve Spanish industry's competitive position.

65. In lowering tariffs, use should be made of sliding-scale duties to provide for a phased reduction over the period necessary for the rationalization of domestic industry. Transitional rates should be replaced with the final duties specified in the tariff at the time quotas are removed, since the indefinite prolongation of transitional duties creates added uncertainty for business. Any tariff exemptions or reductions should be provided only in relation to general objectives of development and through the application of general criteria. Protection of specific industries or firms on an interim basis should be confined to the minimum.

Export Development

66. Substantial progress has been made in developing policies to encourage the expansion of exports. There are, however, further steps

which could be taken. The time required to obtain export licenses could be reduced even further, with the aim of ultimately eliminating licenses entirely. Furthermore, the economic situation no longer warrants export quotas or prohibitions. The system of tax reimbursements to exempt exporters from the payment of indirect taxes should be extended to all exports and applied in full and with the minimum delay. Finally, the regulations concerning tariff concessions on materials imported for later export should be brought up to date, simplified and applied more liberally.

67. Adequate facilities for export credit and credit insurance, on a basis comparable with those in countries with which Spanish exports compete, are essential particularly in view of the need for increased exports of manufactured goods. The recently established system of export credit should be extended and made more flexible in its operations, and the coverage of risks under the credit insurance system should be raised.

68. A separate Foreign Trade Center should be established to be responsible for the general strategy of export development, to assist exporters by means of market studies, publicity, information and the like. The Center should receive more funds and personnel than are presently provided for such purposes and should be accorded a greater degree of financial and operating autonomy.

Foreign Private Investment

69. Foreign private investment has an important part to play in development. It should be recognized that the international capital market is highly competitive. Since foreign investment legislation invariably leaves a wide area of administrative discretion, potential investors will consider the spirit of the law, and how it is administered, as much as the letter of its contents. In any event, the long-run outlook for foreign capital will depend less on the legislation itself than on more general economic considerations.

70. So far as the legislation is concerned, a great deal of progress has been made in recent years and the conditions offered to foreign investors now compare favorably with those in other countries. It would now be useful if the complexity of the existing legislation were reduced by consolidating it into a single clarified and consistent text.

71. If the Government should remove the requirement of prior authorization for industrial investments as is recommended below, it would be desirable to establish some procedure through which proposed foreign investments above a designated size (such as 500 million

pts) would be subject to Government consideration even in cases where more than 50 percent ownership is not involved. This consideration, for example, would be for the purpose of ascertaining whether the terms and conditions of the investment present any particular problem that should be worked out in advance. The review procedure, which might be administered by the Presidency of the Government, should take place within a designated time period such as three or four months.

72. In order better to draw the attention of foreign investors to the various possibilities that exist in Spain, an enlarged office of foreign investment should be established that can provide all the services expected of such a center.

Section III

TRANSPORTATION

THE TRANSPORT ECONOMY

73. Geography, history and the distribution of areas of economic activity have made it difficult to achieve an integrated transport system. Transport moves primarily along a small number of high-volume lines radiating from Madrid to the other main areas of economic activity on the periphery or linking these areas with each other. This basic network is already well established.

74. Transportation as a whole has been growing at a fairly rapid rate. Important shifts in the pattern of traffic have been taking place, in part through the process of economic development but also as a result of rate and investment policies.

75. The demand for transportation will continue to grow and large-scale investments will be required. More important than the magnitude of future investment, however, is the proper balance among the various components of the investment effort.

76. Each of the various modes of transport will continue to have a vital function to perform. Regulatory policy should be directed toward ensuring that the user is free to select from among the alternatives that combination of price and service which is best for him while enabling each carrier to cover its full costs.

77. This regulatory approach should rely, to the maximum possible extent, on market forces to relate prices to long-run costs, to distribute

traffic among the services on an economic basis and to relate investment decisions to demand and cost considerations. The principal role of the Government should be to ensure that market forces operate freely and that costs are as low as possible. To perform this role, more information is required.

78. In view of the Government's wide interest in and responsibility for the development of transportation, it is important to ensure that the requisite administrative machinery exists and functions properly. The principal need is for a permanent body at the higher official and technical level that would provide a forum in which the development of the transport system as a whole is watched, future needs are assessed, and policies and programs for meeting them are planned. Such a transport committee might consist of a permanent chairman of standing and experience in transport matters and committee members drawn from the interested government departments and from the transport operators. It should be served by a permanent secretariat that would perform important day-to-day functions.

RAILWAYS

79. Faced with a continual loss of traffic to other forms of transport, with large deficits and with a decline in service, the railways are not able to make their essential contribution to economic development. The Government has been increasingly preoccupied with this situation and has initiated a number of expert investigations.

80. Action will need to be taken to improve administrative and operating arrangements and to modernize and rationalize the railway system. The latter will entail both increased capital expenditures and a different emphasis among the various types of investment.

Organization

81. Many present difficulties can be traced to problems of organization. Accordingly, Red Nacional de los Ferrocarriles Españoles (RENFE) should be reorganized so that its Board of Directors has full responsibility for operating the national system and preparing all phases of the railway investment program. The General Management would be responsible for carrying out the Board's policy. Public supervision could be assured by the appointment of non-voting government supervisors to the Board of RENFE.

Investment Needs

82. Because the existing network is in general more than sufficient for present and probable future traffic demand, before carrying out any additional work on new lines a study of their justification should be made. Some decisions could be reached at once on closing existing lines or limiting them to goods traffic. There would remain a basic network of lines on which investment funds should be concentrated over the next five years.

83. Of prime importance on this basic network is track renewal. Besides being unsafe, the poor condition of the track results in loss of time, excessive wear of rolling stock and high operating expenses. Given top priority, track renewal could proceed at a faster pace. About 4,500 km of the most important lines should be renewed in the next five years.

84. Track maintenance could be made more effective by merging a number of the existing maintenance organizations into a consolidated system. This would reduce the dimensions of the task of track renovation in subsequent years. Increased reliance should be placed on single-track lines, using modern traffic control techniques.

85. Most locomotives are old and steam-powered. They should be replaced by diesel electric or straight electric locomotives. Reliance should be mainly on diesel locomotives which are not only economical but require a relatively small investment and can be used on all lines. Fixed investment for electrified lines is costly and is only appropriate where traffic is heavy; further expenditures of this kind should be limited to linking already electrified sections.

86. Large-scale replacement of steam power will require a major reorganization of locomotive maintenance. The opportunity should be taken to reduce the number of repair shops and consolidate the system.

87. Replacement of rolling stock should be carefully phased in relation to other plans. While older cars should be withdrawn, new passenger cars might not be needed if passenger lines are reduced and modern diesel and electric train units acquired. Old freight cars will have to be replaced, but no increase in their number should be necessary because of reduced turn-around time.

88. A substantial increase in expenditures on modernization is called for. Average annual expenditures of 7 billion pts—a rate which is both technically and financially feasible—would make possible the completion of more than half RENFE's modernization program in the next

five years. The augmented program would entail a shift in the distribution of expenditures: while expenditures on new lines would be eliminated, greater importance would be given to track renovation and to dieselization. Proportionately less funds would be provided for passenger and freight cars and for electrification.

Operational Problems

89. The speed and reliability of the railway could be notably improved. A number of proposals to this end are made, including a reduction in the number of marshalling yards, passenger and freight stations and other facilities. The construction of a few modern marshalling yards in place of the present ones would have a particular bearing on the speed and reliability of freight service.
90. The railway staff is in excess of present needs and further reductions in the number of personnel will be necessary as modernization proceeds. Also, RENFE needs the flexibility which would accompany control over its personnel in order to deal with the disposition of the working force, its recruitment and training.

Financial Policy

91. RENFE's annual deficit, after allowing for financial charges and depreciation, is about 3.5 billion pts. A significant part is accounted for by the provision of reduced rates to various classes of users. Furthermore, other government agencies receiving services from RENFE do not pay for them in full. RENFE should not be expected to bear such losses. If reduced rates to some users are considered necessary, the Government should reimburse RENFE for them.
92. RENFE's financial position would also be improved by changing its rate policy toward a differential system reflecting differences in the costs of transporting various types of goods. In this way, the railway would be able to attract that traffic for which it has an economic advantage. The timing of rate adjustments should be coordinated with those for other transport modes.
93. The revision of railway rates, together with the added efficiency and improved service resulting from modernization and the proposed organizational changes, could substantially reduce RENFE's deficit over the years and enable the railway to play its full part in economic development.

ROADS

94. While there is little need for new roads, apart from the east coast autopista, an enormous amount has to be done on repairs, on ordinary maintenance and on construction and reconstruction along existing routes. Many key roads were not designed for the traffic they are now bearing, and regular maintenance work has generally fallen behind. Increased budget allocations, better data for highway planning, more coordination of projects and improved design work are all necessary.

95. Top priority should be given to the urgent repair of the most traveled roads; unless this work is done quickly, they will deteriorate rapidly. The priority applied to any road should take into account traffic density and its actual condition. Because the work is urgent, it should be completed within four years, with the bulk of the expenditure in the second and third years. The cost would be 8 billion pts. To carry it out, a special organization under an able organizer, supported by a technical adviser, should be set up within the Ministry of Public Works. Contracting firms should be employed using mobile construction teams.

96. There is a heavy backlog of repair work on other roads, which should gradually decline as maintenance is improved. Expenditure on this work over a four-year period is estimated at 3 billion pts.

97. Lack of ordinary maintenance has been important in contributing to the poor condition of roads. Maintenance has been largely based on the *caminero* system, under which roads are maintained by local manual laborers. In recent years, organized groups and contracting firms have also been used. The Government is now considering setting up an organized and well-equipped maintenance system. The extent of mechanization should vary according to local conditions. Equipment for ordinary maintenance for a four-year period might require 2.3 billion pts.

98. Construction and reconstruction to upgrade standards over existing routes should be based on future traffic needs and on the state of existing roads. Until more studies have been made, construction and reconstruction requirements cannot be determined, but they are certainly very large and will have to be spread over a long period. Because urgent repairs should have priority, expenditure on construction and reconstruction in early years should be modest and concentrated on the completion of uncompleted projects. However, such expenditure could be increased later so that for the five-year period it could total 15.5 billion pts (including traffic studies).

99. The only major new road necessary in the near future is the east coast autopista which would eventually extend from the French border to Murcia and pass through areas of the greatest traffic density and traffic growth. Although conceived as a whole, it should be carried out in stages, with first priority given to the section from Barcelona to the frontier. Its size, complexity and high cost suggest that it should be carried out by a special organization with its own finances and able to employ its own consultants and contractors.

100. It is important to obtain more and better data on such subjects as the origin and destination of traffic, vehicle fleet location and fuel consumption, and to prepare forecasts of traffic growth. Some steps in this direction have already been taken. With better data, the planning and design of roads, which have been improving in recent years, could be further improved.

101. If the road system is to serve adequately the demands that will be placed upon it, the organization responsible for roads must be strengthened. Independent units should be consolidated, four or six regional offices should be established to supervise the 50 provincial Jefaturas, and other organizational changes considered.

102. The capacity of the construction industry to handle the increased work recommended should be expanded: improved designs, better planning of work, employment of foreign contractors in some cases and more and better equipment are necessary. The pool of construction equipment that the Government rents to contractors is largely old and worn, while much contractor-owned equipment needs to be replaced with larger items and standardized. Contracting firms should be encouraged to specialize.

103. Traffic administration in such matters as safety and prevention of over-weight vehicles should be tightened up.

PORTS AND SHIPPING

Ports

104. The central problem facing the ports is that of achieving the proper balance in their facilities. In general, existing wharf and breakwater capacity is sufficient for present and foreseeable traffic needs and in some cases it is excessive, while other elements that determine the effective capacity of a port such as cranes and handling equipment, are inadequate. The Plan for Port Development 1962–69 shows the same

emphasis. Attention needs to be given to the fuller use of deep-water wharves and maintenance of depth by dredging.

105. Purchase of equipment should be stepped up, while new wharf construction should only be undertaken if the need for it has been established. Port investment during the period 1962–69 should total 5.8 billion pts of which 3.9 billion pts would be for infrastructure and 1.9 billion pts for equipment and related high-priority projects. Expenditure on small ports should probably be curtailed and consideration given to the possibility of some port consolidation. This program is designed to provide the most effective use of existing port facilities, thereby reducing the time spent in port and, as a consequence, transportation costs.

106. Proposals for new dry docks and for the Sevilla-Bonanza Canal should be scrutinized carefully; for the former, in order to ascertain whether future demand would justify construction and, for the latter, to determine whether the benefits would cover its heavy annual cost and whether the much cheaper alternative of increased dredging would be preferable.

107. While the Ministry of Public Works should retain general responsibility for reviewing port operations and investment plans, port operations should be left to the local port authorities. The effectiveness of the Junta de Obras y Servicios at principal ports would be increased by more contacts with users. Utilization of port equipment should be improved by collecting more statistics. Customs procedures could be expedited in certain respects.

108. The general level of port charges should be raised so as to reduce the aggregate port deficit, which in 1958 was about 1 billion pts including capital charges. Port tariffs, which are uniform for the whole of Spain, should be replaced by tariffs reflecting the costs at each port. Preferential rates to various public bodies should be discontinued. In this and other ways, port accounts would reveal the economic cost of and return from port operations.

Shipping

109. The merchant marine, nearly half of which is over 25 years old, needs to be modernized, but the pace of modernization should be governed by future traffic prospects and by the program of port improvement.

110. Overage tramps and ocean liners should be replaced over a period of years. Some increase in and improvement of the territorial

service to the Balearic and Canary Islands and in the use of specialized fruit vessels should be brought about.

111. Even though surplus capacity in coastal shipping has depressed freight rates, the slower speed of old ships and delays in port have resulted in the loss of trade to road transport; coal is the main cargo, but return cargoes are irregular, and prospects are uncertain. With modern ships and speedier handling in ports, the trade could be done by a much smaller fleet and offer better returns. But this partial replacement should be dependent on market prospects at the time that the ports are modernized.

112. Except for territorial lines, new building should be for replacing old ships rather than adding to the fleet. The planned assistance to shipowners to be provided over the next few years by Credito Naval is reasonable. In subsequent years, the need for public funds may be less.

113. Shipbuilding capacity is surplus to Spanish needs and recent progress in obtaining export orders should be encouraged, through export credits for example.

AIR TRANSPORT

114. Air transport has a bright future in Spain.

115. Fares for internal and territorial services are probably too low to cover the costs of adequate services. They should be increased. If very low fares to the Canaries are necessary, the airlines should receive a direct subsidy for this purpose. The airlines should be allowed more flexibility to adjust rates to costs and demand for different services.

116. The possibility of expanding freight and charter services should be studied.

117. Airports and navigational aids have been inadequate, but present modernization plans are well conceived and should remedy the deficiencies.

Section IV

AGRICULTURE

118. With the expansion of agricultural production in recent years, there are no longer any important food shortages and farm prices have been relatively stable. Now that supply and demand are in better

balance, agricultural development should be largely determined by the future growth of domestic and export demand for farm products.

119. The central objective of government policy toward agriculture should now be to produce the right amounts of particular crops at the lowest possible cost. This requires the careful study of demand patterns so that public policy can be oriented to assist the forces already at work to shift resources from declining to expanding types of production and to increase productivity. A complementary objective should be to facilitate the transfer of excess manpower from agriculture to other parts of the economy where its contribution to growth can be greater.

Increase in Productivity

120. Irrigation is an important method of increasing agricultural yields. There are others: the reform of farm units to achieve optimum sizes; soil conservation; improved seed and livestock; disease and pest control; better fertilizer use; and increased mechanization. Underlying all these is the need for augmented research and extension services and an expansion of education to farmers.

121. There is no doubt that irrigation can produce impressive results in raising productivity and making it possible to cultivate higher-value crops. But irrigation is relatively costly and due consideration should be given to the aforementioned alternative methods, to determine which will provide the greatest returns in increased production and income for the costs involved.

Irrigation

122. Irrigation will in any event have an important place in the agricultural program. Financial and other resources should be concentrated on a sufficiently limited number of irrigation projects so that all can be completed expeditiously and capital will not be locked up in uncompleted projects. Furthermore, the irrigation projects to be carried out should generally be those which provide the highest benefits relative to their costs and a higher return on the invested capital than is possible in alternative uses. This policy will require careful analysis of individual projects that should be based on improved economic data. Next, the provision of adequate credit for secondary works and technical assistance to improve cropping patterns will be necessary to ensure full production in new and existing irrigation projects.

123. The changing pattern of demand makes it important that the

Government make a fresh appraisal of its irrigation plans on a priority basis. While this appraisal is going on, an interim irrigation program should aim primarily to complete rapidly some of the projects that are clearly of high priority. From tentative data, it appears that only a moderate additional acreage under irrigation would be required for high-value crops, since these are cultivated very intensively and there are opportunities for increasing production on existing irrigated land. The more extensive crops are of lower value so that only in those cases where capital costs of irrigation are also low would there be much likelihood of an adequate return. Moreover, the future market outlook for wheat—the most important extensive crop—suggests a decline in demand in the long run as standards of living rise.

124. There are, of course, considerations other than economic ones. The Government naturally wishes to assure a stable supply of such basic commodities as wheat. Severe droughts can cause wide fluctuations in production. However, as yields are increased on land already irrigated and on dry land less susceptible to drought, the land most susceptible can gradually be withdrawn from wheat, particularly when total wheat consumption falls; in this way, year-to-year output should be more stable. In any event, stability of supply can be assured by adequate storage facilities, together with moderate recourse to imports and exports.

125. Another noneconomic consideration is the welfare of the rural population. Irrigation has often been associated with land settlement to assist regional development. Such "coordinated" projects are impressive. But, being costly, they can only benefit a limited number of people, and there are other means of improving rural welfare on a wider scale. Colonization is possible without irrigation in a number of areas and, generally speaking, irrigation should be included only if economically justified in itself.

126. Until the appraisal by the Government is finished, it is impossible to determine what the future trend of expenditure on irrigation should be. It is reasonable to assume that there will first be a period of consolidation, during which the Government will concentrate mainly on raising the level of productivity of land already irrigated and on those projects or parts of projects in the course of construction which can most readily be completed to produce a high return of marketable crops. Landowners should be able to repay loans for these purposes on reasonable terms, provided that the period of repayment is relatively extended. In particular, it will be important to increase the public credits for secondary and ancillary irrigation works so that land already irrigated can be brought rapidly into full production.

Other Measures to Increase Productivity

127. Among the other measures for increasing yields, one of the most promising is the change in the size of farm units. Increased attention should be given to stimulating the effective use of large farms, within the limits set by the need for extensive farming in dry areas. The excellent program of voluntary land consolidation, which combines units now too small for economic operation, should receive much larger budgetary appropriations. In addition, the Government should re-examine its rental legislation with a view to removing disincentives to land improvement. Finally, ways should be found to make better use of common land.

128. Added support should also be provided for soil conservation programs, the improvement of seed and livestock, disease and pest control and the wider use of fertilizer; all these programs will require augmented budgetary allocations if the best use of agricultural resources is to be obtained.

129. Mechanization can increase yields and production. This process should be supported by public credit, but not at subsidized interest rates which lead to uneconomical reductions in the demand for farm labor. The price of tractors and other farm machinery is relatively high and consideration should be given to reducing the tariff on these items.

130. Technical research and extension services and agricultural education are especially important for improving production methods and bringing them to the farm community. There is a close association between extension and education, since technological improvements are most likely to be adopted by those who understand their advantages. Government support of these programs should be expanded.

The Shift in Resources

131. Changes in demand will require significant shifts in resources. These shifts will raise farm incomes, provided that agricultural policies are oriented to ensure that they take place promptly and with minimum dislocation. Controls and regulations which make it difficult for farmers, processors and distributors to react correctly to market forces should be lifted. Market intervention by the Government should be directed primarily toward stabilizing prices by ironing out seasonal fluctuations within the crop year. Increased mobility of farmers and laborers should be encouraged so that farm resources can be put to their most productive uses. Greater reliance should be placed on international trade so that Spain can gain from its comparative advantage

in some crops for export and so obtain other crops more cheaply abroad.

132. Some of the land that will not be required in the future for wheat production should be devoted either to livestock or to forestry. The increased demand for animal products should make it possible, for example, to shift some marginal wheat land to sheep grazing. This transition from wheat to animal husbandry and forestry is a natural one which has already started, but it will be gradual and farmers will need help during it.

133. One of the major challenges facing agriculture during the next decade will be to increase the supply of animal proteins (meat, milk, cheese, poultry) for human consumption. This will require a much closer integration of animal husbandry with agriculture as well as the provision of more and better pasture land. The growing demand for animal proteins will make it possible to expand the production of cheese from sheep milk and of broilers and eggs, provided that these programs receive the requisite public support.

134. Forestry is a natural outlet for large parts of the territory, particularly since an increased demand for timber products can be anticipated. Forestry is also an important source of rural employment. A twofold change in the direction of forestry policy is called for: some of the low-lying land now in the forestry domain should be developed into pasturage; and the excellent National Forestry Service should shift the center of its reforestation work toward the South in order to facilitate the movement of land from wheat into forestry.

Distressed Areas and Low-Income Groups

135. Increases in productivity from these shifts of resources and from their better use will raise the general level of farm incomes. The Government has been attacking the problem of rural poverty directly through the programs of the Instituto Nacional de Colonizacion (INC). These programs are commendable and have achieved important results. But since they reach a relatively small number of rural families and tend to fix agricultural resources in areas where, for natural reasons, their return is relatively low, alternative approaches should also be considered.

136. One such approach would be to facilitate the movement, already taking place, of families either to other rural areas where returns are higher or to industry and services. Relocation should be supported by other programs such as education and vocational retraining and the concentration of grants and credits in areas of greatest need. A single

agency is required to coordinate these efforts in favor of the most needy rural areas. INC has the experience most adaptable to this work.

Organizing for Development

137. The large tasks ahead will require important adaptations in the organizational structure. Better coordination should be achieved both in Madrid and in the field among the various elements concerned with formulating and carrying out policy.

138. Action should be taken to prevent excessive compartmentalization. Each of the various services in the field should not be independent of the others, communicating only with its own headquarters. The services in each provincial capital should be concentrated in a single Jefatura, so that they can deal collectively with local problems to the solution of which each has something to contribute. Furthermore, groups of provincial Jefaturas should be placed under regional offices which would relieve some of the work load at the center and assist in intraregional and interregional planning.

139. By the same token, the administration of the Ministry itself should be so adjusted that the various skills and specializations could complement each other in the formation of a coordinated approach to agricultural problems. There is also need for a clearer definition of functions between the Ministry of Agriculture and the Ministry of Public Works with respect to the various aspects of the irrigation program.

Financing Agricultural Development

140. To achieve the rate of agricultural development that Spain's resources make possible, additional capital will be required, both in the form of increased private and public credit and of increased budgetary appropriations.

141. Changes proposed elsewhere should enable the Cajas Generales de Ahorro to lend to agriculture in increasing amounts. At the same time, the Servicio Nacional de Credito Agricola (SNCA) should expand its activities, but SNCA loans to farmers should be made at interest rates approximating the cost of money in alternative uses. The additional funds that the SNCA will require should be provided in full directly by the Government, rather than through the intermediary of the commercial banks. To an increasing extent, credits now provided by the Servicio Nacional del Trigo and the INC should be extended either by the banks and savings associations or by the SNCA.

142. Budgetary allocations for agricultural purposes should increase in amount and reflect the main shifts in policy emphasis: greater emphasis on technical developments, on education and extension services, on better land use and on improvements in farm organization; more emphasis on completing high-priority irrigation projects and on bringing existing irrigation works into full production while an appraisal of the needs as a whole is going on; special programs to facilitate the shift of resources to meet the changing pattern of demand; and, as an alternative to land settlement, consideration of other programs designed to reach and assist a larger number of families in low-income groups and distressed areas.

Section V

INDUSTRY AND POWER

INDUSTRY

143. A continued growth of industry is essential to raise living standards, increase employment and promote regional development. Prospects for further industrial expansion are very good. Natural resources provide a broad base for industrial development. There is ample electric power. Most important is the abundant supply of industrious and easily trained manpower.

144. As a result of the expansion over the past 20 years, the industrial sector is quite extensive. It has been concentrated in a relatively few regions—the north coast, the Barcelona area and Madrid. Growth has been most rapid in some of the newest branches of industry.

Basic Problems

145. Two basic problems face Spanish industry. First, while there are numerous efficient firms, many others are too small to operate efficiently even in industries in which there could be important economies in large-scale production. Second, because many firms are insufficiently mechanized, or equipped with old or nonstandard machines, much of industry has a low productivity and high costs.

146. These problems arise from various causes. Inflation in an economy isolated by import and exchange controls has encouraged and protected industries designed to serve only the Spanish market and

hence often too small to be efficient. Foreign exchange shortages have limited the access of firms to imports of raw materials, machinery and equipment needed for modernization. Capital for investment in industry has been short. In addition there has recently been some uncertainty as to future economic policies and as to the future role of state-owned enterprises.

Objectives of Government Policy

147. Public policy can help in various ways to achieve a more modern and competitive industry. First, by progressively removing the remaining interventions and controls, by increasing labor flexibility and mobility and by other measures, it can create an environment in which industry is free to turn its resources to the most productive uses. Second, it should define clearly the role of public enterprise and the conditions under which it will operate. Third, there is need for public assistance, both to increase the availability of funds to finance private industrial expansion and to deal with special problems such as regional development. All of these activities require an improvement in the flow of statistics and economic studies on which informed business decisions can be based.

Controls

148. Improving the industrial climate will necessitate action with respect to controls of two kinds. First, there are what might be termed equilibrium controls, under which industrial materials have been allocated or rationed or subjected to price controls. These are at best short-term palliatives, and the problems which gave rise to them have now been successfully overcome. Their continuation would tend to produce further distortions, and the remaining controls should be removed.

149. Second, there are what might be called structural controls established under the Law for the Protection of Industry of 1939. The principal of these controls involves the prior approval of the Ministry of Industry for investment in new industrial plants or for the expansion or relocation of existing plants. The administration of the investment authorization has presented a number of problems, and since the requirement is no longer necessary it should be discontinued.

150. The 1939 legislation also established a category of "industry of national interest" to stimulate, by special benefits, industries needed for national defense or self-sufficiency. The criteria of "national interest"

specified in the legislation are very broad and, as in the case of the investment authorization, it has proven difficult to apply well-defined economic standards. The category should be eliminated, or, at least, be applied automatically to whole branches of industry rather than to individual firms and only to overcome short-term or institutional obstacles.

151. Another of these controls is the requirement that a wide variety of public organizations use exclusively articles of Spanish manufacture. The requirement has often obliged these organizations to equip themselves under disadvantageous conditions as to price, quality and delivery time. If the Law is retained, it should be interpreted liberally, a price factor should be introduced and the requirement should be limited to a published list of items.

Labor Flexibility and Mobility

152. The expansion and modernization of industry will involve not only an increase in total employment but also changes in employment among industries and in particular trades within industries. These changes will demand considerable flexibility in the use of the labor force.

153. Dismissals for "economic" reasons can be made only through a procedure involving governmental approval. Wage rates and other conditions of employment are regulated in considerable detail. This system has tended to impede changes in the employment pattern; it has also made it difficult to adjust wages to changes in productivity and reduced the incentive to introduce new machinery or to undertake new ventures.

154. The Government has already taken some steps toward greater flexibility and these point the direction for future policy. Establishment of a nationwide employment exchange and of a fund to assist in moving industrial labor from surplus to deficit areas is an important element of this policy. The widespread use of collective bargaining agreements is a recent development in the right direction. While greater flexibility and mobility of labor will increase its productivity, there will also be a need for more intensive vocational training.

The Role of Public Enterprise

155. How rapidly industrial development takes place will also depend on the relationship between public and private enterprise, and in particular on the role of the Instituto Nacional de Industria (INI). INI

has made a number of important contributions, not only to the reconstruction of industry after the war but also to its subsequent development. With changed conditions, however, a definition of the role of public enterprise is a matter of priority. This definition involves three issues: the scope of INI's operations; equality of competition between public and private enterprises; and accountability and control.

156. The Law establishing INI in 1941 provides, on the whole, a reasonable definition of such a role, but much depends on how the law is reflected in administrative practice. The more broadly INI's mandate is interpreted the more uncertainty is created among private investors, thus retarding the growth of private industry and the inflow of foreign capital. Accordingly, the Government should periodically decide and announce publicly what new activities, if any, should be assigned to INI for a coming period. In making these decisions, the Government should generally be guided by the principle that INI should not enter into any field in which private enterprise is already operating profitably or which private enterprise has active plans for entering. The new activities of INI should be essentially those of an industrial pioneer, opening up and developing new fields; this pioneering role would be particularly relevant in matters of regional development. At the same time, the original intention of reducing INI's participation in some of its activities could be further implemented by increased public sales of INI's holdings, with special emphasis on selling INI's shares in companies where it has a minority interest.

157. It is also desirable that INI enterprises should operate, insofar as possible, under the same conditions as private firms with which they compete. Each INI company should be treated as an autonomous unit responsible for its own financial management. Those companies which are profitable should be expected to obtain their capital financing on the same basis as private firms, without special advantages in borrowing conditions. Those companies which are not profitable—and some could not be expected to be, particularly in defense or pioneering fields—should obtain financial assistance directly from the State budget where it would be clearly identified and subject to budgetary review. INI should also not have any special advantages with respect to inclusion in the category of "national interest," to subsidies from other public organisms, or to administrative and regulatory matters.

158. If the Government is to exercise effective control over public enterprises and if the public at large is to be kept informed of their situation, financial information on these enterprises needs to be disseminated more widely. More readily available public accounts would

also help to stimulate cost consciousness. Accordingly, the Government should require each INI company to publish a comprehensive annual report and an analysis of the results of its activities, including a statement of its future plans and a detailed financial account of its operations.

Finance for Industry

159. An increasing volume of investment will be required if industrial expansion is to be rapid. Much of this will come through private sources, but the flow of private capital is affected by the impact of public policy on the economic environment. More directly, the Government provides public funds to finance private industrial investment, primarily through the Banco de Credito Industrial (BCI).

160. More funds should be allocated to BCI and its scope of lending operations should be widened through the establishment of branches in the principal industrial centers outside of Madrid. BCI should modify its approach to make it possible for smaller firms to borrow. While not relaxing its careful project appraisals, BCI should assume somewhat greater risks in order to spur industrial development. Under appropriate circumstances, BCI should be permitted to make equity investments. Furthermore, BCI should enlarge the scope of its technical assistance to borrowers.

Regional Development of Industry

161. The Government has stated that its primary objective is the maximum rate of growth of the economy as a whole, and that regional development should be pushed only when it does not interfere with that objective; this approach will undoubtedly provide the maximum benefit to the Spanish people.

162. It is, of course, recognized that much can nevertheless be done to encourage regional development and lessen regional disparities in income. The essential elements of a regional development policy in the industrial sector are twofold:

a. careful selection of a limited number of regions with the best prospects for development;

b. adoption of measures that will accelerate development of these regions without interfering with growth elsewhere in the economy.

163. The types of industries most appropriate for these regions are those that have a high level of employment per unit of investment and also operate at a minimum of cost disadvantage as a result of location vis-a-vis markets and suppliers.

164. One important way in which the Government, and INI in particular, can assist the process of selective regional development is through the establishment of industrial estates. These can provide new industries with the external economies that are customarily found in large centers and thus would offset the attraction of more plants to already overcrowded areas. INI could not only establish such industrial estates but could also provide entrepreneurs with technical assistance on such matters as design of machinery, production methods, quality control and marketing techniques.

ELECTRIC POWER

165. The demand for power has been growing rapidly as the economy expands, with generation of electricity increasing threefold between 1949 and 1959. At the end of 1959, about 70 percent of installed capacity was hydroelectric and there are still considerable hydroelectric resources to be exploited. Generation, transmission and distribution are still largely in the hands of private companies; the Government's principal functions are regulatory and rate-setting.

166. Regulation of power dispatching is entrusted to Unidad Electrica SA (UNESA). The low priority it gives to thermal generation based on imported fuel should be discontinued; the favorable priority given to production from distressed coal mines is also questionable.

167. In effect, power rates for different categories of consumers are uniform for the whole of Spain. In order to ensure that industries are located where electricity can be generated most cheaply, price differentiation for large consumers in different areas should be encouraged.

168. Funds are collected by the Oficina Liquidadora de Energia Electrica (OFILE) through a surcharge on sales of electricity (recargo) and are distributed as contributions to the capital and operating costs of new generating plants. The way in which contributions are distributed has not always encouraged investment where it was most needed, and the whole case for subsidizing new capacity should be reviewed in order to avoid a bias toward investment in one form of generation as opposed to another or toward investment in generation as opposed to distribution.

Section VI

OTHER SECTORS

THE INTERNATIONAL TOURIST TRADE

169. The growth in Spain's international tourist trade has been very encouraging. Spain has many inherent advantages for tourists, having a favorable climate and many touristic attractions. Hotels and services are generally excellent and comparatively cheap. Furthermore, Spain has been able to share in the general growth of the international tourist trade.

170. Nevertheless, continued expansion of tourism will not take place automatically, and to maintain—and, if possible, increase—Spain's share in the total travel market, vigorous action will have to be taken. Additional hotel accommodation will have to be provided; existing capacity needs to be better utilized by combating the seasonality of the market. Improvement in transport and other infrastructure will be needed. Augmented publicity abroad should be planned. And, most important, price stability must be maintained throughout the economy.

Hotels

171. The majority of new hotels will be built by private enterprise, but investment will need stimulus and assistance from the Government through the Credito Hotelero, to which additional funds should be allocated. The Credito Hotelero no longer needs to offer the incentive of concessionary interest rates; its main functions should be to augment the total volume of hotel investment and to make sure it takes place where most needed.

172. Price controls on hotels could be eliminated without leading to an excessive rise in prices. Any increase in hotel prices would be kept in check by the intensified competition from an increasing number of hotels which, in part, the removal of price controls would itself stimulate. Competition from other Mediterranean countries would also induce hotel operators to maintain comparatively low prices. Furthermore, price discipline should be maintained by allowing hoteliers to fix their own schedule of prices—including varying rates at different seasons—and then compelling them to maintain the published rates during the year.

173. The state-owned chain of hotels provides useful services; its ob-

ject should be to supply facilities where private initiative is not likely to do so. It should not compete with private facilities on unequal terms.

Infrastructure

174. Investment in transportation and other infrastructure is essential to the long-term prosperity of the tourist trade and should be considered on a priority basis. There is a two-way relationship involved: plans, policies and assessments of trends by the tourist interests should be taken into account by those responsible for planning transport and other public services and vice versa.

175. Resort areas should be planned to take advantage of opportunities for external economies. Generally speaking it is relatively less expensive to provide public services for an intensively developed resort than for small or scattered developments. Accordingly, the loan policy of the Credito Hotelero should be geared to encouraging hotel construction in areas where priorities have been established taking these factors into account.

Administrative Organization

176. A forward-looking policy to expand tourism can only succeed if there are specific arrangements for taking a comprehensive view of its problems, and if there is a close coordination among the various authorities concerned. Accordingly, a small interdepartmental committee should be established to keep the main problems of tourism under systematic review and to bring to the attention of all agencies concerned those tourist trade developments which impinge on their particular interests.

177. The Government should also consider how tourism can be given a more prominent and assured place within the administration and its affairs brought fully within the purview of economic discussions. A separate sub-secretariat might be worth considering.

178. Increased budget allocations for publicity and other expenditures to promote Spanish tourism abroad are required. Local and regional initiative in tourism should also be encouraged.

EDUCATION AND SCIENTIFIC RESEARCH

179. The Government is participating in the Mediterranean Regional Project organized by OEEC (now OECD) and is undertaking long-term studies of priorities in educational planning. In making such

plans, the Government will undoubtedly keep the strategy for economic development in mind.

180. Primary education should be extended to reach all those of legal school age (6–12), its quality should be improved and its curriculum and organization so arranged that it can form a suitable basis for further specialized training.

181. In planning future construction requirements, internal migration trends must be taken into account and, since these are affected by economic developments, there should be joint consultation between the Ministry of Education and the Planning Commission.

182. In order to stem the drain of qualified teachers from the profession, salaries and other conditions of employment should be improved.

183. The Government is considering raising the school-leaving age to 14. While this is a worthy objective, its achievement should be timed to follow the improvement in the quality of the existing primary school system. Also, the question of the content and purposes of the additional two years of studies would have to be considered because for many new pupils these years would provide their terminal education.

184. The supply of trained technical specialists at the secondary level needs to be expanded on the basis of projections of manpower requirements. Before any large-scale additional investment is made for these purposes, there should be a clearer plan of the types of specialization required, the appropriate types of training establishments and their location.

185. Wastage rates are a matter of concern. It is very wasteful to expand facilities merely to accommodate added initial intakes of students without a commensurate increase in the output of fully qualified students. A number of possible solutions should be considered.

186. In the universities, there is still too small a proportion of students in the science faculties. Moreover, there is doubt as to whether existing capacity is being fully utilized.

187. Of particular concern is the small number of graduates from the higher technical institutes. There is some evidence that the numbers admitted to professional training are being unnecessarily and arbitrarily restricted, and the Government should see that this practice is reversed. While existing facilities should be used to the full, there is probably also a case for increasing the number of institutes in different parts of Spain.

188. Adult education can help make surplus labor more mobile by aiding the retraining process. Vocational courses should be coordinated with literacy and other general courses for adults. Efforts should be

made to keep unit costs within bounds so that some sort of training may be provided for the maximum number of adults.

189. The formulation of a national policy for scientific research should be pressed. Coordination between various agencies should be assured. To make the various research institutes fully effective, additional and up-to-date equipment must be acquired and the salaries and conditions of employment of research scientists improved. Thus, a substantial increase in budget allocations for scientific research should be foreseen.

HOUSING

190. Because there has been an impressive increase in housing construction, the Government can turn away from a policy of general stimulation of housing to one which is more selective. The principal deficiency now appears to be in housing for the low-income groups, and a significant improvement in housing conditions could ensue if the Government concentrated its financial and construction efforts on alleviating this deficiency. Other tasks could be left mainly to the private market with public authority providing financial support where necessary.

191. Efficiency would be increased by a reduction in the number of public and quasi-public agencies operating in the housing field and by more coordination and specialization in the functions of those which remain. Close contact should be maintained between housing authorities and economic planning officials so that housing activities parallel economic growth trends, both with respect to geographical location and the likely pattern of consumer demand.

192. Since lower-income housing inevitably involves substantial subsidy, the Government should take direct responsibility for such construction, without the interposition of intermediaries.

193. Because of their dispersion, low-income families in rural areas have benefited less than others from public housing programs in the past. New techniques must be considered if this large problem is to be met with any reasonable speed. One of the most hopeful possibilities is a self-help program under which the public authorities provide minimum housing facilities, while the occupants improve their units with their own labor and with the support of technical and financial assistance from a central organization. Cooperatives and other non-profit groups can usefully assist in such programs. The whole system

could be coordinated at the center by a special new section within the Instituto Nacional de Vivienda (INV).

194. The principal forms of public support for the private sector should be, first, the establishment of a national system of mortgage insurance to guarantee the repayment of first mortgages from the private sector, and, second, the provision of second mortgages from public funds. The object of the second mortgage system is not to subsidize the individual owner but to augment the total amount of capital available for housing in the private sector and to inject it where it can be most effective. Concessionary rates of interest should thus be avoided, since any such subsidy should be concentrated on low-income housing. The social purposes of the public credit mechanism in the private sector could be achieved in other ways, such as extending the amortization period for those in need.

195. The gradual removal of rent control would also stimulate private housing investment. Removal of rent control could be made conditional on repairs and improved maintenance.

196. The contracting process within the building industry should be reviewed to put more of a premium on compliance in all respects, especially construction schedules, since delays in completion both deny use and impose added costs. Better credit facilities should be available to contractors to enable them to acquire modern equipment and machinery. Public lending agencies should make an effort to speed up certifications and payments on completion of works, so that contractors can avoid the heavy costs of short-term private loans.

SECTION **I**

DEVELOPMENT POLICY

CHAPTER 1 *ECONOMIC GROWTH AND OBJECTIVES*

Antecedents

The Spanish economy has had many difficulties to contend with during most of the past 25 years. It was disrupted by nearly three years of war, and when hostilities ceased in April 1939, the problems of reconstruction were formidable. There were no gold or foreign exchange reserves; productive capacity was much reduced; and the scarcity of food, raw materials and equipment could only be made good by increasing imports for which there was insufficient purchasing power. A few months later, the outbreak of the Second World War made it still more difficult to procure essential supplies and the possibilities of shipment were strictly limited; in consequence any major work on reconstruction had to be postponed.

During these critical years the Government was compelled to impose a strict and far-reaching system of controls and to intervene in many aspects of economic life. Prices, foreign trade and payments, investment, employment and the allocation of raw materials were among the items subjected to regulation. And since Spain could no longer count on receiving certain indispensable products from abroad, the Government tried to meet the emergency by encouraging the exploitation of indigenous resources which had hitherto not been regarded as economic propositions. It also laid plans to build up a number of basic industries, if necessary through state-controlled enterprises, to enable the work of reconstruction to proceed as soon as opportunities occurred.

The end of the World War in 1945 did not bring promise of an early return to normality or of any easy solution of Spain's economic problems. European countries were grappling with their own grave problems of reconstruction; there were shortages of foodstuffs and essential materials throughout Europe; and although the countries directed their efforts toward restoring the freedom of international trade, the exceptional conditions forced them for some years to regulate it through a network of bilateral agreements. Spain did not participate in the Marshall Plan, and while other Western European Governments were seeking multilateral solutions to their problems, the Spanish Government persevered with its own plans. All this tended to accentuate the isolation of the economy, which events of the previous 12 years had brought about.

In these circumstances, the growth of the economy from 1940 to 1950 was very slow, and accompanied by severe inflation. By 1950 it is doubtful whether national income—and *a fortiori* income per head—had recovered even to the depressed level of 1935. But a distinct quickening of growth took place in the next decade. In 1951 a loan was obtained from the United States, and substantial economic aid followed the Pact of Madrid in 1953. With the supply position easing, a more rapid expansion occurred, but though growth was at first achieved without the inflation characteristic of the past, prices later began to rise and foreign exchange reserves to disappear. The intensification of controls and recourse to multiple exchange rates could not reverse the trend. Throughout this period, the domestic market, in an ambience of shortages and inflation, presented little or no problem to producers, and except for the few traditional export products there was little inducement for them to enter the foreign market, at a time when other European countries were progressively freeing trade and payments and restoring competitive conditions.

By the end of 1958 Spain's foreign exchange reserves were at a low ebb and still falling, and it was evident that drastic measures were called for. Spain had for some time been seeking closer association with other Western countries through international organizations concerned with economic cooperation, and in July 1959, the Government drew up a stabilization program in cooperation with the OEEC and the IMF. The peseta was devalued, restrictions were imposed on both public and private spending, and a program of trade liberalization adopted, according to the standards set by OEEC in which full membership was sought. The stabilization was supported by credits from the OEEC, IMF, the U.S. Government and private banks, and Spain became a member of OEEC on July 20, 1959.

These decisions were significant both politically and economically. In its presentation of the program to the two organizations, the Spanish Government declared that "the time has come to redirect economic policy in order to place the Spanish economy in line with countries of the Western world, and to free it from interventions inherited from the past, which do not correspond to the needs of the present situation." And the Government recognized that a more liberal system of trade and payments required a considerable relaxation of controls which hampered productivity and flexibility, and an increased reliance on the price mechanism. In other words, these decisions marked the end of economic isolation and cleared the way for a freer economy, based on international trade and economic cooperation with other countries.

The stabilization program was immediately successful, and has continued to be so, in restraining inflation and recouping foreign reserves. Prices have risen very little. The surplus in the balance of payments has been sufficiently large to bring the foreign reserves to over $850 million by the end of 1961. Trade was progressively liberalized, some price controls were removed and a greater freedom given to both domestic and foreign investment. The forces of competition have emerged again and manufacturers are, after a long interval, concerned as much with markets as with production. There has been renewed interest in the export market. On the other hand the growth of the economy, which was running at about 5¼ percent per annum from 1951 to 1958, virtually stopped between 1958 and 1960 as the readjustment took place.

Interest in official and business circles accordingly shifted to the reactivation and development of the economy. The Government was anxious to press on with economic expansion and modernization, founded on the financial stability which had been achieved, in order to raise the standard of living of the people.

Another factor influencing policy has been the movement among European countries toward economic integration and the enlargement of the market in Europe, which has recently gained in momentum.[1] This movement imparted a greater sense of urgency to the completion of the transition toward a freer economy, and to making progress in development and modernization, without which Spain would not be equipped to play her part in the European scene.

It was against this background that the Spanish Government decided to prepare a development program and to ask the International Bank for Reconstruction and Development to appoint a mission to make recommendations to that end.

Economic Planning and Objectives

In accordance with its terms of reference, the mission conceived of its task as threefold:

a. to make recommendations on economic policy for development;

b. to propose criteria for investments in the public sector for the next five years and, where circumstances permit, the specific investments themselves;

[1] More recently the Spanish Government has requested the European Economic Community to negotiate some form of association.

c. to suggest how the Government might improve its organization for economic development.

Our recommendations in these various respects will be found throughout the rest of the report under the relevant sector headings. They are also discussed in terms of the principles underlying them later in this section.

At the outset, the mission believes it important that consideration be given to the kind of development plan that is most appropriate for the Spanish economy at this juncture. In our view—and we believe that the Government concurs in this—planning at this stage should be what has come to be called "indicative." In planning of this kind, the Government would have a twofold role: first, to propose a policy for the rate of growth of the economy and to work out the implications for the future development of the economy as a whole; and, second, to state the actions it proposes to take, with respect both to public investment and to public policy as its own part in the fulfillment of that rate of growth. Together these might be said to constitute a development program, not spelled out in small detail but indicative of the main lines of future growth of the economy and the main actions necessary to bring them about.

The forward view of the economy, which would be arrived at in consultation with the private sector, would normally be confined to important economic magnitudes such as the over-all rate of growth, private and public consumption and investment, foreign trade and payments and production in major subdivisions of the economy. The amount of supplementary detail under each heading might vary widely; in the initial stages it would be likely to be limited by the confidence which could be placed in the available data. A necessary part of the planning process would be constant improvement of data and of methods of handling it.

The Government would, as a logical consequence of this forward view of the economy, draw certain conclusions as to its own program for action over the next four or five years. This program would consist of two parts.

The first would be the important policy measures it foresees as necessary to promote the growth of the private and the public sectors of the economy. These policy measures might cover a variety of fields, such as taxation, tariffs, economic controls and social insurance. The second would be a forecast of its own current and capital expenditure in the various sectors. The Government would thus make itself responsible for the creation of a consistent and realistic view of the future development of the economy, together with a statement as to how it intended to bring about that development through its economic and social policies and its program of public expenditure.

A perspective of the future of this kind can be of very great value to all those who have to make investment decisions, whether they be in the public or the private sector. In the absence of such a perspective and of knowledge of the Government's intentions for the future, private entrepreneurs may be hesitant to take action.

Planning of this kind is not rigid, and under it the Government does not attempt to order every aspect of economic life. The private sector is left free to place its own interpretation on the predictions implicit in such a forward view of the economy, and to make its own plans for investment accordingly. If explicit predictions of production of key commodities, such as steel, are made, they are intended more as indications for general guidance as to orders of magnitude than as targets necessarily to be fulfilled. But knowledge of the Government's intentions is, of itself, an important element in enabling the private sector to make decisions which will help to fulfill those intentions.

Open discussion and interchange of views can stimulate a more general understanding of the process of economic development and the relation of each individual part of the economy to the whole. Adaptation to changing circumstances will continually be necessary, since human vision is limited and external circumstances especially may change. Economic planning of this kind must therefore be a continuous process, not a series of isolated acts four or five years apart. A development program is an instrument to make the process work, not an end in itself.

We hope that our report can serve as a step in this process. In addition to making various recommendations in detail, we try to present a view of the future as a common basis for them. We are conscious of the fact that there are many gaps in the picture we present. There are some elements that we have consciously omitted. We have, for example, concentrated more on the Government's own program for action than on the general perspective for the future, although we do in very general terms sketch the nature of development. We have not attempted to give indicative targets in particular sectors unless, as in agriculture, they appear crucial to the argument. In a first attempt there are bound to be deficiencies of this sort, which can be remedied by improved information and closer consultation within the private and the public sectors and between them.

In a number of places we recommend that certain studies be made, that information be collected to make those studies possible and that suitable units be created to collect the information and analyze it. All this will take time. We envisage that, in one to two years' time, sufficient information will be available to make new, more detailed forecasts of the development of the economy and to revise and amplify the various recommendations that we have made in tentative or general terms. There is no doubt that Spain has the human resources to create more detailed and more accurate programs as more information and more experience are acquired.

An important purpose of any kind of planning is to reconcile objectives. The objectives of national policy, of which economic policy is only a part, are always manifold and may often be conflicting. Different policies, for example, might be followed according to the weight that is attached to economic growth on the one hand and economic security on the other. It is only against a common perspective that the choice between different objectives can, first, be seen and secondly, be made.

In a statement given to the mission, the Government set forth a list of the principal lines of policy it intends to follow, namely: to promote a high rate of growth; to base development on foreign trade; to confine public activity to typically public investments except in special cases; to encourage competition; to maintain stability; and to make the most efficient use of savings. We are in thorough agreement with these objectives, which do not, in general, appear to be incompatible.

The Government does, however, recognize that there are two objectives which may conflict under some circumstances with the promotion of rapid economic growth. These are the objectives of employment and the development of particular regions. In view of the large number of underemployed agricultural workers in Spain and the big gap between the incomes of the poorer areas and those of the richer areas, these subsidiary objectives cannot be dismissed lightly, even though they may at times conflict with the larger purpose. The Government's view is that priority should be given to activities favoring these objectives *per se,* only when the differences between this course and the more general one of economic growth are not very wide. The mission concurs with this view; since the rate of growth will be the determining factor in increasing employment and in reducing the disparity between regions, there should be no diversion from the effort to promote growth except in cases of great hardship or when the economic cost is very small.

Growth and Structural Change

The problems of rural poverty, of disparity in income between regions and of the need to create jobs for the underemployed are not unique to Spain. These problems, which are closely related to each other, are characteristic of the stage of economic growth which Spain has reached. Even though the many structural changes that economic growth brings about are bound to vary from country to country, there is a certain common pattern. It is, therefore, useful to set the position of Spain today in the historical perspective of this pattern, since it provides valuable insight into the course that economic development in Spain has followed in the past and may be expected to follow in the future.

In the early stages of development, agriculture is the predominant sector, being much larger than the industrial and service sectors combined, especially in terms of employment. Even though the industrial and service sectors may be growing, they are initially too small to make large demands on agriculture either for its products or for its manpower. Similarly, as population grows, the industrial and service sectors do not, in the first instance, take up the increase in the labor force. Consequently, the number of people in agriculture continues to grow and there is likely to be considerable unemployment or underemployment of the farm population.

At this early stage of development, therefore, agricultural income grows relatively slowly, and, *a fortiori,* the average income of people employed in agriculture grows more slowly still. The larger the non-agricultural sectors become, the greater are the demands they make on the agricultural sector and consequently the greater are the possibilities for the incomes of farmers to rise. But for a long time incomes outside of agriculture grow faster, with the consequence that agricultural income per head tends to fall relatively to the average for the economy as a whole, very often to as little as half that average.

Sooner or later turning points are reached in respect of both agricultural employment and relative income. First, the growth in the nonagricultural labor force becomes sufficiently large to take up the annual increase in the labor force as a whole, and the number of people employed in agriculture starts to fall. The second turning point, which usually comes later, is when agricultural income per person employed begins to grow as fast as or faster than average income in the economy.

How long this process takes and the timing of the two turning points depend on many factors, which vary from country to country. Two important factors are the rate of increase in population and the rate of economic growth in the economy as a whole. The faster the population grows, the longer it will take to reach the turning points. The faster the rate of economic growth, the quicker they will be reached.

At the beginning of this century, Spain was still largely an agricultural country. From the evidence we have, growth of income in Spain appears to have been slow in the first half of this century and it was, of course, interrupted by the war. But population has also grown slowly (about 8½ percent per decade), to a considerable extent because of migration overseas.

In these fifty years there have been great changes. In 1900, Spain was a country of 18½ million people; two-thirds of the working population got their living from the land. In 1950, the population was 28 million or half as much again; the number of people in agriculture was then less than half the labor force. Growth in employment was concentrated in industry and services and, with it, went a parallel growth in urbanization, especially in the larger cities. But the agricultural labor force still continued to grow, if only slowly.

In the last decade, 1950–60, population increased at about the same rate as before, but income grew faster. There was, for the first time, a large reduction in the agricultural labor force of the order of half a million. In 1960, some 42 percent of the force was engaged in agriculture and they produced 27 percent of the national product. These figures, which suggest that income per head in agriculture is about 65 percent of the national average, demonstrate the relative poverty of agriculture in the economy. They are not untypical of a country where the net income per head is somewhat in excess of $250.

What will happen to agricultural income and employment in the future depends on what assumptions are made about the growth of population and income. Population is likely to grow, if anything, more slowly than in the past; the demand for Spanish labor in Western Europe may be an important element in this respect. An even more crucial question is the growth of income.

For the purposes of the mission's forecasts, where we have made them in this report, the assumption has been that there will be an annual rate of growth in national product of 5.0 percent per capita from 1960 onward. This is higher, but not much higher, than the rate of growth of the economy from 1951 to 1958 (4.4 percent per capita). This past growth was achieved at the cost of some inflation and was made possible by a flow of resources from abroad, which amounted, in very rough orders of magnitude, to some 2 percent of the GNP. We assume that at least part of this flow of foreign resources will continue, though not necessarily in the same form. We also assume that a somewhat higher rate of savings will be available to the economy in the coming years and will, more or less, make up the difference.

Our reason for assuming an increase in the rate of growth does not, therefore, rest on the assumption of a greater relative volume of resources for investment. It rests on the widespread opportunities for better use of these resources, as the rest of the report will show, and on the belief that the Government can readily adapt its development policy to grasp these opportunities. An increase from 4.4 percent to 5.0 percent implies something less than a 15 percent higher yield on the same level of investment (relative to GNP). This should be well within the bounds of possibility.

The "target" of 5 percent is intended to be optimistic, but realistic. Without optimism, growth will not be stimulated. Without realism, there is the risk of disillusionment. Much higher figures have been recorded in other countries in recent years, e.g., in Japan and Yugoslavia, but a better comparison is probably with Italy where, in a period of active economic expansion over the last decade, the rate of growth, taking one year with another, averaged about 5 percent per capita.

On the basis of this assumption, the mission has made a very general projection of the future development of the economy in terms of agriculture on the one hand and industry and services on the other. This projection should be regarded as an illustration of general direction rather than as a detailed forecast. The results of the projection are given in Table 1.1. At the present stage of development in Spain, the demand for agricultural products will continue to grow relatively slowly—on our assumptions, at about half the rate of the growth of the economy as a whole. Thus, the estimated agricultural product in 1970

TABLE 1.1: Illustrative Projection of the Growth of the Spanish Economy, 1960–1970

	1960	1970
Population: (million)	30.4	33.0
Gross Product per head (thousand pts)	17	27
Gross Product at factor cost (billion pts)		
Agriculture	136	180
Industry and services	368	720
	504	900
Labor force: (million)		
Agriculture	4.8	4.0
Industry and services	6.8	8.6
	11.6	12.6

is only about a third higher than in 1960 compared with a twofold estimated increase in the rest of the economy.

In spite of this rapid growth in the industrial and service sectors, the increase in the labor force in these two sectors has been assumed to be little more than one-quarter—in absolute figures 1.8 million people. This would still exceed the increase in the labor force by 800,000 and so would draw off that number of workers from agriculture. With this large reduction in the number of farmers, agricultural income per worker might increase by as much as 60 percent, which is a far higher figure than in the previous decade and comparable to the increase in the economy as a whole. The increasing momentum of the structural changes taking place could even open the possibility that there would be a closing of the gap in the following decades.

Whatever happens to the relation between agricultural and nonagricultural income, the over-all rate of growth will in any case be important in determining how fast agricultural income grows. On the assumptions we have made, a reduction (or increase) in the rate of growth of 1 percent from 1960 to 1970 might mean a comparable, if not greater, reduction (or increase) in that of agricultural income per worker.

Hypothetical exercises of this kind are, of course, based on many assumptions and dubious statistics. In particular, treating agriculture as the residual recipient of the labor force is an oversimplification. Consequently, less significance attaches to the absolute figures than to the kind of comparison we have just made. The latter underlines the conclusion that rural poverty and underemployment are not isolated problems: they are problems of economic growth and are best attacked by achieving the highest possible rate of growth.

Much the same can be said of regional development. Indeed, the two problems largely overlap. Agriculture is not a homogeneous sector. There are great disparities in income between dynamic and traditional agriculture, between the citrus farmer of the Levante and the landless laborer of Andalusia. The problem of surplus labor in agriculture is particularly acute in certain regions, notably in Galicia and Andalusia, though manifesting itself in the different circumstances of *minifundia* and *latifundia*.

Past experience in other countries suggests that these problems are part of a process of historical development which is to a large extent inevitable. The Government is unlikely to be able to affect the process more than marginally, and the greatest contribution that it can make is, again, by increasing as much as possible the over-all rate of economic growth. In this way, the rapid development of industry and services, and of agriculture itself in some regions, will draw manpower and other resources from the poorer regions, thereby increasing the income both of those who leave the region and of those who remain.[2] Even so, in view of the wide disparities in the resource base, population density and growth potential of different regions, it must be expected that economic growth will continue to be unevenly divided among the regions of Spain.

We are not, however, advocating a policy of letting nature take its course. There will certainly be opportunities for the Government to influence the way in which change takes place, even within the criteria it has set itself. But it should use its influence not to combat change, but to promote it and to help people to adjust to it. We return to this subject at some length in the sections on Industry and Agriculture, where specific recommendations for assisting the less developed regions will be made.

We would caution, however, against massive investments in a particular sector or region based on no other criterion than its poverty. In the first place, these investments often only touch the welfare of a few. Furthermore, in an economy where the resources available for investment are scarce, investments not based on productivity as a criterion are necessarily made at the cost of investments that are so based, with the inevitable result of a decline in the growth of production and income for the economy as a whole. When there is so much to be done in most places on strictly economic grounds, which would contribute more to economic growth and would materially affect the welfare of the many, any policy of investment which ignores productivity will tend in the long run to be self-defeating.

[2] In this connection, see the discussion on regional changes in Annex A, at the end of this section (pp. 84–89).

CHAPTER 2 *POLICIES FOR ECONOMIC GROWTH*

Cost Consciousness and Economic Development

The war years and the years following with their accompanying shortages, controls and inflation were not conducive to cost-consciousness. Essential goods had to be procured without counting the cost. Selling was easy and cost control secondary to the problems of obtaining raw materials and capital goods.

These conditions have passed. Shortages have disappeared and, in some cases, been replaced by surplus capacity. Foreign exchange is abundant. Reactivation rather than inflation has more recently been the problem. As we point out in the section on agriculture, the task now is no longer to produce at any cost, but at the least cost in order to reap the fullest advantage from the economy's resources.

The change in circumstances has naturally brought about a change in outlook in this respect in many quarters, especially in view of the move toward greater economic integration with the rest of Europe. Although this move adds point to the need for greater cost-consciousness and, in some degree, makes it more important, we believe that closer attention to costs in any event is important to economic growth. As we point out at various places in this report, Spain's resources are sufficient to promote substantial economic growth. Perhaps more than anything else, how rapidly growth in fact takes place will depend on how wisely the public and the private sector take advantage of the means already at their disposal. This, in turn, is in large part a question of considering closely the costs of alternative ways of using these resources, to ensure that they make the maximum contribution to development.

As many of our recommendations made toward this end are scattered throughout the report and the same themes recur in different forms in different places, we have summarized some of the principal ones in this chapter. The need for greater cost-consciousness exists in both the market and the non-market economy, but the economic discipline necessary to promote cost-consciousness differs from one to the other. We have accordingly distinguished between the two, although in some cases the same point may apply to both.

The Market Economy

In the market economy, economic discipline should be enforced by a freely functioning price mechanism that brings about the best allocation of resources through the force of competition. We do not pretend that the price mechanism always works perfectly or that individual entrepreneurs always respond to its signals in the right way. Nor would we suggest that a laissez-faire attitude is desirable from the social point of view. But these qualifications merely mean that the price-mechanism should not be the master; they do not preclude it from being a good servant.

Although, as a result of stabilization and the accompanying moves toward liberalization, many distortions in the cost and price structure were eliminated, some still remain. Distortions may arise in various ways. Price controls are one source. While it is true that the majority of these controls have been removed, a minority still persist. We have in some cases made specific recommendations for removal of them; in general it would be our feeling that the case would have to be extremely strong to justify retention. The fact that a rise in prices would follow relaxation is not sufficient reason to continue controls; a rise in price may in fact indicate the existence of a distortion that can best be corrected by bringing in new resources, as the rise in prices is likely to do. In some cases, where the bounds of distortion are uncertain and where the possibility of widespread social repercussions might attend removal of controls, it may be necessary to proceed circumspectly. But the only clear-cut case of this kind that we are aware of is rent control.

There are, in addition, widespread forms of price distortion by cross-subsidies among state enterprises. For example, the ports make land and other installations available to government-owned enterprises at highly subsidized rates. Government enterprises also pay for some petroleum products at prices which involve a subsidy to the producer, whereas prices paid for electricity sometimes involve a subsidy to the consumer. As such practices make it likely that resources are used uneconomically, the mission recommends their abolition.

Among the most insidious forms of distortion in a developing economy is subsidization through the interest rate, implicitly or explicitly. Interest rates are the device by which capital is allocated through the price mechanism. They are therefore a cost of fundamental importance. Failure to observe this fact can lead to misuse of capital without anyone being aware of it. It may, for example, introduce a bias toward capital-intensive projects at the expense of the employment of labor, which is not in Spain's interest at present. It should be noted that the danger is just as great in the agricultural sector as in any other. In advocating more rigorous criteria for selecting public investments, therefore, we have indicated the need for a realistic appraisal of the cost of capital. In addition, we have, in various places in the report, stressed the need for a more fluid capital market, in which both private and public institutions compete for capital resources on the same terms.

Though the ultimate objective is to create a price mechanism which will promote, as far as possible, the best allocation of Spain's resources, this does not mean that all subsidies or other special forms of assistance should be eliminated. The state has a duty to relieve hardship, for example. It does mean that, in whatever form, subsidies should be given as directly as possible to those in need. They should not be made indiscriminately through the price mechanism, where they can create serious and unknown distortions in the economy.

As we have said, response to the price mechanism is not always adequate. Industrial enterprises may not be possessed of information which would lead them to take advantage in due time of future possibilities or they may be uncertain of the government's intentions. There are various things the Government can do to overcome this. It may, in some areas, be justified in instituting incentives. They should not have the effect of favoring one firm against another nor, unless there is a clear economic reason, one type of activity against another. We have, therefore, recommended against the practice whereby firms which are declared "of national interest" are permitted to import free of duty and are freed from the normal income tax obligations for certain periods. As a second example, tax reimbursement (*desgravacion fiscal*) is made to exporters in certain industries, but not all, as compensation for sales taxes and similar indirect taxes paid in the course of production. A third example is the system of payments for electricity which tends to introduce a bias toward investment in generation as against transmission and toward investment in generation of particular kinds.

It may still be desirable to give special incentives or compensation in certain conditions, but in that event the conditions should be broad in scope and the advantages should be available to all those satisfying the particular conditions, e.g., *desgravacion fiscal* should be allowed to all exporters.

The classic example of inadequate response to the price mechanism is resort by producers to restrictive or monopolistic practices. Although the mission was aware of the widespread preoccupation with this problem in Spain, we found it difficult, in the time at our disposal, to identify such practices with certainty. However, it is our impression that, where they did appear to exist, they were often buttressed by existing laws or controls or procedures. For example, the existing laws on the control of investment, mainly in industry, but to a limited extent in agriculture, would be a serious impediment to economic expansion if they were rigorously enforced. As things stand, to the extent that they are effective, they are arbitrary in effect and tend to encourage monopoly. As we believe that their rationale belongs to a past condition that no longer applies, we have recommended their abolition. Furthermore, we believe that our recommendations for a free market for capital will, in the same way, lead to greater competition.

In fact, our emphasis has been less on curbing monopoly than on encouraging competition. In the majority of cases, the best cure for such practices is a progressive exposure to foreign competition. We recognize that the tradition of protectionism and the previous period of economic isolation have left a legacy of economic activities which are unable to compete at international prices and that it would cause widespread hardship to expose the producers concerned and their employees to full international competition right away. In order that Spain obtain the best advantages from foreign trade, however, the mission has recommended progressive reduction of tariffs and abolition of quotas, especially for capital goods and raw materials, since the price and quality of these products have wide ramifications. In general, we have made a number of recommendations for facilitating imports from abroad. By the same token, we recommend greater freedom of purchase, as between domestic and foreign suppliers; RENFE, for example, has been particularly hard hit by restrictive practices in this respect. We also feel that the present emphasis on producing individual goods entirely within Spain may fail to take into account the possible economic advantages of partial production within the country. It may often pay to manufacture part of a particular product within the country, while importing the rest.

Foreign investment is of particular importance in this connection, since it can afford a valuable addition to domestic savings and technical knowledge as well as stimulating competition. It is, of course, understandable that the Government would wish to regulate the flow of foreign funds, but for the sake of the growth of the economy regulation should have as little deterrent effect as possible.

The Government can also do much to encourage the market economy by clarifying its intentions and introducing more certainty into its regulations. One instance of this is the present status of the tariff structure, which is in a state of transition. We have, therefore, recommended that the initial level of tariffs be set forthwith and that a schedule of reduction be published, on which people can depend as a reasonably reliable forecast. A second important case is taxation. The difficulty, under the present tax system, of predicting tax liabilities must necessarily be a serious obstacle to the quotation of firm prices and, therefore, a deterrent to investment and trade both internally and externally.

Finally, we have at various points recommended that government enterprises operating in the market economy not be insulated from its impact. This is not to say that, in the case of some government enterprises, there may not be considerations of a social or economic nature that justify the operation of the enterprise in certain respects without reference to ordinary commercial norms. We do say that these exceptional activities require justification, that they should be costed and decisions taken on the base of the true cost. Furthermore, when unprofitable activities are carried on in the broad national interest, a suitable formula should be found, whenever possible, to compensate the enterprise from the general revenues.

Transportation, which is particularly important in Spain with its widely dispersed markets, is a good case. In order to have a fully competitive multi-mode transport system, we have recommended that both the railways (Red Nacional de Ferrocarriles) and the present port administrations (Juntas de Obras de Puerto) be given greater responsibility for their current operations and the planning of their future investments. We believe that the best way of ensuring that the essential connection between investment planning, costing of operations and rates charged is realized in the future, and a more economically minded transport system obtained, is to make the organizations themselves responsible for decisions and for their consequences.

On the other hand, the government-owned industrial holding company, Instituto Nacional de Industria (INI), already enjoys a high degree of autonomy. In this case we recommend greater exposure of INI to market forces and removal of its special privileges, for two reasons. First, special privileges can only lead to uneconomic use of resources. Secondly, the Government's intention to encourage private initiative in the industrial field and to replace it only when it is lacking will not be fulfilled if private initiative is threatened by subsidized public competition.

In all cases, we believe that government enterprises should be subjected to thorough accountability. The Government should set its standards in this respect so as to offer an example to the private sector and insist on external auditing of its own enterprises and timely publication of their accounts. The accounts of public utilities, such as the RENFE and the ports, should include such items as depreciation and capital charges in order to give a truer indication of the surplus or deficit incurred. Full information on the accounts of the individual firms of INI and of INI as a whole should be publicly available.

The Non-Market Economy

Investments made directly or financed through loans by the central government, its autonomous agencies, official credit institutions, public enterprises and local government, probably amount to somewhat less than half of all investment in Spain. Public investment policy and practice is therefore of great importance. As we have just indicated, we believe that where government investment is to be made in sectors directly affected by the market, market considerations should apply. No less attention, however, is necessary in controlling costs and basing decisions on them in the case of investments less directly subject to market forces.

In the motive behind public investment there is often a social element. This does not in any way detract from the need to make just as careful an examination of investment proposals as in the private sector. Social objectives cannot be immune from analysis, simply because they are social. It is just as important to obtain whatever social benefits are desired at the lowest possible cost and to weigh the benefit against the cost, even though the former cannot be put in numerical terms.

In the non-market economy, some other form of discipline than the price mechanism must be imposed. The Government should ensure that all proposals for expenditures are subjected to some form of scrutiny to see that public money is being used to the best advantage. Responsibility for this has to be placed on the ministries themselves, and be delegated within ministries. Enforcement of this scrutiny should be part of the budgetary process. Only by this combination of delegation and discipline can the Government ensure that it considers programs of expenditure rather than individual projects, and that it is in a position to call for a thorough examination of the implications of these programs.

The mission found little evidence that investment proposals (or, indeed, proposals for current expenditure) are examined and analyzed in terms of cost and objective in any systematic way. The RENFE has made a careful study of the rentability of its lines but investments actually carried out have not always been in accordance with the results of the study. The Centro de Estudios Hidrograficos in the Ministry of Public Works has made a praiseworthy attempt to analyze the relative merits of irrigation projects, but, as the Centro itself points out, the data on the land to be irrigated are inadequate.

The consequences of not obtaining the highest economic return for the investment of public money are extremely serious. The less the return, the less is the increment to national product and consequently to savings for reinvestment. Therefore, the less will be the rate of growth of the economy, with consequences which have already been discussed. By improving the return on public investment funds the Government could, even without any increase in the magnitude of these funds, make a decisive contribution toward accelerating the rate of economic growth.

Although the mission's views on particular past investments and its recommendations for the future appear in detail in later chapters of the report, we have felt it desirable to describe at this point some of the consequences of inadequate review of public investment. In thus emphasizing investment we reflect the principal preoccupation of the mission. We would not exclude the application of our remarks, *mutatis mutandis,* to current expenditure.

Fewer starts and more rapid completions. In several sectors, many projects are begun with limited funds so that all of them take a long time to complete. Outstanding examples are irrigation works and railway lines. Housing is another example. The average time for completion appears to be about three years, which it should be possible to cut in half. This may not appear a large reduction in time, but the volume of expenditure affected, about 20 billion pts, is very large.

The cost of an excessively long period of construction is high. Including interest at 8 percent during construction, a project which takes ten years to build costs one-third more than the same one built in three years. As the interest is only part of the cost to the economy in terms of production foregone, the annual loss of income to the economy in various sectors for this reason alone must have run into many billions of pesetas annually.

Long delays also involve other risks. Deterioration of the parts of the construction finished early may occur before the works as a whole are completed. Changes in technology or in the market for the product may occur which alter the purpose for which the project was originally designed. A conspicuous case of this is the new railway lines which have been and are still being built. Some of them, when first conceived, may very well have had a function, but with increasing use of the automobile and the airplane, the need is rather to reduce the number of rail lines than to add to it.

Need for complementary investments. Some projects are completed without adequate provision for complementary investments. In certain cases, where the latter have been provided for, there has been a difference in the timing of completion of the various parts of a project. In other cases, no provision has been made. In either event, there is necessarily a period during which no benefits accrue to the project.

For example, the mission observed housing developments lacking public utility services such as water. Irrigation projects have also been delayed, because one agency with ample funds has completed its part, while another, less well supplied, has been unable to carry out its part at the same pace. In this particular case measures have been taken to prevent this from continuing.

The reason is not always lack of coordination between different authorities. Investment in the ports has been heavily on the side of construction work such as quays and breakwaters. Wharves, however, remain underused for lack of cranes. A comparatively small expenditure on cranes and other equipment would have saved much time in loading and unloading ships and so brought a higher return.

Projects with an intrinsically low return. A number of substantial investments have been made or proposed with no prospect of more than a negligible return. The consequence of this is clear; capital, the most scarce of the resources required for the growth of the economy, is wasted. We have already referred to the new railway lines, which the mission has recommended should be stopped forthwith.

Although we do not consider that the information available is sufficient to judge the large number of irrigation projects with any precision, it is clear that there is an extremely wide variation in their cost and yield.

Overinvestment. In a few cases, there is a danger of a relatively new phenomenon in Spain, overcapacity. Time does, of course, cure this problem, but the economy may in the meantime derive inadequate benefit, if special measures have to be adopted to dispose of the surplus. There appears to be a danger of this in the plans for increasing the number of dry docks and, to a limited extent, in the generation of electricity.

Overinvestment may be due to a failure to assess the market. In the mission's view, any irrigation program requires a proper assessment of the country's domestic requirements, the products to be produced under irrigation, the export possibilities and the potential for increasing production to meet these requirements by means other than the new projects. We think the existing program ought to be appraised with these considerations in mind.

Maintenance. In two major sectors normal maintenance has been neglected. The railway's budget for maintenance and normal improvement of track has never been adequate for its needs and, since the stabilization program, has been reduced even further. The condition of the track is one of the principal reasons for the poor service offered by the RENFE and the diversion of traffic to other modes. Adequate maintenance and fast service on the railways would not only save the country a large amount of capital expenditure in other types of transport equipment, but would even reduce the need for railway equipment itself.

The other case is the roads. Road traffic in Spain has grown very rapidly in the last ten years, and can be expected to do so in the future. Extensive repair of the heavily traveled roads is therefore essential if they are not to break up and thereby involve the Government in very heavy reconstruction expenditure. The urgent repair program we have recommended for these roads will be an expensive item and will make a heavy claim on the capacity of the road administration. While these two are the outstanding cases, the mission observed other cases of neglect, e.g., the painting of bridges, the upkeep of the few existing cranes in the ports, the maintenance of old houses.

Social investment. While it is impossible to measure "social" returns, cases exist in which investment appears out of proportion to the social benefits accruing. Obviously there are many cases in which social benefits are desirable, but it is in the interest of the country to provide such benefits as economically as possible. In this way, social benefits can be extended to reach as many people as possible rather than being concentrated on relatively few.

A particular instance of what we have in mind are the colonization projects of the Instituto Nacional de Colonizacion (INC). While these projects are, in various ways, admirably conceived, the standard of housing and other amenities provided for the colonists and the cost of bringing some of the land under irrigation appear in some cases to be high. In the field of public housing, more use of the well-known technique of "self-help" would enable the benefits of better housing to reach more people, particularly in rural areas.

It will be obvious from the foregoing that the mission believes that a much greater return in terms of both social and economic benefits from the Government's capital investment should be obtained. Elsewhere in the report, we make suggestions how this might be done in particular cases. The really important thing, however, is that the administration so organize itself as to be able to make the necessary choices on a continuing basis.

We have already spoken of the devolution of certain kinds of government activity, so that they are more responsive to market forces. We are confident, for example, that cranes rather than docks would have been installed, had the port authorities been responsible both for the choice of investment and also for the service payments on the capital required to make these investments. We also feel that, in similar circumstances, RENFE would follow a different investment policy.

Economic discipline has, however, still to be enforced within the government organization itself. Accordingly, we recommend the establishment within the spending ministries of small program and project review units to examine projects to be submitted for inclusion in the budget. Review would necessarily include a review not only of isolated projects but of the totality being planned in relation to projected needs. There would necessarily have to be a complementary central unit for this purpose in the Ministry of Finance; this unit would not, of course, replace the work of the Planning Commission, but would, on the contrary, be intended to work closely with it in order to ensure that budgetary decisions were in accordance with the spirit of the development program. A recommendation for the control of investment expenditure corollary to this is the detailed itemization of investment projects in the annual budget instead of allocation in large lump sums, as under the present system. Moreover, we believe this type of control in detail should extend just as much to autonomous organizations as to the central administration.

CHAPTER 3 *ORGANIZATION FOR ECONOMIC DEVELOPMENT*

There can be no doubt that the Government is embarking on an ambitious undertaking which will involve the administration in a vast amount of work; and the question now to be considered is how this operation can be directed to ensure success; its very complexity demands careful organization.

The successful guidance of an industrialized economy at the present day is a very demanding task. For the Government has, as we have seen, responsibility for economic activity at two different levels. In the first place, it has responsibility for the efficient guidance of the economy as a whole, including both public and private sectors. Secondly, it is manager, so to speak, of the large body of activities which call for direct public expenditure and it is the owner of a large number of government enterprises operating in the market economy. In order to carry forward a successful development program, the higher organs of Government must remain free to consider broad issues of economic policy. They cannot do this satisfactorily if they are constantly called upon to make *ad hoc* decisions on individual matters. Delegation of decision is, therefore, of the utmost importance, but it must be accompanied by some form of economic discipline to ensure that those to whom the decisions are delegated are responsible for the consequences. First-class staff work will be necessary to bring before the higher organs of Government the right issues in the right perspective at the right time. The Government should not have to consider, for example, individual projects, but programs of expenditure and their relation to the growth of the economy.

The way in which the administration should be adapted to the needs of the development program is a matter for the Government's decision; but it is the development program which should determine the shape of the administration, not the reverse. Furthermore, no matter how carefully it is planned, any organizational structure will be of little use unless all sections of the administration concerned show a readiness to work together in the interests of the program, according to the directives of the Government, and a willingness to cooperate by supplying information, working for joint solutions in committee, observing timetables and so on. Each ministry responsible for the investment of public funds will have a part to play, but departmental initiatives will have to be governed by the needs of the program as a whole; there

66

will be no place for isolated action in what must be a concerted effort to achieve the Government's objectives. In a long-term undertaking, coordination should become one of the constant themes of policy and administration requiring all concerned with economic affairs to harmonize their efforts in the interests of the development program as a whole.

The highest organ of State through which the direction of coordination of policy can be effected is the Council of Ministers (Consejo de Ministros) under the Prime Minister (Presidente del Gobierno). Five years ago Delegate Committees (Comisiones Delegadas) of the Council were established under the same chairman to draw up joint proposals for Cabinet decision on matters affecting several ministries and so relieve the full Council of some of the pressure of business.

Of particular relevance in the present context is the Delegate Committee for Economic Affairs (Asuntos Economicos) which is composed of the Ministers of Finance, Agriculture, Industry and Commerce, other Ministers being co-opted at need. This Delegate Committee has been meeting regularly about once a fortnight. The two other Delegate Committees concerned with economic questions are for Transport (Transportes y Comunicaciones) and for Health and Social Affairs (Sanidad y Asuntos Sociales). The mission was informed that they had not often had occasion to meet.

To the extent that it is considered necessary for the Council of Ministers to delegate to a smaller specialized group among its members, the Delegate Committee for Economic Affairs seems to be the obvious choice for handling all major questions of policy relating to economic development. In this case there would obviously be advantage in its having the opportunity of expressing its views on any proposals which might emerge from the two other Delegate Committees mentioned above, before final decisions are taken.

The focal point below the Delegate Committee for Economic Affairs for consideration of questions of long-range economic policy was established on February 1, 1962, when the office of Planning Commissioner (Comisario del Plan de Desarrollo Economico) was created in the Prime Minister's office (Presidencia del Gobierno) with the responsibility for elaborating and supervising the program for economic development on behalf of the Delegate Committee, and for ensuring the coordination of the work of ministries, the Sindicatos and private interests concerned. The Planning Commissioner may be asked to attend meetings of the Delegate Committee and advise Ministers of measures to be taken to achieve the necessary coordination.

Two of the units already in the Prime Minister's office will be administratively dependent on the Planning Commissioner: the Oficina de Coordinacion y Programacion Economica (OCYPE) which already has certain planning responsibilities and the Instituto Nacional de Estadistica (INE). The Commissioner will (by delegation of the Minister Subsecretary of the Prime Minister's office) be empowered to preside over the existing Governing Committee (Junta Rectora) of OCYPE, consisting of high-level officials from the various ministries. It is not entirely clear to us what the function of this Committee will be under the new auspices, but insofar as it will act as a coordinating committee to review proposals or discuss problems before they are submitted to the Delegate Committee, and in view of the probable pressure of business, we feel that there is much to be said for entrusting this work to a steering committee of four or five of its members, which could be convened on short notice.

We believe this reduction all the more necessary as the Commissioner is to be advised by six "horizontal" committees (Ponencias) responsible for studying certain general subjects (Finance, Commerce, Labor, Productivity, Regional Development and Flexibility of Economy) and 20 "vertical" committees (Comisiones) responsible for studying particular sections of the economy. The private sector will be represented in most of these committees. We comment on these committees later in the chapter.

The mission welcomes this new appointment which, given the necessary cooperation of all branches of the Government, should ensure central consideration of the manifold problems of economic development and effective staff work before ultimate decisions are made.

The Role of the Planning Commission

We have already described, in general terms, the kind of economic planning we envisage. But we believe it opportune to make a few further observations on the work that the Planning Commission will be undertaking. In our view there will be three principal types of work, which are intimately connected, although we here make a distinction between them:

a. prognosis of the nature and the pace of change in the structure of the economy;

b. reconciliation and revision of investment programs in the public sector;

c. staff work on policies for economic development.

The first task would be prognosis of the long-term (say ten years) direction and pace of change in the structure of the economy, as the mission has attempted to do for illustrative purposes, but in somewhat more detail and on the basis of more up-to-date information. In the first instance, the prognosis would largely be for the guidance of the advisory committees and other working groups within the Government. We believe that this should be done as early as possible and without trying to achieve more than a very rough approximation in order to provide a common basis for subsequent work. The lack of such a common basis in the past has been most marked, with different ministries often preparing plans on quite different assumptions. In any event, it will be necessary for the Planning Commission to revise its original macroeconomic prognosis in the light of the more detailed investigations carried out by the various committees. Planning is essentially a two-way process, from the general to the particular and back again to the general. When the various committees have reported, it will be necessary to review the indicative targets or forecasts of each sector for internal consistency.

At this point, it will also be necessary to see whether the various sector programs or estimates of investment expenditure can be satisfied from the available resources and whether they are consistent with the projected rate of development. There may well be competing claims on the savings of the economy, its foreign exchange resources, or the available skilled labor which it is difficult to reconcile because of different emphasis on the weight to be attached to different objectives. We have already mentioned the possible conflict between economic growth in the long run and social objectives in the short run. It will be up to the Planning Commission to test the various components of the program for consistency in these regards, to reconcile conflicting claims where this is possible and to present the issues and alternative lines of policy to the Delegate Committee when necessary.

After this stage, the Government may wish to embody the results in a development plan in more or less detail. We do not, on the basis of experience elsewhere, expect that work of this kind can be done at all quickly. For the first "round," so to speak, of prognosis and revision, one year is likely to be the absolute minimum necessary. The goal, in the first instance, might very well be consideration of plans for the period from 1963 onward, with the idea that by the time a consistent plan is arrived at, the period of the program is likely to be from 1964 onward.

Most of the observations that we have to make may be summarized by saying that in this process of planning the Commission and its advisory committees should not attempt too much. In the first place, we doubt the need for highly sophisticated techniques, mainly because we doubt their relevance.

In the second place, we would warn against an attempt to program future government expenditure in too much detail.[1] This is largely a matter of judgment in the various sectors. Though too little detail may be virtually useless, too much may be self-defeating. Long-range planning is not a substitute for an effective annual budget. The purpose of a plan is to set the framework within which the annual budget is cast. But planning and budgeting are also a two-way process. With each succeeding budget, there will have to be changes in the plan for the future. Experience elsewhere has all too frequently shown that any attempt to plan which ignores the need for intimate collaboration between planning and budgeting is apt to end up as an academic exercise.

In our view, the planning document as such is less important than the planning process, which is a continuous interchange of views between those responsible for the working of particular sectors, who know best their own particular problems, and officials working at a central point at which the economy can be viewed in its entirety. The process should, therefore, be a continuous one with regular revisions, undertaken, for example, every two years, which would be a convenient interval coincident with that of the budget. Even if the term of the development plan is four or five years, a biennial revision would still be necessary. In this planning process the Government and the private sector should derive great benefit from having a consistent perspective against which to form their policies.

The most decisive reason for the Planning Commission not attempting too elaborate a plan is the vital importance of its third function, staff work on general economic policy, including the organization necessary for the implementation of policy. Many of the recommendations we have made are concerned with selection of the policies that will most effectively serve Spain's developmental goals. Even where they are more specifically directed toward particular investments, they reflect a more general view on the appropriate economic policy for development. We believe, that, in the first instance, a large part of the work of the Commission, and also its advisory committees in many cases, must inevitably be concerned with advice on policy and with seeing that the measures necessary to implement it are carried out

---

[1] We have ourselves appeared to violate this principle in certain instances. However, in most such cases the purpose was usually illustrative of a particular policy.

by the ministries or other bodies responsible. Many of the mission's recommendations, moreover, are concerned with the preparation of special studies, designed to give a securer foundation for investment decisions in the future. These studies will also occupy much of the Commission's time, whether they are carried out by the Commission itself or by others.

Furthermore, any new proposals for economic action placed before the Comision Delegada para Asuntos Economicos ought to be considered in the light of their consistency with the long-term programs and objectives of the Government. Wherever the proposals originate, the planning staff should comment on them and express its views before they reach the Comision Delegada. The Comision Delegada would thus be assured that the long-term interests of the economy were taken into account in arriving at a decision.

The Role of Other Government Bodies

As we have pointed out, coordination will be an essential ingredient of development. This is especially true of coordination between the Planning Commission and the various ministries. However, a program of this kind can be handicapped if the means adopted to ensure coordination and planning are too complicated, and the permanent structure of committees in the central administration too elaborate, with the result that the responsible officials have no time to attend to their departmental work, because they are constantly attending meetings of one interdepartmental committee or another. Although there must be a permanent system for facilitating interdepartmental consultation at the center, we think the aim should be to keep it as simple as possible and to rely where practicable on *ad hoc* arrangements. For this reason, although the establishment of the 26 advisory committees may be a desirable move to get the process under way, we would hope that in future the need for such committees to carry out the principal planning and policy work will be reduced and the Government will come more to rely on established units within the administrative machinery. We would still foresee a place for a number, but probably a reduced number, of committees specifically for liaison with the private sector. We have ourselves, moreover, suggested the need for retaining coordination committees in certain special cases (e.g., transport and tourism).

For any particular problem, the ministry chiefly interested should be responsible for producing a report or answering a questionnaire, in consultation with other interested parties, rather than establishing formal committees, which often cover too wide a representation and tend to drag on after their useful life is over. We believe that the program and project review units that we have suggested would be a suitable focal point within a ministry for liaison with the planning staff, in addition to their budgetary function. This would mean that within each ministry there would be a system analogous to the one already introduced into the central administration itself.

Each Minister whose competence comes within the scope of the development program will have a double responsibility in the coordination of policy. On the one hand, he will have to watch the interests of his sector of the economy during the formulation of the program and its adjustment from time to time; on the other hand, he will have to ensure that the decisions taken by the Government on economic policy, and all that they imply, are observed within the ministry. Therefore, when the Minister is asked to make decisions on departmental programs, he should have the benefit of advice not only from those officials responsible for presenting them, but also from those whose task is to see the Ministry's operations in perspective, and who are in close touch with the Planning Commission.

These considerations apply just as much to the autonomous organizations and public enterprises which are responsible to the various ministries. The specific functions of some of these bodies in relation to economic development are referred to elsewhere in the report, but the point to be made in the present context is that, since they do have some independence, it is all the more important to ensure that they are covered by any arrangements approved by a minister to promote coordination within his ministry.

Whatever advantages may be found in this system of autonomous public bodies, of which there are a large number, they could, in present circumstances, be a source of weakness if there is no clear understanding about their role in relation to the government's economic policy. There should be something more than a formal attachment of the organizations to particular ministries; their plans must be consistent with the program assigned to that ministry; and their operations must be closely coordinated with its operations, both at headquarters and in the field.

The arguments in favor of providing for an efficient system of coordination, which would embrace both the departments within a ministry and the autonomous public bodies attached to it, apply equally to its operations in the field, especially for those ministries whose operations and expenditures on public investment are spread widely throughout Spain and have a direct bearing on the economic development program.

The provincial agencies enable the ministries to have contact with the community in all the principal centers. Their function, in accordance with the program, is likely to be less concerned with promoting policy through direct control and more with offering advice, giving incentives and otherwise stimulating enterprise in the interest of greater productivity and economic expansion. In no sector will this be more apparent than in agriculture. In Section IV we explain in some detail why we foresee the need for overhauling the present arrangements in provincial capitals, under which the various services are working as separate units responsible to their different departments or autonomous agencies in Madrid. In the new conditions we are discussing it is plain that the provincial agencies cannot make the effective contribution required of them in the interests of the agricultural community unless all the services work together in one place and on one program, and are coordinated under one authority representing the Ministry of Agriculture. It is clear, moreover, that irrigation needs will have to be decided in the light of agricultural requirements as a whole, so that liaison between the provincial agricultural authorities and the Confederaciones Hidrograficas of the Ministry of Public Works will be necessary.

Since the pattern of public expenditure cannot be judged without a forward look at the economy as a whole, it seems essential that the investment proposals of each ministry should be considered by the Delegate Committee from the point of view of the longer-term program of economic development which, as we have explained, will require adjustment from time to time. One method of facilitating this process would be to require each of the economic ministries to prepare an annual report for the Government on agreed lines. It might, for example, cover a summary by each ministry of the operations in its sector for the previous year, its comments on any changes foreseen in the long-term prospects and an explanation of how its investment proposals for the coming 12 months are to be reconciled with the Ministry's own long-term plans and of how they might be expected to contribute to the Government's development objectives. This annual report, which would be submitted to the Delegate Committee for consideration, would be examined first by the Planning Commission at about the same time as the ministry's investment proposals were being scrutinized in the Ministry of Finance. We believe the aim should be to enable the Delegate Committee, on the advice of the Comisario, to review each ministry's plan of operations for the coming year in the light of the needs of the Government's economic development programs and of the evaluation by the Ministry of Finance of the investment expenditures.

Finally, there are one or two general points to be made. The first is that organization for economic development should be as flexible as possible, and once a program of action has been agreed upon, the organs of administration concerned with it, whether they be ministries, autonomous bodies, or provincial agencies, should be ready to adapt themselves to its requirements. They should see themselves as partners in a concerted effort, and not merely as custodians of some special sector or area, operating as self-contained units. Those responsible for the direction of economic policy will indicate where resources can most usefully be employed for the good of the whole economy—which is the purpose of a program—and from this will follow the apportionment of responsibility for its execution among the various organs of the administration. These shares will not be equal and they will not necessarily bear any relation to past responsibility or performance. There may be need for more construction in one sector and less in another; some projects already prepared may have to be postponed or abandoned, and others accelerated; maintenance may supersede new works; the Government's intervention in one place may give way to private enterprise and be concentrated elsewhere; the pressure of work in one ministry may increase, and decrease in another; specialized departments or agencies may have to be regrouped with others to secure a comprehensive policy; and so on. In such circumstances, it must follow that the administrative organs cannot remain unaffected and that more flexibility in the system and more mobility would make for efficiency and better coordination. As we stated at the outset of this chapter, the program of development should determine the shape of the administration, and not the reverse.

Remuneration of the Civil Service

This should be no great problem for a public service which, in the mission's experience and by repute, contains so many highly qualified, loyal and competent civil servants, who are alert to new ideas and anxious to profit by them. But it does seem that in some respects existing arrangements may hamper efficiency, and since the importance of the role of the civil service in achieving the aims of the program cannot be gainsaid, we believe everything possible should be done to remove disabilities. In our view, there is a pressing need for changing the present system of remunerating civil servants. This is essentially a delicate question of internal policy, but since we are convinced that it is important in organizing for economic development we wish to draw the Government's attention to it. In point of fact, the basic salaries of civil servants have not been adjusted *pari passu* with the fall in purchasing power, and they no longer provide adequate means of subsistence. Consequently, ministries must either allow their officials time to augment their income from employment outside, which is not satisfactory for the administration, or they must make provision themselves to supplement the basic salaries of their officials to bring their total emoluments more in line with the cost of living. Both these expedients are used: but we are concerned more with the latter in this context.

Under the present system a ministry obtains supplementary funds either from levies which it is authorized to impose or, for example, in ministries responsible for public investment, from recoveries from public funds of a surcharge on the cost of construction work or other capital expenditure falling within their competence. In some cases, remuneration is partly dependent on the work done by the official himself; for instance, engineers or surveyors in the government's service, working in a professional capacity, earn fees for drawing up plans and, if the plans are adopted, for inspecting their execution.

The possibilities of raising funds in these several ways vary considerably from Ministry to Ministry. As a result, anomalous situations are created in which government officials with the same experience and professional training, but working in different ministries, may receive very different compensation. Similarly, a high-ranking official in one Ministry may, in practice, receive substantially less remuneration in total than an official of lower qualification in another Ministry. In addition to the inequities that may result from these situations, the question inevitably arises whether the system creates incentives that may be in conflict with sound investment policies, and specifically whether it is related in part to the emphasis on new construction and the relative lack of attention to maintenance as well as to the bias toward new construction as against completion of existing construction that the mission has commented upon at various places in this report.

We believe that this system of remuneration could be disorganized by, and become incompatible with, the policy which we regard as essential for the success of economic development, whereby public expenditure by departments has to be governed solely by the needs of a national program and is in keeping with its objectives. For instance, we shall recommend that construction of new lines on the railways should be halted, and that urgent repairs on the main roads should have precedence over new road construction, which will mean that these capital works will no longer provide for a contribution to the ministry's funds for augmenting salaries, or for the fees of the professional staff, at least not in the same measure. It will plainly be embarrassing for the authorities who will be expected to make decisions on investment proposals on their economic merits, in order to ensure that public funds are used as productively as possible or that investment should be concentrated in one area rather than another, if these same decisions are to affect adversely the staff's emoluments. By the same token, it would be unfair to a conscientious public employee who wishes to limit public expenditure to the necessary minimum and to direct it in the most effective way, if his remuneration should be more adversely affected the greater the service he renders in this regard.

For these reasons, we believe that it would be far better to break the link that exists between the two questions. And in any case it seems to us that such a system, dependent as it is on fortuitous sources of revenue, makes the reward uncertain, where it should be certain; and it is bound to give rise to anomalies and to militate against the cohesion of the public service and its objectivity.

We believe that much would be gained in the execution of a national program of economic development, under which the operations of each ministry and all its dependencies must be subordinated to the general objectives of the government's economic policy, if this system for remunerating civil servants were replaced by a centrally administered system which would remunerate them on a uniform basis on a scale appropriate to their status, and conducive to their following a career in the public service and giving their full time to it. This would have the undoubted advantage of relating the emoluments of civil servants to their service to the State, and not to the nature of the operations of their ministry, department, or agency; and by removing anomalies and giving a greater sense of security, it would redound to the efficiency and objectivity of the public service as a whole, and simplify problems of location and interservice transfers. As a first step, the funds now used by the ministries should be paid over to the Ministry of Finance. The Government would then be in a position to re-examine the various parafiscal taxes, license fees and levies through which supplementary revenues are obtained, and the procedures followed in their collection, to consider which should be preserved and which eliminated in the light of their effects on investment costs and incentives.

In connection with these changes in the system of remuneration, there are two other points which we would commend to the attention of the Government. The first concerns pensions; although increased recently, they do not provide sufficient funds for civil servants to retire at the normal age for doing so. We believe that the scale of pensions should be re-examined at the same time as that of direct salary payments, to provide a system in which, through normal retirement, opportunities are opened up for advancement within the civil service ranks and for increased flexibility in the use of personnel, and which would make a government career more attractive. The second point concerns the relationship between the pay system and the various special corps or *cuerpos* into which officials of the civil service are organized. We would consider it preferable to break the link that apparently now exists between the base pay of a civil servant and his position in the *cuerpo* to which he belongs, in the interests of achieving a centrally administered and unified system of compensation based on experience and qualification.

Statistics

The need for good statistics both in long-range planning and in the shorter-run guidance of the economy scarcely needs emphasis from the mission. Official recognition has from time to time been given to this fact in Spain. Recent changes, especially the closer incorporation of the Instituto Nacional de Estadistica (INE) into the planning organization, attest to the continuance of this recognition.

When the INE was established in 1945, the law indicated that its objective was to rectify the inadequate authority of the then existing organization and the general lack of coordination, leading to a multiplicity of effort toward the same end and uncoordinated plans for collection of the same types of data. Although the mission recognizes that, in certain respects, there has been outstanding improvement in the statistical field, we cannot say that the deficiencies prevalent in 1945 have altogether disappeared.

There is still a serious problem of coordination. This particularly applies to classification of data collected by different agencies. In order to collate information from various sources, it is essential that the classifications used be the same in each case; at the very least, the differences should be clearly understood. It is also important that there be a clear understanding of the extent of coverage in each field. The fact that statistics in a particular field cover only a part of it obviously robs them of some of their usefulness, but far from all. They can still be very useful, but only if the parts of the field being covered are clearly identified and if, as far as possible, that coverage remains consistent with time. We refer to these problems elsewhere in the report.

Secondly, it appears that, in a number of cases, statistics are collected by some government agencies without reference to INE. Sometimes the statistics are not distributed at all and sometimes they are distributed within the Government without informing INE. There is also a multiplicity of effort, notably in the production of derived statistics such as indices. There has been more than one cost-of-living index, several explicit industrial production indices, published or unpublished, apart from those implicit in national income estimates. There are also two national income estimates, a fact we return to later. To some extent, this duplication of effort is apparently due to lack of confidence by one part of the administration in statistics produced in another because of discrepancies in the results obtained.

In these respects the INE is not yet fully performing the centralizing function it was supposed to under the law, although it has no doubt improved matters considerably. It still remains, to a large extent, a collecting agency of the classical type, gathering and publishing statistical data on an extraordinary variety of subjects. But it has not been able to contribute adequately to the kind of information necessary for economic development: it has not had the money; it has not had the machines; and it has not had the staff.

For example, population censuses have been held now for many years, but economic censuses were not authorized until a law of June 8, 1957. Even then, lack of money and machines has delayed the program for carrying out these economic censuses in industry and agriculture.

The trouble is certainly not a dearth of talented Spanish statisticians. But the INE is not in a position to offer them a career. This is an outstanding case of the general problem, mentioned above, of the present system of remuneration of public servants. As a consequence, most of the best talent is working either whole-time or part-time in the universities, in other branches of the Government or for private firms; some have gone abroad. This, in our view, is one root of the problem, the other being inadequate budgetary allocations. Remedying one of these deficiencies, however, will not be particularly helpful without remedying the other. We believe that the whole outlook on the purpose of INE needs to be revised. Its purpose is not simply to produce statistics, but statistics which are going to be useful for economic development. This will require an effective demand from the Government as a whole, as opposed to individuals in different parts of it. It is our impression that this effective demand has not hitherto existed.

Under the new organizational arrangements the opportunity clearly exists now to change this state of affairs. It is essential to break the vicious circle, whereby confidence in INE is weakened because it cannot provide the required services, and INE is deprived of the means to do so because of the lack of confidence. We doubt whether there is any better place to break it than in the national accounting field. It is unusual to find the principal macroeconomic national statistics produced outside the central statistical organization, not in one, but in two different places. National income statistics are prepared by the Comision de la Renta Nacional of the Consejo de Economia Nacional with an extremely small staff. The national accounts are prepared by a group of university professors under the auspices of the Ministry of Finance.

The national accounts bear little relation to the national income figures in those respects in which comparison is or should be possible.[2]

In our view, this is an unsatisfactory situation, which is bound to make potential users of statistics skeptical of their value. It is not simply that national accounts are of value in themselves for a general understanding of the economy. The preparation of them is a very revealing process in that it brings out sharply where the principal deficiencies in the statistical raw material lie. For this reason, it is most desirable that they be prepared by the organization responsible for collecting, directly or indirectly, analyzing and publishing that raw material, namely INE. National accounting and related work ought to be centralized and INE given the responsibility. We would hope that this would go a long way toward curing the present lack of coordination and sense of purpose toward a common goal.

We recognize, however, that no centralization of this kind can be done at all effectively without reinforcement of INE. In fact, it would probably be of value to create an entirely new wing of INE, devoted to the production of development statistics, while the existing organization continues with substantially the work it is doing now. This raises very difficult questions of pay and seniority. We would not want to suggest any concrete solution, but would stress the need for finding a prompt solution even on an interim basis.

Administration and Development

The purpose of this chapter has been to stress that organization in the public administration is important for the success of economic development at all stages of preparation and execution. There is a need for central direction and coordination, which has been fully recognized by the Government in the appointment of a Comisario del Plan to support the Delegate Committee. Each ministry has to act in accordance with the program and coordinate in its own area of responsibility, covering autonomous public bodies and other agencies attached to it. All this calls for flexibility in the administration, which has to be shaped to meet the demands of the program, and the conditions of employment in the civil service have an important bearing on this. How these organizational problems should be solved is a matter for the Government to decide, but we hope that the foregoing suggestions will be helpful to it in arriving at a decision.

---

[2] We should also mention a third, but private initiative in this field, namely, the interesting pioneering effort of the Banco de Bilbao to prepare income estimates on a provincial basis.

CHAPTER 4 *BUDGETARY IMPLICATIONS OF DEVELOPMENT EXPENDITURE BY THE CENTRAL ADMINISTRATION*

The public sector in Spain can be defined in a variety of ways, as we explain in the next section. We would have liked to have drawn the financial implications of the various recommendations contained in this report on as broad a basis as possible, but in view of data problems and our uncertainty as to the interpretation of the public accounts, we have found it preferable to concentrate on the revenues of the central administration and the expenditures which it finances directly or indirectly, leaving out of consideration expenditures financed by autonomous organizations and other government agencies through their own resources.

Our first step was to forecast the feasible growth of revenue of the central administration. Exclusive of certain large *contra* items which appear as both revenue and expenditure, revenue in 1960 amounted to some 70 billion pts, mainly in taxes but to some degree in income from public property. In projecting this revenue forward, we have not attempted to forecast receipts in detail on the basis of a particular tax structure. Instead, we have taken a view as to the elasticity of fiscal receipts in relation to national income, which would indicate an increase in receipts from 1960 to 1966 of the order of 50 billion pts. This is based on the assumption that national income would grow by a little over 5¾ percent per annum (including the growth in population) and that fiscal receipts would grow at between 9 percent and 10 percent annually. This percentage increase in receipts is roughly in line with comparable experience elsewhere and with past rates of increase in Spain, although the latter are affected by changes in the tax structure and by inflation.

The implications of our recommendations as to expenditure vary greatly in the precision that can be attached to them. In a number of cases in subsequent sections of the report, we have suggested a figure for the estimated cost of putting our recommendations into effect. As we point out in the accompanying text, however, these figures are often largely illustrative in the absence of more detailed information on costs than was available to us. In various respects, the expenditures are conditioned on studies or actions to be undertaken by the Government, and in order to understand them it is necessary to refer to the relevant portions of the report. These expenditures, which we shall

80

henceforth call "listed" expenditures, are summarized in Table 4.1. These listed expenditures cover the main elements of public expenditure in the basic fields of agriculture, industry and transportation. They form a small part of total government expenditure, however, and it remains to be seen what the implications of these projections are for the total.

TABLE 4.1: Estimated Increase in Listed Expenditures, 1960–1966

(billion pts)

Item	1960ᵃ	1962	1966
Transport:			
Railways	4.0	5.2	6.9
Roads	1.9	3.8	8.0
Ports	0.9	1.5	0.5
Shipping creditᵇ	1.4	1.2	1.2
	8.2	11.7	16.6
Agriculture:	7.5	7.5	10.0
Industry and Tourism:			
Creditᵇ	0.7	2.0	2.0
Other	—	0.3	0.3
	0.7	2.3	2.3
Total	16.4ᶜ	21.5	28.9

ᵃ In many cases these are only rough estimates of public expenditure on specified items in the particular field and do not necessarily include all expenditure in that field.

ᵇ Net of reimbursements.

ᶜ Of which approximately 1 billion pts not covered directly or indirectly by the central administration budget.

Although we have made no detailed estimates of expenditure for housing, urbanization and education, we feel that it is possible to put an order of magnitude of 5 billion pts against the increase between 1960 and 1966. This is based on an assumed drop in expenditure on housing and housing credit by the Government (to be taken up by private sources of financing) and a considerable increase in expenditure on urbanization and also on education. The figure of 5 billion pts would not include an allowance for an increase in teachers' salaries, a point we come to more generally later.

The implications of these very rough estimates are shown in Table 4.2. It shows that, without borrowing or American aid, which together financed the deficit in 1960, an increase of the order of two-thirds is possible in expenditure other than in the categories we have mentioned. Some of the remaining categories that we have not attempted to project specifically will undoubtedly require less than this kind of

TABLE 4.2:   Estimated Increases in Revenue and Expenditure of Central
Administration, 1960–1966

(billion pts)

Item		1960	1966
Revenue:[a]		70	120
Expenditure:[b]			
Listed Expenditure from Table 4.1		15[b]	29
Education, Housing, Urbanization		16	21
Non-recurring[c]		3	0
Military, Internal Security	17		
Public Debt	6	42	70
Pensions and similar expenditure	4		
Other unlisted	15		
		76	120

[a] Net of large *contra* items (service of Instituto de Credito para la Reconstruccion Nacional debt; revenues of the postal service). Expenditure includes credits by the Banco de Credito Local in 1960, although financed directly by Bond sales.
[b] See footnote [c] of Table 4.1.
[c] Two large items (financing of a very large increase in short-term credit by the Instituto de Credito para la Reconstruccion Nacional and subventions by the Ministry of Commerce to counteract the effects of stabilization).

increase. It appears, therefore, that the mission's recommendations for increases in expenditure on the various items listed herein and described at greater length elsewhere in this report are reasonably within the financial capabilities of the Spanish Government. This underlines a point that we make repeatedly, namely, that the rapid development of the Spanish economy is dependent less on an increase in the resources available for investment (or in the share of the public sector in these resources) than on a more effective use of resources.

In our view one of the first priority claims on additional expenditure by the Government is increased pay and pensions for the civil service. We have enlarged on the reasons for this earlier in this section and need not repeat them here. It may, however, be of some value to point to the orders of magnitude involved. The cost of personnel services to the central administration (including pensions), other than the three armed services, was about 15 billion pts in 1960. To this must be added the personnel costs of autonomous organizations amounting to 4 billion pts (although not all of this is effectively financed by the central administration), making 19 billion pts in all (excluding extrabudgetary remuneration).

We are not in a position to say what the size of the increase should be over-all, although some idea of the orders of magnitude involved may be gathered when we say that the increase for teachers (present and future) alone might well be of the order of 2 billion pts. In any event, it is clear that the increase could be substantial and still leave a sizable sum over for increases for other purposes.

About the purposes other than those that we have specified, there is one point in particular that we wish to make. We doubt whether it is possible to predict far in advance just what the balance between public and private expenditure should be or indeed how both should be financed. If the private sector responds actively to the government's liberalized policies, it is entirely possible that resources should be shifted away from the public sector and the possibility of tax remission would then have to be considered. This is particularly likely to be the case if the capital market develops satisfactorily, thus making it unnecessary for the Government to act to the same extent as a financial intermediary.

ANNEX A   *NOTES ON POPULATION*

Age Structure

The age structure of the Spanish population has certain peculiarities, as a result of various past events and changes in the rates of reproduction. Table A.1. shows the structure of population at the last available census date, 1950. The most noticeable feature of this age-structure is the "bulge" in the age-group 15 to 24 (and to a lesser extent 25 to 29). These were the people born in the decade before the civil war.

The next oldest age-groups are smaller not only for the usual natural reasons but also because, among men at least, they were those affected principally by the civil war; in addition, the 30 to 34 age-group was affected by the low birth rate (and high death rate) during the influenza epidemic of 1918. The youngest age-groups, 0 to 14, are also smaller than the two following ones, which is unusual. This does not only appear to be the result of dislocation during the war, which would affect mainly the 10 to 14 age-group. There appears at the same time to have been a more permanent reduction in the fertility rate among women of child-bearing age.

The "bulge" will naturally continue but in successively older age-groups with each passing decade. Two significant consequences will follow from this. The first is that in 1960 this large group will be aged 25 to 34, which is the most important child-bearing age-group for

TABLE A.1: Age Structure in 1950

(millions)

Age-group	Total	Men	Women
0–4	2.57	1.32	1.26
5–9	2.44	1.25	1.18
10–14	2.33	1.18	1.15
15–19	2.69	1.33	1.36
20–24	2.67	1.33	1.35
25–29	2.38	1.16	1.22
30–34	1.94	0.91	1.04
35–39	1.86	0.86	1.01
40–44	1.83	0.88	0.94
45–54	3.06	1.44	1.62
55–64	2.18	0.99	1.19
65 and over	2.02	0.83	1.19
Total	27.96	13.46	14.50

women; after 1960 the size of this age-group will be smaller for a number of years. Although this will be partly offset by changes in other age-groups, the net effect should be a comparatively small growth in the number of births between 1960 and 1980 and in the number of children aged 5 to 14 between 1970 and 1980.

The second significant effect will be in the number of men and women aged 15 to 64, the economically active age-groups. Between 1940 and 1950 the "bulge" age-group came into the labor market and the number of men aged 15 to 64 increased by 1.1 million (see Table A.2). An increase on this scale cannot be expected in the following decades, even without taking into account a much higher rate of emigration.

Emigration

Adjustment for emigration is not easy to make. Before World War II, Spaniards emigrated mainly to South America and predominantly from those provinces facing the Atlantic, the Canaries and Galicia. The pattern has changed in recent years; Spanish workers like the Irish and the Italians, now seek employment in Western Europe. It is certain that, with this geographical change, many other characteristics, such as the age distribution, the number of accompanying dependents and the permanence of the emigration, have also changed.

Statistics in Spain still apply only to transoceanic emigration and we understand that they are not complete even within this category. As there is every likelihood that the shift toward European migration will

TABLE A.2: Population Changes, 1940–1950

(millions)

	1940 Census	1950 Census
Total:		
All ages	25.9	28.0
15–64	16.4	18.6
Men:		
All ages	12.4	13.5
15–64	7.8	8.9
Women:		
All ages	13.5	14.5
15–64	8.6	9.7

persist, it appears to us that steps should be taken as soon as possible to establish records of this movement.

We have assumed that the net number of men and women leaving Spain each year would be 50,000 between 1960 and 1970 or about the same as in the previous decade. Deductions from an unadjusted projection have been made on this basis, taking into account also the estimated births and deaths of the emigrant population.

On the assumptions we have made, which are necessarily somewhat precarious, we estimate that the total population, which was 30.4 million according to the 1960 census, will increase to 33.0 million in 1970. We would also expect the increase in the number of men in the 15 to 64 age-group between 1950 and 1970 to be 1.3 million or not much more than in the single decade 1940–50.

Regional Changes

The three principal industrial areas in Spain are the provinces of Madrid and Barcelona and a group of five provinces along the Cantabrian coast (Oviedo, Santander, Vizcaya, Guipuzcoa and Alava[1]). Together these seven provinces account for over half the industrial output of Spain. Other concentrations are on the east coast (Valencia) and in the southwest (Sevilla/Cadiz). The main industrial areas are also those, by and large, with the highest incomes (see Map 1). Outside these industrial concentrations, incomes tend to be higher in the north of Spain than they are in the south.[2]

The rate of growth of population has, as might be expected, been highest in the industrial centers, since they have attracted people from other areas. But as Map 2 shows, some southern provinces had a fairly high rate of growth of population in the first half of the century. Accordingly, we may distinguish three areas in Spain in 1950 (apart from the isolated Canaries which are a special case):

a. the main industrial provinces with high incomes and a relatively rapid growth in population (7 provinces);

b. the rest of the north and center with moderate incomes and a slowly growing population (27 provinces);

c. the south with low incomes and a moderate growth in population (14 provinces).[3]

[1] The last three of these may be identified in the following maps by their capital cities of Bilbao, San Sebastian and Vitoria.

[2] These data are taken from *Renta Nacional de Espana*, 1957, Banco de Bilbao.

[3] In using the term "south" here, we refer to the provinces of Caceres, Ciudad Real, Albacete and Alicante and the ten others to the south of them.

All such divisions are bound to be more or less arbitrary. The last two areas shade into each other gradually rather than abruptly and neither is, by any means, homogeneous. Nevertheless, there are certain characteristics, to which we will point, which are generally speaking more typical of the south than other parts of the country. One is the high proportion of casual laborers (*obreros eventuales*) among agricultural workers—about half compared with less than one-quarter in the rest of the country; concomitantly, output per agricultural worker is relatively low.

The decade 1950–60, which was, as far as can be ascertained, a period of much faster economic growth than hitherto brought significant changes in regional rates of population growth. The contrast between the more rapidly growing industrial areas and the remainder was sharper than before (see Map 3). In many provinces there was actually a fall in population. Although the most conspicuous cases of loss of population were still in the center (Teruel, Soria and Guadalajara all about 9 percent), there were also several instances in the south. The significance of this change is that the south, for the first time, has the prospect of relief from growing overpopulation.

A second feature of the change in 1950–60 is the general exodus from the rural areas. Table A.3 compares the changes in population in the principal areas from 1900 to 1950 and from 1950 to 1960, distinguishing between major cities and the remainder.[4] Except in the main industrial areas, where there are a number of rapidly growing smaller industrial towns, and the Canaries, the population outside of the major cities was static. In fact, there was an increase of about half a million in the semi-urban population (nuclei with a population of two thousand to ten thousand) and a corresponding decrease in rural areas (nuclei with a population below two thousand).

Migration has a dual effect. The immigrant cities grow first of all by virtue of the influx of people. But, in addition, this influx is likely to consist preponderantly of young adults. Consequently, the proportion of old people in the immigrant cities tends to fall, the birth rate (per thousand) to rise and the death rate (per thousand) to fall compared with an area in which there is no migration. In the emigrant areas, exactly the opposite would happen, the population becoming generally older. These changes should be reflected in differences between the natural rates of increase in population (difference between births and deaths per thousand). Map 4 shows the range of these rates for

[4] The figures shown might be expected to exaggerate the change between 1950–60 and the previous decades. This is so for the south, where the increase in population in 1940–50 was about 7 percent compared with 9 percent for 1900–50. However, there was little difference in other areas.

TABLE A.3: Population Growth by Areas

	Population (millions)			Per decade growth rate (percent)	
	1900	1950	1960	1900–50	1950–60
Main Industrial Provinces:[a]					
14 cities[b]	1.48	3.98	5.24	22	32
Rest	1.86	2.54	3.03	6	20
Total	3.34	6.51	8.28	14	27
Rest of North and Center:					
17 cities[b]	0.78	1.99	2.25	21	13
Rest	8.09	9.35	9.22	3	−1
Total	8.86	11.35	11.47	5	1
South:[c]					
19 cities[b]	1.13	2.26	2.56	15	13
Rest	4.91	7.07	7.18	8	2
Total	6.04	9.33	9.74	9	4
Canaries:					
2 cities[b]	0.08	0.26	0.33	25	28
Rest	0.28	0.54	0.62	14	15
Total	0.36	0.79	0.94	17	19
Total:					
52 cities[b]	3.47	8.48	10.38	20	22
Rest	15.13	19.50	20.05	5	3
Total	18.60	27.98	30.43	8.5	8.8

[a] Oviedo, Santander, Vizcaya, Guipuzcoa, Alava, Barcelona, Madrid.
[b] All those with a population over 50,000 in 1950.
[c] Caceres, Badajoz, Huelva, Ciudad Real, Sevilla, Cadiz, Malaga, Cordoba, Granada, Jaen, Albacete, Almeria, Alicante, Murcia.

1959. The difference between the rates in the industrial provinces, where the rates are mainly high, and the others in the north and center, where they are low, would be quite consistent with a history of immigration in one case and emigration in the other.

Many of the provinces in the south, however, still have a relatively high rate of natural increase. We do not know why this is so. Investigation into rates of migration during the 1940–50 decade[5] reveals no conspicuous difference between north and south. It is quite possible that the explanation lies at least partly in higher fertility rates. This could be determined by further examination of past age-structures

[5] See A. G. Barbancho, *Los Movimientos Migratorios en Espana,* Madrid, 1960.

and, more particularly, the age-structures in 1960, when the full results of the census became available.

In any event, the geographical position of the south in itself appears to have been a greater barrier to internal migration than in the north and center, where most provinces are contiguous to industrial areas. Accordingly, in other parts of the report, we have stressed the need to help the mobility of labor as a partial solution to regional problems.

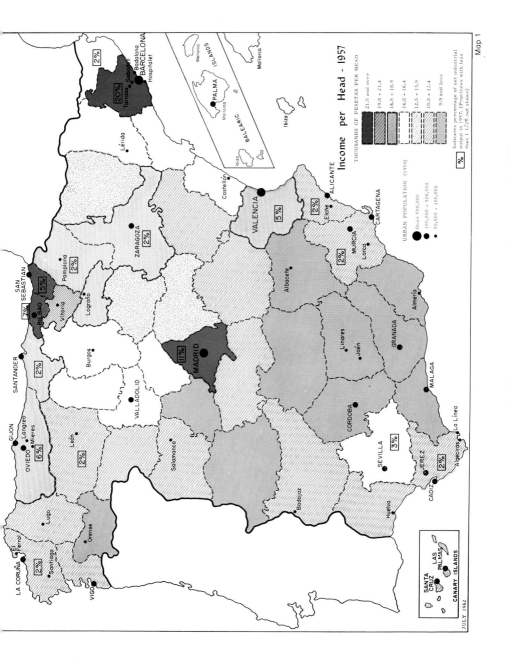

Income per Head - 1957

THOUSANDS OF PESETAS PER HEAD

21.5 and over
19.0 - 21.4
16.5 - 18.9
14.0 - 16.4
12.5 - 13.9
10.0 - 12.4
9.9 and less

% Indicates percentage of net industrial
output in 1957. (Provinces with less
than 1 1/2% not shown)

URBAN POPULATION (1950)

Over 500,000
100,000 - 500,000
50,000 - 100,000

Map 1

JULY 1962

2%
20% Terrasa · Sabadell
BARCELONA
Badalona
Hospitalet

BALEARIC

PALMA ISLANDS

Menorca

Mallorca

Mallorca

Ibiza

Lérida

Castellón

VALENCIA 5%

ALICANTE 2%
Elche

CARTAGENA

ZARAGOZA 2%

Pamplona 2%

SAN
SEBASTIAN 5%
7% BILBAO
Vitoria
Logroño

MURCIA 2%
Lorca

Albacete

MADRID 11%

Burgos

Almería

GRANADA

Linares
Jaén

VALLADOLID 2%

SANTANDER 2%

GIJON
OVIEDO Langreo
Mieres 6%

León 2%

Salamanca

CORDOBA

MALAGA

La Linea

SEVILLA 3%

JEREZ 2%
Algeciras
CADIZ

Badajoz

Huelva

Lugo

El
Ferrol

Orense

LA CORUÑA 2%
Santiago

VIGO

SANTA
CRUZ LAS
PALMAS

CANARY ISLANDS

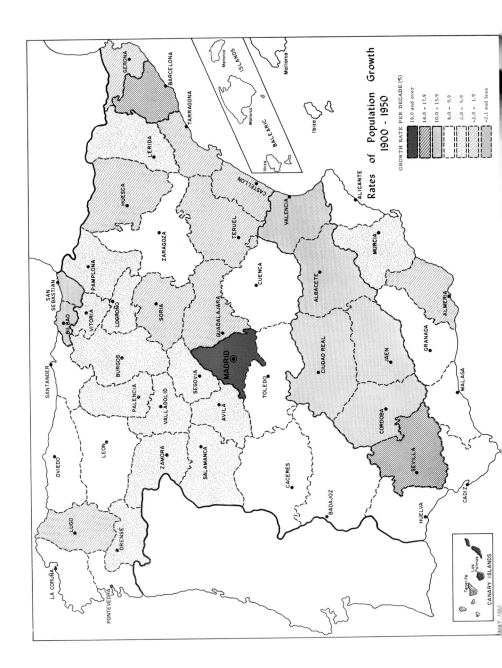

Rates of Population Growth
1900 - 1950

GROWTH RATE PER DECADE (%)

18.0 and over
14.0 - 17.9
10.0 - 13.9
6.0 - 9.9
2.0 - 5.9
-2.0 - 1.9
-2.1 and less

GERONA
BARCELONA
TARRAGONA
LERIDA
HUESCA
CASTELLON
VALENCIA
ALICANTE
TERUEL
ZARAGOZA
SAN SEBASTIAN
PAMPLONA
VITORIA
LOGROÑO
SORIA
BILBAO
CUENCA
ALBACETE
MURCIA
ALMERIA
GUADALAJARA
MADRID
GRANADA
SANTANDER
BURGOS
SEGOVIA
TOLEDO
CIUDAD REAL
JAEN
MALAGA
PALENCIA
VALLADOLID
AVILA
CORDOBA
OVIEDO
LEON
ZAMORA
SALAMANCA
SEVILLA
CACERES
BADAJOZ
HUELVA
CADIZ
LUGO
ORENSE
LA CORUÑA
PONTEVEDRA

ISLANDS
Menorca
Mallorca
Mallorca
Ibiza
BALEARIC
Ibiza

Tenerife
Los Palmas
CANARY ISLANDS

MAY 1962

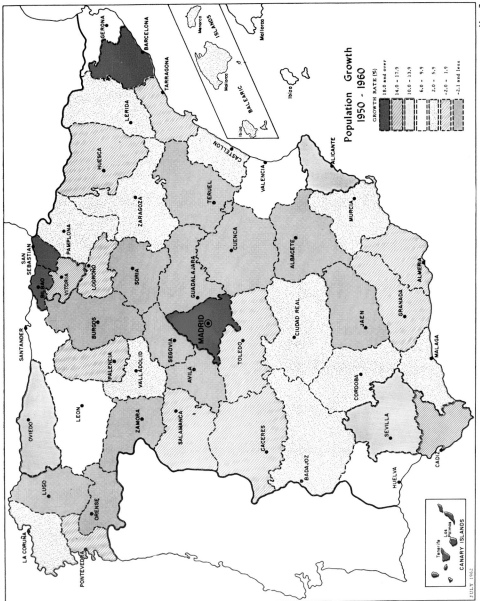

Population Growth
1950 - 1960

GROWTH RATE (%)

18.0 and over
14.0 - 17.9
10.0 - 13.9
6.0 - 9.9
2.0 - 5.9
-2.0 - 1.9
-2.1 and less

Map 3

JULY 1962

GERONA
BARCELONA
TARRAGONA
LERIDA
HUESCA
CASTELLON
ALICANTE
VALENCIA
TERUEL
ZARAGOZA
PAMPLONA
SAN SEBASTIAN
CUENCA
ALBACETE
MURCIA
VITORIA
BILBAO
LOGROÑO
SORIA
GUADALAJARA
MADRID
ALMERIA
GRANADA
CIUDAD REAL
JAEN
SANTANDER
BURGOS
PALENCIA
SEGOVIA
AVILA
TOLEDO
MALAGA
VALLADOLID
CORDOBA
OVIEDO
LEON
ZAMORA
SALAMANCA
CACERES
SEVILLA
LUGO
ORENSE
BADAJOZ
HUELVA
CADIZ
LA CORUÑA
PONTEVEDRA

BALEARIC ISLANDS
Menorca
Mallorca
Ibiza

Tenerife
Las Palmas
CANARY ISLANDS

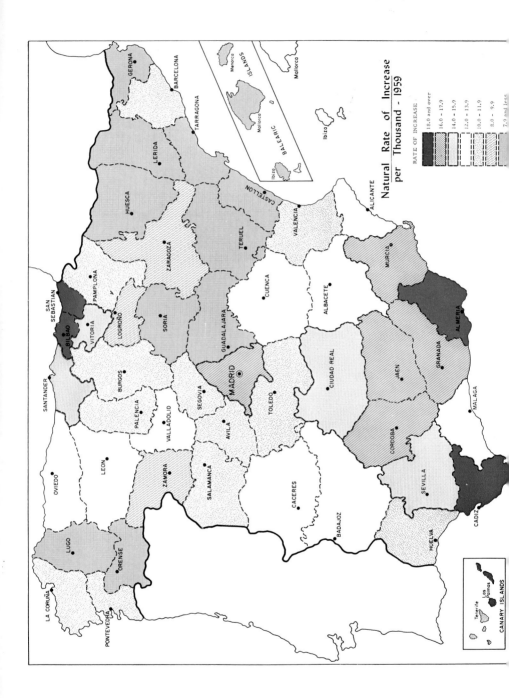

Natural Rate of Increase per Thousand - 1959

RATE OF INCREASE:

18.0 and over
16.0 – 17.9
14.0 – 15.9
12.0 – 13.9
10.0 – 11.9
8.0 – 9.9
7.9 and less

ISLANDS

Menorca

Mallorca

BALEARIC

Mallorca

Ibiza

Ibiza

Ibiza

GERONA

BARCELONA

TARRAGONA

LERIDA

CASTELLON

HUESCA

VALENCIA

ALICANTE

TERUEL

ZARAGOZA

MURCIA

SAN SEBASTIAN

PAMPLONA

VITORIA

LOGROÑO

SORIA

GUADALAJARA

CUENCA

ALBACETE

ALMERIA

BILBAO

GRANADA

SANTANDER

BURGOS

PALENCIA

VALLADOLID

SEGOVIA

MADRID

AVILA

TOLEDO

CIUDAD REAL

JAEN

MALAGA

OVIEDO

LEON

ZAMORA

SALAMANCA

CACERES

CORDOBA

SEVILLA

LUGO

ORENSE

BADAJOZ

HUELVA

CADIZ

LA CORUÑA

PONTEVEDRA

Tenerife

Las Palmas

CANARY ISLANDS

SECTION **II**

GENERAL GUIDANCE OF THE ECONOMY

CHAPTER 5 *THE INTERDEPENDENCE OF*
PUBLIC POLICIES

Subsequent chapters of this section are concerned with monetary and fiscal management of the economy and with foreign economic policy. These different sides of the general guidance of the economy are the responsibility of different organs of government and it is, for this and other reasons, convenient to discuss them separately. Nevertheless, the fact must not be overlooked that they are not isolated subjects. In a quantitative sense, there is a direct interconnection between monetary movements, public finances and the foreign balance.

This interconnection can be illustrated in summary form by a brief review of developments in the Spanish economy since 1957. Between 1958 and 1960 the economy shifted from a deficit in its foreign account, which became critical in 1959 and led to the stabilization plan, to a large surplus in 1960. As item A in Table 5.1 shows, the reason for this was twofold: a reduction in the large deficit of the public sector to a near balance; and a large increase in the surplus of the private sector.[1]

In the public sector, this drastic reduction in the deficit was a result of the efforts made as part of the stabilization plan to contain the amount of public expenditure and to increase revenues. The increase in the surplus of the private sector was due initially to the credit restraints imposed as part of the stabilization plan. These did not persist throughout 1960, as item B in Table 5.1 shows. Although credit was freely available to the private sector, the consequences were quite different from those in 1958, a year of inflation and strain on the foreign reserves. The private sector was hesitant and private saving (in the financial sense) was very large. With the addition of the substantial credit extended to it, the private sector's liquid assets increased by some 50 billion pts, nearly all in time deposits with the commercial banks or deposits in the savings banks.

In 1961, some reactivation of the economy took place. Both the extension of credit to the private sector and the accumulation of liquid assets were very much larger than in 1960, while the increase in foreign exchange reserves was smaller. In the two and a half years following

[1] Surplus (or deficit) as used here includes both the excess (or deficiency) of income over expenditure of the sector plus inflow of capital from abroad, which it is not easy to identify except for U.S. aid, which is shown separately. Short- or long-term capital from abroad was an important element in the increase in the financial surplus of the private sector.

TABLE 5.1:　Financial Position of the Public and Private Sectors

(billion pts)

Item	1957	1958	1959	1960	1961
A. *Financial position of sectors:*					
Surplus of private sector	11.4	7.3	20.1	23.3	22.6
Deficit of public sector	−17.2	−13.3	−14.0	−2.0	−6.5
Net inflow of U.S. aid[a]	3.6	4.9	3.5	4.2	3.3
Increase in foreign exchange reserves[b]	−2.2	−1.2	9.6	25.5	19.4
B. *Change in liquid assets:*					
Surplus of private sector	11.4	7.3	20.1	23.3	22.6
Net credit to private sector	24.4	32.3	1.6	28.9	44.2
Increase in liquid assets	35.8	39.6	21.7	52.2	66.9
C. *Composition of change in liquid assets:*					
Sight deposits and currency	23.6	23.8	9.1	2.9	25.7
Time and savings deposits	12.2	15.8	12.6	49.3	41.2
	35.8	39.6	21.7	52.2	66.9

[a] Donations to the Spanish Government plus increase in unused part of U.S.-owned counterpart.

[b] Increase in counterpart account in the Bank of Spain of holdings of the Instituto Español de Moneda Extranjera (IEME). The correspondence between this account and foreign exchange reserves is not exact. In 1959, particularly, there was a large discrepancy.

SOURCES:*Informe sobre la Evolucion de la Economia Espanola en 1961,* Banco de España, p. 105; and information supplied by the Bank of Spain. (For detailed notes, see Table 7.1).

stabilization, sight deposits and currency increased by about 20 percent and liquid assets as a whole by about 45 percent.

If an expansionist policy is pursued by the Government, as is eminently desirable for the growth of the economy, and if there is corresponding private confidence in that growth, private investment will be encouraged. In that event, there is an evident possibility of demand exceeding available resources and of a slowing down or reversal of the present trend in the balance of payments in spite of growing tourist receipts and foreign investment. It will therefore be important, in planning the future expansion of the economy as a whole, to keep constantly in view the interrelationships between monetary and financial movements and the external payments position.

In order to ensure that expansion does not get out of hand in the future, the instruments for controlling the economy should be ready; the lines of authority for applying those instruments must be clear;

and the mechanism for coordinating action in the various fields of authority well established. Control implies adequate statistical information on the state of the economy. This information may emanate from different sources, but it should, nevertheless, be in a form in which the interconnection between the different sectors is readily apparent.

If the need emerges to control the allocation of resources in the economy, it is more than ever important to ensure that the methods used, direct or indirect as the case may be, make for allocation in the most efficient way and that restrictions are not placed on those economic activities that are promoting the growth of the economy. However important control of the quantity of public and private expenditure may be, it is equally important, if not more so, that it not be at the expense of quality. It will be necessary to exercise discretion as between the public and private sectors; a government program to encourage expansion does not necessarily have to be a big one and restraint may at times be the wisest course. In controlling credit to the private sector, it will be necessary to exercise control gradually and generally and not merely where it is most easily applied. If adequate steps are taken in good time, there should be no need to jeopardize the progressive liberalization in foreign economic relations which enables the Spanish economy to make better use of its domestic resources.

This question of control has particular importance in the public sector, because the public sector in Spain has wide ramifications and includes a very large number of institutions. Perhaps more than in most countries, it is not altogether easy to define where the public sector leaves off and the private sector (or the financial sector, through which both the public and private sectors obtain their credit requirements) begin. Many public institutions perform functions which are similar to, and in competition with, the private and the financial sectors. There are many public enterprises operating in the market economy and public credit institutions in the financial sector.

The mission has already expressed the view that the economic discipline to be applied to different parts of the public sector should depend on the function of each part. For this and other purposes, it is desirable to have a clear and consistent definition of the public sector and its various component parts. It is necessary from the point of view of general control of the economy and the statistical information necessary for it. It is also necessary for the laying down of general rules of conduct, such as accounting and accountability to the central authority.

In the present context we think it useful to make an initial distinc-

TABLE 5.2: Public and Financial Sectors

Public Sector	Financial Sector
Central Administration (Administracion Central)	Bank of Spain (Banco de Espana)
Autonomous Organizations[a] (Organismo Autonomos)	Foreign Exchange Institute (Instituto Espanol de Moneda Extranjera)
Local Authorities (Entidades Locales)	Commercial Banks (Bancos de Deposito)
Social Security Organizations (Seguridad Social)	Savings Banks (Cajas de Ahorro)
Syndicates (Sindicatos)	Official Credit Institutions[b] (Entidades Oficiales de Credito)
Public Enterprises (Empresas Publicas)	Committee on Medium- and Long-Term Credit (Comite de Credito a Medio y Largo Plazo)
Spanish Provinces in Africa (Provincias Espanolas en Africa)	

[a] Except for official credit institutions.
[b] Official credit institutions include the following: Banco de Credito Local, Banco Hipotecario, Instituto de Credito para la Reconstruccion Nacional, Banco de Credito Industrial, Servicio Nacional de Credito Agricola and Servicio Nacional de Credito Maritimo y Pesquero.

tion between the financial sector, which includes some public institutions, and the public sector, more narrowly conceived. The financial sector which has various functions as a financial intermediary between the several parts of the economy, should be conceived of as a whole, irrespective of the ownership and control of its individual institutions. Therefore, we have separated out a number of institutions, public or private, which might properly be considered the financial sector. These are shown in the right-hand column of Table 5.2. Future reference to the public sector will be confined to the institutions in the left-hand column.[2]

[2] Much of the statistical information will, however, cover only a part of the public sector, so defined. Table 5.2, for example, covers only the first three groups.

CHAPTER 6 *FISCAL MANAGEMENT*

The Public Accounts

The budget in its broadest sense is a vital step in the planning process. It is the annual working document through which the Government gives concrete form to its general intentions toward the development of the economy and to its specific intentions toward the part that the Government itself will play in that development. It must be a document which expresses those intentions clearly and decisively.

The document must be clear in its intentions, not only to a limited number of ministers and government employees, but to a wide circle of people in influential positions in the productive economy and in the financial sector. For these people must act, at least in part, on the basis of what they expect the Government to do. What is true of the initial estimates is also true of the final results. The public accounts should be a comprehensive, consistent, timely body of information, both as to results in retrospect and as to forecasts.

Public accounts should be clear in various different ways. First, they must be clear as to definition. Since the public sector has wide ramifications in Spain, for many purposes it is most conveniently considered in a number of subsectors according to the nature of the business of the individual institutions. A comprehensive definition should be supported by a logical division into subsectors which is consistently used in all official documents.

Secondly, although different systems of accounting may well be necessary for each subsector, it should be possible to consolidate the accounts of the whole public sector or any major part of it. It should also be possible to do this in such a way that these accounts can be integrated with information received from other branches of the economy and used in the preparation of aggregate statistics for the whole economy such as the national accounts and the flow of funds.

Thirdly, it should be possible to analyze the accounts, so that income and expenditure can readily be classified according to useful and consistent categories. For example, current and capital expenditure should, as far as possible, be identifiable not only in total but also by function. In these three respects clarity of information is needed for the exercise of general policy, to gauge the impact of the Government on the economy and on particular sections of it.

Fourthly, the use of public money should be identifiable in sufficient detail for control of the actual spending authorized for each part of the Government. This is a matter of internal management of the Government's own business. Every part of the Government should have its program marked out. Each should know what its own obligations are and what are those of others. These obligations should, of course, be coordinated in the first instance. A budget is, essentially, an instrument of coordination.

The task of presenting clear and meaningful public accounts is never easy, in any country, since the public sector typically includes not only the central government but a large number of local government bodies together with parastatal bodies of various kinds. In Spain the problem is compounded by the large number of so-called autonomous organizations, each of which is at least nominally dependent from a particular ministry. There are some 1,600 of these autonomous organizations, in most cases with special sources of income of their own, in addition to public enterprises and other public bodies which are not so designated.

Difficulties also arise for a number of other reasons:

a. The relevant information is not all assembled in one place or even in a few places.

b. There is a great variety of functions among the various public bodies and no clear and consistent classification of them.

c. The timing of publication of budgets and final accounts varies.

d. There are many internal transfers from one institution to another and many *contra* items appearing on both sides of the accounts of a particular public body.

e. The system used to classify accounts and the form in which they are presented make them difficult to analyze.

The principal source of information on the public accounts is the *Informacion Estadistica* of the Ministry of Finance. This document covers only the central administration, the autonomous agencies, Spanish provinces in Africa and local authorities. It does not include information on many important public enterprises such as the component firms of INI, the railways (RENFE), the government petroleum distribution monopoly (CAMPSA), the social security organizations (Instituto Nacional de Prevision and Mutualidades Laborales) and the Sindicatos.

While these are significant omissions for some purposes, the groups that are covered in *Informacion Estadistica* might be considered, with certain important reservations which are specified later, as a first approximation to the bodies performing typically governmental functions. A summary of income and expenditure for 1960 assembled from this document is shown in Table 6.1. The total on each side comes to about 150 billion pts. However, this is an unconsolidated account and there are also some serious omissions.

TABLE 6.1: Unconsolidated Account of Part of the Public Sector, 1960[a]

(billion pts)

Income:	
Central Administration (budget)	72.7
Central Administration (extrabudgetary)	14.5
Autonomous Organizations	45.6
Local Authorities (except Alava and Navarra)	14.9
Alava and Navarra	.5
Spanish Provinces in Africa	.4
	148.6
Expenditure:	
Central Administration (budget)	67.1
Central Administration (extrabudgetary)	20.3
Autonomous Organizations	44.9
Local Authorities (except Alava and Navarra)	14.9
Alava and Navarra	.5
Spanish Provinces in Africa	.4
	148.2

[a] Final results for central administration: budget estimates for other organizations.
SOURCE: *Informacion Estadistica del Ministerio de Hacienda*, 1961. In detail: (i) Central Administration, p. 139. (ii) Autonomous Organizations, pp. 179, 193. (iii) Local Authorities, pp. 224, 226. (iv) Alava and Navarra, pp. 245–247. (v) Spanish Provinces in Africa, pp. 145–147.

The only available consolidated account of this same part of the public sector is published in the Annual Report of the Bank of Spain. It is reproduced here as Table 6.2. In the process of consolidation, many items of income and expenditure have been eliminated, thereby reducing the total by over 30 billion pts. (The principal reduction is in the expenditure of the central administration and the income of autonomous organizations, which to a considerable extent is a result of eliminating subventions from one to the other.)

Even if this table is only approximately correct, it is clear that the Government's role in the economy is an important one. Total expenditure is about one-quarter of GNP and government investment somewhat less than half of gross investment. It is noteworthy that the greater part of the investment is carried out by the autonomous organizations.

As the Bank of Spain report acknowledges, however, the table is only an approximation. In the first place, both accounts, the consolidated and the unconsolidated, are a composite of final results (for the central

TABLE 6.2: Consolidated Account of the Public Sector, 1960[a]

(billions of pts)

	Income	Expenditure
Current	98.7	54.8
Transfers	1.0	11.5
Capital Formation	1.7	34.4
Financial Capital[b]	13.8	14.0
	115.2	114.8

[a] Excluding social security and syndicates.
[b] Amortization of debt has here been deducted from both sides.
SOURCE: *Informe sobre la Evolucion de la Economia Espanola en 1961*, Banco de España, 1962, p. 85.

administration) and budget estimates (for the autonomous agencies and local authorities).

Since the difference between budget estimates and final results is often very large, the absence of comparable information is a serious deficiency. The mission feels that, if the central administration (which is by far the largest single unit in the public sector) is capable of providing a timely budget and timely accounts, other public institutions should reach the same standards. It is essential that the Ministry of Finance should have the necessary powers to call for, and review, the accounts of public institutions which should be delivered within determined time limits and according to the established forms. A particular effort should, in our view, be made by the autonomous organizations, some of which are very large. Among the 194 groups of organizations (covering a much larger number of individual organizations) which are listed in *Informacion Estadistica*, 7 groups have a budget of over 1 billion pts and another 37 groups have a budget of more than 100 million pts (see Table 6.3). In some cases, the expenditure of the dependent organizations dwarfs that of the parent ministry.[1]

It is evident that no meaningful description of government activity is possible without a proper consolidation of the activities of the central administration and the autonomous organizations, at the very least. However, in addition to the difficulties of timing, the task of consolidating the accounts of these various bodies is made extremely complex by the bewildering labyrinth of cross-transfers between different institutions. In addition to the large capital and current grants

[1] The expenditure of the Ministry of Agriculture (other than subventions) in 1960 was only about 200 million pts compared with over 13 billion pts by its dependent autonomous organizations.

TABLE 6.3:   Budgeted Expenditure of Autonomous Organizations, 1960

(billion pts)

Ministry	Total Number[a]	Amt.	Over 1.00 pts Number[a]	Amt.	0.10 to 1.00 pts Number[a]	Amt.	Under 0.10 pts Number[a]	Amt.
Agriculture	38	13.42	3	10.91	4	1.95	31	.55
Prime Minister's Office	5	9.35	1	9.09	1	0.24	3	.02
Housing	6	8.41	1	7.03	4	1.36	1	.01
Education	52	4.09	1	1.49	6	1.69	45	.91
Public Works	19	2.60	1	1.26	5	1.13	13	.21
Interior	16	1.85	—	—	4	1.62	12	.24
Finance	9	1.36	—	—	4	1.20	5	.16
Army	8	0.96	—	—	2	0.95	6	.01
Air	5	0.81	—	—	2	0.72	3	.09
Commerce	5	0.51	—	—	1	0.34	4	.17
All Others[b]	31	1.59	—	—	4	0.98	27	.61
Total	194	44.95	7	29.78	37	12.20	150	2.97
Percentage		100		66		27		7

[a] Number of groups as listed in *Informacion Estadistica*.
[b] Industry, Justice, Navy, Labor and Foreign Affairs.
SOURCE: *Informacion Estadistica del Ministerio de Hacienda*, 1961, pp. 193–204.

or loans from the central government to autonomous organizations, the latter in turn make such grants or loans to each other and to other branches of the public sector. Similar complications of cross-transfers, though smaller in magnitude, arise from the operations of official credit institutions and local authorities.

A further problem arises because, within these organizations and, indeed, the public sector as a whole, there is also a great diversity of function. Many organizations are engaged in typically governmental activity, that is, the provision of goods or services financed directly or indirectly by taxation. But the most important of the autonomous organizations are engaged in other sorts of activities, such as the provision of goods or services for sale in the market economy or the making of loans to the private sector.[2] A list of the more important ones is given in Table 6.4.

Given these difficulties of timing, of internal transfers and of diversity of function, it would require a very carefully conceived system of classification of public agencies and of the accounts they use to bring all these manifold transactions together in such a way as to give a clear

[2] This also is true of the Post Office, which is part of the central administration.

TABLE 6.4: Partial List of Autonomous Organizations with Commercial or Financial Functions

Principal Activity	Ministry On Which Organization Is Dependent	Name	Budget Expenditure 1960 (million pts)
Buying & Selling Commodities:			
	Prime Minister's Office	Comision de Compras de Excedentes de Vinos (Wine)	241
	Agriculture	Servicio Nacional del Trigo[a] (Wheat)	952[b]
	Agriculture	Instituto de Fomento para la Produccion de Fibras Textiles (Textile fibers)	4,990
	Commerce	Comisaria General de Abastecimientos y Transportes (Government trading abroad)	342
Real Estate:			
Construction of ⎫ Housing for ⎪ Government ⎬ Employees ⎭	Army	Patronato de Casas Militares	162
	Navy	Patronato de Casas de la Armada	267
	Public Works	Patronato de Casas para Funcionarios del Ministerio	121
Purchase and ⎫ sale of land ⎬ ⎭	Housing	Comisaria General de Urbanismo de Madrid	854
	Housing	Comisaria General de Urbanismo de Barcelona	101
Public Utilities:[c]			
	Public Works	Canal de Isabel II (Water)	454
	Public Works	Juntas de Obras de Puertos y Comisiones Administrativas (Ports)	1,258[b]
	Public Works	Jefatura de Explotacion de Ferrocarriles del Estado (Narrow-gauge railways)	230
	Air	Junta Nacional de Aeropuertos (Airports)	598
Credit Agencies:			
	Agriculture	Servicio Nacional de Credito Agricola	2,101
	Housing	Instituto Nacional de Vivienda[a]	7,029
Miscellaneous:			
Industrial holding company	Prime Minister's Office	Instituto Nacional de Industria[a]	9,086
Foreign exchange institute	Commerce	Instituto Espanol de Moneda Extranjera	61[b]
Mint	Finance	Fabrica Nacional de Moneda y Timbre	231[b]
Mercury mine	Finance	Consejo de Administracion de las Minas de Almaden y Arrayanes	173

Table 6.4 *(cont.)*

Principal Activity	Ministry On Which Organization Is Dependent	Name	Budget Expenditure 1960 (million pts)
Betting Agencies for charitable purposes	Finance	Patronato de Apuestas Mutuas Deportivas Beneficas	799
Total			30,050

[a] Institutions with important ancillary functions.
[b] Institutions for which the statement of expenditure is known to be seriously incomplete.
[c] One of the largest single enterprises in Spain, the national railways (RENFE), is not classified as an autonomous organization and its accounts are not summarized in *Informacion Estadistica*.

summary of the public sector's activity. This subject we deal with at greater length below. As the situation now stands, it is very difficult to attach any clear meaning to even the total of income and expenditure in a consolidated account such as that reproduced in Table 6.2. Moreover, in the process of consolidation, the possibility of identifying the nature of income received and the purpose of expenditure is lost.

The mission believes that the absence of adequate information on the finances of the public sector deprives the Government of an essential tool for economic planning. The absence of adequate information implies the absence of adequate control. We cannot say which is cause and which is effect, but one cannot exist without the other.

Classification of Public Accounts

The greatly increased size of public expenditure, the consequent difficulties in comprehending and controlling it and the revolution in economic thought have impelled many governments to reconsider the format of their accounts to make them more useful and understandable. A new system of classification of public accounts in Spain was introduced by an order of the Council of Ministers, dated July 26, 1957,[3] and represents, in statement of purpose and in conception, a great advance. Considerable progress along the lines of this new classification

[3] Presupuestos. Nueva Estructuracion—Normas para 1958.

has been made in subsequent years, but a further effort in the same direction is necessary in order to correct certain deficiencies in its application for these reasons:

a. The system is not suitable in its present form for institutions with a commercial or financial function.
b. The information available is not summarized in the most useful categories.
c. The system has not been applied completely or consistently.

The present system applies to the central administration and the autonomous organizations. As a more detailed account of the system and its application is given in Annex B, the comments which follow are of a general nature.

The first difficulty arises because of the application of a single system of accounts to agencies with diverse functions. In so doing, the functions of the Government as producer, as financial intermediary and as final consumer of goods and services become confused.[4]

The present system does not provide for this type of distinction, especially in the case of institutions producing goods and services, and consequently leads to certain anomalies in the classification. It seems clear that the first requirement is a new and authoritative definition of the public sector and of its subsectors. For this purpose, it is not necessary to change the present titles of the subsectors:

a. Central Administration
b. Autonomous Organizations
c. Local Authorities
d. Public Enterprises
e. Public Financial Institutions
f. Social Security Organizations

All public agencies should be incorporated in one and only one subsector and the official definition used more consistently than in the past. Subsector b., Autonomous Organizations, should be confined to

[4] As producer, a government agency purchases materials and in combination with the various factors of production sells the product to others. The product may be an intermediate one entering into the cost of production of other goods or it may be sold for final use by the private sector or to the Government itself. Transportation services, for example, fall into all these categories. But when the Government, in its typical activity, buys materials and personal services and uses them in combination for various purposes, it is at the same time the final user, whether as consumer or investor. In the third case—the Government as financial intermediary—interest attaches much less to the purchase and sale of goods and services, which is usually very small. The main interest lies in the inflow and outflow of capital funds, in the source and destination of these funds and in the purpose for which these funds are used.

branches of the public sector engaged in typically government activity. It is the mission's view, expressed subsequently, that there is a strong case for incorporation of these organizations into the *corpus* of the central administration. Other presently autonomous organizations should be classified, according to their nature, under c., d., or e. Organizations in categories d., e., and f., which have a commercial or financial function should have standard forms prescribed for their accounts and for their annual reports, which should be published. Summarized information on these accounts should be made publicly available.

A second difficulty arises because several of the chapters include two or more types of transaction (e.g., sales and loans, interest and amortization, income and cash balances) the sum of which is not very meaningful. The most important cases are listed in Annex B.

Thirdly, the information in *Informacion Estadistica* is broken down by ministry, for the central administration, and by the various groups of autonomous organizations. But one ministry may have several different functions and this is also true of the larger autonomous organizations. Both the Ministry of Public Works and the Instituto Nacional de Colonizacion, for example, are in part engaged in the construction or operation of irrigation works. Because there is no breakdown within each, no functional classification of expenditure is possible.

Other difficulties in the use of the information in *Informacion Estadistica* are inconsistent usage of the classification system and the omission of important items of income and expenditure. To some extent this arises because, as was pointed out before, the classification system is ill-adapted to the activities of certain institutions. There are, however, large extrabudgetary transactions of the central administration and some autonomous organizations which are either not listed at all in *Informacion Estadistica* or are listed outside the main accounts with very little description of their nature. The details are given in Annex B.

The mission believes that a machine-coding system for all the accounts of the public sector should eventually be introduced. This is, however, a complex task to be undertaken only after careful examination of methods in use in other countries. In the meantime, some useful reforms could be carried out with the existing system as a basis. A revised form of summary of income and expenditure, details of which are given in Annex B, should be published for the central administration and the newly-defined autonomous organizations, which in effect constitute the central government. The object of this revised form would be twofold:

a. to eliminate the difficulty caused by the inclusion of more than one type of expenditure under a single heading;

b. to provide a closer, though far from perfect, approximation to a functional breakdown by showing expenditure of different branches of ministries separately.

This revised summary would apply to *all* income and expenditure with the possible exception of purely transit items.

Expenditure: Information and Control in Detail

Information on and control of public money in detail, though fulfilling a different purpose, is just as important as it is in the large. The quality of expenditure requires careful scrutiny. First, expenditure should be the right kind of expenditure, designed to meet the purposes dictated by the government's development policy. Secondly, expenditure for any given purpose should be at the lowest possible *cost* consistent with that purpose. It is not enough to judge expenditure in a particular category by the percentage increase over the previous year. All expenditure requires the same kind of scrutiny whether it is going up or going down.

Good judgment on the suitability of various budgetary proposals for expenditure can only be exercised if these are put forward in a readily comprehensible form. In considering the form, there is bound to be some conflict with the requirements of traditional accounting control. The categories under which individual items of expenditure by the ministries are authorized by the Ministry of Finance often cut across functional lines of demarcation. Some compromise is necessary, but it is essential that the presentation of the budget should not be determined solely by its relevance to subsequent fiscalization.

We may illustrate this point by reference to the expenditure budget of the central administration, which in some respects contains too much detail and in others too little. The budget document for 1960/61 contains 638 pages of detailed description of the general expenditure of the State (Letra A) with some 200,000 individual entries ranging from as little as 60 pts (part of item 351.185) to as much as 1.6 billion pts (item 413.324) and totaling some 56 billion pts. Our first recommendation would be to reduce drastically the enormous number of entries in the detailed account of expenditure (Pormenor del Presupuesto de Gastos). A very large part of these entries consists of an extremely detailed account of salaries and salary supplements.[5] Although we do not dispute the necessity for detailed control of the civil

[5] There are 70 pages for the Ministry of Education alone.

service organization, the place for this does not appear to be the budget document itself. Such a degree of detail swamps the reader and robs the document of all perspective.

At the same time that the expenditure on personnel is summarized, its purpose could be identified more clearly. Some personnel are employed in the general administration of a ministry, others on rendering a particular government service such as primary or secondary education and still others on the preparation, construction, or maintenance of investment projects.

On the other hand, there are some extremely large items which are not explained in detail at all. In addition to general expenditure under Letra A, six special items of expenditure in the form of grants or loans to autonomous organizations or public enterprises are listed under the so-called Letra C. In 1960 these six included one item of 5 billion pts and in all totaled 10 billion pts. Other large subventions to autonomous organizations are included in Letra A. In addition, there are a number of large items of direct expenditure by the Government itself, examples of which are quoted in the Annex. Many of these are items of investment expenditure, embracing a large number of projects.

The past history of investment expenditure in Spain convinces us that it is of the utmost importance to exercise much more detailed control. We would recommend that all investment projects costing more than 10 million pts *in total* be listed separately and that the following information be placed in juxtaposition to the expenditure allocation for the year:

a. total estimated cost of the project;
b. remaining estimated cost of the project at the beginning of the budget year;
c. time required for completion.

This recommendation might, unlike the previous one, considerably increase the size of the document. If so, it would have served a useful purpose, since it would reveal the number of projects being undertaken at the same time and their rate of progress. As we point out at various places in this report, the mission is persuaded that the number of projects is too large and the rate too slow in several sectors, and suspects that the problem is widespread.[6]

---

[6] It might be objected that such detailed presentation would reduce the flexibility necessary to each ministry in view of the uncertainty inherent in construction projects. This could be taken care of by simple rules for *virement* up to a limit at the discretion of the ministry concerned and beyond that at the discretion of the Ministry of Finance. Such latitude would permit flexibility between projects but not in the number of them.

The mission sees no good reason why the budgets of remaining autonomous organizations should not be subject to the same rules and be published, either in association with that of the central administration or at least in a supplementary document. In our view, a beginning should be made with those of the largest autonomous organizations. Furthermore, since a substantial volume of public money is transferred to public enterprises for investment purposes, it would also be desirable to assemble and publish capital budgets and accounts of these organizations. The same degree of detail would be desirable in describing investment projects. We understand that much of the forward information on investment projects needed for carrying out these recommendations is becoming available to the Ministry of Finance (as a result of the order of January 24, 1958) and is being elaborated by the Junta de Contratacion Administrativa.

Another valuable kind of information for budgetary control is a statement of unit costs for those services which are regularly performed. This information is useful for what is now known as performance budgeting. The order of July 26, 1957, of the Council of Ministers, already referred to, called for this type of information from ministries and autonomous organizations. The mission can only recommend that this thoroughly desirable innovation be put into practice.

Organization for Fiscal Control

Information is only useful if it is used. The mission believes that for unified, effective control of the public sector there should be one central unit within the Ministry of Finance responsible for advising the Minister on the kinds of information required, for seeing that it is collected, for analyzing it and for making policy recommendations on the basis of that analysis.

For present purposes, we shall call this unit the Central Budget Office. We do not thereby suggest that a new section is necessarily needed in addition to the present departmental structure. It may well be possible to evolve an office of this kind out of the present structure. This is a matter on which the mission does not feel qualified to pronounce.

The purpose of this office would be twofold, corresponding to the functions of over-all and detailed control already discussed. In its first function, the office would be looking outward to the general guidance of the economy. It would necessarily have to consider fiscal policy as a whole in relation to the level of economic activity in view of the Ministry of Finance's responsibility for short-term policy in conjunction with the Bank of Spain. More specifically, the office would be responsible for considering the impact of taxation, borrowing and expenditure on the balance of payments, monetary and credit conditions, regional development and the pursuit of long-range objectives as embodied in a development plan.

For these purposes, the Budget Office would necessarily be the focal point of liaison with the Planning Commission, the Bank of Spain, and the Ministry of Commerce, all of which are involved in the over-all guidance of the economy.

The second function would involve looking inward on the government's own expenditure policy. This consists, first, in ensuring that expenditure proposals are presented in coherent programs and, secondly, that the Government is getting adequate value for the expenditure of public money. We cannot stress too highly the need to look at expenditure in terms of programs. The subsequent section on agriculture, for example, reflects our views on this in much more detail.

This will mean that some existing procedures will require modification. A typical case is irrigation. Individual irrigation projects are now considered at all levels of government as isolated projects. Approval for a project is given without reference to subsequent budgetary availability of funds. When the time for budgeting comes, a lump sum is allocated to irrigation, the amount to be spent on individual projects being decided later. Since both the Instituto Nacional de Colonizacion (Ministry of Agriculture) and the Directorate General of Obras Hidraulicas in the Ministry of Public Works are involved, a mechanism has been introduced recently by the Ministry of Finance to coordinate their expenditure through a special committee. While this type of coordination is, of course, necessary, it is not sufficient. Irrigation allocations should be determined in the light of the whole agricultural program.

Examination of specific proposals within a program of expenditure will also be necessary. The mission has already drawn attention to the serious lack of economic criteria for investments undertaken by the Government and has also endorsed the government's view that there is a need for performance budgeting. We believe that the responsibility for ensuring adequate control of this kind over expenditure would appropriately fall on the Central Budget Office.

However, the Central Budget Office cannot itself undertake detailed investigation of the manifold expenditure proposals put before it, nor should it be expected to weld them all into programs of expenditure. It will have to rely on the spending ministries and organizations to do the investigation and compilation according to prescribed standards and procedures. When the time comes for review, the Central Budget

Office will check that its standards have been met and its procedures followed.

The idea that the process of ensuring the economical and judicious use of public money should begin with the spending units themselves may require a certain shift of emphasis, but the shift would be in the direction in which many other governments have moved in recent years. A first step would be to establish in all the more important ministries special project and program review units staffed by a small team of engineers and economists. In Sections III and IV of the report we point to the need for units of this kind to ensure more centralized economic control of transport and agricultural policy and investment programs. Although specific recommendations are made in these two cases, the recommendation is really a general one.

We do not wish to try to characterize the work of these units in detail, but would rather illustrate it with the example of investment project analysis. There is considerable controversy as to the appropriate methods of assessing the relation between cost and benefit of projects; the interpretation of these assessments in comparing unlike projects is, on the whole, difficult if not impossible to make. Nevertheless, methods have been developed which often make it possible to come to firm conclusions on the rival merits of projects in like fields and, more especially, when there is more than one way of achieving the same objective. In the first instance, therefore, the units should make a special effort to study alternatives. It will frequently be unnecessary to resort to any very sophisticated analysis to reveal that one way of doing something is much less expensive than another.

Analysis of individual projects makes little sense without some study of present and future requirements as a whole. It will, therefore, be part of the responsibility of the units recommended to look at the sum of projects in a particular sector in terms of the total need or market. We develop this point in somewhat more detail in the section on agriculture. The review of sector programs as a whole has the additional advantage that their future costs can be assembled in one place and compared with the probable resources available to the public sector.

We may, therefore, sum up the work of these units, in respect of investment projects, as follows:

a. an analysis of the market for whatever goods or services are to be produced (even if there may be no market in the normal sense, assessment of needs by some agreed standards is necessary);

b. comparison of costs, including initial investment and future recurrent costs, with benefits to be obtained, whether measurable or not;

c. review of alternative ways of reaching the same objective;

d. clear statement of the financial requirements over time, including all aspects of the investment proposal, whether they are a direct part of it or not.

The responsibility of the Central Budget Office would then be to concern itself with methods used by the various ministries, with the exercise of choice between different claims on the public resources, and, in close collaboration with the Planning Commission, with the reconciliation of individual sector programs with the long-term objectives of the Government.

Tax Policy and Administration

The Central Budget Office that we have proposed would have an important function on the revenue as well as the expenditure side. There is clearly an opportunity still to be grasped for profitable exchange of information and ideas, with due regard for confidentiality, between the tax authorities, the statistical services and the planning authority to which the statistical services are now responsible. As taxation reaches into every branch of economic activity, tax returns can be a useful source of economic information on savings, investment, consumption and the distribution of income. As they are not always a reliable source, it is conversely the case that statistical information derived from other sources may be of help to the tax authorities. Furthermore, the study of tax returns and trends in comparison with other economic indicators is necessary for the better forecasting of revenue.

As in many other countries, the Government faces difficult problems of tax administration, the solution of which cannot be reduced to a simple formula. Some solution will, however, have to be found if taxation is to be an effective instrument of policy. The mission has little doubt of the need to generate reasonably reliable statistical information, related more than hitherto to the functioning of the economy as a whole, in order to lay the groundwork for continuing analysis of the problems of policy and administration. The proposed Central Budget Office would be a logical place for centralizing the necessary collection of data, for analyzing it and for channeling the kind of two-way flow of information that we have described.

Beyond this, the mission feels it must necessarily confine itself to some rather general observations in view of the impossibility of delving at all deeply into the tax system itself, which is complicated, and in view of the over-riding importance of the administrative problems.

The mission has considered the tax system in relation to certain social and economic purposes. The social purpose is to place the burden of government expenditure on those who can most afford it and to do this in the most equitable manner. There are two aspects to equity. The first requirement is an equitable distribution as between high and low incomes, which concerns the extent of progressivity of the tax system. The second is an equal burden for equal incomes of the same general character.

From the economic point of view, the tax system, while necessarily drawing an increasing volume of revenue from the more dynamic sectors of the economy, should not go so far as to destroy the incentive and the means to growth. Nor should there be arbitrary discrimination, especially between firms in the same industry, but even between different industries, except for very well-defined purposes. Finally, a tax system should be sensitive to the growth of the economy and to fluctuations in it.

The revenue of the central administration in 1960 amounted to some 73 billion pts, of which about 64 billion pts was tax revenue.[7] Indirect taxes accounted for over 60 percent of tax revenue in 1960 and the proportion has, if anything, tended to increase in recent years (see Table 6.5).

The Spanish tax structure is sometimes criticized for an undue reliance on indirect taxes, on the ground that they are inequitable because regressive. The question is not, however, quite as simple as a straight comparison between direct and indirect taxes would imply. It is possible for indirect taxes as a whole to be progressive and direct taxes regressive. Much depends on the system and its application. In fact the Government, in recent years, has been eliminating or reducing some of the taxes falling most heavily on articles of general consumption such as salt, soap and shoes. It has also introduced some luxury taxes. Among the taxes on specific goods (other than import duties, in which there is a protective element), there is a heavy and growing reliance on petroleum products and, to a lesser extent, tobacco (see Table 6.6). Even here, there is likely to be a progressive element and the tax on petroleum products can be considered, in part at least, as a user charge. It is, in fact, very difficult to say just how progressive these

---

[7] Part of the difference of 9 billion pts was not genuine revenue, since it included charges for postal service (offset by expenses) and interest received from financial institutions (offset by interest payable on bonds).

TABLE 6.5: Central Administration Revenues

(billion pts)

	1958 (Actual)	1960 (Actual)	1962 (Estimates)
Direct Taxes:			
Taxes on income from real property	2.7	3.1	3.3
Tax on income from capital	2.8	2.4	2.7
Industrial and commercial taxes[a]	1.7	2.5	4.5
Tax on personal employment	4.2	5.3	6.5
Personal income tax (Contribucion sobre la Renta)	0.7	1.1	0.9
Corporation tax (Impuesto sobre la Renta de Sociedades)	7.2	7.4	9.0
Inheritance taxes	1.2	1.4	1.6
Other	0.2	0.3	0.3
Subtotal	20.9	23.5	28.8
Indirect Taxes:			
Transfer taxes (derechos reales)	2.2	2.7	3.0
Taxes on securities	1.4	1.5	1.5
Stamp taxes	3.9	4.5	5.3
Import and related taxes	2.6	5.2	9.3
Export taxes	—	1.5	0.4
General tax on expenditures	10.4	12.5	14.4
Luxury taxes	4.1	6.5	7.9
Fiscal monopolies	5.4	5.2	6.8
Other	0.4	0.5	0.3
Subtotal	30.4	40.1	48.9
Other Revenue:			
Charges for postal services	1.2	1.7	2.0
Lotteries	1.1	2.4	2.0
Other income[b]	2.2	4.9	5.0
Subtotal	4.5	9.0	9.2
Total	55.8	72.7	86.9
Indirect taxes as proportion of total taxes	59	63	63

[a] On corporations and unincorporated enterprises.
[b] Mainly income from property.

taxes are without much more understanding of their relation to consumption; this underlines the plea made earlier for more analysis of taxation in relation to the economy as a whole.[8]

If a criticism is to be levied, it is rather that there is too much reliance on taxes on intermediate goods such as cast iron, on which the

[8] In this connection, we believe that special attention might be given to taxes on food at the municipal level, which are both regressive and, in combination with certain rules, distorting in their economic effect.

TABLE 6.6:   Detail of Receipts from General Expenditure and Luxury
Taxes and Fiscal Monopolies

(billion pts)

	1960 (Actual)	1962 (Estimates)
Petroleum*	10.8	19.7
Tobacco*	4.8	
Motor Vehicles	1.2	2.5
Other Luxury Taxes	1.0	
Alcohol, Wine and Beer	0.8	0.9
Cast Iron	1.3	1.5
Yarn	0.8	0.9
General Consumption Goods^b	0.9	0.4
Other General Expenditure Taxes	2.8	3.2
	24.2	29.1

ᵃ Including proceeds from general expenditure tax, luxury tax and fiscal monopoly in the case of petroleum products and the latter two in the case of tobacco.
ᵇ Sugar, salt, shoes, soap and preserved food.

tax in 1960 was 1¼ billion pts. In these days, when there is acute competition between different intermediate products, such as steel, wood, aluminum and plastics, a tax on any one of them is discriminatory and will have the effect of reducing its competitive position. It is difficult to see what the resultant economic distortions will be, but it is hardly likely that they can be of any foreseeable benefit to the economy. Although such taxes are universally used, especially in the case of fuels, we believe that their use should be reduced as far as possible.

Among the most serious criticisms of indirect taxes in general is the proliferation of many small taxes. A particular target in this respect is the stamp tax (Timbre del Estado), which is really a conglomeration of numerous minor taxes which in general have a reputation for complexity and uncertainty of application. Minor taxes with complicated regulations absorb an undue amount of the time and energy of both taxpayer and tax collector. No tax system is likely to be crystal clear, but the mission believes that in a period of rapidly rising revenues, a significant and cheap contribution to the encouragement of initiative could be made by simplification and reduction in the number of taxes.

Some of these small taxes are levied by autonomous organizations and municipalities. While we appreciate the need for revenues for local authorities, we would suppose that it is possible to accomplish this end in other ways.[9] Moreover, we doubt that there is any good case for what are, in effect, earmarked taxes for autonomous organizations, for a vested interest is likely to be created in a particular tax, irrespective of its merits. Except in special cases, the notion of earmarked taxes does not appear to us to have merit, unless there is so close a connection between payer of the tax and recipient of the benefit as to make the tax equivalent to a user or service charge. Otherwise there is no reason to presume in advance any relation between tax receipts and the expenditure for which they are earmarked.

The question of equity and progressivity arises most acutely in the case of direct taxes and, especially, direct taxes on individuals. Direct taxation in Spain is based on a schedular system. Individuals and corporations pay separate taxes on income and property according to the source (income from real property, capital income, income from personal employment, income from industrial or commercial enterprises) *plus* a complementary tax on income as a whole after deduction of taxes paid under the separate schedules (the Contribucion sobre la Renta or the Impuesto sobre la Renta de Sociedades). The scheduled taxes are mainly at fixed rates without differentiation for size of income. The rates vary, not only according to the schedule, but within a schedule according to more detailed subdivisions of the type of income received. The tax on income from personal employment, which broadly speaking affects both employed and self-employed professional people, has an element of progressivity in the very lowest brackets, but is nevertheless comparatively high (15 percent above 60,000 pts a year) for quite modest incomes. One other element of progressivity is, in our view, an undesirable one. The tax which an individual pays on dividends is graduated steeply according to the percentage relationship the dividend bears to the capital. There does not appear to be equity in the tax so far as the individual recipient is concerned. Nor, as long as the concept of capital used does not correspond to net worth, does an economic justification appear possible.

Taxes on income from property are characterized by a low tax base and a high rate. Revenue has been sustained in the face of inflation by raising the rate instead of revising the base. It may be reasonably assumed that the tax base is now out of date, not only in absolute, but also in relative terms as between one property and another. For this reason, the tax is not a satisfactory instrument from either an economic

---

[9] Because of various exemptions, for example, municipalities are now deprived of considerable revenue from land.

or a social point of view. The view is widely held in Spain that an up-to-date assessment is needed, and the mission agrees.

Except in the case of taxes on capital income, collection of direct taxes has been a serious administrative problem. In order to increase receipts, a system has been introduced under which the Ministry of Finance each year establishes the tax base for the income received under certain schedules (for the tax on income from personal employment and for the tax on the income of industrial and commercial enterprises) within each industry, trade, or profession (either by provinces or for the country as a whole) and the tax thereby assessed is shared within the group according to some agreed formula.

There is, of course, no certainty that individuals with identical incomes have a similar tax liability. Nor is there necessarily a direct connection between income and tax liability as between different industries or even within a particular industry, since the basis of assessment is often some simple but arbitrary unit such as the number of machines of a particular type installed or the quantity of electricity used. Nevertheless, the connection is undoubtedly much closer than before, particularly as this system of global assessment (cuota global), as it is called, has succeeded in its purpose of gathering into the tax net a large number of new taxpayers.

One inherent disadvantage is that the share of an individual or corporation in the global assessment in a particular sector is not only applicable as a base for the tax on the corresponding part of his or its income, but it is also applicable as the base for taxes assessed on his or its whole income (the Contribucion sobre la Renta or the Impuesto sobre la Renta de Sociedades). When the tax base is lower than the individual's real income, which it is commonly agreed that it often is, the effect is, of course, to reduce substantially the possibility of obtaining revenue from the Contribucion sobre la Renta, especially on high incomes, where marginal rates are high.[10]

This and other disadvantages were, of course, well recognized and it was always intended that the system would be continuously evolved. The mission can only recommend that the original intention be sustained. For example, reducing the rate on schedular taxes, like the tax on personal employment, and raising the assessed income used as a basis for the global assessment would have the effect of allowing greater latitude to the tax authorities in assessing incomes as a whole. This would permit the shifting of emphasis of direct taxation in the direction which the Government clearly intends, and with which the

---

[10] The Corporation Tax is at a flat rate.

mission agrees, namely, toward total income and away from a large number of highly variable schedules.

In practice, this will not be an easy task, at least for the taxation of individuals. Collections of the Contribucion sobre la Renta have been disappointing. The latest year for which we have data broken down by income brackets is 1957 (before the introduction of global assessments). Although the revenue from this tax has increased since 1957, the total revenue is still small. Table 6.7, which shows the breakdown, is by no means a satisfactory guide for two reasons:

a.   It shows only initial contributors in 1958 in respect of the 1957 tax. There are many more in subsequent years, but the number of initial contributors must be at least half the total.

b.   The tax bracket is not the same as income. It is income after exemptions.

TABLE 6.7: Contribucion sobre la Renta, Initial Contributors in 1958 Classified According to Tax Base

Tax Bracket (Thousand pts)	Number of Contributors
100–200	26,286
200–500	10,526
500–1,000	1,339
over 1,000	342
Total	38,493

Nevertheless, such rough unofficial estimates of the distribution of income as we have seen suggest, even with these deficiencies, that the income distribution figures inferred from tax collections are a large underestimate of the true position. The total taxable income of these contributors was some 12 billion pts, representing an actual income, before exemptions, of the order of 20 billion pts. In fact, we would suspect the true order of magnitude for all potential contributors to be nearer double this amount and, quite possibly, very much higher. This again points to the need for closer collaboration between the tax authorities and the statistical services.

Many of the direct taxes have exemptions of a specific character as, for example, for income invested in low-cost housing or INI securities. Some industries enjoy particular exemptions (e.g., the film and record industries) as do certain types of agricultural activities (e.g., cotton growing). We believe that many of these special exemptions reflect particular shortages in the past. We doubt, for example, whether in the present economic situation, industry should be given tax incentives to invest in housing, when its own needs for investment are likely to be great. We would recommend a re-examination of all these special exemptions and would expect that the greater part could be eliminated.

The Role of Autonomous Organizations and Public Enterprises

Underlying our earlier statements in this chapter about autonomous organizations is the belief that their role needs to be more clearly defined, according to the nature of their business. Those that are really public enterprises operating in the market economy should be permitted the flexibility of action typical of their business. But they should also be accountable to the Government and to the public at large for the conduct of their affairs in the same way that a private company is accountable to its shareholders. The Government should, in fact, act like a shareholder and, whenever appropriate, legal expression should be given to its role as such. In practice, different treatment has been accorded to different organizations. This is why in one part of the report we stress the need for greater independence (RENFE) and in another more accountability (INI). In suggesting that the conduct of public enterprises should more closely approximate that of private enterprises, we do not in any way exclude the possibility that economic considerations transcending the operation of the enterprise itself, or social considerations, will have a part in determining public policy, especially in the case of public utilities. But if so, the Government as such should both know the cost of whatever external burden it places on the enterprise and, for the efficient operation of the enterprise, should bear this cost.

There remains the question to what extent there is a place for autonomous organizations which do not have a commercial or financial function. While we recognize that there may very well be cases where a measure of autonomy is desirable (e.g., the universities), the case for reintegrating the autonomous organizations into the Government is a strong one.

The case for leaving them outside rests on a number of arguments. Greater flexibility through the offer of better conditions in hiring staff is one. The answer to this is, we believe, the improved conditions within the Government proper that we have suggested in Chapter 3. Much of the same applies to the whole system of letting contracts or authorizing payments to contractors. The system is more expeditious within the autonomous agencies than it is in the central administration, which has consequently set up a system of compensating contractors more quickly by permitting them to discount the so-called *certificaciones* through the Banco de Credito Industrial. It is our view that the answer to this problem should be an improved system within the central administration, not the creation of agencies with more flexible rules. Autonomous agencies have, typically, been given much greater freedom in establishing their own programs of expenditure and have consequently been less susceptible to the normal process of coordination that the budgetary procedure should ensure. We feel that, in present circumstances, this may prove more of a disadvantage than advantage, since a primary object of the government's planning for development is to improve coordination.

While the mission is clearly unable to take all the relevant administrative considerations into account, it does recommend that the Government seriously consider how far the present administration can be simplified and a more unified control exercised and welcomes the decree of June 14, 1962, which is a significant step in this direction.

CHAPTER 7 MONETARY MANAGEMENT

The advances that Spain has already made toward a more industrialized and complex economy and its potential for continued, more rapid advance make it imperative that there be a fluid, sensitive market for long- and short-term capital. Such a capital market has the vital task of allocating savings, through the price mechanism of interest rates, to their most profitable uses. The market should provide the maximum degree of transferability so that savings with various degrees of liquidity can be adapted to the demands for investment funds with different schedules of maturity. Financial institutions should be responsive to evolving needs, if necessary by the creation of new ones when the opportunity for a new specialized function emerges. They should be as free as possible to transfer funds and should be aided in this process by the creation of whatever financial instruments are most amenable to the purpose.

The market requires continuous, unified and effective control, which only the Government can supply through an agency with delegated powers adequate to the purpose. The Government can, furthermore, aid the free functioning of the market by eliminating special privileges or restrictions and by ensuring that subsidies, when it is considered necessary to grant them, are made openly and not indiscriminately through the interest rate. It can supplement the market with specialized institutions to round out the private sector when particular needs are not being met and as long as the need persists. But as the needs are constantly changing, the role of the Government in this respect requires periodic review.

In the last few years the Spanish Government has taken several strides toward the establishment of these conditions, both by changes in its own financial practice and by measures designed to change the legal basis of the financial system. Chief among the latter are the law of December 26, 1958, on medium- and long-term credit institutions and the bank reform law enacted in April 1962.[1] Under this 1958 law six official medium- and long-term credit institutions were made dependent for their funds directly or indirectly on the Ministry of Finance. A Committee on Medium- and Long-Term Credit was established with powers to authorize capital issues and grant special credits. The new bank reform law may be briefly summarized as follows:

[1] *Ley de 26 diciembre de 1958 sobre entidades de credito a medio y largo plazo; Ley de bases de ordenacion bancaria.*

120

a. The Bank of Spain is to be nationalized and transformed into a fully fledged central bank.

b. Rules are to be established for the closer regulation of banking, for the separation of the two functions of commercial and investment banking and for the encouragement of new banking institutions.

c. The three official credit institutions with remaining private interests are to be nationalized.

d. The Committee on Medium- and Long-Term Credit is to be transformed into an Institute with supervisory powers over the official credit institutions.

e. The Credit Institute of the Savings Banks (Instituto de Credito de Cajas de Ahorro) is to take a more active role in promoting the extension of credit by the *Cajas* to small industry and agriculture.

f. The Governor of the Bank of Spain will serve as President of the two Institutes for medium- and long-term credit and for savings banks.

The Central Bank and the Government

The nationalization of the Bank of Spain brings to a logical conclusion a long-existing trend. The Government will now have an agency that can be independent of both special private and special public interests and that is responsible for the technical management of the money market and for advising the Government on major issues of policy. The central bank will also absorb some of the functions of the Foreign Exchange Institute (IEME) and become the depository of foreign exchange. This, too, we regard as a desirable integration of the management of foreign exchange and monetary control.

The relations between a government and a central bank demand scrupulous regard for the roles of each by the other. The interests of the Government are necessarily paramount and since it must retain responsibility for the stability of the economy it should be free to accept or reject the advice of its own agency. On the other hand, the Government must have due regard to the day-to-day conduct of its own financial operations in order to avoid undermining the authority of the agency to which it has delegated the responsibility for monetary control.

A government's own operations are of such importance in determining the course of the economy that there can be no such thing as monetary policy isolated from fiscal policy. This fact adds emphasis, if it be needed, to our observations in the preceding chapter about the need for more unified control over public expenditure and more comprehensive information, both before and after the fact, on the outcome of the government's finances.

Whether the public sector's finances are in surplus or in deficit, careful diagnosis of the cause is necessary to determine to what extent the balance of government payments is the result of isolated but temporary causes, of normal seasonal movements, or of the development of a long-run trend. This diagnosis will influence the technique by which the government surplus or deficit of the moment is to be financed and the action to be taken for the future, which may be a reinforcement or counter-action of the current trend.

As Table 7.1 shows, the actual borrowing from the central bank has been very greatly reduced between 1958 and 1960, principally because of the thoroughly commendable policy of restricting the access of autonomous agencies, especially the INI. However, there are still a number of financial operations in which a financing agency is given automatic rediscount privileges with the Bank of Spain. For example, "prefinancing" and other special credits by private banks have been authorized by the Medium- and Long-Term Credit Committee with rediscount privileges at the Bank of Spain and similar privileges for hire-purchase (ventas a plazos) paper are envisaged in the Bank Reform Law. The main part of the operations of the Servicio Nacional del Trigo, which depend largely on the weather, is financed directly by the Bank of Spain.

Independent action by a multiplicity of government agencies must weaken the authority of the central bank and frustrate its ability to cope with the exigencies of the situation in the most appropriate way. Automatic recourse of public agencies to the central bank outside the purview of the general operations of the Treasury should be reduced to the absolute minimum. This is not only the case when these agencies are drawing on the Bank of Spain for additional financial resources but also when they are in surplus and replenishing their current accounts. It is essential that the central bank be in a position to advise the Government as to the technique by which a surplus or deficit is to be financed and act as its agent accordingly. At any given time a choice will have to be exercised between operations which impinge on the cash resources of the banking system or on its holdings of short- or long-term government securities. This is essentially a technical matter for the monetary authority, not a matter for independent judgment by different government agencies.

TABLE 7.1: Sources of Finance, 1958–1960

(billion pts)

Item	1957	1958	1959	1960	1961
Public Sector:					
IEME	6.5	–1.0	–	–	–
Bank of Spain[a]	–0.4	7.9	6.0	0.5	–4.3
Commercial Banks	4.0	2.1	1.2	0.3	0.1
Savings Banks	3.5	4.7	3.6	7.6	8.4
Counterpart Funds	0.5	0.9	3.8	2.5	4.8
Capital Market	0.5	–2.9	0.3	2.4	5.7
Official Credit Institutions	–0.5	0.3	–	–6.7	–8.9
	14.1	11.9	14.9	6.7	5.8
Transactions of Bank of Spain on behalf of SNT	3.1	1.4	–0.9	–4.7	0.7
Total	17.2	13.3	14.0	2.0	6.5
Private Sector:					
Bank of Spain	0.9	2.5	–3.4	0.6	–1.0
Commercial Banks	19.9	23.4	7.2	23.4	43.0
Savings Banks	3.4	4.2	2.3	3.2	4.3
Official Credit Institutions	4.5	4.0	4.2	7.1	6.6
Subtotal	28.7	34.1	10.3	34.3	52.9
Capital Market Trans. to Pub. Sector	–0.5	2.9	–0.3	–2.4	–5.7
Capital Market Trans. to Fin. Sector	–3.2	–5.5	–2.9	–1.0	–0.2
Other Transfers to Fin. Sector	–0.6	0.7	–5.5	–2.0	–2.8
Total	24.4	32.3	1.6	38.9	44.2

[a] Excludes transactions of Bank of Spain on behalf of the Servicio Nacional del Trigo (SNT).

SOURCE: *Informe sobre la Evolucion de la Economia Espanola en 1961*, Banco de Espana, p. 105, (April 1962); and information supplied by the Bank of Spain.

NOTES: (i) This table, which is an amplification of certain figures in Table 5.1, differs from the table in the Bank of Spain report in the following ways:

a. In the public sector, changes in bonds pledged with the Bank of Spain (Dispuesto en pignoracion) have been eliminated so that the credit extended by banks to the public sector includes only the gross changes in "Fondos Publicos." Issue of coinage has also been included under the Bank of Spain.

b. In the private sector, only direct credit has been included under the appropriate institution. Under the Bank of Spain, this has been offset by changes in importers' deposits. Other bank accounts on the asset side (including "activo real") have been consolidated with capital and reserves and other accounts on the liability side to form the residual item (other transfers).

c. The self-financing of the private sector through the capital market, amounting to about 16 billion pts annually, has been omitted.

(ii) Differences in totals are due to rounding.

Accordingly, we recommend that the Government move away from the practice of financing short- and long-term movements in its balance with the Bank of Spain solely by means of payments into or overdrafts on its current account with the Bank of Spain. This form of financing would be reinforced by the floating of short-term and long-term securities on the open market. Not only would this give the central bank more opportunity for monetary implementation through open market operations, but it would also, in the case of short-term securities, add a useful liquidity instrument to the money market and provide a means of gathering excess short-term funds from official institutions for centralized use.

As part of the new policy outlined in the 1958 law, the Government announced its intention of issuing a new form of long-term security (the old form is discussed below) known as the investment certificate (*cedula de inversion*). These certificates enjoy certain tax exemptions which have very probably permitted their issue at rates below the market. The true cost of capital to the Government is thereby obscured and, if corresponding interest rates are used as a guide to the government's own lending policy, a hidden subsidy is likely to result. As pointed out elsewhere, we believe that as a general rule this should be avoided, except in special cases.

The Private Banks

The 1958 law gave the Ministry of Finance power to fix the minimum quantity of government securities held by private banks as a percentage of their deposits, both as a whole and for the new investment certificates in particular. In 1960 it was decreed[2] that the Minister of Finance, in consultation with the Bank of Spain, could order the private banks to constitute reserves, up to 10 percent of their deposits, in the Bank of Spain in the form of cash or free government securities. These powers have not so far been exercised. However, in the Bank Reform Law of 1962, it is clearly envisaged that the Bank of Spain will intervene more actively in the regulation of money through the establishment of rules governing rediscount operations and the deposits of private banks in the Bank of Spain, through open market operations and other instruments of monetary control, such as variable liquidity coefficients.

The mission is in complete agreement that effective control by the Bank of Spain is necessary. The Bank of Spain is technically well equipped to exercise it and we recommend that it be given the neces-

[2] Decree of 15th December, on currency control.

sary powers as soon as possible. However, we do wish to draw particular attention to the reference in the Bank Reform Law to measures related to the pledging by the banks of public debt.

The long-term debt formerly issued by the Government consisted of long-term securities which could be automatically pledged with the Bank of Spain. At the end of 1960 the formidable amount of 90 billion pts of this debt was outstanding, the greater part being in the hands of the private banks. The existence of the privilege of automatic pledgeability has been recognized as a very serious impediment to control of the liquidity of the economy. The period of amortization of this type of debt will mean that it will be a long time before it is significantly reduced. So long as there are *any* securities in this category outstanding they will constitute a problem. Differential rediscount rates, unless the difference is a large one, will not help. The mission finds it difficult to conceive of any measures which would circumvent this threat to stability that would not have concomitant disadvantages.[3] In any event, to be effective, the measures would have to be tantamount to a revocation of the privilege. In the circumstances, it seems better to recognize the fact that the privilege is an anachronism and that the Government and the banking community should come to some reasonable agreement for a conversion operation (or series of them) or the equivalent.

Nearly two-thirds of the resources of Spanish private banks, whose balance sheets are shown in Table 7.2, are concentrated in five large banks. These banks, which like most Spanish banks are mixed banks, have financed many of the largest industrial enterprises in Spain by equity participations, as well as by short-term credit and holdings of bonds. In so doing they have been responsible for much of the growth of modern industry in Spain. Nevertheless, three allegations are commonly made against the banks: first, that they exercise excessive control over the enterprises they finance; secondly, that they discriminate unduly in favor of their own dependent enterprises; thirdly, that they are apt to finance long-term needs by rolling over short-term credit.

It is for these reasons that the Government in its bank reform bill proposes to establish the legal basis for investment banks (*bancos de negocios*), to limit the equity participation of the present private banks (if necessary by enforcing the sale of existing holdings), to lay down percentage rules for the banks' holdings of liquid resources and to place the responsibility for inspection of private banks in the Bank of Spain. The Government states its intention, with which the mission agrees, to move circumspectly in the direction of greater specialization. The

---

[3] For example, rules governing minimum percentages of assets to be held in the form of this debt would have constantly to be changed, would tend to penalize the more dynamic banks and would be difficult to apply in the case of new banks.

TABLE 7.2: Private Banks Balance Sheets (End of Year)

(billion pts)

ASSETS	1959	1960	1961	LIABILITIES	1959	1960	1961
Commercial port-folio	88.9	103.9	130.5	Sight deposits	124.3	122.4	144.4
Advances	64.3	71.5	86.9	Time deposits	75.3	111.3	134.9
Government securities[a]	60.6	61.0	61.1	Foreign deposits	3.0	2.2	3.0
Not deposited with Bank of Spain	(20.2)	(27.6)	(23.4)	Advances by Bank of Spain	25.6	14.6	16.3
Deposited but not used	(24.8)	(18.8)	(21.4)	Capital and reserves	15.7	17.4	19.5
Deposited and used	(25.6)	(14.6)	(16.3)	Other liabilities	5.8	6.7	6.4
Other securities	19.6	20.7	21.7				
Cash and deposits in Bank of Spain	6.8	7.1	9.7				
Other assets[b]	9.6	10.3	14.6				
	249.7	274.6	324.6		249.7	274.6	324.6

[a] The three categories distinguish those securities not deposited as collateral with the Bank of Spain, those deposited against which credit is available but unused (disponible) and those against which advances have been made (dispuesto).

[b] Including *net* balances with other banks.

SOURCES: *Boletin Estadistico*, February 1962, Banco de Espana, February 1962; *Informe sobre la Evolucion de la Economia Espanola en 1960*, Banco de Espana, April 1961.

advantages of any abrupt fission of the dual function of the present private banks might prove more theoretical than practical.

The promotion of greater competition through the opening up of alternative sources of finance is likely to be the most effective means of ensuring that all creditworthy applicants have adequate access to funds. In this respect, the relaxation of the so-called "Status Quo Bancario"[4] in order to facilitate the creation of new banks, including foreign banks, is, in our view, a more important innovation. Certain other measures designed to widen the opportunity for credit are discussed below under other headings.

Savings Banks

The savings banks (Cajas de Ahorro) are a potent source of savings in the economy. Deposits have been growing with remarkable reg-

[4] Since 1936 the establishment of new banking institutions has been prohibited. Since many small banks have been absorbed by the larger ones, the number has consequently been reduced.

ularity year by year, regardless of the degree of inflation or the rate of growth of the economy (see Table 7.3). The only serious check was in 1959, the year of stabilization, but the shortfall in that year has been made good in the two subsequent years. It would, on that account, be unreasonable to expect the high rate of increase of the last two years (21 percent) to continue and it may be that the rate will tend to fall in the future. Even so, it would hardly be fanciful to expect an increase of 100 billion pts in the resources of the savings banks in the five years 1960–66 and annual deposits at the end of that period of the order of 25 billion to 30 billion pts, which would be around 4 percent of GNP. This would constitute a very sizable part of national savings.

TABLE 7.3: Savings Banks Deposits

	Absolute Amount	
	(billion pts)	
1946		7.75
1950		15.36
1954		30.75
1958		$\left\{\begin{array}{l} 59.35 \\ 59.79 \end{array}\right.$
1959		66.41
1960		80.48
1961		97.27
	Rate of Increase per Annum	
	(percent)	
1946–50		18.6
1950–54		19.0
1954–58		17.9
1958–61		17.6

SOURCES: 1946–58 (first series): *Anuario Estadistico 1961;* 1958–61 (second series): *Banco de España.*

The rapid growth of deposits in the past and the prospect that it may continue in the future illustrate how rapidly regulations based on fixed percentages can become out of date in a developing economy. The savings banks are required to put 65 percent of the increase in their deposits in government securities, which in recent practice has meant largely the securities of INI and INI enterprise.[5] The supply of new securities in the last two years has been less than the corresponding proportion of the increase in deposits. This may have some connection with the substantial increase, beyond normal liquidity requirements, in the savings banks' cash assets or bank accounts (Table 7.4).

[5] INI securities accounted for 92 percent and 86 percent of the new government securities in 1960 and 1961 respectively.

TABLE 7.4: Savings Banks Balance Sheets

(billion pts)

ASSETS	1959	1960	1961	LIABILITIES	1959	1960	1961
Loans & Advances[a]	18.6	21.0	24.3	Deposits	66.4	80.5	97.3
Government Securities	40.5	48.1	56.6	Capital and Reserves	2.7	3.0	3.5
Other Securities	3.2	4.0	4.9	Advances from			
Cash and Bank				Bank of Spain	2.4	1.6	1.1
Accounts	3.0	5.0	8.2				
Fixed Assets	5.7	6.8	7.7				
Other Assets (net)	0.5	0.3	0.3				
	71.6	85.2	102.0		71.6	85.2	102.0

[a] Including polizas of the Credito Agricola.

SOURCE: *Informe sobre la Evolucion de la Economia Espanola en 1961*, Banco de Espana, April 1962.

In any event, there has been little change in the financing of the private
sector by the savings banks between 1958 and 1961 (see Table 7.1).
As we point out in the section on industry, we believe that, in any
case, public enterprises competing directly in the market economy with
private enterprises should not have special advantages such as a captive
market for their securities. Furthermore, any such rules as now govern
the investments of the savings banks greatly reduce the opportunity
for transferability of savings in the economy. We do not, in any way,
dispute the need to respect the fiduciary position of the savings banks
and to ensure that they are guided by prudent policies in their investments. But we do not consider that inflexible rules that, in addition,
favor a particular borrower are the way to accomplish this end and
therefore we recommend that they be abandoned.

The savings banks are well suited, by virtue of their local character
and their experience of local conditions, to extend greatly their lending
activity in the fields of agriculture, industry and housing, as we point
out in later sections of the report. They have a particular role to play
in fostering small enterprises, as the Bank Reform Law points out. The
mission agrees that there is an important gap to be filled in this respect,
but it also feels that the savings banks, though having certain social obligations, should be regarded as financial institutions and granted the
necessary flexibility to form an integral part of the whole financial
system. For example, within limits which might vary according to circumstances, they could invest to a greater degree in high-grade indus-

trial securities, thus providing a wider and more competitive market. And, also to a limited extent, they might be permitted to experiment, if necessary in combinations, with new forms of regional lending institutions to meet particular needs in the financing of medium-size industry, agriculture, or services. As we have pointed out elsewhere, there are some types of lending by official credit institutions which the savings banks could be expected to take over.

There are a number of things that the central organization, the Credit Institute of the Savings Banks, could do to help this evolutionary process. In the first place, if the savings banks are to be allowed greater freedom, which we think is highly desirable in a changing economy, the counterpart must be regular portfolio inspection. This inspection should be motivated, not by strict observance of predetermined rules, but by a flexible interpretation of prudent banking principles in the light of local conditions. A corollary function worth serious consideration would be a deposit insurance scheme for savings up to a particular limit paid for by premiums from the savings banks themselves.

The Institute could also assist the transferability of funds by making arrangements for the easy transfer of funds from a surplus area to a deficit one. While there will always be a proper incentive to invest local savings in their place of origin, the needs of development will, as we have already pointed out, demand geographical transferability.

Finally, the Institute could be the initial point for negotiation of placements of a large block of industrial securities, which could not be absorbed by any one institution.

Official Credit Institutions

There are six credit entities designated under the Bank Reform Law as official credit institutions,[6] as follows:

Institutions	Sphere of Operations
Banco Hipotecario	Urban and rural real property
Banco de Credito Local	Municipalities
Banco de Credito Industrial	Industry, hotels
Instituto de Credito para la Reconstruccion Nacional	Shipping, housing, schools
Servicio Nacional de Credito Agricola	Agriculture
Caja Central de Credito Maritimo y Pesquero	Fishing

[6] The six are not the same as those designated under the 1958 law, which included the Instituto Nacional de Vivienda, but not the Banco de Credito Local.

The first three are long established and private in form, with private shareholders, but even before the passage of the 1958 law the Government had a strong interest in their affairs. This interest took the form, in one or more cases, of the appointment of senior officers, provision of capital, or sharing in the profits (other than through shareholding). The Credito para la Reconstruccion is essentially a government bank, founded in 1939, as its name implies, to finance postwar reconstruction, although this is no longer its function. The last two (Credito Agricola and Credito Maritimo) are now classed as autonomous organizations, dependent on the Ministries of Agriculture and Labor respectively. The scale and nature of their operations varies greatly as Table 7.5 shows, the Credito para la Reconstruccion being the largest in longer-term lending, while the Credito Maritimo is very small. Three of the institutions have a sizable volume of short-term lending. In the case of the Credito Agricola, short-term agricultural loans are the normal run of business. The short-term loans of the Credito Industrial are some-what special in that they have little to do with industry, but are in

TABLE 7.5: Lending Operations of Official Credit Institutions, 1960

(billion pts)

Institution	Medium- and Long-Term Loans			Short-Term
	Increase in Out-standing Loans	Reim-burse-ments	Total	
Banco Hipotecario	0.90	n.a.	n.a.	–
Banco de Credito Industrial	0.77	0.40	1.17	1.5
Banco de Credito Local	1.89	n.a.	n.a.	–
Instituto de Credito para la Reconstruccion Nacional[b]	3.10	0.50	3.60	1.8[a]
of which:				
Ships	1.42	0.33	1.75	
Housing	1.36	0.13	1.49	
Schools	0.26	–	0.26	
Other	0.06	0.04	0.10	
Servicio Nacional de Credito Agricola	(0.60)[a]	n.a.	n.a.[a]	(1.6)[a]
Caja Central de Credito Maritimo y Pesquero	0.04	0.06	0.10	–
	(7.3)[a]	n.a.	n.a.	(5.3)[a]

[a] Order of magnitude only.
[b] Excludes 0.90 billion pts included in the 1960 Memoria as "abonos realizados" and offset in the balance sheet by "cuentos corrientes prestatorios."
SOURCE: Annual Reports and material supplied by the institutions.

effect discounts of government certificates presented by government contractors. The short-term loans of the Credito para la Reconstruccion in 1960, which were a new departure on this scale, consisted mainly of advances to shipbuilders. With this latter exception, however, the volume of short-term lending outstanding has not increased much from year to year and constitutes only a small part of the total credit outstanding, which at the end of 1960 amounted to some 64 billion pts (Table 7.6), of which 14 billion pts was to the public sector (mainly loans by Credito Local to municipalities).

TABLE 7.6: Consolidated Balance Sheets of Official Credit Institutions

(billion pts)

ASSETS	1958	1959	1960	1961	LIABILITIES	1958	1959	1960	1961
Cash	4.6	3.3	4.9	7.6	Capital & Reserves	2.4	2.6	2.9	3.2
Government Securities	1.0	1.1	0.3	0.3	Treasury	4.7	6.1	13.5	23.8
Loans to Public Sector	8.1	9.5	11.0	12.4	Bond Issues	37.4	40.3	41.3	41.6
Loans to Private Sector	35.5	39.7	46.8	53.3	Bank Credit (drawn)	4.5	4.2	4.4	4.3
					Other (net)	0.2	0.4	0.9	0.7
	49.2	53.6	63.0	73.6		49.2	53.6	63.0	73.6

SOURCES: *Informe sobre la Evolucion de la Economia Espanola en 1961,* Banco de Espana, April 1962 and information supplied by the Bank of Spain. The table includes direct operations of the Medium- and Long-Term Credit Committee.

The financing of these institutions was varied in the past; the Banco Hipotecario and Credito Local have been financed by their own bonds on the market, the Credito para la Reconstruccion by government-guaranteed issues, the Credito Industrial by direct grants from the Treasury (outside the budget) and Credito Agricola and Credito Maritimo by drafts (polizas) sold to the private banks and savings banks but subsequently rediscounted for the most part at the Bank of Spain. Under the 1958 law, however, official credit institutions therein designated were to receive allocations of funds from the Treasury with general direction as to their use on the advice of the Medium- and Long-Term Credit Committee.[7] As Table 7.6 shows, the principal source of

[7] The Committee also had the power to make and authorize special credits on its own. Official credit institutions or private banks actually processed these loans. In the former case additional allocations of funds were made for the purpose; in the latter, the credits were rediscountable with the Bank of Spain.

funds in 1960 and 1961 was the Treasury, the main exception being Credito Local, which was not covered by the 1958 law and which continued to float its own securities.

The proposal to nationalize the three institutions with remaining private interests is a not illogical conclusion to a process of increasing public influence. The mixture of public and private interest has created a feeling which, right or wrong, is not salutary, that private interests are incompatible with institutions having a public purpose and supplied to a varying extent with public funds.

In any event, the Government will now have under one roof the new Instituto de Credito, a battery of credit institutions which it can use without impediment to fill the undoubted need for long-term funds. In these circumstances, the mission has several observations to make on organization and policy.

In the first place, common standards should be set for accounting and information. In the case of the autonomous organizations (Credito Agricola and Credito Maritimo) the present accounting is, as we have already said, unsuitable and should be recast. But, in other cases, there is an inadequate account of the flow of funds into and out of the institutions and the balance sheets are complicated by the existence of esoteric accounts; it is very difficult to reconcile the figures contained in them with those in the Treasury accounts. Some funds appear to flow through an institution to the Treasury without being recorded. In other cases, the relationship between loans granted and loans actually disbursed, between short- and long-term loans, or between loans disbursed, reimbursements and loans outstanding is not clear.[8] Some institutions publish breakdowns of their loans by function and others do not. As we pointed out in the beginning of this section, we believe that it is of the greatest importance for the successful guidance of the economy that there be an orderly flow of consistent information between the various arms of the Government and to the public at large.

The principal financial need in Spain is for long-term capital and we believe that public credit institutions should concentrate as far as possible on filling this need. We would not wish to be dogmatic on this point, since some short-term needs closely connected with the normal business of the institution will undoubtedly emerge. But every effort should be made to shift short-term lending to other financial institutions.

Indeed, this recommendation on short-term lending is really only a part of the policy adumbrated earlier. The role of official credit in-

[8] In this respect, the Credito para la Reconstruccion has excellent data, broken down by loans for a variety of purposes.

stitutions is to fill existing gaps in the financial structure. They should constantly be looking for ways to close these gaps, not only through their own lending, but by bringing suitable credit applications to the attention of other financial institutions whenever possible. Accordingly, the way will be prepared for them to tackle new types of requirements as they emerge.[9] A case in point, more fully dealt with in the section on agriculture, is credit for secondary irrigation works.

This process of change, in which the official credit institutions pioneer in filling new requirements and turn over old ones to other institutions, can only work well if the terms of lending are comparable. We do not believe that there is any case for generalized subsidy through the interest rate and have referred above to the hidden subsidy implicit in some of the present government borrowing rates. What actually constitutes the schedule of market rates is currently difficult to say in the absence of a fluid capital market, but it is certain that the real cost of capital is high in Spain and the interest rate should be used to allocate it to the most productive borrowers. Furthermore, we doubt whether it is a proper function for a lending institution to be granting direct subsidies at the same time, except purely as a matter of administrative convenience.

Closely related to this is the question of risk. As we point out later in Section V in the case of the Banco de Credito Industrial, official credit institutions would be well advised to take more risk. We do not mean by this that they should lend with the prospect of low returns on their investment. We do mean that they should be prepared to invest without collateral security, where the latter is not obtainable. The dynamism of an economy depends more on personal initiative than on personal possessions. The success of public credit institutions should be judged by the over-all success of the projects they invest in, which would automatically ensure a high rate of recovery of the funds. By this criterion, the fact that 100 percent recovery is not achieved is not relevant.

It would also be worth considering the opening of more regional offices. This would make it more feasible to seek out those opportunities for lending which depend on a knowledge of local conditions and of the character of the borrower. The advantages of decentralization include greater convenience and speed for the borrower and it may well be that some borrowers will approach a regional office who would, for one reason or another, be deterred from approaching a central office.

In the short time that the official credit institutions have been oper-

---

[9] The Credito para la Reconstruccion, for example, has greatly changed the nature of its lending according to circumstances.

ating under the new regime, there has been a tendency, implicit if not explicit, to regard them as a balancing factor in the economy. In 1960 and 1961 allocations were increased towards the end of the year as it became evident that the budget of the central administration was in greater surplus than had been expected. We do not dispute the ends of this policy to offset the deflationary effect of the finances of the public sector, but we believe that changes in the volume of lending of official credit institutions should be only one of a number of means toward it.

The level of activity of the official credit institutions is the easiest to adjust to the conjunctural needs of the economy but that does not necessarily mean that it is the best instrument for the purpose. In our view the ultimate test of the appropriate level of lending should be whatever the institutions are able to lend wisely at unsubsidized rates of interest. As the occasion demands, they should be able to compete in the market for investible funds, indirectly through government borrowing operations. Allocations at the beginning of the year should be the best estimates that the institutions and the parent Instituto de Credito are able to make of their annual requirements for various purposes. But if they fall short or surpass the estimates in detail or as a whole, the opportunity should be open to the Instituto de Credito to advise the Government that allocations be switched or that it reduce or increase its prospective call on the market. Otherwise the institutions will be starved of funds at some times and have more than they can promptly use at others without lowering their standards.

The Instituto de Credito will, under the Bank Reform Law, be empowered to continue the various functions attributed to the Committee under the 1958 law. One of these functions is the consideration, in conjunction with the Bank of Spain, of applications by private banks for permission to extend credits beyond the normal time limit. The present purpose of this review is to provide certain broad categories of industry, for example, exporters of capital goods, with financing facilities that cannot otherwise be obtained and to withhold these facilities from less essential industries. This kind of control may well be desirable for the time being and may remain so in certain categories, but we would hope that it can be exercised in the form of general rules and in such a way as not to weaken the authority of the Bank of Spain. In particular, we believe that the granting of automatic rediscount privileges in this connection should be kept to a minimum.

The Committee has also authorized individual special credits from government funds, the credits being administered by one of the official credit institutions. The new Instituto de Credito will have an important function to play in matters of policy, which ought not to be diluted by day-to-day operations. The concession of these credits by the Instituto, therefore, ought to be limited to those isolated or exceptional cases where it is not feasible to fill the necessary gap through existing or new credit institutions.

In our view, the new Instituto de Credito ought to be concerned with the whole range of public lending policy and not only the operations of the six designated institutions. A number of other autonomous organizations are engaged in lending, most notably the Instituto Nacional de Vivienda, but also the Instituto Nacional de Colonizacion, the Servicio Nacional del Trigo and the Instituto Nacional de Industria. Unless there are very good reasons to the contrary, we feel that the lending function should be performed by a lending agency and not by an agency whose primary purpose is something else. Public lending agencies, whatever their field, ought to be supervised as a whole.

The Government has expressed its conviction, with which we fully concur, that a major expansion of the external sector is essential to the development of the Spanish economy. The level of both exports and imports during the postwar period has been lower, in real terms, than that reached more than 40 years before, prior to the First World War (see Table 8.1). Comparisons of time series over so long a period are of limited value, but it is reasonably clear that foreign trade has occupied a declining rather than expanding position in the economy; the extent of the decline is suggested by the fact that exports in 1959 amounted to less than 4 percent of the GNP, a lower proportion than in any other member country of the OEEC except Turkey.

Numerous factors account for the declining role of foreign trade. The highly protectionist tariffs of 1891, 1908 and 1922 began to isolate Spanish industry from the rest of the world. The economic crisis of the 1930's, and the difficulties of the next two decades (described in Chapter 1) reinforced this isolation. Recurrent inflation increased the demand for imports, while diverting potential exports to the domestic market where prospects for high quick profits were more attractive. The traditional export sectors (agriculture and mining) suffered from the slow growth of farm production, war damage, a series of disastrous harvests and gradual depletion of some mineral deposits. Exchange rate adjustments did not keep pace with the depreciation of the currency, while the system of multiple exchange rates further distorted the cost and price structure and hampered the growth of exports. Foreign investors were discouraged by the controls and found the terms and conditions applying to foreign investment unattractive.

During most of the postwar period, there has been an acute shortage of foreign exchange, and the consequent strict rationing of imports through quantitative controls meant that there was a shortage of essential raw materials and equipment which retarded the growth of various sectors of the economy. In the absence of the competitive stimulus of imports, some domestic industries developed along high-cost and inefficient lines.

A first and major step in the direction of reversing these trends was taken through the stabilization plan adopted in July 1959. The devaluation of the peseta and unification of the exchange rate structure brought about an immediate increase in foreign exchange receipts

136

TABLE 8.1: Balance of Trade, 1901–1960

(million pts[a])

Year	Imports (A)	Exports (B)	Surplus (+) or Deficit (–)
1901	908	757	–151
1905	1,058	955	–103
1910	999	970	–29
1915	977	1,258	+281
1920	1,423	1,020	–403
1921	2,836	1,580	–1,256
1922	2,716	1,319	–1,397
1923	2,926	1,526	–1,400
1924	2,945	1,791	–1,154
1925	2,244	1,585	–659
1926	2,148	1,606	–542
1927	2,576	1,895	–681
1928	3,005	2,123	–882
1929	2,737	2,113	–624
1930	2,448	2,305	–143
1931	1,176	965	–211
1932	976	742	–234
1933	837	672	–165
1934	855	612	–243
1935	876	586	–290
1940	621	394	–227
1941	550	521	–29
1942	604	629	+25
1943	908	878	–30
1944	827	957	+130
1945	863	881	+18
1946	923	813	–110
1947	1,214	937	–277
1948	1,433	1,107	–326
1949	1,389	1,164	–225
1950	1,195	1,190	–5
1951	1,176	1,413	+237
1952	1,584	1,250	–334
1953	1,651	1,306	–345
1954[b]	1,879	1,422	–457
1955	1,890	1,366	–524
1956	2,347	1,353	–994
1957	2,639	1,457	–1,182
1958	2,671	1,487	–1,184
1959	2,433	1,532	–901
1960	2,208	2,223	+15

[a] Gold pesetas, after 1922.
[b] After this year includes the Canaries, Ceuta and Melilla.
SOURCE: *Anuario Estadistico de Espana*, 1960.

from the return of earnings from exports and tourism to official channels and arrested the flight of capital. The first installment of a program for removing import quotas made it possible to import more freely and on more advantageous terms. The law on foreign investment laid the basis for attracting capital from abroad. Most important of all, the stabilization plan halted inflation and restored internal and external equilibrium. It cannot be emphasized too strongly that a continuation of this stability is an essential condition for any long-term growth of the economy.

Since the adoption of the stabilization plan the balance of payments has steadily improved. (Table 8.2 shows the movement in the main elements of Spain's external payments position between 1956 and 1960.) Foreign exchange reserves, which had virtually been exhausted at the time of stabilization, rose by the end of 1961 to close to $900 million. The improvement also made it possible for the Spanish Government to establish in mid-1961 the external convertibility of the peseta into currencies for which reciprocal facilities are offered.

Although the results of the stabilization plan are in many ways encouraging, it must be recognized that there were some exceptional and temporary factors. The leveling-off of production in Spain, accompanied by the running-down of inventories accumulated during the inflation, sharply reduced import demand. With the subsequent gradual recovery of the economy, there has been a disturbing tendency for exports to remain stationary (albeit at higher levels than before stabilization) while the demand for imports has continued to rise, and it would be unwise to assume that payments surpluses will be accumulated at a comparable rate in the future when development proceeds more rapidly.

Against this background it is possible to define the goals of government policy in the foreign sector. Spain has neither sufficient resources nor a large enough internal market to develop its economy in isolation. In the future, as in the past, the rate at which the economy expands will be closely linked to the availability of raw materials, capital goods and technical assistance from abroad. The aims of government policy must therefore be twofold:

a. to facilitate increased imports of goods and services necessary for development, and to procure them at the lowest cost and under the most advantageous conditions consistent with a minimum protection of domestic producers; and

b. to expand earnings from exports, tourism and other invisibles, and to attract the foreign capital necessary to finance increased imports.

TABLE 8.2: Balance of Payments, 1956–1960

(millions U.S. dollars)

	1956		1957		1958		1959		1960	
	Credit	Debit	Credit	Debit	Credit	Debit	Credit	Debit	Credit	Debit
A. Goods and Services:	633.9	839.3	681.0	933.3	732.9	955.6	803.7	905.1	1,177.9	871.8
1. Merchandise, f.o.b.	427.0	730.7	455.3	816.6	527.8	830.5	523.4	766.9	745.1	696.5
2. Non-monetary gold	–	–	–	–	–	–	–	–	–	–
3. Freight and insurance on international shipments	18.9	33.8	15.7	45.2	9.0	28.6	9.3	21.5	15.7	20.0
3.1. Freight	16.5	31.5	14.7	42.6	7.4	25.9	8.2	19.5	14.3	17.8
3.2. Insurance	2.4	2.3	1.0	2.6	1.6	2.7	1.1	2.0	1.4	2.2
4. Other transportation	20.9	12.3	26.0	14.7	25.5	17.1	22.7	17.7	27.8	15.2
5. Travel	94.8	3.3	76.9	3.2	71.6	2.3	158.9	20.5	296.5	50.0
6. Investment income	3.8	8.2	3.2	8.5	3.1	12.4	3.1	12.7	3.4	17.6
6.1. Direct investment	1.0	2.7	1.0	2.5	1.0	2.7	3.1	7.3	3.4	11.5
6.2. Other	2.8	5.5	2.2	6.0	2.1	9.7	–	5.4	–	6.1
7. Government, n.i.e.	51.1	30.7	86.6	23.4	79.5	29.9	61.5	28.6	45.5	29.8
8. Other services	17.4	20.3	17.3	21.7	16.4	34.8	24.8	37.2	43.9	42.7
8.1. Non-merchandise insurance	–	–	–	–	–	–	0.3	1.0	0.6	1.1
8.2. Other	17.4	20.3	17.3	21.7	16.4	34.8	24.5	36.2	43.3	41.6
Net goods and services	–	205.4	–	252.3	–	222.7	–	101.4	306.1	–
B. Transfer Payments:	79.1	0.2	80.1	0.2	78.8	0.2	73.4	0.2	88.1	0.2
9. Private	55.0	0.2	51.5	0.2	58.3	0.2	40.1	0.2	55.6	0.2
10. Central Government	24.1	–	28.6	–	20.5	–	33.3	–	32.5	–
Net transfer payments	78.9	–	79.9	–	78.6	–	73.2	–	87.9	–
Net total (1 through 9)	–	150.6	–	201.0	–	164.6	–	61.5	361.5	–
Net total (1 through 10)	–	126.5	–	172.4	–	144.1	–	28.2	394.0	–
C. Capital and Monetary Gold:	180.9	–	107.6	–	159.3	–	1.8	–	–	342.5

SOURCE: IMF Balance of Payments Yearbook.

These objectives are, of course, fully consistent with the decision of Spain to seek a closer association with the countries of the Common Market. Indeed, the extent of progress toward reaching them will have an important bearing on the rate at which Spain is able to integrate its economy with the others of Western Europe.

Whether or not these objectives are attained will depend in part, as we have indicated, on the policies pursued in the monetary and fiscal fields. In particular, the success of the Government in promoting economic expansion with financial stability and in helping to create the conditions necessary for Spanish industry and agriculture to become competitive will largely determine the course of development in the foreign sector. There are in addition, however, a variety of specific government policies with respect to imports, exports, tourism and foreign capital that will have an important bearing.

Import Controls

Since its accession to OEEC (now OECD) membership, Spain has been progressively liberalizing its import controls. With the publication of the sixth liberalization list in early 1962, approximately 75 percent of the quotas on imports from OEEC member countries have been removed and global quotas substituted for bilateral ones on all but 10 percent of the imports from these countries.[1] Quota reduction has been most extensive in the category of foodstuffs and least in that of manufactured goods (capital equipment and consumer products) where, as in other countries, the pressures for protection of national industry are strongest.

The progress in removing direct controls on imports is not yet fully reflected in trade statistics because of time lags in the administrative changeover and of quotas not taken up. Moreover, the restrictive effect of the remaining controls is not fully revealed by the liberalization percentages, since many categories of goods, particularly consumer goods, were not licensed at all in the standard year on which the percentages are based. On the other hand, the Ministry of Commerce has been increasingly liberal in granting licenses in excess of quotas, especially for capital goods. It can therefore be said that, while there has been significant progress in removing import controls over the last two years, a substantial group of imports and, even more, of potential imports, still remain subject to them. While the grant of import licenses in excess of quotas is to be commended, so long as the quotas and licensing

---

[1] The official base for these calculations is Spanish private trade with the OEEC member countries in 1950.

system exist they are bound to have some restrictive effect on the demand for imports. Moreover, industrialists are still handicapped in making their investment plans since they cannot be sure that licenses will be as readily available in the future.

The mission therefore fully endorses the government's aim to remove all quantitative restrictions on imports and recommends the extension of its program of liberalization as rapidly as possible. The present payments position makes it possible to take further measures now. The new tariff, adopted in 1960, provides a further reason to remove quotas rapidly; the tariff obviates the need for quotas in many sectors, and the effectiveness of individual tariff rates cannot be tested so long as the quotas are in force. The Government should establish a schedule of its own for further liberalization, specifying targets by category and, wherever possible, by individual articles so that producers will have the necessary information on which to base their plans. Liberalization should be extended to cover more manufactured goods; as we point out in the section on Industry, it is important for the development of Spanish industry that it be assured the possibility of importing freely not only the raw materials but also the capital equipment which it needs. It would also be desirable for the Government to introduce the beneficial effects of foreign competition into the consumer goods sector, as envisaged in its declaration to the OEEC.

So long as quotas remain, efforts should be made to increase the efficiency of import procedures:

a. the size of global quotas should be adjusted where possible to reflect the effective demand for licenses;

b. global quotas should be made to conform better to the needs of importers, as for example by opening them for longer periods of time, or, if this is practicable, more than twice a year;

c. greater publicity should be given to the liberalized lists, and to the Brussels nomenclature employed; and

d. further steps should be taken to reinforce the progress already made in simplifying and expediting the processing of applications for all types of trade.

A sizable proportion of the goods still under bilateral arrangements is imported through state trading, which accounts for from 10 percent to 20 percent or more of total imports. The principal articles under state trading are tobacco and petroleum products (handled by government monopolies), textile raw materials of agricultural origin and basic foodstuffs, particularly cereals. Within limits set by the particular financing provided for some of the commodities (notably those financed by American aid), state trading is conducted on a non-discriminatory basis. Many of the state-traded products are under price supports in Spain, at or above world market levels. The Government has explained the continuation of state trading on the grounds that it is necessary to maintain a certain control on trade in the products in question, both to ensure a sufficient and continuous supply and to avoid speculative price movements. In most cases, however, it does not appear necessary to conduct trade through state channels in order to achieve these purposes. On various occasions the Government has declared its intention to reduce state trading as far as possible, and during 1960 and 1961 a number of products were transferred to private channels. We believe further efforts should be made in this direction.

Another special limitation on imports arises in connection with Article X of the Law of November 24, 1939, on the Protection of National Industry. Article X requires a large number of important public and private firms and establishments to use exclusively articles of Spanish manufacture. Exceptions are provided for reasons of quality or timing, but not of price. Recently the Ministry of Industry has been administering the legislation in a more liberal spirit; nevertheless, the law requires Spanish enterprises to purchase equipment in Spain when it could be acquired more advantageously abroad. Our recommendations with respect to this requirement are given in Section V.

Tariff Policy

Adjusting the new tariff to the needs of development is perhaps the key problem in the external sector. Protectionism has a long tradition in Spain. The 1922 tariff, according to a League of Nations study, was the highest in the world, but with the passage of time the specific duties became ineffectual and import quotas were relied upon instead. The new tariff was designed to make possible the early suppression of quotas and to constitute the only means of regulating imports; at the same time, it was not intended to jeopardize the effects of the liberalization of imports. The legislation adopted in June 1960 provides Spain with an up-to-date tariff instrument, based on the Brussels nomenclature and employing *ad valorem* duties almost exclusively.

The tariff contains a number of special features. Transitional duties of two kinds are provided: (a) for goods not yet produced in Spain, in which case a duty of only 5 percent is applied; and (b) for goods not yet liberalized, for which the transitional duty is generally about two-thirds of the final one, on the grounds that the quota itself provides some protection. The first category has been interpreted very narrowly, with the result that there are only a small number of transitional duties in it, but the second covers about 25 percent of the tariff, applying in particular to iron and steel products, tools and machinery and equipment. The final duties are supposed to replace the transitional ones when the goods in question are liberalized, but this requires administrative action which has not always been forthcoming. In addition, sliding-scale duties have been established in cases where Spanish prices are particularly high relative to international levels. The duties are reduced, usually by 5 to 10 percentage points, over a period of time which is typically five years, and are intended to provide additional protection during the time necessary for the industries to invest and modernize. The law has temporarily carried over the earlier—and by now obsolete—legislation relating to special exemptions and reductions in the tariffs (*bonificaciones* and *franquicias*) which can be granted for a variety of reasons, including "national defense" and the "public interest." These provisions have given rise to strong pressures for special tariff favors.

It is difficult to measure the degree of protection afforded by a tariff, and international comparisons of tariff levels can be misleading. The average (arithmetic mean) level of the Spanish tariff is stated by the Government to be 24–25 percent, which is compared with 18–19 percent in the case of France and Italy. The most typical, or modal, tariff value is 30 percent, and the median value is 27 percent. Individual duties vary widely, being lowest for animal and vegetable products, minerals and other raw materials, and highest for manufactured goods. While Spain clearly ranks among the high tariff countries in Europe, the more significant point is that the duties are particularly high on capital goods required for development, such as iron and steel products, machine tools, machinery and equipment. Duties on these products commonly range between 30 percent and 45 percent.

Tariff policy should be considered primarily in the context of its effect on economic development and on the possibility of integrating the Spanish economy into Western Europe. While it is still early to pass judgment on individual items, it is apparent that the rates for basic steel products and for capital equipment are incompatible with the development needs of Spain. Spanish production is not adequate to meet the expanding requirements in these fields, and imports must be made available, at competitive prices, for the growth of industry. Continuation of the present tariff levels will have two serious consequences for the competitive position of Spanish industry: (a) it will raise production costs and prices for the industries that will have to modernize with high-cost imports, or with equally high-cost or qualitatively inferior domestic production; and (b) it will direct the scarce funds available for new investment into less productive channels. Moreover, a high tariff structure would tend to perpetuate itself by failing to discourage high-cost inefficient enterprises and thereby increasing the non-competitive character of Spanish industry, which would then in turn reinforce the argument in favor of maintaining high protection.

There are sectors of Spanish industry, or particular firms within a sector, that would be adversely affected by a sudden or drastic lowering of tariffs at this time. But if the Government feels that such industries must be protected for the present, it is essential: (a) that this protection be granted selectively and only in cases of manifest need; (b) that the protection be limited to the minimum period of time necessary for the industries to modernize and adapt themselves to the new economic situation; and (c) that the protection be provided, insofar as possible, in ways that will not raise the costs of imports.

We would therefore urge the Government to re-examine its tariff policy in this light. To this end, the administrative procedures for making changes in tariff rates, which at present are complicated and time consuming, should be modified to provide greater speed and flexibility. It is important, however, that the Government proceed to lower tariffs in a systematic rather than piecemeal fashion, and that Spanish producers have a firm knowledge of tariff plans and timetables so that they can adjust their plans accordingly. Maximum use should be made of sliding-scale duties, to provide for a phased reduction over the period necessary for the rationalization of domestic industry. The time-phased reductions should relate to each other in an orderly fashion, beginning with raw materials or semi-finished products and then moving to finished equipment goods. First attention should be given to the needs of industries that are capital-intensive and/or particularly dependent on imports. The selective use of tariff quotas should be considered as a means of providing duty-free imports while still according the necessary degree of protection.

The mission is also of the view that transitional rates should be replaced with the final duties specified in the tariff at the time that quotas are removed, since the indefinite prolongation of transitional duties creates added uncertainty for business. If the final rates are too high, they should be lowered through the streamlined procedures referred to in the preceding paragraph; this can also be done, of course, even while the quotas are still in effect and the transitional rates apply. Also, any tariff exemptions or reductions should be provided only in relation to general objectives of development (e.g., export promotion or regional development), through the application of general criteria to branches of industry (or regions) and not individually to firms.

A further point of some importance concerns the valuation of goods in customs, which inevitably involves an element of judgment. With the tariff viewed as an instrument of development, revenue considerations should occupy only a subsidiary role. The customs valuations should not, therefore, have the effect of adding an extra margin to the cost of imports.

Export Development

Substantial progress has been made in developing policies to encourage the expansion of exports. The progress has been along two principal lines: (a) removal of some restrictions and controls on exports; and (b) adoption of fiscal, credit and other measures to stimulate the growth of exports. More remains to be done, both along these lines and through indirect measures that will enhance the competitiveness of Spanish industry, establish a climate conducive to exporting and help to create an export mentality.

The various controls on exports, a legacy of the years before stabilization, are gradually being relaxed. All exports remain subject to license, and although the formalities have been streamlined and now generally entail only a few days' delay, the mission believes that policy should be aimed at reducing the delays even further, and eventually at eliminating export licensing entirely. As a first step, consideration might be given to removing the licensing of exports below a minimum value. A system of global licenses, valid for a whole season, has been applied to a few of the major commodities that are exported over an extended season. We believe that this system could be extended to other products, as the Ministry of Commerce is now undertaking to do. Complaints are sometimes heard, however, that export registers maintained by the syndicates have been closed in some instances against the entry of new exporters; the mission does not know whether there is any substance to these complaints, but it is clear that the registers should be used only for statistical purposes.

During the period of shortages, a considerable number of export commodities were subject to individual quotas, and in some cases absolute prohibitions, in order to ensure adequate supplies for the domestic market. The number of such commodities has since been reduced and the Government has stated that it intends to abolish the absolute prohibitions at the earliest opportunity. Controls remain on perhaps a dozen, the principal ones being lead ore and undressed hides and skins. Some agricultural products are also still subject to occasional prohibitions or quotas. The mission believes that the economic situation no longer warrants such quotas or prohibitions. Although not strictly an export control, mention should be made of the Ministry of Agriculture regulation restricting the planting of new citrus trees, which has retarded the development of Spain's principal export product. Elsewhere in this report we recommend that this regulation be rescinded.

A system of tax reimbursement (*desgravacion fiscal*), in effect since the end of 1959, exempts exporters from the payment of indirect taxes in Spain. Granting the reimbursement is discretional rather than automatic, and the ministries concerned have been applying it selectively on the basis of the purported need of each sector in order, it is said, to avoid excess profits or inflationary price rises. The list of tax-exempt products has gradually been extended; it now covers about three-fourths of the industrial products, but only a few agricultural products. Such tax reimbursements should be extended to all exports at the earliest possible date; to the full amount permitted by the law; and without reference to purported "need." Even if profits should rise in the short run as a result, this should have the favorable consequence of attracting additional resources into the export sectors.[2]

The procedure for tax reimbursement has proven to be slow and complicated and on the whole it is not yet working as well as might be desired. To some extent, this may be due to the problems inherent in establishing a new procedure. But it appears that the tax authorities have sometimes interpreted the system of provisional liquidation as entailing a new transfer tax obligation on the part of the exporter, the payment of which consumes further time. It is also stated—and the mission has not been able to investigate this—that some tax officials have held up reimbursement pending a verification of the over-all tax status of the exporter. The mission believes that procedures for granting tax reimbursement could be made more rapid and automatic, particularly by establishing that reimbursement does not raise any additional tax questions or involve the exporter in any additional tax obligations.

Spain, as other countries, provides tariff concessions on imported materials incorporated into goods subsequently exported. The concessions may take the form of duty-free temporary admissions, or of reimbursement of the duty after the goods are exported (a type of "drawback"). Although one aspect of the legislation has recently been modernized, in other respects it is still complicated and out of date, and the procedures cumbersome. Moreover, the application for exemption or rebate may be denied in practice if it is considered that the materials to be imported can be produced in Spain. These regulations should be brought up to date, simplified and applied more liberally.

[2] In this connection, it is important to adopt the mission's recommendation in Chapter 14 that the limitation on the planting of new citrus trees be removed.

Spain has been later than most countries in providing its exporters with the facilities necessary for them to extend medium- or long-term credit to their foreign customers. The system of export credit dates from the beginning of 1960, and is now functioning for shipbuilding, machine tools and some other machinery and equipment goods. In the interest of speed, existing banking and credit channels were used instead of establishing a specialized institution for the purpose. Credits are granted in the first instance by commercial banks (or the Banco Exterior) with the approval of the Medium- and Long-Term Credit Committee and upon the advice of the Ministries of Finance and Commerce. If approved by the Committee, the credit is eligible for rediscount at the Bank of Spain. The commercial bank may lend up to 80 percent of the value of the equipment, and the Bank of Spain may discount up to 80 percent of the bank's credit. Interest rates are 4.6 percent for the Bank of Spain and 5.5 percent for the commercial banks, excluding insurance premiums which have provisionally been fixed at about 1 percent. The maximum term is five years, the same as that of the credit insurance, except for shipbuilding where special facilities are available for seven years.

The companion system of export credit insurance only began to operate at the end of 1961. The legislation provides for a parastatal company to handle commercial risks, and a public institution to handle political and extraordinary risks. As in most other countries, transfer risks are covered but not exchange risks or losses from internal cost and price rises. However, coverage for commercial risks is limited to 75 percent, and for political and extraordinary risks to 65 percent; these are lower than the averages for other European countries, which are 80 percent and 85 percent, respectively. The lower proportion of coverage on political and extraordinary risks is apparently due to the opinion that the geographical structure of Spanish trade entails somewhat greater risks than in the case of other European countries. It was concluded that these greater risks should be borne by the exporter rather than the Government; it may be questioned whether such risks in fact exist but, if they do, it would be preferable to deal with them by increasing the premium rate rather than by reducing the insurance coverage. The present arrangements have the further disadvantage that the extent of insurance coverage (75 percent and 65 percent) is lower than that of the export credits (80 percent) to which they apply, thus leaving the commercial banks without insurance for a portion of their credit.

Adequate facilities for export credit and credit insurance, on a basis comparable to those in other countries with which Spanish exports compete, are a prerequisite to the restructuring of exports in the direction of manufactured goods. While export credit terms vary substantially from country to country, those in Spain may be considered about average. In its practical operation, however, the Spanish procedure was described to the mission as slow and lacking in flexibility. This may be due in part to unfamiliarity with the new system, which has resulted in delays at various stages, and to a lack of public awareness of its existence. The delays in establishing export credit insurance may also have been a retarding factor.

We feel that it is important for the existing system of export credit to be extended, and for steps to be taken to make it more flexible and automatic in its operations. Consideration should be given to channeling the export credit system through one of the official credit institutions for medium- and long-term lending provided for in the banking reform legislation. We also believe that, in the interests of the competitiveness of Spanish exporters, the Government ought to consider raising the coverage for commercial risks under the credit insurance system to 80 percent, and for political and extraordinary risks to at least 80 percent.

The Ministry of Commerce has been enlarging its assistance to exporters in such forms as market studies, publicity and information. These activities take on particular importance in Spain, where the organization for exporting often does not exist, and where deficiencies in packaging, labeling, standardization, or quality control have often resulted in the loss of export business. While these activities appear to be well conducted, and the Ministry enjoys the confidence of the export community, the resources devoted to them have so far been very limited. The mission suggests that a separate Foreign Trade Center be established, which would have general responsibility for the strategy of export development. Such a center should be organizationally dependent on the Ministry of Commerce, but with greater financial and operating autonomy than is now possible and with closer association of exporters and trade groups in the management. The center should have more funds and personnel at its disposal, and should have a president of national stature.

Foreign Private Investment

Foreign private investment has an important part to play in the development process. Foreign investors can provide additional investment capital to supplement domestic savings. Moreover, this capital is transferred in the form of foreign exchange, which can be used in turn to finance imports. A concomitant feature is often the provision of valuable technical, marketing and managerial assistance. The concern sometimes expressed that a flood of foreign investment will damage uncompetitive Spanish industry can readily be exaggerated. Much of the investment is likely to be in new fields. Competition, in those instances where it takes place, may help to break up monopoly positions and to stimulate firms to modernize. Credit facilities and foreign exchange can now be made available in larger amounts to assist in the modernization process, as we propose in the subsequent Chapter 15 on Industry.

The international capital market is highly competitive. Capital will only be attracted to Spain if the long-run prospects of return compare favorably with those of other countries. The provisions of the laws enacted in 1959 and 1960 are neither more nor less advantageous than those of other countries. The Spanish legislation was patterned on the Italian law of 1956, but a number of changes were introduced resulting in less liberal terms and a loss of clarity. On the other hand, a number of important improvements have been introduced by subsequent modifications or additions to the basic legislation.

In the long run, the outlook for foreign capital will depend less on the legislation itself than on more general economic considerations. Spain offers a number of important advantages to the foreign investor. The prospects for economic growth, and the corresponding opportunity for favorable returns on capital, are potentially high. On the other hand, it must be recognized that there are a number of factors at present that might deter the foreign investor. These will only be enumerated, since they are all discussed elsewhere. They include: uncertainty as to the future direction of economic policy; the existence of controls and restrictions, particularly those requiring prior authorization of investments and the labor regulations concerning redundant workers; uncertainty as to the future role of INI in fields in which private capital is also interested; and the difficulties of ascertaining the true value of Spanish firms because of accounting and tax problems. These are matters on which the mission has submitted recommendations in the various parts of this report and it is to be hoped that the Government will be able to consider them at an early opportunity.

All foreign investment legislation leaves a wide area of administrative discretion, and potential investors will consider the spirit of the law, and how it is administered, as much as the letter of its contents. The restrictiveness of the 1939 legislation and the subsequent experiences of foreign investors were not conducive to the creation of confidence, which is so necessary today, and it cannot be said that the new legislation of 1959 and 1960 is entirely free of ambiguity in this regard.

It is therefore encouraging that the authorities responsible for administering the new legislation appear anxious and willing to apply it in a liberal fashion. On the other hand, considerable attention has been given to the applications of several foreign concerns, in competition with INI, to establish petrochemical facilities in Spain, and the disposition of this case may have an influence on the attitude of potential investors.

With respect to the legislation itself, the 1959 and 1960 laws, together with the numerous changes that have taken place subsequently, clearly constitute a major advance. A number of problems remain however. One concerns the complexity of the present legislation. Foreign investment is now governed by a large number of acts, decrees and orders which suffer to some extent from a lack of clarity and consistency, and parts of which remain subject to future interpretation. It would clearly be advantageous if the various existing texts were to be combined into a single and definitive statute. This statute should clear up the inconsistencies and ambiguities in the existing legislation, cover the gaps now outstanding, clarify the status of prior investments and implement matters still in abeyance.

The legislation requires prior approval for foreign participation in excess of 50 percent of the capital of a company and is undoubtedly an obstacle for some investors interested in obtaining control. On the other hand, control can often be obtained with ownership of 50 percent or less, and so far the Council of Ministers has granted virtually all of the applications in excess of this limit. If the Government wishes to maintain the 50 percent limit as a means of control, we would suggest that it continue to grant exceptions as freely as possible and that the procedures for considering these cases be arranged so that applications could be assured of a decision within a specified period, say two months.

The legislation has been based on a distinction, not entirely clear, between direct investment in firms and "portfolio" investment in securities. Originally the terms provided for these two types of investment were different, but subsequent amendments have liberalized them both and the distinction, for most purposes, is no longer significant. These amendments, which are to be commended highly, have advanced the Spanish legislation to a very favorable point. With minor exceptions, no limitation is now placed, with respect to either timing or amount, on the repatriation of dividends, original capital, or capital gains on investments subsequent to July 1959. The original legislation on direct investment made a distinction between investments qualified as of preferred economic and social interest and those not so qualified.

This distinction appears now to have been eliminated *de facto,* but we recommend that it be done *de jure* since, in our view, there is no sound economic rationale for it.

Direct foreign investment is subject to the same requirement as domestic investment with respect to the prior authorization of the Ministry of Industry. Although the foreign investment legislation establishes a time limit for the authorization process, this limit has not always been observed in practice. In any event, it is our recommendation that this requirement be eliminated completely with respect to both domestic and foreign investors (see Chapter 15).

Removal of the requirement for prior authorization of industrial investments would mean that prior government approval of direct foreign investments would only be required in cases where more than 50 percent ownership was involved. We recognize, however, that when large foreign investments are being proposed, the Government may wish to have the opportunity to consider them in advance even where majority ownership is not at issue. This consideration, for example, might be for the purpose of ascertaining whether the terms and conditions of the investment present any particular problems that should be worked out in advance. We would suggest, therefore, that the Government establish a procedure, which could be administered by the Presidencia del Gobierno (as has been the case with the system of preferential classification) for obtaining the views of interested organizations and bringing them before the Government for consideration within a designated period of time, such as three or four months. The size of the foreign investments to be placed under this review is a matter for the Government to determine, but as an indication of the order of magnitude we would suggest a figure of 500 million pts or more.

An office has been established in the Presidencia del Gobierno to assist prospective investors, but we doubt whether it is on a sufficient scale for the tasks that it should be performing. We recommend that an enlarged office be established, either in the Presidencia or in the Ministry of Commerce, that would be in a position to provide all the services to be expected of a center for foreign investment. An important function of the center would be to draw the attention of foreign investors to the various possibilities for participation in Spanish enterprise.

The acid test of the new policy is, of course, its ability to attract foreign capital. A great deal of interest has been generated and there is no doubt that the potential of foreign private investment is quite high. As of September 1961, 123 applications requiring government approval (either for more than 50 percent ownership or for preferential classification) had been received, and the total value of the investments covered by the applications was $172 million. However, the largest investments were in the petrochemicals field and, although 92 applications had been approved, these covered only $60 million. Actual foreign investment in 1961 amounted to $37.5 million, and of this only about $4 million was direct investment and the remainder investment in stock exchange.

These results, which are still very modest, appear to indicate that the majority of potential foreign investors have, for the moment at least, adopted a "wait and see" attitude. The evidence does not suggest to us that the problem is one of stemming a flood of foreign capital so much as of encouraging additional capital to enter in proportions consonant with the needs of the economy. This will require both that the legislation be revised and that some of the other obstacles to foreign investment be reduced along the lines that we have indicated.

Balance of Payments Prospects

The last question to be considered, in the light of all the others, is what the balance of payments prospects are in the coming few years. Much will depend of course on the success of the Government in orienting its development policy along the lines suggested in this report. Much will also depend on factors beyond Spain's own control, on the weather—particularly important to Spain because of its predominantly agricultural economy—about which all that can be predicted is its unpredictability, and on world events, notably the level of economic activity in Western Europe and the United States.

Despite the elusiveness of these considerations, it appears to us that Spain should be able to afford the liberal import policy that the demands of economic expansion will entail. Most of the increase in imports should come from increases in the capital equipment and raw materials—particularly petroleum—needed for industrial development. There may be some increases in consumer goods imports, although increasing import substitution following on the growth of domestic output may limit this upward trend.

Given a vigorous export promotion policy, together with various measures to promote the rationalization of industry discussed in Chapter 15, Spain can look for substantial gains in its export of manufactures in the coming years. Furthermore, weather permitting, there are favorable prospects for the output and export of fruits and vegetables. It is very unlikely, however, that the total value of exports will reach that of imports in the near future, but the positive balance on other current transactions, due for the most part to tourist receipts, is likely to increase and largely offset the trade deficit. Thus, the deficit on current account should, on the average, be relatively small.

It should be possible in normal circumstances to cover this expected deficit without a loss of reserves. Capital outflow is small: external debt is relatively low and therefore the servicing burden is light. If the policies we suggest above for the encouragement of foreign investment are followed, the prospects for capital inflow are good, and there is the possibility of external loans and other financial assistance, either bilaterally or from international agencies. Even if these judgments prove to be too optimistic, we would expect that any payments deficit that might be incurred could be covered, over some period of time, without excessive loss of reserves. In any case, it is doubtful whether Spain, with its vast need for capital resources, should continue indefinitely to accumulate reserves beyond a prudent margin of safety, say sufficient to finance six to nine months of imports.

The foregoing analysis serves to underline certain points:

a. the importance of a comprehensive program to develop exports;

b. the vital role of tourism as an equilibrating factor; and

c. the need to attract a larger inflow of private capital from abroad.

If reasonable progress can be made on these points, it should be possible to import substantially more of the capital equipment, materials and services required for development.

ANNEX B BUDGETARY CLASSIFICATION AND PRESENTATION

As pointed out in Chapter 6, we think it is desirable to consider further reform of the classification system and of the presentation of the budget. The mission is in no position to make any detailed recommendations as to how this should be done. In any event, there are in existence very helpful guides to types of classification which would meet the requirements.[1] Meanwhile the better should not be allowed to be the enemy of the good. The suggestions or comments which follow are intended as a further explanation of the main text.

The Need for More Informative Summaries

Summary of Expenditure in the Budget of the Central Administration: The budget for the central administration (Presupuestos Generales del Estado) is published every two years and remains valid for a period (bienio economico) beginning with the even-numbered years. Taking 1960/61 as an example the estimates first published cover income and expenditure for 1960 only. A list of modifications to it for 1961 is subsequently published which have to be added to or subtracted from the original budget for 1960 to arrive at the budget for 1961.

There are three main headings in the budget: Letra A (expenditure); Letra B (income); and Letra C, which is a short list of six capital grants or loans to autonomous organizations.

A summary of Letra A is published in the "Boletin Oficial del Estado" and subsequently in the Budget document itself. This summary, which is about 50 pages long, lists expenditure under the following headings:

a. First by section (seccion), i.e., ministry or other main subdivision such as public debt. There were 25 of these in 1960 (a new one has since been added, making 26).

b. Under each section, by chapter (capitulo), i.e., main description of the purpose of expenditure as shown in Table B.1.

c. Under each chapter, by article (articulo), i.e., more detailed description of purpose of expenditure such as subventions to other organs of the State, to local authorities and private

---

[1] For example, *A Manual for Economic and Functional Classification of Government Transactions,* United Nations, New York, 1958.

154

TABLE B.1: List of Chapters in the Spanish Public Accounts

Chapter	Income	Expenditure
1	Direct taxes	Staff
2	Indirect taxes	Materials and equipment, rent and maintenance of premises
3	Charges for services rendered and other income	Departmental expenses
4	Subventions, aid payments and participations in income	Subventions, aid payments and participations in income
5	Financial operations	Financial commitments
6	Sale of investments not producing income	Investments (not producing income)
7	Sale of investments producing income	Investments (producing income)
8	Income from property	Closed accounting periods

parties. There are, in all, 38 articles under the eight chapter headings.

d. Under each article, by service (servicio), i.e., branch of a section such as Directorate-General of Roads or Hydraulic Works in the Ministry of Public Works. The number of services varies with each section. In all there were 211 service headings in 1960.

It is not, however, possible to tell at a glance how much is being spent under the heading of a particular servicio, which would be a first approximation to a functional breakdown, nor under a particular articulo (except for each ministry separately), which would be a guide to the type of payment and, in certain cases, the recipient. A way of setting forth the same information in order to make both these things possible is shown in Table B.2. In this table it is possible to tell quickly how much is charged to the Directorate-General of Roads (CCV–323) and how it is distributed.

An example of a second type of summary is shown in Table B.3. This brings together all payments by article under the various sections, the detail, of course, being shown in the previous summary. At present information of this kind can only be obtained by laboriously adding up the entries under the 200-odd services. In practice we would doubt the necessity for so many service headings in the summary (there

TABLE B.2: Budgeted Expenditure of the Ministry of Public Works, 1960
(million pts)

		Services[b]						
Chapter and Article[a]	Total	Min. 321	SGT 322	CCV 323	FTTC 324	PSM 325	OH 326	PPEA 327
100 Staff:								
110 Salaries	81	64	–	–	6	8	3	–
120 Other remu- neration	25	22	c	c	c	1	1	c
130 Daily allow- ances, travel and transfers	20	1	–	9	2	1	7	c
140 Daily wages	139	–	–	117	3	1	18	–
150 Social action	137	98	–	39	–	–	–	–
160 Retirement payments	7	–	–	7	–	–	–	–
	409	185	c	172	11	11	29	c
200 Materials and equipment, rent and maintenance of premises:								
210 Office materials (expendable)	8	5	–	1	1	c	1	c
220 Office equip- ment (inven- toriable)	1	1	–	c	c	c	–	c
230 Rent and works at leased buildings	1	1	–	–	–	–	–	–
	10	7	–	1	1	c	1	c
300 Departmental expenses:								
310 Ordinary pur- chases	c	c	–	–	–	–	–	–
320 Special pur- chases	c	c	–	c	c	–	–	–
330 Maintenance and repair work	656	1	–	617	9	9	20	c
340 Publications	1	1	–	–	c	–	–	–
350 Other ordinary expenses	2	1	–	c	–	c	1	–
360 Appropriations for new depart- ments	2	–	2	–	–	–	–	–
	661	3	2	617	9	9	21	c

Table B.2 (*cont.*)

		Services[b]						
Chapter and Article[a]	Total	Min. 321	SGT 322	CCV 323	FTTC 324	PSM 325	OH 326	PPEA 327
400 Subsidies, aid payments and participations in income:								
410 To autonomous bodies and public organizations and undertakings	1,857	12	–	–	1,685	91	68	–
420 To provincial and local corporations	325	–	–	112	–	2	211	–
430 To private individuals	40	–	–	c	38	–	2	–
	2,222	12	–	112	1,723	93	281	–
500 Financial Commitments:								
520 Interest on advances and loans from public bodies	252	–	–	–	–	252	–	–
560 Amortization of loans from public bodies	110	–	–	–	–	110	–	–
570 Amortization of bank advances and loans	96	–	–	96	–	–	–	–
	458	–	–	96	–	362	–	–
600 Investments (not producing income):								
610 Constructional and installation work and extension and alteration of existing installations	1,276	2	–	1,002	1	35	231	5
620 Initial establishment purchases	91	91	–	–	–	–	–	–
630 Advances to third parties	67	c	–	–	67	–	–	–
	1,435	93	–	1,002	68	35	231	5

Table B.2 (cont.)

Chapter and Article[a]	Total	Services[b] Min. 321	SGT 322	CCV 323	FTTC 324	PSM 325	OH 326	PPEA 327
700 Investments (producing income): 710 Constructional and installation work and extension and alteration of existing installations	2,728	–	–	–	747	67	1,914	–
	2,728	–	–	–	747	67	1,914	–
800 Closed accounting periods:	–	–	–	–	–	–	–	–
Total	7,922	300	2	2,000	2,559	577	2,477	5

[a] This is not a complete list of articles, but only of those appearing in the budget of the Ministry of Public Works.

[b] The letters are abbreviations of the names of the servicios and the numbers the functional numbering system already used.

[c] Less than 500,000 pts.

TABLE B.3: Detail of Chapter 4 of the 1960 Budget Subventions

		Articles			
Section	Total	410	420	430	440
National Council	155	155			
Prime Minister	138	36			102
Foreign Affairs Office	37	27		10	
Justice	95	95			
Army	44	31		13	
Navy	28	27		1	
Interior	647	642	1	4	
Public Works	2,222	1,857	325	40	
National Education	968	918	6	44	
Labor	223	223			
Industry	446	297	12	138	
Agriculture	74	47	17	10	
Air	91	91			
Commerce	1,545	2		1,542	
Information and Tourism	106	18		87	
Housing	287	287			
Finance	11	11			
Expenses of the Revenue Service	39	1	37	1	
	7,156	4,765	398	1,890	102

NOTES: (i) Details may not add up to totals because of rounding. (ii) Titles of Articles: 410 To autonomous bodies and public organizations and undertakings. 420 to provincial and local corporations. 430 to private individuals. 440 to the State.

are, for example, 28 separate headings for the section on public debt, which might well be reduced to two or three).

We understand that very similar summaries have been worked out recently for internal use in the Ministry of Finance. We would, therefore, recommend their publication as soon as possible.

Summary in Informacion Estadistica

This document summarizes both the estimates (original and as amended during the year) and the final results very briefly. There is a dual breakdown by (a) section (i.e., ministries and similar headings), and (b) chapter.

As we have pointed out, this is not an adequate summary. It discloses no information of a functional nature. It is impossible to distinguish capital from current transactions or financial expenditures from expenditure on goods or services. It is also impossible to distinguish, in the very important subvention chapter, who the recipients are, even by broad groups.

We would advocate something part way between the present over-condensed presentation and the form of summary suggested above. In respect of functions, some sections should be broken down into their component services. Obvious examples are the Ministry of Public Works and the Ministry of Interior. There would not, however, be the same need for the Ministry of Finance, for example. A choice would have to be made based on distinctiveness of function and size of expenditure.

The present chapter headings should be replaced by new and more headings on both the income and expenditure sides (see Table B.1). We would regard the minimum requirement to be as follows:

a. *Chapter 3* (Expenditure). Maintenance (Article 330) would be separated from the remaining articles. Consideration might be given to consolidating the remaining articles with Chapter 2.

b. *Chapter 4* (Income and Expenditure). All four subvention articles should be shown separately in order to disclose the recipient.[2]

c. *Chapter 5* (Income and Expenditure). Interest (Articles 410 to 440) and Amortization (450 to 480) should be shown separately. Other commitments (490) would be allocated according to whether they were of a current or capital nature.

d. *Chapters 6 and 7* (Income and Expenditure). Articles 610, 620, 710 and 720, which constitute capital formation,[3] on the expenditure side should be shown together in one item. Articles 630, 730, 740 and 750 which are financial items (credits to third parties) should be shown together in a single item. We doubt the value of the distinction between income-producing and non-income-producing assets.

e. *Chapter 8* (Income). Article 840 (other income) should be shown separately and cash balances left over from previous years should be excluded altogether since they are not income.

f. *Chapter 8* (Expenditure). Expenditure on account of closed accounting periods should, to make it most informative, properly be included under whichever is relevant of the other headings. Pending this change, non-investment and investment expenditures (Articles 810 and 820) should be shown separately.

---

[2] In order to make it possible to consolidate the budget of the central administration with other budgets or groups of budgets, Article 410 needs to be broken down into more component parts (autonomous organizations, social security organizations, official credit institutions, public enterprises) corresponding to other subdivisions of the public sector.

[3] With the exception of purchases of land and other existing assets which should be shown separately, if they can be isolated.

This would, of course, take up more space. Much space could, however, be saved by eliminating most of the data on the distribution of expenditure by province and month, which in the 1961 document takes up 36 pages. This information is, on the whole, not revealing, because one-quarter of the income and two-thirds of the expenditure falls under a catch-all heading, *Direccion-General del Tesoro*.[4]

Concepts Which Are Too Comprehensive

Individual items of expenditure are known as concepts (conceptos). Each item bears a six-figure code number, e.g., 611.323. The first half (611) identifies it as the first item in a particular service's budget falling under Article 610 (non-income-producing investments, construction and installation).[5] The second half of this code number (323) identifies the item uniquely as being part of the budget of a particular service, in this case the Directorate-General of Roads (DGCCV) in the Ministry of Public Works.

Some large concepts, other than subventions to autonomous organizations are described only in very broad terms. Examples are:

Ministry	Concept	Amount ('000 pts)	Purpose
Presidencia del Gobierno	712.101	1,000,000	Provincial plans (investments)
	151.103	1,008,000	Family aid for all officials
Obras Publicas	619.323	710,800	Road modernization
	613.326	217,400	Water supply
	716.324	480,000	New railway lines & electrification
	711.326	451,374	Irrigation works
Aire	611.423	288,147	Airfields

---

[4] See pages 71–78 and 95–122. Useful information that could be retained would be the distribution of certain tax payments where there is no catch-all item and the distribution of income and expenditure as a whole by month, with a breakdown of the latter by sections.

[5] There is, however, no other significance attached to the figure 611; two items numbered 611 have no more in common than do one numbered 611 and another numbered 613.

There are really two problems here. The first is the question of control and the principle of not spreading money over a large number of capital works and, as a result, not finishing any of them expeditiously. This is not only a matter of size of the allocation. There are, for example, smaller allocations for investment by the Ministry of National Education, which are equally general and which require more specification.

The other problem arises from a conflict between the functional nature of the expenditure and the department of the Government legally responsible for disbursing it. The Presidencia del Gobierno in the case of the first two items disposes of money which is actually spent on behalf of other parts of the Government. It is difficult to see what can be done about this problem pending a general reform, but we would at least suggest that, in addition to identifying such items in more detail, they be included in financial summaries under the appropriate functional section.

Inconsistent or Misleading Usage

If an accounting system with a particular classification is to be useful, its meaning must be clear and usage consistent. One difficulty which has already been mentioned is the lack of definition as to what is included in the various public subsectors. Thus, Article 440 includes subventions to the State (El Estado). In the 1960 central administration budget there is one item under this article, a subvention to the Spanish provinces in Africa, which have their own sources of income in addition. Part, however, of the expenditure in Africa is carried on the budget of the central administration under a particular servicio in a number of the ministerios. It is difficult, under these circumstances, to say what the State means or what its financial relationship with the provinces in Africa is. Similarly, in the 1962 budget, under a new Section 8, Fondos Nacionales, there are only four items, all classified as subventions to the State. It is difficult to assign any meaning to items in the budget which, in effect, are classified as a subvention to itself. Another example concerns the Servicio Nacional de Credito Agricola and the Caja Central de Credito Maritimo. These institutions are considered at this same time to be official credit institutions and autonomous organizations. They ought to fall under only one classification.

Usage of particular articles is not always consistent: Articles 610, 620, 710, 720 are intended to include new physical investments and additions to existing ones. In a number of cases, however, subventions to or financial investments in autonomous organizations have been included under this heading. Examples in the 1960 budget of the central administration are:

Section	Concept	Amount ('000 pts)	Purpose
Ministerio de Educacion Nacional	613.347	500,000	Subvention to Junta Central de Construcciones Escolares
Ministerio de Vivienda	621.505	200,000	Subvention or advance to Corporaciones Locales
Ministerio de Hacienda	611.544	43,000	Capital investment in Fabrica Nacional de Moneda y Timbre

Somewhat the same thing happens in the budgets of the autonomous organizations, in particular in respect to two of the items mentioned above. The subvention to Junta Central de Construcciones Escolares in *Informaciones Estadistica* is under Chapter 3 instead of Chapter 4.[6] The investment in the Fabrica Nacional de Moneda y Timbre does not appear at all.

Similar problems occur in the case of the items in Letra C of the budget. These are all classified under Chapter 7 (Investments) whereas they are really subventions (Chapter 4) or in one case loans (Chapter 5). The recipient agencies so classify them, except for one, the Juntas de Obras y Comisiones Administrativas de Puertos, which does not include the subvention at all.

Extrabudgetary Transactions

It is, in fact, clear that the figures in *Informacion Estadistica* are only partial records. In a brief summary table (p. 141) the *Informacion Estadistica* lists the extrabudgetary operations of the central administration (see Table B.4). Some of these are purely a matter of

---

[6] This may, however, be a clerical error since loans from the Instituto de Credito para la Reconstruccion Nacional to the same institutions also appear in Chapter 4 instead of Chapter 5.

TABLE B.4: General Balance of the Treasury, 1960

(billion pts)

	Receipts	Payments
Budgetary	72.7	67.1
Annex Section:		
U.S. counterpart funds	2.8 ⎱	3.1
Other income	0.3 ⎰	
For the account of local authorities	3.7	3.5
Special Section^a	3.1	3.0
Loans and advances	1.0	1.6
Official credit institutions	1.5	9.2
Other items (net)	0.5	–
	87.2	87.4

ª This is an accounting regularization of the 1957 budget.

NOTE: Details do not add to totals because of rounding.

SOURCE: *Informacion Estadistica del Ministerio de Hacienda,* 1961, pp. 135 and 141.

accounting (e.g., special section), or are transit items (e.g., local authorities; some loans and advances). The two remaining expenditure items nevertheless add up to some 12 billion pts.

A list of the items in the so-called Annex Section, which consists mainly but not wholly of investment projects financed from American counterpart funds, is shown elsewhere (pp. 135–136). These, however, suffer from some of the defects described above (e.g., a global figure of 740 million pts for hydraulic works) and, in certain cases, are classified as investments when they are in reality subventions or loans to autonomous organizations. There appears to be no reason why both the income and expenditure should not be treated in the same way as ordinary budget items and incorporated therein. If, for administrative reasons, the estimates (as opposed to the final results) cannot be included in the original budget, a supplementary addendum could be issued.

It may, of course, be useful to have a separate list accounting for projects financed from American counterpart funds, but this should be considered as an *extract* from the general accounts.[7]

[7] The reason for including projects financed by the "Otros Ingresos" in this annex is unclear. The income item for Barcelona water supply, for example, appears to have a counterpart on the expenditure side of the central administration budget (Concept 421.326) as a subvention to local corporations.

There is no detailed accounting anywhere of the other two items. Financial investments in official credit institutions are an extremely large and important item. The only information given is the total figure without a breakdown into the recipient institutions.[8] Furthermore, there is a large income item from the Banco de Credito Industrial (BCI) which consists of discounts of certificates (*certificaciones*) issued by the Ministry of Public Works, which are subsequently redeemed by the Government and appear therefore as a *contra* item on the expenditure side.[9] There is no explanation of this, however, in the document.

The Loans and Advances also require further explanation. Advances constitute net treasury payments for expenditure to be authorized in subsequent budgetary allocations, while receipts are net payments out of current budgetary authorizations for past advances. While the difference in these two items may be an accurate reflection of the additional expenditure involved, it is clear that the character of the actual expenditure may, as a consequence, be rather different from that set forth in the main accounts.

Finally, there is one class of income and expenditure which does not appear in *Informacion Estadistica* at all. These are the extrabudgetary supplements to civil servants' incomes referred to in the main text. These are clear-cut items of government expenditure. In some cases, no doubt, the expenditure is already included, though not shown separately, in the cost of individual projects. In others, however, there is a special income in the form of special exactions from the public (*tasas y exacciones parafiscales*). In such cases, they do not necessarily pass through the budget,[10] but through special funds which in some cases have the status of an autonomous organization. The mission has no reliable information on the magnitude of the omissions.

Information on important autonomous organizations such as the Servicio Nacional del Trigo and the Instituto Espanol de Moneda Extranjera, as recorded in *Informacion Estadistica,* evidently does not include certain important transactions. The first institution makes very large purchases (or sales) of wheat and additions to (or releases from) stocks, running into billions of pesetas in any one year. The second, which hitherto has held the country's foreign exchange, has even

[8] A more detailed list is published elsewhere (Datos Complementarios), but the figures are still difficult to reconcile with those appearing in the balance sheets of the recipient banks.

[9] There is not always a precise correspondence in the amounts, so that in some years the BCI may extend some short-term credit to the Government.

[10] The mission understands that steps are being taken to bring more of them into the ambit of the budget.

larger transactions with the rest of the world, with the Bank of Spain and with the Government itself, which remain unrecorded. Obviously it is impossible to forecast these transactions in advance, but the results should be available in a readily usable form.

SECTION **III**

TRANSPORTATION

CHAPTER 9 *THE TRANSPORT ECONOMY*

The Evolving Pattern of Spanish Transport

Geography, history and the distribution of areas of economic activity have made a rational and integrated transport system difficult and expensive to achieve in Spain. The main physical feature of the country is a large, high central plateau (meseta) deeply cut by rivers and streams and encircled by rugged mountains often extending down to the coastline. Spain developed over the centuries in a number of widely separated regions, located mainly in the coastal lowlands, between which there were—and still are—areas of sparse population and relatively limited activity; furthermore, once Madrid was established as the capital in the center of the meseta, many important functions were attracted to it in addition to its political and administrative tasks, even though the city is remote from the other main concentrations along the coast. The main areas of intensive economic activity—Barcelona-Gerona, Valencia-Alicante, Sevilla-Cadiz and Oviedo-Santander-Bilbao-San Sebastian—are all more than 400 kms from each other as well as from Madrid.

This peripheral development has meant that transport moves primarily along a relatively small number of high-volume lines radiating from Madrid or linking the other main areas of economic concentration with each other. This basic network is already well established. Further economic growth is likely, for the most part, to place additional burdens on this already established network, although some secondary regions can be expected to develop further and new ones to emerge. It is for this reason that, in dealing with the various types of transport in subsequent chapters, we constantly urge that top priority be accorded to the improvement of the high-volume routes and to the means of conveyance operating along them.

Transportation as a whole has been growing at a fairly rapid rate, as can be seen from the statistics on freight and passenger traffic (see Tables 9.1 and 9.2). As is to be expected at the present stage of Spain's development, transportation activity is increasing somewhat more rapidly than is the total national product. More striking than the overall movement, however, are the very different rates of growth of the different modes of transport. Thus, while railway traffic (both freight and passenger) increased at a slow rate between 1950 and 1958, and coastal shipping trade (apart from tankers) remained more or less stationary, highway freight traffic (ton-kilometers) grew almost threefold

169

and highway passenger traffic (passenger-kilometers) doubled. Even more remarkable is the fact that highway transport continued to increase in 1959 and 1960 despite the recession which adversely affected the other forms of transport. While only one-sixth of the freight traffic moved over the roads in 1951, more than one-third did in 1960.

To a considerable extent these shifts in the pattern of traffic are inherent in the process of economic development. Technological changes, both within the transport sector and in the economy as a whole, have

TABLE 9.1: Estimates of Freight Transportation, 1951–1960[a]

	Railway (RENFE only)	Highway (Inter-city only)	Coastal Shipping	CAMPSA Tankers	Total Intercity Traffic
Ton-Kilometers: (billions)					
1951	7.0	2.8		8.0	17.8
1952	7.6	3.5		9.5	20.6
1953	7.6	4.5		10.2	22.3
1954	7.1	4.7		9.3	21.1
1955	7.0	5.1	7.5	2.0	21.6
1956	7.6	6.4	7.6	2.1	23.7
1957	7.9	6.9	8.2	3.4	26.4
1958	7.9	7.5	8.5	3.5	27.4
1959	6.6	8.5	8.5	3.5	27.1
1960	5.1	10.0	7.7	3.8	26.6
Tons Loaded: (millions)					
1951	25.0	14.2		10.6	49.8
1952	28.3	17.3		12.7	58.3
1953	27.7	22.5		13.6	63.8
1954	29.5	23.4		12.4	65.3
1955	29.3	25.7	10.0	2.3	67.3
1956	31.5	32.1	10.1	2.5	76.2
1957	34.1	34.4	11.0	4.0	83.5
1958	35.1	37.5	11.3	4.1	88.0
1959	31.3	42.5	11.4	4.1	89.3
1960	25.5	50.0	10.2	4.4	90.1

[a] Airline traffic is not included since it amounted to only 2 million ton-kilometers in 1960.

SOURCES: Railway: From *Annual Memorias of RENFE.* It should be noted that in the 1958–59 period the narrow-gauge lines, public and private, carried an additional 1.2–1.4 billion ton-miles, mostly of coal and minerals. Highway: From *La Situación del Transporte Terrestre en España,* Ministerio de Obras Publicas. 1959 and 1960 ton-kilometers have been estimated by the mission. All tons loaded have been estimated by the mission. Coastal Shipping and CAMPSA Tankers: Tons loaded furnished by Mercante Marina. Includes traffic to and from Baleares and Canarias.

had a major impact on transport requirements. One of the most important of these is the shift in sources of energy for industrial and domestic use from bulky solid fuels (wood, and especially coal)—which have represented a very high proportion of the tonnage carried by rail and coastal shipping—to petroleum-based liquid and gas fuels which

TABLE 9.2: Estimates of Intercity Passenger Transportation

	Railway (RENFE only)	Highway			Coastal Shipping	Airlines (Iberia & Aviaco)	Total Intercity Traffic
		Total	Buses	Private Vehicles			
Passenger Kilometers: (billions)							
1951	7.3	5.1	1.7	3.4	a	.1	12.5
1952	7.9	5.4	1.8	3.6	"	.1	13.4
1953	8.0	5.9	2.1	3.8	"	.2	14.1
1954	7.9	6.5	2.3	4.2	"	.2	14.6
1955	8.0	7.3	2.5	4.8	"	.2	15.5
1956	8.6	8.6	2.8	5.8	"	.3	17.5
1957	8.6	10.0	3.1	6.9	"	.3	18.9
1958	8.7	11.0	3.3	7.7	"	.3	20.0
1959	8.5	11.6	3.4	8.2	"	.3	20.4
1960	7.3	12.2	3.5	8.7	"	.4	20.0
Passengers Carried: (millions)							
1951	108.4	156.7	107.7	49.0	.8	.3	266.2
1952	114.6	167.3	114.8	52.5	.8	.4	283.1
1953	115.7	192.7	134.2	58.5	1.0	.4	309.8
1954	114.4	217.4	150.0	67.4	.9	.5	333.2
1955	117.2	242.6	160.0	82.6	.8	.5	361.1
1956	123.3	281.9	178.0	103.9	1.0	.8	407.0
1957	124.3	343.4	202.5	133.8	.9	.8	469.4
1958	127.6	382.9	209.6	173.3	.8	.8	512.3
1959	124.3	404.3	218.0	186.3	.9	.8	530.3
1960	108.8	427.0	226.7	200.3	.9	.9	537.6

a Less than 100 million passenger-kilometers in all years.

SOURCES: Railway: From *Annual Memorias of RENFE*. It is likely that the narrow-gauge passenger traffic, not included, was 300–500 million passenger kilometers in 1958–59. Highway: From *La Situación Del Transporte Terrestre En España*, Ministerio de Obras Publicas. 1959 and 1960 passenger kilometers for private vehicles and 1960 passenger-kilometers for buses have been estimated by the mission. The number of passengers for private vehicles in all years was estimated by the mission. Coastal Shipping: From *Annuario Estadistico*, 1960, for number of passengers. Passenger-kilometers estimated by the mission. The majority of this traffic is to and from the Baleares. Airlines: From *Annual Memorias of Iberia and Aviaco* and from the INI report *Plan de Desarrollo de Iberia y Aviaco*, INI.

can also readily be transported by truck and, increasingly in the future, by pipeline. Another factor is that, as the economy expands, an increasing proportion of the national production takes the form of consumer goods. These frequently are high value items that are transported in small volumes; the cost of transport tends to be a small part of the selling price, and therefore only a secondary consideration, whereas speed and reliability of service are of paramount importance. Finally, with the growth of the motor vehicle many companies are no longer obliged to rely on public carriers but can own and operate their own trucking services.

Not all of the loss of traffic suffered by the railways and coastal shipping can be attributed to this process of economic and technological change. As we mention below, and discuss at greater length in succeeding chapters, rate policies have not always been designed to attract the traffic that should be expected to move by rail and sea, and investments have been made in such a way that costs are considerably higher than they might be. The changes that we propose should make it possible for the rail and coastal shipping systems to compete with roads on a more equal footing in the future.

The demand for transportation will continue to grow, and large-scale investments will be required if the transport system is to handle efficiently and at minimum cost the volume of traffic to be expected. It will not be necessary to increase over-all the size or extent of the transportation system; as we have mentioned, the existing network of highways, railway lines and ports is adequate—and in some cases more than adequate—for present and foreseeable needs. What is required is a better-balanced investment effort, with greater emphasis on cargo-handling equipment for the ports, on urgent repair and improved maintenance of the main highway network and, in the case of the railways, on modern track and motive power and improved systems for classifying and moving traffic.

Implications for Public Policy

Despite the changing pattern of demand for the various types of transport, each continues to have a vital function to perform. However, the governmental policies necessary to ensure the proper performance of these functions have to be adjusted continuously in the light of technical and economic changes which themselves are continuous. The government's approach to transport regulation must be flexible.

Public regulatory policy is still based officially on the concept that the railroad system remains the principal mode of transport, and that other modes should be made subordinate to it. This concept originated in 1940, at a time when Spain did not manufacture motor vehicles or refine petroleum products and was gravely short of foreign exchange. On the other hand, Spain had a railway system that was functioning well and was assured of domestic supplies of coal for fuel. Consequently, the road transport laws of 1947 and 1949 aimed at stimulating rail development and restraining road transport by limiting the use of buses and trucks and relegating road transport services to the role of an auxiliary to the railroads.

Conditions have, of course, changed since the 1940's: domestic production of motor vehicles has expanded rapidly; the foreign exchange position has vastly improved in the past few years, and petroleum can readily be obtained; and coal is regarded as being less efficient than other sources of power for railway locomotives.

Although the statutory regulations have not been revised to take account of these changing circumstances, it would be misleading to conclude that official policy has handicapped the growth of road transport, as is readily evident from the statistics already presented in Tables 9.1 and 9.2. The restrictions on the use of road transport have not, for the most part, been rigorously enforced in practice; while at the same time the difficulties experienced by the railways, which we describe later, have prevented them from taking full advantage of their favored position. Regulatory policy should be framed with adequate attention to the possible economic consequences, including the effect on competition among the various transport modes, rather than on an *ad hoc* basis.

A regulatory approach directed toward achieving a balanced and coordinated transport system should enable passengers and goods to move by the type of transport, or combination of types, offering the desired quality of service for the lowest cost. Quality of service is taken to include speed, frequency and reliability, freedom from loss and damage, convenience and, for passengers, comfort. Inherent in this policy are rates and fares reasonably related to the actual costs of transport movement to the economy. These "costs" are the long-run marginal costs of providing service, taking into account the costs of facilities furnished by public agencies, as well as depreciation and interest. Consequently, government policy should seek to establish a transport economy in which the user is free to select from a variety of alternatives the combination of price and service that is best for him and which, at the same time, allows the rates charged by each carrier to cover its costs.

The Government can only use this basic policy to guide the allocation of public resources in the transport sector if it possesses accurate information on the costs of movement by the various modes and on the service needs of users. At present, RENFE produces the best transport data in Spain and it is well analyzed. There are adequate traffic data for coastal shipping, but data on costs and prices charged are almost non-existent. Since both Spanish airlines adhere to the International Civil Aviation Organization (ICAO) reporting and accounting practices, the companies have presumably compiled adequate information, although their published revenue and expense data are not in the same detail as their traffic data. As in other countries, it is with respect to road transport that the lack of data is most serious. The only current reports are from the operators of regular bus services and these are inadequate since they include no operating cost data. All holders of *tarjetas* (permits) for any type of public service should be required to file accurate and complete annual reports indicating the important facts of traffic, revenues and expenses. We might mention in passing that such statistics as those presented in Tables 9.1 and 9.2 are not readily available.

This regulatory approach should rely, to the maximum possible extent, on market forces to relate prices to long-run costs and to distribute traffic among the services on an economic basis: the principal role of the Government should be to ensure that market forces operate freely and that the real costs of each service are as low as possible. In Spain, many rates for transport services are in fact being set by the market and, with some exceptions, they appear to have been quite close to actual costs. It is highly significant that road and water freight transport operate with a minimum of regulation as compared with other countries. Railway and air rates are fixed by the Government, but in later chapters we recommend that RENFE and the air line companies be granted greater freedom to adjust rates to take account of market factors and to provide services suited to the needs of users.

We recognize that there will be a continuing need for the Government to supervise the general level of transport rates, and in some instances to fix particular rates on the basis of broader considerations of the public interest. But the need for detailed government regulation arises mainly in conditions of serious imbalance between supply and demand. Spain is very fortunate that such an imbalance does not exist today, and with judicious policies it can be avoided in the future.

If the pricing structure for each transport service is thus related to costs, then the level of demand for the various services can be taken as the basis for determining investment needs; with reasonably accurate forecasts of trends in demand, appropriate decisions can be made as to what sort of investment in transport facilities, and where, when and how much, is required. Investment decisions in the future, particularly with respect to the railways and the ports, will need to be based to a much greater extent on such demand and cost considerations. In subsequent chapters, we discuss our views on appropriate future investment programs for each of the various transport sectors.

Given such programs within each sector, as well as certain organizational arrangements that we discuss below, we believe that Spain is in a good position to achieve a well-balanced and efficient national transport system.

Government Organization

The Government has wide responsibilities for, and a close interest in, the investment needs, the operations and the welfare of each of the different modes of transport, which will be considered in some detail in the chapters which follow. But something more than this is needed if there is to be a properly balanced and well-coordinated national transport system. Central direction and supervision are needed in order to provide for the contingencies of the changing economic scene and their impact on competing modes of transport. Otherwise, there will be an overlapping of interests and a misapplication and wastage of investment resources.

It is therefore not only necessary for the Government to devote its energies to making each mode of transport efficient, but to have a view of the future demands on the transport system as a whole, and the ways in which those demands can most usefully and economically be met. A long-term transport policy should be an essential part of the long-term program for economic development, and the recurring operational problems and investment plans must be viewed in the light of that long-term policy.

With these considerations in mind the mission believes that machinery should be set up to enable such an over-all view to be taken on a continuing basis. Although this possibility already exists at governmental level through the Delegate Committees of Ministers, the principal need seems to be to have a permanent body at the higher official and technical level. The precise form this should take is a matter for the Government to decide; but for our present purposes we can stress the salient points by assuming that there would be a standing committee (hereafter referred to as the Transport Committee) with a permanent chairman, preferably a person of standing and experience in transport matters, and a permanent secretariat, including some economists and engineers, drawn from the staff of the various ministries concerned with transport. The members of the committee would be the senior departmental officials with executive responsibilities for the various modes of transport; and others with responsibility for operating the system, such as representatives from RENFE, INI and senior technical experts on roads and ports, should be closely associated with the Committee and have an opportunity for making their views known.

The permanent staff of the secretariat would be assigned certain day-to-day functions:

a. collecting and analyzing data on general transport developments, and supervising the collection of sector data by individual ministries or agencies;

b. forecasting the future trends in the demand for transport both generally and for different modes;

c. establishing the long-term goals of transport development and the general guidelines and criteria of public regulation;

d. reviewing major policies and decisions on rates, services, etc., in the light of these goals and criteria;

e. reviewing investment programs of the individual transport sectors in the light of these goals and criteria; and

f. preparing periodic reports for the Government and the public on transport problems and developments.

These functions would oblige them to maintain close contact with the transport ministries; they would also act as the liaison group on transportation matters at the technical level with the staff of the Planning Commission and the Ministry of Finance.

On the basis of the work done by its permanent staff, the Transport Committee would brief ministers on questions of national transport policy, and see that those responsible for the operations are advised of any consequential action to be taken. In particular, when the ministerial reports to the Cabinet on the following year's investment program are prepared under the procedure recommended in Chapter 3, we suggest that departmental proposals for each branch of transport should be examined by the Transport Committee to see that they are consistent with one another and with the country's over-all requirements; and that the Committee's covering report should be in the dossier on transport destined for the Delegate Committee for Economic Affairs and the Comisario del Plan.

We have indicated our views on what the main function of the Transport Committee should be; its mandate will have to be drawn up more precisely when the competent authorities have given more thought to it. We should not expect the Committee to intervene in the execution of the individual programs for the various modes of transport unless they appear likely to run counter to national policy. But there will be overlapping problems of interest to more than one mode of transport (e.g., whether highway services are ready to replace railway services, in cases where lines are to be closed to traffic), which might be referred to the Transport Committee unless some *ad hoc* arrangement is preferred. But its essential purpose is to provide a forum in which the development of the whole transport system is watched, future needs are assessed and methods of meeting them are planned.

CHAPTER 10 *RAILWAYS*

There are many difficult problems facing the Spanish railways which are manifested in a continual loss of traffic to other modes of transport, in large deficits and in a decline in performance and service. Such problems are not peculiar to Spain; they have harassed most Western countries and have demanded drastic measures of reorganization and large investments for modernization, and they are by no means solved in all cases. It may be said that Spain has been behind other countries in grappling with these problems, although some of the reasons for this have been unavoidable. But though efforts have been made in recent years to modernize the system, they have not succeeded in getting to the root of the problem. The Spanish Government has been increasingly preoccupied with this situation, recognizing that unless the decline can be arrested, the railways cannot make their essential contribution to the economic development of the country, and may indeed act as a brake on it. The Government has initiated several expert investigations in the last few years, culminating in those undertaken by Mr. Louis Armand with whom the mission was closely associated while conducting its own studies, and with whose conclusions it is in general agreement.[1]

The origins of the present difficulties are numerous and complex; in this chapter we attempt to analyze them and to suggest remedies. We share Mr. Armand's views that many of them can be traced directly or indirectly to problems of organization, which can only be resolved by a fundamental change in the effective division of responsibility between the national railways and the Government. We hope that our recommendations, together with those made by Mr. Armand, will enable the Spanish Government to take prompt action to overcome the difficulties facing the railways and thereby make it possible for them to regain their competitive position within the transport sector.

---

[1] Mr. Armand served as an expert consultant to the Spanish Government during the first half of 1961 to advise on major matters of organization of the railways and their operational policy. Furthermore, he worked in conjunction with Mr. Dorsch (see Chapter 11) on questions of coordination with the road transport system. His recommendations have been presented to the Government in a memorandum. The International Bank for Reconstruction and Development assisted in arranging for Mr. Armand's services.

178

Traffic Trends

The national railway system, operated by the Red Nacional de los Ferrocarriles Espanoles (RENFE), consisted in 1960 of 13,444 kms of lines, of which 1,876 kms were double track and 1,968 kms electrified. As in the case of the other modes of inland transport, the main arteries of the rail network radiate from Madrid to the principal production and consumption centers of the periphery, with some cross connections and local routes.

Two-thirds of railway traffic, as measured by revenues, comes from freight and one-third from passenger service (see Table 10.1). Coal and ores are the principal commodities handled, but these move in bulk over relatively short distances in the north from the mines to industrial centers and ports. Large volumes of fertilizers, cement and petroleum are also transported by rail. South and west of Madrid traffic densities are low and average hauls quite long. As can be seen from Table 10.1,

TABLE 10.1: RENFE Traffic, 1948–1960

Year	Passenger Kilometers (billions)	Freight[a] Kilometers (billions)	Passenger Revenues (bill. pts)	Freight[b] Revenues (bill. pts)	Total Revenues (bill. pts)
1948	7.6	5.5	1.0	1.8	2.8
1949	7.3	5.5	1.0	1.8	2.8
1950	7.1	6.4	1.2	2.8	4.0
1951	7.3	7.0	1.3	3.3	4.6
1952	7.9	7.6	1.4	3.6	5.0
1953	8.0	7.6	1.4	3.2	4.6
1954	7.9	7.1	1.6	3.4	5.0
1955	8.0	7.0	1.7	3.4	5.1
1956	8.6	7.6	1.8	3.7	5.5
1957	8.6	7.9	2.3	4.8	7.1
1958	8.7	7.9	2.6	5.4	8.0
1959	8.5	6.6	2.5	5.5	8.0
1960	7.3	5.1	3.0	5.1	8.1

[a] Does not include mail or company service.
[b] Does not include mail and company service after 1952.

SOURCES: *Annuario Estadistico de Espana, 1960* and *Memorias del Consejo de Administracion de RENFE 1954–1960.*

the trend of freight traffic was upward during most years between 1948 and 1958; this growth, however, masked a continuing loss of the railways' share of the total traffic to other forms of transport, particularly trucking. The sharp drop in goods traffic between 1958 and 1960 was due to the impact of the recession and trucking competition, aggravated by the rate increase of 1959. The growth of passenger traffic has been slow but steady. Compared with other European countries, the volume of traffic handled is large, and the load factor relatively high. Passenger traffic has increased partly as a result of the installation of new equipment such as TAFs and TALGOs.[2]

Technical Conditions

Extent of Network. The existing network is more than sufficient for present and probable future passenger and freight traffic demands. Experience in other countries indicates that high traffic densities are required for profitable railway operation, but the construction of new lines in Spain seems to have been undertaken without regard to existing or potential demand in areas never likely to develop sufficient traffic density. Map 5 shows traffic densities on the existing network[3] while Map 6 indicates the numerous lines with unfavorable operating ratios.[4] It is significant that in 1959 close to 80 percent of the kilometers of line comprising the RENFE network had operating ratios in excess of 100; 40 percent of all the lines showed operating ratios greater than 160. Losses have been larger on passenger than on freight traffic, mostly because RENFE has had to provide service to thinly-populated areas that could be served more advantageously by bus and to carry many passengers at reduced rates.

The 1960 budget authorization for new lines to be constructed by the Ministry of Public Works was about 750 million pts. We do not know how much was spent in previous years, but it seems likely that at least this amount has been spent annually (in constant prices). A RENFE estimate, prepared in 1958, indicated that 7.5 billion pts of additional expenditure would be required to terminate the lines then under construction.

None of these lines is likely to generate sufficient new traffic to justify its operation; the principal effect of the new lines will be to divert

---

[2] The TAF is a three unit, diesel-powered passenger train; the TALGO is a light-weight articulated train of special design powered by a diesel electric locomotive.

[3] The map is based on total tonnage of trains, including car weight. It would be preferable to use data on traffic in passenger-miles and ton-miles if they can be obtained.

[4] The operating ratio is measured as operating expenses divided by revenue; a ratio of more than 100 means that revenues did not even cover operating costs. Profitable operation requires ratios below 100, since non-operating costs (depreciation, interest) must also be covered from the revenue.

traffic from existing lines, further reducing average traffic densities and increasing the size of the network with unprofitable operating ratios. The Armand report recommended that all lines under construction be re-examined to decide on which lines work should be stopped. It also recommended that the existing network be divided into three categories:

(a) lines to be retained in normal freight and passenger operation;

(b) lines to be closed to passenger traffic, but to be retained for restricted goods traffic; and

(c) lines to be closed to all traffic.

Since the examination and classification of lines will take some time, the report suggested that priority be given to determining the new lines on which work should be stopped and which part of the network would definitely fall into category (a).

On the basis of its further examination, the mission strongly recommends that all work on new lines, including all uncompleted lines, be suspended until the study proposed by Mr. Armand is completed. Materials on order for uncompleted projects could be diverted for the renovation of existing track (see below), while some portions of unused railroad right-of-way might be used for highway improvements (one such possibility might be the double track tunnel in the Somosierra pass on the Madrid-Burgos highway).

We also believe that some decisions can be reached now as to the existing lines to be closed immediately to all traffic and dismantled (with replacement service by trucks and buses organized at the appropriate time) so that investment funds can be concentrated over the next five years on the modernization and re-equipment of a basic network of lines that will undoubtedly continue to remain in service after the study proposed by Mr. Armand is completed. The mission has therefore presented its suggestions on Map 8 with respect to the main network to be retained and modernized, the lines to be closed immediately and the lines falling into an intermediate group to be classified after the proposed study by RENFE.

Narrow-Gauge Railways. The RENFE network consists of broad-gauge lines (1.672 meters). In addition, there are a small number of narrower gauge lines, mostly one meter gauge with some of the European standard (1.435 meters). Under the present law these privately owned lines revert to the State 99 years after original concession. Some of the concessions have already expired and a large proportion of the remainder will have reached the 99-year period within the next 10 or 20 years. So far, only those lines with deficit operations have in practice been taken over by the State. These are operated by the Ministry of Public Works (not by RENFE).

A number of the 53 private railway companies still operating are important carriers of coal and minerals, with a financially sound future; some of them would like to make new investments, which would clearly be in the public interest. But the 99-year reversion law makes private financing difficult or impossible for them, and we suggest that the law be amended to allow these privately owned railways to be continued under their present ownership so long as they are potentially profitable. There seems no advantage to further public acquisition since the high cost of conversion to the broader gauge would prevent their being consolidated into the RENFE system. But for the majority of these companies, which cannot be regarded as potentially profitable, we think that operations should be discontinued when the concessions expire and the companies are due to revert to public ownership, or even sooner if the owners want to be released from the terms of their concessions on account of the losses they are incurring. Similarly, those lines that have already been taken over by the State and which have little prospect of operating except at a loss should be wound up and replaced by highway services.

Single vs. Double Track. It is fortunate that there are not many double track lines, since with modern techniques for traffic control most of the single lines can carry much more than their present volume of traffic. Savings could be realized by operating some existing sections of double track lines on a single track. Any projects for new double track lines should be scrutinized very closely (e.g., the tunnel at Zaragoza) before adoption, since there appears to be little or no need for them. The following figures from RENFE illustrate the advantages of using central traffic control (CTC) rather than double track to increase train handling capacity:

	Original Construction Cost per km	Annual Increase in Maintenance Cost per km	Annual Savings in Operating Personnel per km
		(thousand pts)	
Addition of 2nd track	5,100	63	0
Installation of CTC	1,000	7	19

On many lines, even CTC systems are not required. Block signal systems are sufficient for the volume of traffic and have the advantages, relative to CTC, of being much cheaper and using more labor, of which the railroad has an abundance.

Condition of the Track. Generally speaking, the track of the RENFE network is in bad condition. Much of it consists of older, lighter rails. Even the bare minimum of maintenance and repairs necessary for safety reasons is not being carried out on the majority of the lines and broken rails, of which there were 2,500 in 1959, are causing an increasing number of derailments. Such conditions have necessitated both compulsory reductions in train speeds in order to reduce accident risks, with the resultant loss of valuable time, and the imposition of weight limits on locomotives that prevent them from being used to maximum efficiency and impede the introduction of modern motive power. They have also resulted in premature wear of rolling stock and the need for extensive repairs. We estimate, for example, that track improvements could save almost 40 percent of the present expenses (more than 3 billion pts in 1960) for rolling stock repairs. Passenger comfort has also been affected, as has the handling of freight, which is subject to excessive damage.

While considerable improvements have been achieved recently with the limited funds available, the highest rate of track renewal attained has been less than 500 kms yearly; at this rate, it would take over 20 years to renew 10,000 kms of track. We believe that track renewal can and should proceed at a much faster pace, through the provision of more funds and the employment of additional manpower, and that it should be regarded as an objective of top priority. All of the necessary metal and construction materials exist in Spain, and the work can be accomplished by a wide variety of combinations of men and machines, with specialized equipment coming from abroad. Map 8 shows the extent of track renovation, totaling about 4,500 kms, which the mission considers possible over the next five years.

At present no Spanish companies are doing large scale track renovation for RENFE, since the latter has not been able to plan its program of work for a sufficient period ahead or in sufficient volume to make it worthwhile for important companies to equip themselves for it. However, the vast needs for the years to come should make it possible to remedy this. The assurance of a stable volume of business should also make it possible for properly equipped companies to lower the price of rails, an important factor in determining the rate at which track renewal can take place.

We also suggest that while track renovation is going on, track maintenance should be reorganized. Although the national network of RENFE was formed by amalgamation of the numerous private companies some 20 years ago, the old organizations responsible for track maintenance have never been merged and consolidated. Some cities (e.g., Zaragoza) have three or more separate maintenance organizations. Other cases where advantage has not been taken of the economies made possible by the amalgamation of the separate railways under RENFE are cited below in connection with classification yards, locomotive and other repair shops and railroad facilities in the main cities.

Motive Power. It is generally recognized that operating costs of motive power are excessive. More than 80 percent of RENFE's engines are still steam-powered, and many of the steam engines are overage; 40 percent are more than 40 years old and some over 100 years.

The delay in converting to more efficient motive power is due in part to the fact that limited investment funds have been used primarily for other purposes. But it is significant that RENFE is still acquiring steam locomotives, in part under ten-year contracts, and in this and other respects RENFE's interests have been made subservient to those of the national supplier industries. In the future reorganization of RENFE (see below) we think it important that the railways should be in a position to deal with manufacturers at arms' length; they should be free to cancel obsolete contracts and change suppliers if performance is unsatisfactory, and to purchase abroad if necessary. RENFE should also be able to purchase its engine fuel supplies, notably fuel oil and gas oil, on the same terms as other consumers, with due allowance for the economies of bulk buying. It appears that this may not always have been the case in the past.

The mission recommends that steam engines be replaced by more economical motive power as rapidly as possible, and that the conversion of heavy steam locomotives from coal to fuel oil be used only as a temporary expedient. As Table 10.2 shows, the operating costs per ton-kilometer of train weight are substantially lower for diesel electric and straight electric locomotives than for steam locomotives, particularly when powered by coal. Modernization of the locomotive fleet poses the choice between electrification and dieselization. While electrification makes it possible to use power produced from Spanish resources, it is a costly proposition involving large fixed investments. Now that there is no longer a shortage of foreign exchange, it is justified only where a high volume of traffic may be expected; this traffic potential exists only for a very limited number of the most important lines. Since there are already extensive electrified sections, we recommend that there should be no enlargement of the basic electrified network. On the other hand, some further electrification is required to link the presently electrified sections into large continuous lines in order to improve the utilization of electric locomotives and provide the best speed of train service. In the future, electrified lines might extend (as shown in Map 9):

a. from Madrid to the north and northwest (Irun, Bilbao, Santander, Leon, Asturias, Monforte);
b. from Madrid south to Cordoba;
c. within Catalonia.

TABLE 10.2: Comparison of RENFE's Steam, Electric and Diesel Motive Power Costs in 1960

	Cost Per Train Kilometer (pts)	Average Weight Per Train (tons)	Cost Per Gross ton-km of Train (pts)
Passenger Service:			
Steam Locomotives			
Coal	112.9	198	0.57
Fuel Oil	97.9	349	0.28
Electric Power			
Locomotives	71.7	309	0.23
Train Units	38.4	192	0.20
Diesel Power			
Locomotives	79.5	325	0.24
TAF	50.6	137	0.37
Rail Cars (excl. TAF)	31.5	39	0.81
TALGO	53.8	120	0.45
Freight Service:			
Steam Locomotives			
Coal	171.0	381	0.45
Fuel Oil	146.0	510	0.29
Electric Locomotives	127.7	497	0.26
Diesel Locomotives	137.0	601	0.23

NOTE: Average prices of Fuels and Electric Power:
Coal   930.87 pts/ton
Fuel Oil   1,027.70 pts/ton
Diesel   6.6516 pts/liter
Kwh   0.4228 pts
SOURCE: Based on information supplied by RENFE.

Diesel power is dependent on fuel imports, but it is an economical form of power requiring relatively small initial investment and it is suitable for all lines of the Spanish railway network. The mission believes that dieselization should be pushed forward rapidly. Diesel switch engines should be substituted for antiquated steam locomotives, and even put into service on lines which will eventually be electrified.

Greater use should also be made of modern rail cars such as TAF's to eliminate passenger trains now made up of obsolete rolling stock drawn by over-powered, under-efficient steam locomotives. If subsequent analysis should demonstrate that there is an important future for first-class rail passenger service in competition with air lines and private motor vehicles, TALGO trains might be used to replace rail cars and steam-powered trains. For the present, however, improved service and lower experimental fares should be tried before the TALGO trains—now in operation between Madrid-Barcelona and Madrid-Irun—are extended to points other than Sevilla.

Large-scale replacement of steam power will require a major reorganization of locomotive maintenance. This reorganization is long overdue, since there has been no consolidation of the locomotive repair shops taken over from the private railway companies. Map 10 shows that many cities have from two to four locomotive repair shops; this must lead to inefficiency, over-staffing and duplication of facilities. Map 11 contains RENFE's proposals, with which the mission concurs, for a reduced number of maintenance shops and reserve depots for diesel and electric power. In addition to this reorganization, improved equipment for locomotive maintenance should be installed. There is, for instance, a 106-year-old wheel lathe in the new depot for electric locomotives at Leon.

Rolling Stock. Many passenger and freight cars are too old and in poor condition, and the older ones should be withdrawn as soon as possible. But we suggest that in view of the probable reduction in the number of passenger lines and the introduction of diesel and electric train units, new passenger cars only be purchased when a future need for them becomes apparent. When freight cars are withdrawn from service, they should be replaced with modern types, but no increase in the number of freight cars used for domestic traffic seems justified since turn-around time could be appreciably reduced—with corresponding savings in the number of cars required—by improved traffic handling (see below).

Operating Problems

The speed and reliability of operation of the Spanish network could be notably improved. We suggest that RENFE undertake further

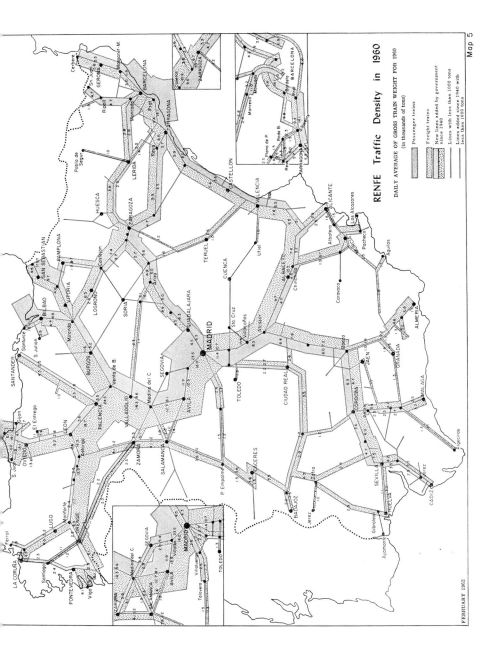

RENFE Traffic Density in 1960

DAILY AVERAGE OF GROSS TRAIN WEIGHT FOR 1960
(in thousands of tons)

Passenger trains

Freight trains

New lines added by government
since 1940

Lines with less than 1000 tons

Lines added since 1940 with
less than 1000 tons

FEBRUARY 1962

Map 5

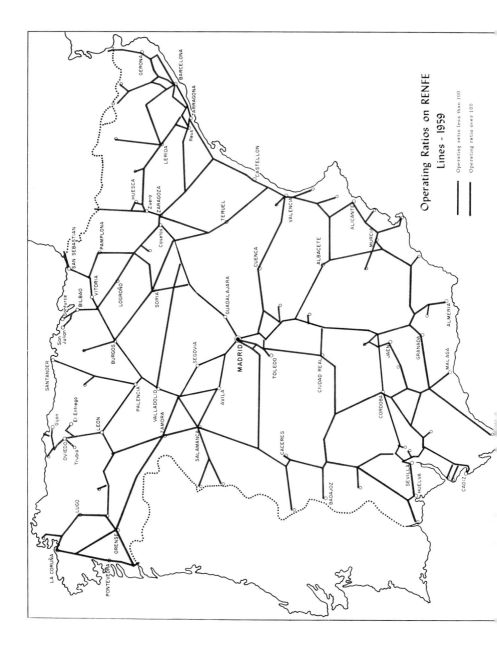

Operating Ratios on RENFE
Lines - 1959

——— Operating ratio less than 100
▬▬ Operating ratio over 100

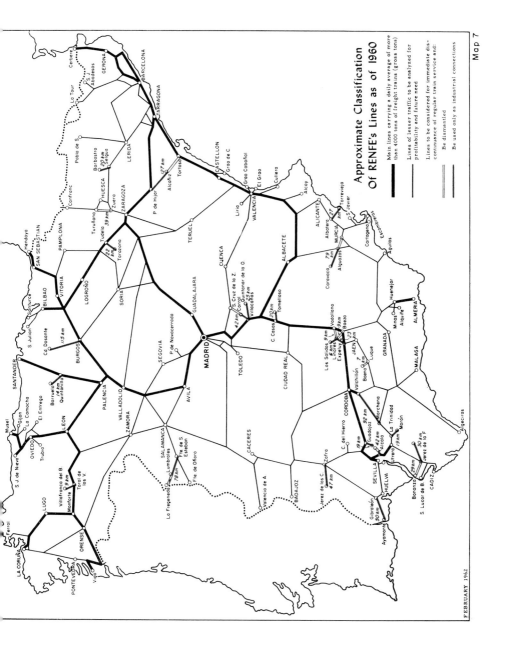

Map 7

Approximate Classification
Of RENFE's Lines as of 1960

Main lines carrying a daily average of more
than 4000 tons of freight trains (gross tons)

Lines of lesser traffic to be analyzed for
profitability and future need

Lines to be considered for immediate dis-
continuance of regular train service and:

Be dismantled

Be used only as industrial connections

FEBRUARY 1962

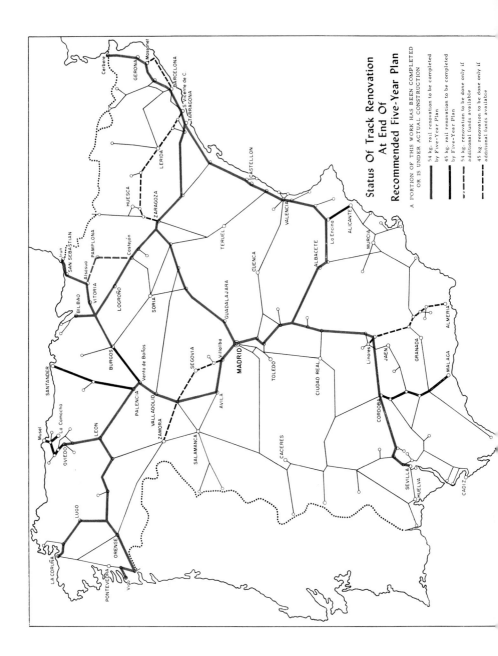

Status Of Track Renovation
At End Of
Recommended Five-Year Plan

A PORTION OF THIS WORK HAS BEEN COMPLETED
OR IS UNDER ACTUAL CONSTRUCTION

54 kg. rail renovation to be completed
by Five-Year Plan

45 kg. rail renovation to be completed
by Five-Year Plan

54 kg. renovation to be done only if
additional funds available

45 kg. renovation to be done only if
additional funds available

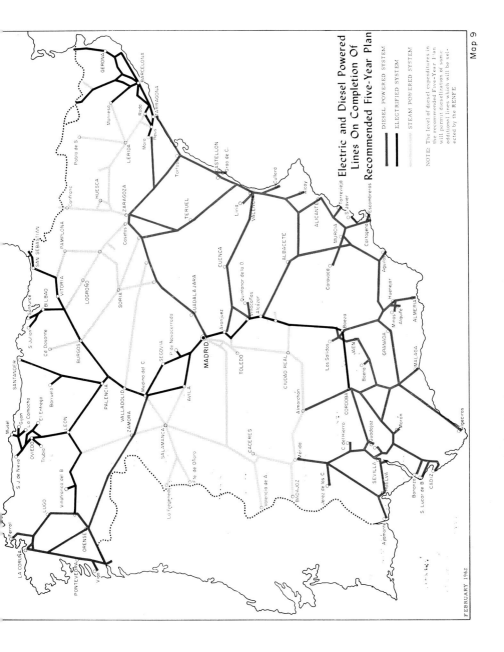

Electric and Diesel Powered
Lines On Completion Of
Recommended Five-Year Plan

——— DIESEL POWERED SYSTEM

———— ELECTRIFIED SYSTEM

·········· STEAM POWERED SYSTEM

NOTE: The level of diesel expenditures in
the recommended Five-Year Plan
will permit dieselization of some
additional lines which will be selected by the RENFE.

Map 9

FEBRUARY 1962

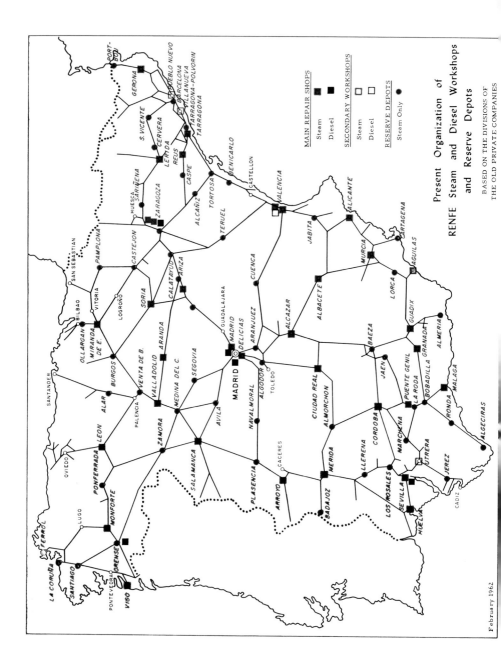

Present Organization of
RENFE Steam and Diesel Workshops
and Reserve Depots

BASED ON THE DIVISIONS OF
THE OLD PRIVATE COMPANIES

MAIN REPAIR SHOPS
  Steam
  Diesel
SECONDARY WORKSHOPS
  Steam
  Diesel
RESERVE DEPOTS
  Steam Only

February 1962

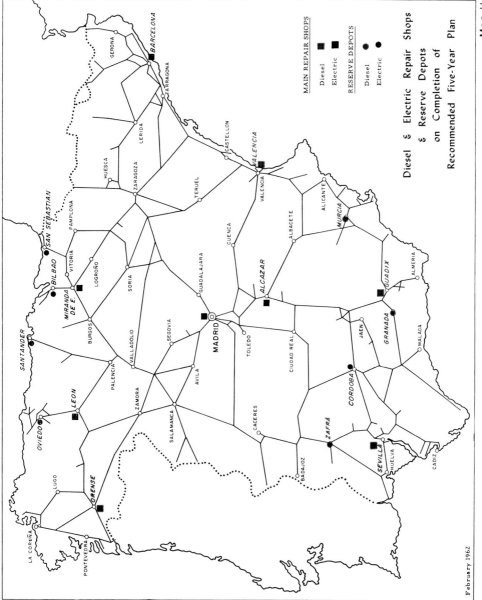

MAIN REPAIR SHOPS

Diesel ■
Electric ■

RESERVE DEPOTS

Diesel ●
Electric ●

Diesel & Electric Repair Shops
& Reserve Depots
on Completion of
Recommended Five-Year Plan

February 1962

Map II

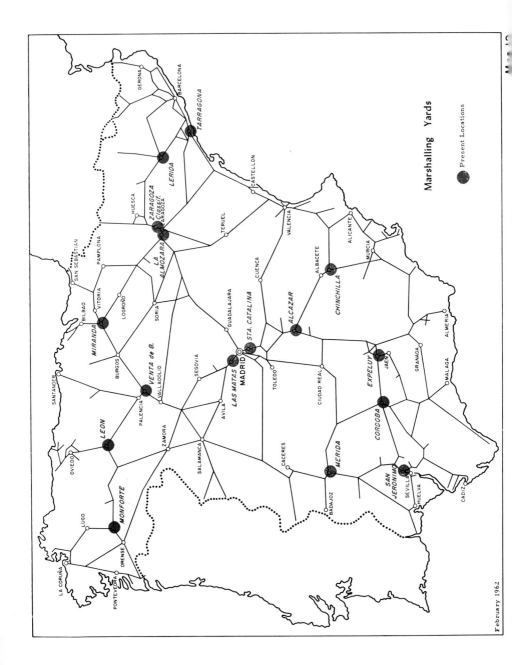

Marshalling Yards

Present Locations ●

GERONA
BARCELONA
TARRAGONA
CASTELLON
LERIDA
HUESCA
ZARAGOZA Classif.
ZARAGOZA
TERUEL
VALENCIA
SAN SEBASTIÁN
PAMPLONA
LA ALMOZARA
ALICANTE
CUENCA
ALBACETE
MURCIA
VITORIA
LOGROÑO
SORIA
GUADALAJARA
STA. CATALINA
CHINCHILLA
BILBAO
MIRANDA
ALMERIA
ALCAZAR
SANTANDER
BURGOS
VENTA de B.
VALLADOLID
SEGOVIA
MADRID
TOLEDO
LAS MATAS
AVILA
CIUDAD REAL
GRANADA
MALAGA
JAEN
EXPELUY
PALENCIA
LEON
ZAMORA
SALAMANCA
CACERES
MERIDA
CORDOBA
OVIEDO
SAN JERONIMO
SEVILLA
HUELVA
CADIZ
LUGO
MONFORTE
BADAJOZ
ORENSE
LA CORUÑA
PONTEVEDRA

February 1962

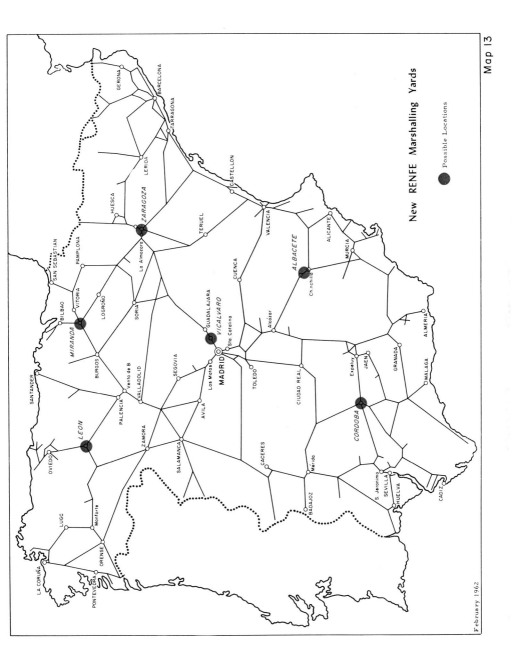

New RENFE Marshalling Yards

● Possible Locations

Map 13

February 1962

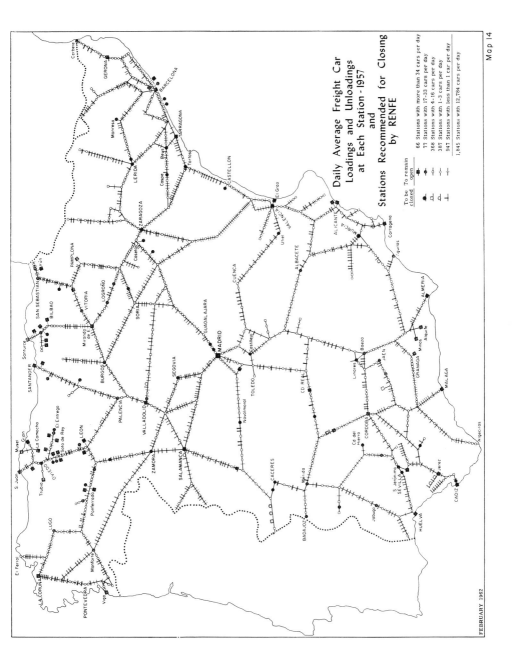

Daily Average Freight Car
Loadings and Unloadings
at Each Station - 1957
and

Stations Recommended for Closing
by RENFE

To be closed	To remain open	
	66	Stations with more than 34 cars per day
	77	Stations with 17-33 cars per day
	368	Stations with 4-16 cars per day
	387	Stations with 1-3 cars per day
	947	Stations with less than 1 car per day
	1,845	Stations with 12,784 cars per day

Map 14

studies with a view to adopting measures that could appreciably reduce costs and improve service thereby helping to arrest the loss of traffic to other forms of transport.

Freight and Passenger Systems. One of these studies should be devoted to the method of shipping freight. The present method, with two separate systems of slow and express freight, is out of date. One possibility which might be considered would be a system employed elsewhere in Europe that has accelerated and conventional shipping using the same service facilities, which is not only less costly for the railroad but more satisfactory for the customers. Terminal operations, including handling of materials and goods, should be studied for speed and efficient use of manpower and capital.

So far as passenger traffic is concerned, consideration should be given to reducing the number of classes from three to two, as has been done throughout the rest of Europe. This would reduce the expense of maintaining the different classes of cars and increase the load factor on the remaining services.

Marshalling Yards. The present marshalling or classification yards, inherited from the former private companies, are too numerous and small; they lack modern equipment and the tracks are too short. Map 12 shows the 16 yards still in service, including 2 at Zaragoza.

Marshalling yards are the key facilities of a rail network, on which the speed and reliability of freight service primarily depend. The creation of a small number of well-equipped yards should result both in substantial savings in operating costs[5] and in a definite improvement in service. Shipping times could be appreciably reduced, and by a faster turn-around freight cars could be used more economically.

Since every marshalling yard requires most trains to stop for some length of time, there should be as few yards as is compatible with adequate classification. Marshalling yards should generally be located at the most important junction points on the system; track length should be adequate to make up the largest trains which system power and track conditions will permit; and there should be a sufficient number of tracks so that work can begin promptly on inbound cars. Pending further study by RENFE, we provisionally recommend that there be six modern marshalling yards, located at Cordoba, Miranda de Ebro, Madrid, Zaragoza, Leon and Albacete or Alcazar de San Juan (shown

[5] The yard at Leon, which at present is probably the only one equipped to handle an adequate volume of traffic, had an average cost per car of 13.6 pts in contrast with an average of 35.5 pts for the nine other yards for which data were available in 1960.

on Map 13). The old yards should be closed as soon as service is available in the new ones. The new yards should be constructed with basic installations that would eventually make it possible to operate with minimum manpower. These yards are a very long term investment, and future manpower costs may be relatively much higher than at present. For the time being, however, the yards can be operated on a labor-intensive basis.

Passenger and Freight Stations. There are too many stations in the RENFE network, and a large proportion of them should be closed. On the other hand, the few passenger and freight stations with heavy traffic should be modernized. Table 10.3 shows the large number of stations with low traffic. Some of these are used only seasonally and should be manned and operated only as needed.

TABLE 10.3: Distribution of Freight Stations by Daily Carloadings, 1957

Daily Rate of Loading and Unloading per Station	Number of Stations	Number of Freight Cars Loaded and Unloaded Daily by Stations in Group
Less than 1 car	947	334
1 to 3 cars	387	944
4 to 16 cars	368	3,662
17 to 33 cars	77	2,320
More than 34 cars	66	5,524
Total	1,845	12,784

SOURCE: RENFE, *La Rentabilidad de las Lineas,* May, 1959.

RENFE has prepared a program[6] (shown in Map 14) for reducing sharply the number of freight stations. In the mission's view, all stations averaging less than four cars per day (more than two-thirds of the stations) should be the subject of immediate study with a view to their closure and consolidation with larger nearby stations. Closing stations with little traffic, reducing the personnel of others and expanding the traffic of central stations will bring about important savings. At the same time, RENFE should study the question of facilitating the terminal exchange of freight between railroad and road transportation through the use of containers, additional spurs and other methods.

In the main cities there are still duplicate railroad facilities which should be merged to increase passenger convenience and reduce costs. In some cases, relocation of facilities as part of an urban development

[6] See *La Rentabilidad de las Lineas.*

plan may be desirable, but should only be undertaken with prior consultation of RENFE, a practice not always followed in the past.

Signaling and Telecommunications. Modernization of signaling, new developments in telephones, teletypes, etc. involve comparatively limited investments but would result in notable improvements in speed and reliability of handling freight and passenger traffic, and in better utilization of cars and engines, etc. Some of this equipment could with advantage be installed in the near future.

Financing Investment Needs

It is evident that a high priority must be accorded to modernizing track, motive power, classification yards and other equipment and facilities that comprise the basic rail network. All of these are important, but track renovation and modernization of classification yards hold the key to reductions in cost and improvements in service, and these have top priority both in time and in allocation of funds.

Over the past six years, gross investment expenditures, exclusive of those for new lines, have moved as follows (million pts):[7]

1955	2,680
1956	2,621
1957	2,288
1958	3,089
1959	2,907
1960	3,273

In addition, somewhat in excess of 700 million pts has probably been spent annually, on the average, for construction of new lines.

RENFE prepared a modernization plan in 1958, which has since been brought up to date (May 1961). It was envisaged that the plan would take 10 to 15 years to complete, depending on the rate of expenditure; a first 5-year installment (referred to as the Plan Quinquenal de Modernizacion or PQM) was prepared on the basis of an annual rate of expenditure for modernization (with no money to be spent on new line construction) of about 5.4 billion pts. While this is an increase over the highest rate of investment in the past (about 4 billion pts), the mission believes that a higher rate of expenditure is both technically and financially feasible. We propose annual expenditures for investment over the period at a rate of 7.1 billion pts. This would make it possible to complete approximately half of RENFE's modernization program over the next five years. The PQM and our recommenda-

---

[7] Based on information supplied by RENFE.

tions for revisions are summarized in Table 10.4, with actual investments during 1955–1960 included for purposes of comparison. As can be seen from Table 10.4, the relative emphasis given to various objectives in the mission's program differs from RENFE's proposed first 5-year installment in that we give greater importance to track renovation and to the dieselization program, with proportionately less funds provided for passenger and freight cars and for electrification.

TABLE 10.4: Railroad Modernization: Original RENFE Plans and Mission Recommended Five-year Plan

A. Values in Million pts

Purpose	Actual Investments 1955–1960ª	RENFE Proposed 5–Year Plan	Mission Recommended 5–Year Plan 1962–1966
Track renovation	3,824	6,545	12,300
Electrification	3,591	4,443	4,480
Diesel locomotives and parts	1,804	4,665	8,480
Diesel-unitized passenger equip.	254	2,250	2,160
Passenger and freight cars	4,311	3,635	1,160
Yards and stations	264	2,430	3,050
Workshops, depots, warehouses	502	1,165	1,770
Wire and telecommunications	18	344	400
Traffic control and signals	601	1,410	1,760
Total	15,169	26,887	35,560

B. Percentage Distribution

Purpose	Actual Investments 1955–1960ª	RENFE Proposed 5–Year Plan	Mission Recommended 5–Year Plan 1962–1966
Track renovation	25.2	24.3	34.6
Electrification	23.7	16.7	12.6
Diesel locomotives and parts	11.9	17.3	23.9
Diesel-unitized passenger equip.	1.7	8.3	6.1
Passenger and freight cars	28.4	13.5	3.3
Yards and stations	1.8	9.0	8.6
Workshops, depots, warehouses	3.3	4.3	4.7
Wire and telecommunications	–	1.3	1.1
Traffic control and signals	4.0	5.2	5.0
Total	100.0	100.0	100.0

ª Excluding investment in new lines, auxiliary investments, financial charges and 436 million pts of unclassified equipment financed by American aid.
SOURCES: 1955–1960 investment data from working papers and other materials supplied by RENFE and the Ministry of Finance; RENFE's 5–year plan from *Plan de Modernizacion.*

The proposed annual phasing of the mission's recommended program is given in Table 10.5. The highest annual rate of expenditure, 8.3 billion pts, is reached in 1964. Although this will be more than three times the average rate of expenditure during the 1955–1960 period for the same investment items, we believe that it can be accomplished. The procurement involved is rather diversified, and contracts will consequently be placed with many different industries. A significant portion of the equipment will probably have to be imported, such as high-powered locomotives or major locomotive components, specialized machine tools for repairs and overhaul shops, telecommunications equipment not produced locally and materials for track renovation, yards and electrification needed in excess of production capacity. Also,

TABLE 10.5: Phasing of Recommended Five-year Program for Railroad Modernization

(million pts)

Purpose	Total	1962	1963	1964	1965	1966
Track Renovation	12,300	1,650	2,000	2,550	2,850	3,250
Electrification	4,480	595	1,145	1,250	990	500
Diesel Locomotives	8,480	980	1,405	1,925	2,070	2,100
Diesel Passenger Units	2,160	300	475	540	490	355
Passenger and Freight Cars	1,160	235	325	100	200	300
Yards and Stations	3,050	500	800	800	700	250
Workshops, Depots	1,770	500	635	460	175	–
Telecommunications	400	75	165	105	55	–
Signals and Traffic Control	1,760	350	360	550	350	150
Total	35,560	5,185	7,310	8,280	7,880	6,905

the track renovation program can be accelerated by utilizing additional personnel and materials formerly used for new line construction; beyond this, more manpower is readily available if it should be required.

The broad purposes of the investment plan with respect to each element (track, motive power, yards, etc.) have already been described. More detailed recommendations with respect to each element, together with the proposed phasing of investments in it over the next five years, are given in Annex C, but a few additional remarks on priorities follow.

Track renovation will receive about one-third of the proposed investment expenditures. The priority attached to this program is due to several factors: the serious condition of large parts of the network; the need to complete track renovation before modern motive power is introduced, particularly where lines are to be electrified; and the need to renovate the main lines before work is done on secondary ones. The program illustrated in Map 8 will make it possible to complete the renovation with 54 kg rails of all segments of the main network, and to renovate with 45 kg rails designated portions of the secondary network.

Dieselization is second in importance in terms of the volume of investment. The change from steam to diesel power is a complex undertaking, requiring retraining of train crews and maintenance personnel, major changes in maintenance procedures and equipment and changes in the type and quantities of fuels and supplies at depots. The magnitude of these tasks will limit the speed at which dieselization can be carried out. The diesel passenger train program, although important, is planned at a moderate rate so that it may be geared into the program for reducing low density passenger services and concentrating traffic on some of the remaining lines in a smaller number of trains.

Although electrification will absorb a substantial amount of funds, the program is designed only to complete the network of lines on which electrification has been started. The additional electrification proposed will require additional locomotives. A number of electric rail car trains would be useful on lines already electrified, especially in Catalonia.

With the proposed amount and phasing of expenditures, it should be possible to complete the planned system of new classification yards by the end of the fourth year. Apart from central freight stations, it is recommended that expenditures for new stations be deferred until the closing and consolidation of low volume stations has been completely planned. Since it is important that RENFE have the industrial capability to do its own maintenance work efficiently, the full RENFE program for workshop and depot improvements is recommended for completion during the five-year period.

Administrative Organization

The vital need for change in the present organization and system of control of the national railways is discussed at length in the Armand report. Briefly stated, the administrative problems facing the railways are threefold:

a. a multiplicity of administrative bodies within RENFE itself, leading to a division of responsibility and to a paralysis of the controlling authority;

b. constant interference by the State in the detailed administration of the railway system. In practice, control of the network has passed from the RENFE management into the hands of the Ministry of Public Works;

c. removal of certain key decisions from RENFE responsibility. Probably the most important example is the construction of new lines; this is the responsibility of a department of the Ministry of Public Works.

The administrative solution proposed by Mr. Armand also contains three elements:

a. reorganizing the RENFE management into two bodies, a Board of Directors responsible to the Government for the administration of the railways and a General Manager responsible for carrying out the Board's policy;

b. granting the reorganized Board and general management full responsibility for operating the national system and for the railway investment program; and

c. reorganizing State supervision through the appointment of two non-voting government supervisors to the Board of RENFE and a reduction in the duties of the Railway Inspection Department of the Ministry of Public Works (without changing its basic function).

The mission wishes to stress the importance it attaches to prompt action on these recommendations, which we strongly endorse. No lasting improvements can be achieved in the technical and financial fields unless and until the administrative situation is reformed on the lines suggested.

Personnel

Number of Personnel. One of the problems facing RENFE is the disposal of staff which have become surplus to its requirements as a result of modernization and rationalization. Although the numbers employed were reduced by 11,200 between 1953 and 1960, it has been estimated that, with some 125,000 employees, there are at least 3,000 personnel (and perhaps substantially more) in excess of present staffing requirements.

Unless remedial action is taken, this problem, which exists in many other countries, will become more acute as modernization proceeds. In an excellent staff study, *Plan de Reduccion de Plantillas,* RENFE has estimated that its proposed Five-Year Modernization Plan, together with certain additional investment, could reduce the labor force by over 15,000 men while handling a traffic increase of 12 percent to 15 percent above the 1958 level. The mission's investment recommendations will provide some additional employment for RENFE personnel, but there will still be a substantial number of persons who can no longer be productively employed. This problem bears on matters of general labor and employment policy discussed elsewhere in this report. To the extent that measures may be required which go beyond the standard regulations for reducing the number of personnel, the Government should give them serious consideration, bearing in mind the importance of modernizing the railway system and reducing operating costs.

RENFE also made proposals to the Ministry of Labor in December 1960, to obtain greater flexibility in the regulation of labor and more freedom in exercising control over its personnel. We would welcome any improvement of the kind which is conducive to a more efficient administration, particularly so far as mobility is concerned; this will become more important in the future, since RENFE should be able to transfer staff as necessary when technological changes are introduced and reorganization gets under way. We have already noted some areas in which additional personnel will be needed, and others where the present staff will become redundant. If RENFE is to operate efficiently, considerable flexibility in its personnel management will be required.

One consequence of the internal reorganization we have proposed is that the General Manager will have the responsibility for building up a competent managerial staff and for deciding upon the policy for recruitment at all levels. Recruitment policy will, of course, be influenced by the problem of redundant manpower, to which we have referred, but in any case it will be an important factor in creating an efficient modern railway system. We therefore believe that the general management should have complete discretion in laying down the standards it deems appropriate for selecting and training staff; this would include whatever action may be considered necessary with respect to the present arrangement whereby, in practice, training and recruitment of new personnel depend to a large extent upon the military services.

The Armand report points out that retaining officials on the active list after they have passed the normal age of retirement and filling higher posts from the outside prevent the promotion of able people within the organization and their training for higher posts. In such circumstances, it is difficult to recruit and maintain an efficient staff, and we believe that the general management should not be handicapped in this way. The problem is due mainly to low retirement pensions, as explained in Chapter 3.

Financial Policy and Results

The Deficit. RENFE's operations have resulted annually in a deficit which, when all the relevant charges are included, has amounted to about 3.5 billion pts in each of the years 1957–1960. As can be seen from Table 10.6, the operating deficit in 1959 and 1960 was substantially lower than in the 1956–1958 period, particularly if allowance is made for increases in prices in the interim.

To the operating deficit (1.4 billion pts in 1960) must be added interest on the outstanding debt used to finance the railway modernization program (about 0.9 billion pts in 1960). Although a 1947 law sought to establish a depreciation and renewals fund, no provision has been made for the depreciation of equipment or fixed installations in

TABLE 10.6: RENFE Financial Results, 1952–1960

(million pts)

	1952	1953	1954	1955	1956	1957	1958	1959	1960
Revenues	4,989	5,001	5,415	5,693	6,175	7,955	9,075	9,589	9,799
Expenses	5,352	5,395	6,297	6,720	7,588	9,863	10,839	11,008	11,217
Operating Deficit	363	394	882	1,027	1,413	1,908	1,764	1,419	1,418
Financial Charges[a]	n.a.	n.a.	416	519	608	670	691	789	875
Deficit before Depreciation	n.a.	n.a.	1,298	1,546	2,021	2,578	2,455	2,208	2,293
Depreciation	539	611	699	815	923	1,005	1,130	1,236	1,358
Deficit after Depreciation	n.a.	n.a.	1,997	2,361	2,944	3,583	3,585	3,444	3,651

[a] Does not include amortization.

SOURCE: Derived from Annual *Memorias de Consejo de Administracion* of RENFE.

the RENFE accounts; this ought to be done if the full cost of the railway to the economy is to be ascertained, since its assets deteriorate and will eventually have to be replaced. Table 10.6 includes RENFE's estimate of depreciation during the years 1952–1960; in the last year, the figure was 1.4 billion pts.

RENFE's financing requirements on current and capital account theoretically include the current deficit before depreciation, fixed capital expenditure, working capital (increase in stocks) and amortization of debt. Capital expenditures are covered by *ad hoc* appropriations from the state budget, by U.S. counterpart funds and, to a lesser extent, by direct loans from U.S. lending organizations and autonomous organizations in Spain. Since RENFE is already in a deficit on its operating account, interest and amortization of RENFE bonds are supposed to be paid by the State (which guarantees the bonds) and the remaining shortfall made good by a subvention from the state budget.

In practice, the position is more complicated, since the State does not, in fact, and has not for many years, paid for the carriage of mail and other goods. The deficiency in 1960 amounted to 650 million pts, which RENFE shows as earned (but not collected) revenue. This necessarily increases the financing requirements of RENFE, which in turn has retained transport and other taxes collected on behalf of the State. The cumulative amounts are very large.

If it is hoped to put the operations of RENFE on a normal commercial basis, the State should pay for the services which RENFE renders it. Although this will not reduce the current deficit, which is now calculated on the assumption that these charges are paid for, it will make it unnecessary for RENFE to resort to the kind of device already referred to. Furthermore, the State owes it to itself to show in the budget of the mail service and other departments of the Government the full cost of the goods or services they buy.

Rates and Social Subsidies. A substantial part of the operating deficit can be attributed to the fact that RENFE is obliged to give reduced rates to other government agencies and a large number of consumers. If, on grounds of social policy, the Government wishes to maintain preferential passenger rates, we suggest that the cost should be borne by the Ministry of Finance on behalf of the Government rather than by the railways. Accordingly, RENFE should be compensated on a contractual basis for the reduced fares that it is required to provide, and the accounts of RENFE should reflect this transaction. The importance of this item is indicated by RENFE's estimate that in 1960 more than 400 million pts of revenue were lost through reduced passenger rates alone.

Other changes in RENFE's rate policy would help to improve its financial position. In general, the present rate structure is based on the value of the goods transported, with various exceptions to provide subsidies to certain goods or regions. This policy has been one of the factors contributing to the loss of high-value goods to competing forms of transportation carrying them at lower rates. As stated in the preceding chapter, rate policy of all of the modes of transport should be based uniformly on the long-run costs of providing service so that each will be able to attract the traffic for which it has an advantage in terms of cost and quality of service. In the case of RENFE, this policy will require that a system of differentiated rates be established to reflect differences in the long-run costs of providing service. To the extent that subsidies are considered necessary for specific products or to aid regional development, they should be provided in some form other than reduced rail transport rates which lead to uneconomical uses of transport. Moreover, the timing of rate adjustments should be coordinated with the other transport modes; this did not take place at the time of the 1959 railroad tariff increases with the result that goods and passenger traffic were lost by the railways to trucking and air transportation.

The investment program and administrative reorganization that we have recommended should make it possible both to reduce costs, and thereby rates, and to improve service materially. Under these conditions, the railways should be in a position to regain the traffic that should be expected to move by rail and that has been lost unnecessarily to other forms of transportation.

Objectives of Financial Policy. The Armand report indicates certain objectives of government policy with respect to the financing of RENFE's operations. Over a period of years, and on the assumption that costs will be reduced through the modernization program, RENFE should be able to eliminate deficits and balance its operating accounts, after providing for an adequate reserve for renewals. But this presupposes that RENFE will have full power to act on its own in the commercial field, to concentrate its operations on the main routes and to control its own tariffs. If, on grounds of the general interest, the Government opposes RENFE's decisions, it should then assume responsibility for the financial consequences of that opposition. Annual loans would be provided to finance capital improvements and new works which would be part of the general investment program for a period of years, prepared by RENFE and approved by the Government.

There will remain an interim period during which a subsidy from the State will still be required. The size of the cash deficit would be reduced, and the railway management encouraged in its efforts to achieve equilibrium, if RENFE were no longer required to pay financial charges on past investments which, as in the case of many other railway systems, bear little relationship to the present value of the system which RENFE operates.

The foregoing recommendations and those contained in Mr. Armand's report have been designed to arrest the deterioration in the affairs of the national railways and to enable them to play their part in the economic development of the country, an objective fully shared by the Spanish Government. We believe that if adequate funds are provided for modernization of equipment and renovation of track, and if a reconstituted RENFE is in control of its own domain, the numerous possibilities for reducing operating costs, improving service and increasing revenue could bring about a marked improvement in RENFE's financial position.

ANNEX C _MISSION'S RECOMMENDED PROGRAM FOR RAIL MODERNIZATION_

Track Renovation (Table C.1)

The segments selected for improvement with 54 kg rail, welded joints, parabolized curves and concrete ties constitute the heavy traffic main lines of Spain and should be completed at the earliest possible time. Only those segments of 45 kg rail improvement listed in the footnote in Table C.1 are clearly of first importance. Any additional 45 kg track renovation beyond these specified lines should be planned near the end of the five-year period when the amount of train service discontinuances and the future transport and traffic patterns have become clearer. Many of the secondary lines are in very serious condition but full renovation should await complete analysis of need. Sufficient funds have been included for the necessary major maintenance and improvement of tunnels and of older bridges. All track renovation on lines to be electrified should be completed before installation of new fixtures.

Electrification (Table C.2)

The recommended program is intended to fill out the network of present lines where electrification has been started. It will complete the lines Madrid-Cordoba, Madrid-Medina del Campo via both Avila and Segovia, Medina del Campo to Monforte, Aviles-Gijon-Musel, Santander, Bilbao and Irun and the worthwhile electrifications in Catalonia. No other lines will have sufficient traffic to support electrification in the foreseeable future. The recommended program further includes the amounts proposed for expenditure on present electrified lines in the PQM.

Diesel Locomotives (Table C.3)

We estimate that the replacement of steam power on the lines will require between 800 and 900 diesel locomotives of 1200 h.p. or larger. Five hundred are in the present RENFE Modernization Plan and we have scheduled 295 for the next five years. If additional funds are available and the maintenance, personnel and supply capabilities for addi-

199

tional locomotives exist, the proposed number could be increased. We have no estimate of the total number of diesel-switching locomotives necessary; 420 are included in the Modernization Plan and we have scheduled 310 during the next five years.

It appears reasonable to plan on manufacturing the switching locomotives in Spain, and funds have been programmed to provide a steady rate of production. In the case of the larger locomotives, it may be desirable to purchase these in Europe or the United States. However, it is possible that Spanish industry might manufacture a substantial part of

TABLE C.1: Railway Modernization Program: Track Renovation

(million pts)

Purpose	Present Revision of 1958 Plan (May 1961)	RENFE Proposed 5–Year Plan	Mission 5–Year Plan	Phasing of Mission's 5–Year Plan				
				1962	1963	1964	1965	1966
Protection against snow, flood, and rebuilding bridges and tunnels	956	250	900	35	50	165	275	375
Overpasses-underpasses	250	150	250	–	50	50	75	75
Quarry mechanization	65	65	65	65	–	–	–	–
Maintenance of way equipment	185	80	185	50	100	35	–	–
Track renovation: Mainline, 54 kg rails, concrete ties	22,709 11,854	6,000 4,500	10,900 10,000[a]	1,500 1,500	1,800 1,800	2,300 2,100	2,500 2,200	2,800 2,400
Principal secondary lines, 45 kg rails, improved curves	7,448	1,500	900[a]	–	–	200	300	400
Other secondary lines, used 45 kg rails	3,407	–	–	–	–	–	–	–
Total	24,165	6,545	12,300	1,650	2,000	2,550	2,850	3,250

[a] This program is intended to include essentially all 54 kg rail improvements, but only those 45 kg improvements on lines of important traffic, i.e.,

Barcelona–Empalme (Granollers)	Linares–Almeria
Cordoba–Malaga	Verina–Abono
La Encina–Alicante	Villalba–Segovia
Palencia–Santander	Zaragoza–Barcelona (via Lerida)
Medina–Zamora	

the less complex components and import the diesel engines and those foreign electrical components which are of high quality and low price compared to the local alternatives. It would also be possible to phase such a program so that foreign purchase of complete units is relied upon exclusively in the first year or two followed by a gradual increase in the number of locally assembled units. However, local production should not interfere with the speed of execution of this program. Rather, local production should be phased into the proposed rates of procurement as its capability increases. By the end of the fifth year,

TABLE C.2: Railway Modernization Program: Electrification

(million pts)

Purpose	Present Revision of 1958 Plan (May 1961)	RENFE Pro- posed 5–Year Plan	Mis- sion 5–Year Plan	Phasing of Mission's 5–Year Plan				
				1962	1963	1964	1965	1966
For New Lines:								
Fixed installations and substations	2,553[a]	1,283	1,300[b]	200	300	500	300	–
Locomotives	3,332	1,480	1,500[b]	–	250	250	500	500
Passenger units	1,418	630	630[b]	100	200	200	130	–
Subtotal	7,303	3,393	3,430	300	1,000	1,200	930	500
For Present Lines:								
Additional passenger units	861	861	860	200	300	300	60	–
Overhaul–present equipment	200	50	50	–	–	–	–	–
Improvement and ex- pansion of existing installations	170	–	–	95	95	–	–	–
Work shops–electric equipment	164	80	50	–	–	–	–	–
Equipment for main- taining catenaries	90	60	90	–	–	–	–	–
Total	8,788	4,444	4,480	595	1,145	1,250	990	500

[a] Refer to Map 9. The modernization plan includes completion of the electrified routes shown on this map and in addition electrification of Madrid-Barcelona, Barcelona-Valencia, Zaragoza-Alsasua and Mirando de Ebro, and additional lines in Catalonia. None of these additional lines is included in the mission's recommended program.

[b] Includes only lines necessary to complete electrification shown on Map 9.

TABLE C.3: Railway Modernization Program: Diesel Locomotives and Parts

Purpose	Present Revision of 1958 Plan (May 1961)		RENFE Proposed 5-Year Plan	Mission 5-Year Plan		Phasing of Mission's 5-Year Plan (million pts)				
	No. of Units	Million pts	Million pts	No. of Units	Million pts	1962	1963	1964	1965	1966
High-powered locomotives (1,800–2,000 h.p.)	500	3,571	1,000	85	2,125	250	375	500	500	500
Medium-powered locomotives (1,200 h.p.)		6,429	1,800	210	3,780	450	630	900	900	900
Switching locomotives (130 h.p.)	82	205	205	60	150	30	30	30	30	30
Switching locomotives (350 h.p.)	273	2,184	1,200	250	1,650	160	240	320	450	480
Road and switching locomotives (700 h.p.)	65	780	—	—	—	—	—	—	—	—
Repair parts (10% of locomotive cost)	—	1,510	460	—	771	89	128	175	188	191
Total	920	14,679	4,665	605	8,476	979	1,403	1,925	2,068	2,101

the proposed program will have produced a high level of procurement and a corresponding level of industrial and managerial ability to effect the change-over from steam to diesel power. These abilities should be the basis for the next investment plan which should carry on at the fifth-year level or higher until dieselization is completed. Eventually, RENFE should use no steam locomotives.

It should be noted that, although the 700 h.p. road-switching loco-motives are not included in our suggested plan, they may be substituted for others if a careful economic and operating analysis justifies their use on the Spanish system.

Diesel Passenger Train Units (Table C.4)

While equal in importance to diesel locomotives in railroad econ-omy, the diesel passenger train program is planned at a moderate rate in order that it may be fitted into the program for reducing low den-sity passenger services and concentrating the traffic on some of the re-maining lines in a smaller number of trains. This timing will provide for maximum, and therefore most profitable, utilization of this mod-ern equipment.

If more funds are available during this period they may well be spent on TAFs. The TALGO program has been limited to the train sets necessary to give daily service on lines from Madrid to three cities: Irun, Barcelona and Sevilla. No other TALGO service should be con-sidered until more experience has been obtained and the above lines have been made to pay their way. TALGO load factors at present are definitely below the break-even point, partly due to the random service —three trains a week each from Madrid to Irun and Barcelona. Exper-iments of various combinations of charges and services should be made in order to find the profitable pattern of operation. The TALGO seat-mile cost may be low for the quality of service rendered, but if a suffi-cient number of seats cannot be filled to ensure profitability, no more trains should be purchased.

The same principles of local manufacture of the less specialized equipment and components and import of the more complex, stated for diesel locomotives, apply here also.

Passenger and Freight Cars (Table C.5)

The recommended program provides only for modernizing and re-building present cars during the first three years. At present there is a surplus of freight cars. The oldest and most worn equipment should be

TABLE C.4: Railway Modernization Program: Diesel-Unitized Passenger Equipment

| Purpose | Present Revision of 1958 Plan (May 1961) | | RENFE Proposed 5-Year Plan | Mission 5-Year Plan | | Phasing of Mission's 5-Year Plan (million pts) | | | | |
	No. of Units	Million pts	Million pts	No. of Units	Million pts	1962	1963	1964	1965	1966
Railcars–TAF	60	1,800	900	32	960	120	180	180	240	240
Light trains–ferrobus	105	893	637	50	425	85	85	85	85	85
TALGO train units	20	500	250	8	200	–	100	100	–	–
TALGO locomotives	27	675	300	10	250	–	–	125	125	–
Modernization of present equipment	–	210	–	–	150	75	75	–	–	–
Repair parts	–	274	163	–	180[a]	20	37	49	42	32
Total	212	4,352	2,250	100	2,165	300	477	539	492	357

[a] Spare parts estimated at 10% of procurement.

scrapped immediately, steps undertaken (aided by other parts of this program) to improve freight car utilization and new cars added only as need develops. If freight traffic increases rapidly enough, new freight cars may be purchased during this period with the funds suggested for the last two years. The same general policy should prevail in regard to passenger cars. During the period of adjustment of the rail passenger service to a self-sufficient basis, the oldest, wooden cars should be retired. When the future passenger service requirements are clearly seen, including the extent to which they should be met with electric and diesel passenger train units rather than locomotive-drawn trains, the

TABLE C.5: Railway Modernization Program: Passenger and Freight Cars

(million pts)

Purpose	Present Revision of 1958 Plan (May 1961)	RENFE Pro- posed 5–Year Plan	Mis- sion 5–Year Plan	Phasing of Mission's 5–Year Plan				
				1962	1963	1964	1965	1966
Steel passenger cars (double axle trucks)	1,750	1,050	150	–	–	–	–	150
Baggage, mail and express cars	250	125	250	50	100	100	–	–
Tank cars	75	75	75	35	40	–	–	–
Freight cars and containers	5,000	1,950	350	–	–	–	200	150
Parts and assemblies for modernizing	335	335	335	150	185	–	–	–
Total	7,410	3,535	1,160	235	325	100	200	300

remaining wooden cars and the bad metal cars should be replaced. This will almost certainly be beyond the end of this five-year period. The planned tank cars and box cars (*furgones*) should be procured immediately.

Yards and Stations (Table C.6)

The planned classification yard system should be essentially completed by the end of the fourth year. The Alcazar, or Albacete, yard should be programmed last in order to provide time for the necessary location studies. Leon is to be brought up to modern standards and the older yards, all inadequate, are to be dismantled except where a *bona fide* local need exists. The central freight stations and their related tracks and handling equipment should be completed promptly and at the level originally assigned in the 1958 Modernization Plan. The improvement of RENFE's door-to-door truck-rail-truck service should be expedited. Other proposed station improvements (expan-

TABLE C.6: Railway Modernization Program: Yards and Stations

(million pts)

Purpose	Present Revision of 1958 Plan (May 1961)	RENFE Proposed 5-Year Plan	Mission 5-Year Plan	Phasing of Mission's 5-Year Plan				
				1962	1963	1964	1965	1966
Expansion of station facilities (longer, heavier trains)	900	400						
Modernization of buildings	400	150						
Central freight stations (for truck distribution and pickup)	230	100	350[b]	50	100	150	50	–
Station equipment-handling	175	50						
Electrical and inter-locking equipment	480	230						
Classification yards	2,500[a]	1,500	2,700[c]	450	700	650	650	250
Total	4,685	2,430	3,050	500	800	800	700	250

[a] See Map 13 showing classification yards approved.
[b] Relates to an original amount in 1958 program sacrificed in subsequent reprograming.
[c] Includes improvement of existing yards at Leon.

sion of facilities and modernization of buildings), while desirable, are not of sufficient priority to be included in the five-year program. The closing and consolidating of low volume stations should be completely planned before making further investment.

Workshops, Depots and Warehouses (Table C.7)

These investments are designed to give RENFE the industrial capability to do its own maintenance in a prompt and efficient manner. The full program for workshop and locomotive depot improvements proposed by RENFE is programed for completion in the first four years.

Emphasis should be placed upon machine tools and equipment to do the maintenance work properly, even at the expense of some quality and decoration in the buildings.

TABLE C.7: Railway Modernization Program: Workshops, Depots, Warehouses

(million pts)

Purpose	Present Revision of 1958 Plan (May 1961)	RENFE Proposed 5–Year Plan	Mission 5–Year Plan	Phasing of Mission's 5–Year Plan				
				1962	1963	1964	1965	1966
New diesel shops (Valencia, Guadix, Salamanca and Zaragoza)	220	120	160[a]					
Expansion of shops (Madrid, Sevilla)	120	100	120					
Reserve depots and parts warehouses	60	60	60	100	200	110	90	–
Machinery and equipment for above three items	185	100	160					
Central diesel motor over-haul shop (Madrid)	300	100	300	50	100	150	–	–
Improvement and modernization of freight and passenger car repair shops	335	200	335	200	135	–	–	–
Machinery and equipment for previous item	635	485	635	150	200	200	85	–
Total	1,855	1,165	1,770	500	635	460	175	–

[a] Excludes Salamanca, an area not scheduled for diesel service.

Telecommunications (Table C.8)

This program should provide the equipment necessary for facilitating dispatch and traffic control in order to quicken the pace of train operations and improve the reliability of freight service.

Signals and Traffic Control (Table C.9)

The most important aspect of this investment is a careful study of the desirability of Central Traffic Control equipment for Spain. Equally

TABLE C.8: Railway Modernization Program: Telecommunications

(million pts)

Purpose	Present Revision of 1958 Plan (May 1961)	RENFE Proposed 5–Year Plan	Mission 5–Year Plan	Phasing of Mission's 5–Year Plan				
				1962	1963	1964	1965	1966
Repair and improvement of lines	506	250	279	75	75	75	54	–
Teletypes	38	38	38	–	38	–	–	–
VHF radio	26	26	26	–	26	–	–	–
Other	57	30	57	–	25	32	–	–
Total	627	344	400	75	164	107	54	–

quick and safe train operations can often be provided with block systems making more extensive use of manpower rather than relatively expensive electrical installations. For this reason CTC has been programed at the level proposed in the PQM installment, while for automatic and manual block signals and remote controls the full modernization program is scheduled to be completed in the five-year period. Further study of the comparative costs and advantages of these two types of train control, as applied to the RENFE, should be made at the earliest possible time.

TABLE C.9: Railway Modernization Program: Traffic Control and Signals

(million pts)

Purpose	Present Revision of 1958 Plan (May 1961)	RENFE Proposed 5–Year Plan	Mission 5–Year Plan	Phasing of Mission's 5–Year Plan				
				1962	1963	1964	1965	1966
Lighted signals	317	200	260	150	110	–	–	–
Central Traffic Control	850	500	500	–	50	150	150	150
Automatic block signals	280	160	280					
Manual block signals	360	250	360					
Remote control of signals and switches	160	100	160	200	200	400	200	–
Other related expenses	346	200	200					
Total	2,313	1,410	1,760	350	360	550	350	150

CHAPTER 11 *ROADS*

The Order of Priority

Road development has had a long history in Spain dating back to Roman times. Despite an often difficult terrain, over the years a comprehensive network of roads has been built throughout the country. There are now more than 130,000 kms of highways of which some 80,000 kms are administered by the central government. The latter are divided into three categories—*carreteras nacionales, comarcales* (regional) and *locales*—and the State exercises its responsibility for their planning, construction and maintenance through a national system of provincial *Jefaturas*, each of which reports to the central office in Madrid. The remaining 50,000 kms of roads are administered by the provinces themselves and are divided into two categories: *carreteras provinciales* and *caminos vecinales* (local roads and lanes). The road network is sufficiently dense (see Map 15) that all points in Spain are less than 20 kms from a nationally administered highway and are, of course, even closer to a provincial road. Thus it may be said that any substantial further extensions to the network as such are not required, although there may be some additions in particular locations.[1]

While the need for work on entirely new roads is minimal, there is an enormous amount of work to be done on repairs, on ordinary maintenance and on construction and reconstruction along existing routes.[2] It is difficult to generalize on the present condition of Spanish

---

[1] A partial exception is the proposed *autopista* to be built on a new right of way along the east coast, which we discuss below.

[2] The semantic distinction between "construction" and "reconstruction" is difficult to discern and for programmatic purposes the two terms can be used interchangeably. The combined term would cover work done to upgrade the standards of an existing route, work which would include, among other activities, the extensive improvement of the road foundations and bases, increasing the width of the paved surface, improving sight lines and permissible speeds by new fills and cuts and by changing curvatures and by building entirely new, but short, stretches of roads to bypass concentrated areas and other obstacles to safe and free flow of traffic. It will also be seen that the distinction between "reconstruction" and "repairs" might also be difficult, especially when the latter is "heavy." However, the object of repairs is limited to restoring a road to its original standards and not to upgrading it. "Ordinary maintenance" consists of the continuing task of keeping a road in the condition to meet the standards for which it is designed. If ordinary maintenance is conscientiously applied, and the volume and type of traffic on it does not go beyond that for which it is designed, then repairs would never be necessary, except in specific instances where the roads were subjected to other unforeseen factors such as subsidence, avalanches, etc.

roads. However, the key to their condition may be found in the fact that most of them have been built essentially to the same standard—that roughly of the 1920's. Even on roads constructed in the 1940's and 1950's, higher standards have only been introduced on some stretches in recent years. However, the volume of traffic has been increasing rapidly over the years; as was shown in Table 9.1, intercity freight traffic increased more than threefold between 1951 and 1960, while passenger traffic more than doubled. Even more important, the growth in the volume of traffic has been distributed very unevenly over the highway system. As can be seen from Map 16 and Table 11.1, most of the state-controlled highways are still lightly traveled; more than three-fourths had an average daily traffic of less than 500 vehicles, and ac-

TABLE 11.1: Traffic Density of State Highway System in 1960

Average Daily Traffic (Vehicles per day)	Length of Highways ('000 kilo-meters)	% of Total Length of Highways	Vehicle Kilometers per Year (millions)	% of Total Traffic
0–100	44.1ᵃ	54.8	806	7.7
100–250	13.1	16.3	835	7.9
250–500	9.5	11.8	1,299	12.4
500–1,000	7.1	8.8	1,943	18.4
1,000–2,000	4.8	6.0	2,625	25.0
2,000–5,000	1.6	2.0	2,043	19.4
5,000–10,000	0.2	0.2	587	5.6
More than 10,000	0.1	0.1	374	3.6
	80.5	100.0	10,512	100.0

ᵃ Including 25,370 kms of unclassified secondary highways which, by and large, have very little traffic (average daily traffic of about 40 vehicles).

SOURCE: Prepared for the mission by Direccion General de Carreteras y Caminos Vecinales.

counted for only about 30 percent of the total traffic. Conversely, more than half of the traffic was carried by some 6,700 kms of highway (less than 10 percent of the highway system) with an average daily traffic in excess of 1,000 vehicles.

The key roads in the network are therefore not designed to a standard high enough for the traffic which they are now carrying. Moreover, the main roads have been subject to the heaviest deterioration as a result of the failure of regular maintenance work to keep pace with the growth of traffic; expressed in constant pesetas, annual expenditures on road maintenance have not increased since 1949.[3] Thus, the present

[3] *El Problema de la Carretera,* p. 3.3.2.

Major National Highways

NATIONAL HIGHWAYS

COMARCALES (nationally-financed provincial roads)

LOCALES (nationally-financed local roads) are not shown

Map 15

APRIL 1962

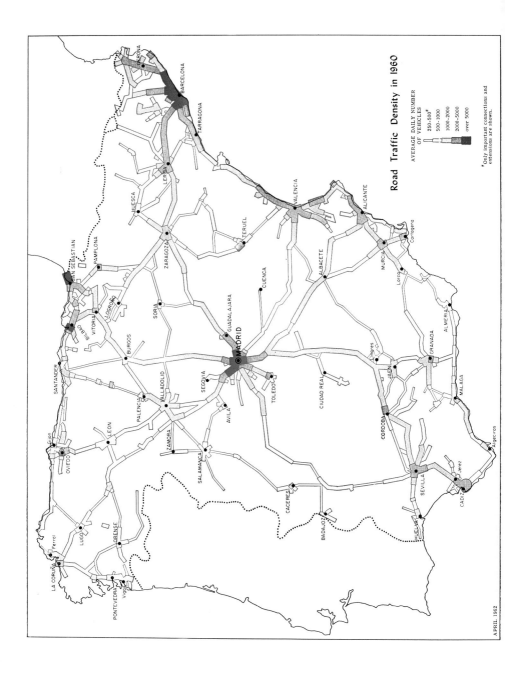

Road Traffic Density in 1960

AVERAGE DAILY NUMBER
OF VEHICLES*

250-500*
500-1000
1000-2000
2000-5000
over 5000

*Only important connections and extensions are shown.

APRIL 1962

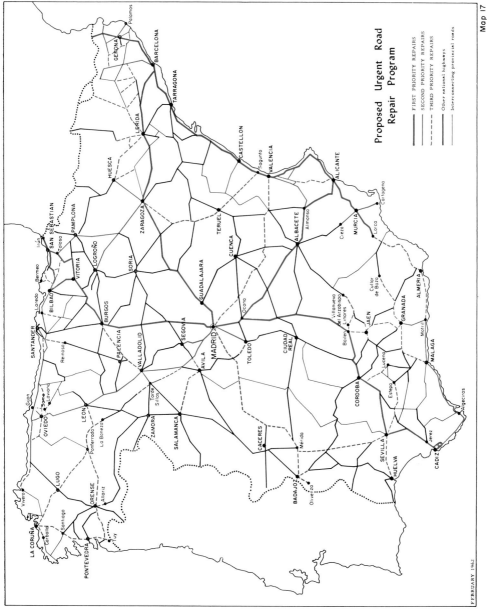

Proposed Urgent Road
Repair Program

FIRST PRIORITY REPAIRS
SECOND PRIORITY REPAIRS
THIRD PRIORITY REPAIRS
Other national highways
Interconnecting provincial roads

Map 17

FEBRUARY 1962

condition of the road network may be characterized as paradoxical: the roads which should be in the best condition—those most heavily traveled—are actually in the worst condition, except in cases where special repair programs have been carried out in the last few years. And, because total traffic volume and its concentration on certain parts of the road network will continue to increase in the future, vigorous action must be taken without delay or the situation will get out of hand.

The mission therefore recommends that top priority be given to a special program of urgent repairs to the most heavily traveled roads. Such a program can brook no delay if heavy economic losses are to be avoided. Within the program, an order of precedence should be established, based on the state of disrepair of the roads and the density of traffic over them.

At the same time, a reorganization and improvement of ordinary maintenance should be envisaged. But, since the urgent repair program should be accorded first priority and since, as explained below, it will take some time to put ordinary maintenance on a sound footing, the increase in the scale of the maintenance program should take place gradually, with the maximum effort being reached only at the end of the five-year period ahead.

Finally, there are important segments of the existing road network, as we have indicated, where the volume of traffic would justify an upgrading of the design standards; furthermore, with the prospect of a continuing rise in traffic volumes, an ever-increasing part of the network will come to qualify for such upgrading through extensive reconstruction. Although there is a good deal of room for expansion in the highway industry, and we suggest below an increasing use of foreign contractors as an interim measure, there are obviously limits, administrative as well as physical, to the speed at which total capacity for work on roads can increase. In view of this, we suggest that the amount of resources to be devoted each year to reconstruction be determined as a residual, with resources allocated first to fulfillment of the urgent repair program and as much of the ordinary maintenance program as is practicable. This implies some initial decline in reconstruction expenditures as compared with recent levels followed by the building up of a massive reconstruction (or construction) program toward the end of the five-year period and the continuance of that program at a high level in subsequent years. Although this policy is dictated primarily by our estimate of prospective technical and administrative capacity, it has the advantage of allowing for the proper advance collection of data and careful planning which construction activity requires, and enables experience to be gained during the urgent repair program which will be invaluable once the construction program reaches massive proportions.

The Urgent Repair Program

Insufficient maintenance and increasing traffic volume on roads of design standards now inadequate for that volume have brought about a situation of near emergency on the heavily traveled sections of the Spanish highway network. A large amount of heavy repair work must be done very quickly to prevent the disintegration of pavements which would result in heavy expense and loss of time to the traffic. The type of work to be done under this program is difficult to define in the traditional terms used in highway work but will vary from large-scale patching to rebuilding. However, no upgrading should be made through the urgent repair program, the purpose of which is to restore the existing right-of-way to its proper condition as rapidly as possible.

The priority in which the urgent repair program is applied to the road network should be based, as we have suggested, on a combination of traffic density and the actual condition of the road. Map 16 indicates the top three groups of highway segments in terms of traffic priority, namely, those roads with an average daily traffic (ADT) of more than 1,000 vehicles, while Map 17 indicates all of the routes to be covered (in whole or in part) under the urgent repair program. With regard to actual road conditions, several sections of the indicated routes, such as from Aranda de Duero to Somosierra on the Madrid-Burgos road, are of the newest construction and would require no attention under this program. The present highway inventory should be used to provide accurate reports on existing conditions along all the indicated roads in order that sites for urgent repairs may be selected.

There are, according to recent estimates, 6,700 kms of roads with an ADT of 1,000 vehicles or more. We estimate that 1,000 kms of these roads are in good condition and do not need to be included in the program. On the other hand, we estimate that some 1,500 kms of roads, which presently have ADT's of less than 1,000, will surpass that point during the next three years and should receive repair work under the program. Thus, there would be some 7,000 kms of roads scheduled for the program.

Because of its urgent nature, the program should not only be started without delay but should also be completed as quickly as possible. We suggest as a target that the program be completed in four years. We estimate that it will cost some 8,000 million pts.[4] The bulk of the expenditures would be expected to occur during the second and third years, with somewhat less expenditure during the first year when planning,

[4] This is based on an average expenditure of 150 pts per square meter of traveled way, the latter having an average width of 7.5 meters.

organization, deployment of resources and letting of contracts have to be undertaken and during the fourth year when the program would be drawing to a close.

Depending upon the specific conditions of paving, subgrade and slopes found at each location, some or all of the following types of work will have to be carried out:

a. laying a new asphalt wearing surface over existing surfaces;
b. where paving is badly broken, laying new paving as thick as the subgrade will support;
c. renewing the subgrade through excavation and refilling it if its load-carrying capacity is insufficient for the traffic;
d. stabilizing side slopes through grading, drainage, pinning and planting;
e. providing for adequate drainage if needed;
f. clearing, widening and compacting shoulders and ditches; and
g. repairing, or replacing if necessary, bridges, retaining walls and tunnels.

In order to carry out a major, short-term program of this type, a special organization within the Ministry of Public Works and careful planning will be required. The program should be placed under a very able organizer supported by a technical adviser with much practical experience in the types of work involved. Since the nature of the work will not permit the cost and time of building up on-site facilities, the major contracting companies should form efficient mobile construction teams specially equipped for these tasks.

Other Repair Work

While our urgent repair program would be restricted to the heavily traveled roads, there is a backlog of repairs required for other roads with less than 1,000 ADT; future repairs to these roads will also be necessary as a result of damage from rock slides, subsidences and other natural occurrences. It will therefore be necessary to continue to budget for ordinary repair work separately, but on a declining basis throughout the five-year period as the backlog is removed. Also, the maintenance service will eventually take over some of the work now handled as "repairs." The budget for 1961 included 890 million pts for repairs, of which it was expected that 125 million pts would actually be disbursed in 1962, leaving a forecasted expenditure in 1961 of 765 million pts. We suggest that an annual allocation of about 700 million pts at the beginning of the five-year period declining to below 500 million pts at the end would be appropriate. We thus estimate a total expenditure for this purpose during the whole period at about 3,000 million pts.

Ordinary Maintenance

While poor conditions on many Spanish roads can be ascribed to design standards inadequate for carrying present volumes of traffic, there can be little doubt that deficient maintenance on a continuing basis has been an important contributory factor. The Spanish Government has recognized this deficiency and is taking steps to improve the situation. The entire system of road maintenance is undergoing study and reorganization; we support this move and urge that it be pressed vigorously.

It seems that insufficient funds have been provided for maintenance of roads, in contrast to new construction. This presents serious difficulty since, from the moment of construction, roads undergo continuous deterioration from usage and from the elements, and consequently require that substantial sums be spent on them each year. We hope that the policy that will emerge from the present studies on reorganizing the system of road maintenance will stimulate a proper interest in this essential work.

Ordinary highway maintenance has been effected by means of the *caminero* system. Under this system, maintenance work is performed by manual laborers living adjacent to the road, each with individual responsibility for a certain stretch of it. The *camineros* have been equipped only with the most elementary hand tools and have not been subject to adequate supervision. In recent years the total labor force has been increased and, in some instances, either organized groups have been used or contractors have been employed for paving repairs, but an organized and consistent system, furnished with the necessary equipment, has yet to be initiated on a nationwide basis.

Since such a system is now under consideration, we will here limit ourselves to a comment on the desirable extent of mechanization of maintenance programs and the financial implications of our suggestions. No matter how the maintenance program is reorganized, some consideration will have to be given to the relationship between the number of workers involved and the amount of equipment with which they are provided. Maintenance work can be done with a variety of combinations of labor and machine intensiveness and undoubtedly the combination that will produce the highest quality of work will vary according to local conditions, such as the nature of the terrain and climate. In general, the mechanization of maintenance should increase in the coming years, but consideration should also be given to the local manpower situation; in regions with surplus manpower and few alternative employment prospects, labor-intensive methods should still be employed. Since most equipment for road maintenance needs to be replaced after eight to ten years, the demand for it will be continuous— first, to bring about a higher level of mechanization and then to maintain that level. The manufacture of soundly priced equipment in Spain might therefore be a possibility.

It is difficult to forecast what increases in ordinary maintenance expenditures might be expected during the next five years. Much would depend on the speed with which the proposed reorganization were effected. Much would also depend on how rapidly, and under what circumstances, the recommended process of mechanization took place. In 1961, only some 6,360 pts per km of nationally administered roads were budgeted for maintenance. Our best judgment is that more than double this amount will be required. In fact, we believe that eventually an allocation of some 15,000 pts per km might be needed. In view of the costs of the urgent repair program and the fact that ordinary maintenance would not be fully effective until after the urgent repairs have been completed, we believe that this upper limit should be approached gradually. However, the mission believes that it would be reasonable roughly to double average maintenance expenditures by the end of the five-year period. Based on these projections, the mission has estimated total investment outlays for the ordinary maintenance program for the five-year period as a whole at about 2,300 million pts.[5]

Reconstruction and Construction Along Existing Routes

We have already stated our belief that the existing network as such is adequate and that no major new roads need to be built, except for the proposed East Coast *autopista* which is discussed below. Otherwise, the emphasis should be on reconstruction to modern standards on existing rights of way, provision of by-passes and re-routing existing roads in urban areas and over difficult terrain. Since the major emphasis of this program would be to bring the network up to the standards required by the volume and speed of traffic, the program should be founded on a careful study of present and expected future traffic loads and of the defects of existing roadways. Just as in the case of the urgent repair program, two factors should be considered in determining pri-

[5] It should be noted that this figure refers to equipment only and does not include payments for labor.

orities in the reconstruction program; where are the greatest traffic densities; and what is the actual condition of the various roads. This will generally mean that the oldest portions of the most densely traveled parts of the present network should be rebuilt first.

In designing the standards to which the various roads should be reconstructed, it should be borne in mind that a road is a very long-term investment and must therefore be designed against future, rather than present, needs. This is one of the reasons why we are recommending below a much improved system for collecting relevant data; the latter are an indispensable element in forward planning, particularly with respect to the forecasting of future traffic volumes, both in general and at specific locations. It is most important that, in each case, studies be made to determine the appropriate ratio between future traffic capacity and present traffic volume so that the correct design standard can be adopted. In this way, the optimum benefit can be derived from the investment over its entire life. As a provisional rule of thumb, to be applied while more accurate projections are being worked out, it might be assumed that traffic will increase at least threefold.

Until the present highway inventory is completed and other factual data are collected, there is no knowing exactly how much reconstruction work is required *in toto*. In the first instance, all roads with an ADT of 1,000 vehicles or more should be considered to determine whether reconstruction is necessary to upgrade their design, with priority given, within this group, to the roads with greatest traffic density. On some of the less traveled roads, traffic densities are now increasing rapidly and the present design standards may shortly become inadequate. Upgrading a road often entails extensive works: additional cuts and fills, changes in curvatures, rebuilding foundations, realignment of bridges and tunnels, extensive redesign of intersections and complete stretches of new construction, sometimes at expensive sites such as in and around urban areas or over difficult terrain. The urgent repair work will have to be coordinated with the reconstruction program so that heavy repairs are kept to a minimum on roads which will shortly be undergoing reconstruction.

It is clear that the reconstruction program will be so large that it would only be practicable to stretch its total execution over a longer period than the five years primarily under review. Moreover, several years will be required before the studies and investigations necessary for some of the major projects have been completed. Finally, we have considered that the urgent repair program, and the programs of ordinary repair and maintenance, should take precedence during the next five years. The amount of reconstruction which can be undertaken over the years 1962–66 will therefore be determined, within broad financial limits, by the capability for road-working which remains after the annual segments of these other programs have been planned for. We believe that the total capability could be expanded quite sizably, given the proper organization, the judicious acquisition of machinery and equipment and some reliance—particularly during the early years —on foreign contractors.

Assuming an expansion in all types of road works of 40 percent the first year, 25 percent the second year and 20 percent in each of the three remaining years, the financial implications would be as shown in Table 11.2 below. It will be noted that some 13.8 billion pts would be required for urgent repairs, maintenance, etc., which leaves 15.0 billion pts as the residual amount available for reconstruction and new construction.

TABLE 11.2: Proposed Capital Expenditures on Roads, 1962–66

(billion pts)

	Budg-eted for 1961	1962	1963	1964	1965	1966	Total 1962–66
Urgent Repairs	–	1.8	2.5	2.8	0.9	–	8.0
Other Repairs	0.8	0.7	0.7	0.6	0.5	0.5	3.0
Equipment for Ordinary Maintenance	0.2	0.3	0.4	0.5	0.5	0.6	2.3
Traffic Studies	0.1	0.1	0.1	0.1	0.1	0.1	0.5
Reconstruction and New Construction	1.7	0.9	1.0	1.6	4.7	6.8	15.0
Total	2.8	3.8	4.7	5.6	6.7	8.0	28.8

Because of the earlier priorities—mainly in repair work—the resources available for reconstruction would be relatively modest during the first three years. The emphasis should therefore be placed on finishing presently incompleted projects; this would avoid the practice, which has occurred in the past, of extending individual projects over excessively long periods of time, marked with frequent interruptions. New starts should be minimized until adequate planning and design studies have been effected, until total road-making capability has been sufficiently expanded and until the top-priority urgent repair program has been virtually completed.

The East Coast Autopista

The only major piece of new construction which is likely to be necessary in the near future is the East Coast *autopista,* a modern limited-access road on a new right of way, with by-passes of, and interconnections with, the major urban areas along the Mediterranean coast from the French border to Murcia, a distance of about 730 kms.[6] This ambitious project is under consideration in Spain, and we endorse the further study and planning of it. The *prima facie* case for building such a road is strong. It would traverse areas of the highest traffic density in Spain (see Map 16) and of the most rapid traffic growth. It passes through important industrial and agricultural areas and serves some of the major tourist regions of the country.

While it is still in an early study stage, the project undoubtedly would be of the first magnitude by any standards. As a very rough estimate, we calculate that total expenditures could be 9 billion pts and perhaps considerably more. Since the program of repairs, maintenance, and reconstruction which we have discussed above has been determined on the basis of the estimated capacity (primarily in terms of administrative and technical resources) to perform road works of all kinds in Spain, it follows that the autopista must be included within the over-all program (although capacity can be increased to some extent through the use of foreign consultants and contractors and on the autopista, as we recommend below). This means that the major construction work on the autopista will have to take place in the latter part of the five-year period and in succeeding years; this will allow time for the extensive study, planning, and design work which must precede it and for the acquisition of land. Although the road should be planned as a single project, it can and should be constructed in stages. The stretch from Barcelona to the French frontier at La Junquera logically has the first priority.

The autopista project far exceeds in planning complexity and magnitude of construction any present or previous individual project in Spain. We therefore believe that it is essential that it be carried out by a special organization or authority. This organization should be relatively autonomous, with its own financial accounts separated from those of all other road-making activities in Spain. Furthermore, if the work is to be completed in a reasonable time, the construction of the autopista would for some years put a heavy strain on the road-making

---

[6] At some point in the future, the volume of traffic on some of the other principal arteries may reach a point where the construction of expressways over some stretches should be considered.

capacity of the country. For this and other reasons we recommend that the proposed special organization be empowered to employ foreign consultants and contractors to the extent necessary.

Data Collection, Planning and Design

The importance of detailed, accurate and current factual data for highway planning cannot be overemphasized. The present administration, led by the Direccion General de Carreteras y Caminos Vecinales (DGCCV), has made commendable progress in the collection of such data in recent years. It is most important that this effort be carried forward, expanded as necessary and adequately staffed and financed. Untold waste of scarce public funds and inconvenience to road users are frequent results of planning without adequate facts. The types of facts required are as follows:

a. Traffic counts on a continuing basis, while already under way, should be expanded to include daily and seasonal fluctuations, and flows at major intersections.

b. Origin-destination surveys (the first pilot survey in a major urban area and on intercity routes was completed in 1961) should be extended to all the important traffic centers; they will be particularly useful in connection with the East Coast *autopista,* and special surveys for this purpose are now being carried out.

c. Current, accurate statistics on the vehicle fleet, particularly as to specific location, should be collected.

d. Fuel consumption figures, by type of fuel and geographic location, should be collected more intensively so as to provide an important index of traffic growth, other than traffic counts, and to serve as an effective comparison check of the latter.

e. Since a major aim of designers should be to reduce or eliminate hazardous situations, data should be accumulated on the important aspects of traffic accidents.

f. The current highway inventory, which is listing the condition and design characteristics of existing roads, should be completed, as we understand will be possible by the end of 1962, and then kept continually up to date.

While these data are a report of the past and present, and therefore excellent guides to future action, another very important planning datum, as we have indicated earlier, is the forecast of the future volume of traffic. Such forecasts in Spain must initially be based on statistics on vehicle population and fuel consumption, the only data available for sufficient years on which to base a forecast. As more and better statistics are accumulated, better forecasts will be possible. When combined with the types of data listed above, it should also be possible in a few years to make accurate traffic forecasts at specific locations.

With more satisfactory data on hand, the quality of planning and design could be improved.[7] So far, there has been a lack of comprehensive plans for harmonizing the work done over a period of years along a lengthy route. It is our impression that the various projects fitting within the general scheme of the 1950 modernization plan have been planned independently of each other. This results in a variety of conditions along different parts of the same route, with sharp transitions and changes of standard. To take one of a number of possible examples, it is noticeable in the north that N. 634 from Bilbao to beyond Oviedo is an old road with poor sight distances, very numerous and sharp curves, narrow bridges and abrupt grades. The portions of N. 634 west of Luarca, and of N. 642 beyond Barreiros are of much later construction and are considerably more comfortable and speedy. Assuming the same ADT along this route, improvement of the eastern portions of the north coast route would obviously be of highest priority. The current road inventory survey, together with the newly available traffic counts and the other data we suggest collecting, would be of great help in planning the work program along this route. In such cases, a comprehensive plan, which would take the long view of the improvement of these routes and make careful analyses of changes in traffic and the economy of the regions traversed, is required so that individual plans may be adjusted accordingly.

According to the Dorsch report[8] and the opinion of Spanish officials, some of the design work carried out in the past does not meet modern requirements. Among the deficiencies referred to are: insufficient attention to surveying and soil testing on construction sites; the omission of many significant details from blueprints, because too small a scale is used; and the practice of compiling some data separately,

[7] This chapter was prepared before the "Plan General de Carreteras" was available. The mission has not been able to examine this new 16-year plan in detail, but no doubt it represents an important contribution to the solution of the problem described here.

[8] Mr. Xavier Dorsch served as an expert consultant to the Spanish Government during the first half of 1961 to advise on the methods of road construction and maintenance and on policies to regulate the road transport system. He worked in conjunction with Mr. Armand (see Chapter 10) on questions of coordination with the railways. IBRD assisted in arranging for Mr. Dorsch's services.

instead of incorporating them in one comprehensive plan, which makes it more difficult for the inspector or the supervising engineer to grasp the full requirements. This lack of detail in plans is somewhat anomalous when contrasted, for example, with the precision used in computing excavation costs to one-hundredth of a cubic meter. It is undoubtedly one of the reasons why a very large number of construction projects exceed their original cost estimates by substantial margins. We believe that these defects are partly due to the fact that the staff available full time to deal with the present volume of work is insufficient, and the supervision of field work is inadequate. It is difficult for one comparatively small central office to keep in touch with the field work of 50 *Jefaturas*. And there is an obvious need to enlarge it in view of the expanded needs of the highway program.

But, if under present conditions some of the shortcomings in planning and design, and indeed in road-making, are due to a shortage of trained personnel, what will the situation be like when the workload is five or ten times greater and higher standards of planning and design are expected? The prospect clearly calls for a vigorous effort to overcome the shortage. We believe that there are a number of ways in which the problem should be tackled. First, it is necessary to obtain more effective use of existing resources through reorganization, which is discussed below, and by ensuring that the Government obtains the services of the engineers in its employ, both in Madrid and in the field, on a full-time basis; this is related to the larger problem of the terms and conditions of employment in the Civil Service to which reference has been made elsewhere, but it clearly becomes acute when higher technical staff are in such short supply. Then again, besides making extensive use of *Ayudantes* (assistant engineers), experienced engineers should, so far as possible, be relieved of administrative burdens, and it would be worth considering whether the nature of the work would permit of a greater use of administrative personnel who could be transferred from other ministries.

A second way to overcome the shortage is to increase the numbers to be trained in the future; this is admittedly a longer-term solution, but one which should not be neglected. The numbers graduating hitherto have been very limited, though there are welcome signs of some increase latterly, which will be effective in the next few years. If the limiting factor is the capacity of the technical schools and faculties, one alternative is to seek opportunities for an important number of Spanish students to attend foreign universities; but if it is the restricted entry to the technical schools, then this restriction should be removed. A third way is to assign some tasks normally carried out by government engineers to consulting firms. Since there are none in Spain at present, foreign firms would have to be used, at least as an interim measure. In any event, it may be necessary to use them if the proposed program is to be promptly executed. The highway authorities are aware of the importance of improving planning and design standards and have already initiated programs along some of the lines indicated above.

Governmental Organization

The Dorsch report deals with questions of organization at length, and in general we endorse its recommendations. In brief, the report recommends reducing the number of organization units in Madrid which are independently involved in planning and programing. Reorganization to increase emphasis on maintenance is suggested. An entirely new echelon is recommended at the regional level, to improve supervision of the 50 provincial *Jefaturas* and to locate certain functions closer to the job and away from Madrid; in this way, those concerned with long-range policy would be relieved of responsibility for supervising field work. The regional offices, of which four to six might be established, would be mainly concerned with detailed design and planning, much of which is now done in Madrid, with construction supervision and administration, and with inspection. In addition, the Dorsch report recommends that the staff in each *Jefatura* be enlarged and reorganized on a functional rather than geographical basis, with five specialized departments established to facilitate concentration on specific tasks such as maintenance and site investigation, including surveying and complete soil analysis. The principal direct responsibilities for maintenance would be at the provincial level within general policies set in Madrid. We particularly recommend that inspection and supervision of contractors be improved so that a larger volume of work can be handled.

In view of the shortage of technical personnel and of the need to gain experience, it might be desirable to introduce the proposed regional organizations, and the changes in the provincial offices, in stages; in this event, we suggest that a start be made in the areas in which the work under the urgent repairs program will first have to be undertaken.

The Role of the Construction Industry

Since contractors do the actual construction work in Spain, improvement in the industry's capacity to handle such work is equal in importance and urgency to improvements in government organization. While much can be done by the industry itself to achieve such improvement, the Government will also be able to stimulate and encourage the industry by establishing a concrete program extending over a period of years. In recent years, many of the larger and more competent contractors in Spain have been discouraged from engaging in this type of construction activity because the volume of work has been too low and the sites too dispersed for road contracts to be financially attractive to them. Our proposed program would greatly increase total funds and speed up the rate of work on specific jobs by reducing the number under way at any one time. Furthermore, improved designs would save contractors much time and money that is now spent in redesigning in the light of unforeseen problems at the actual construction site. Prompt payment to contractors upon completion of agreed stages of the work would also assist the industry and help in the long run to reduce costs.

The construction industry by necessity employs a large number of engineers, but this number should not have to increase, if the quality of public planning and design is improved. The important manpower limitations are in managers and skilled laborers. In this respect, the use of foreign contractors with training duties and the use of demonstration sites in Spain, under both Spanish and foreign contractors, would be very helpful. The urgent repair program may also make a major contribution to increasing the number of experienced managers and workers.

There is also a shortage of equipment which is likely to become more acute in the future unless prompt action is taken. While an equipment shortage is easier to remedy than a shortage of trained personnel, nevertheless certain changes will be needed. The State has acquired a large pool of construction machinery which it rents to contractors; the maintenance of this pool is understaffed and inadequate, and much of the equipment is quite old and worn. Much of the machinery that is owned by contractors is also in urgent need of replacement. The Dorsch report points out that the most efficient basis for mechanization is in fact private ownership, because there is then an incentive to maximize utilization and to provide adequate maintenance of this important investment.[9] If credit is necessary to encourage private contractors to own their equipment, then the Government should ensure that it is available in adequate amounts at normal interest rates. Lack of standardization of makes and sizes is also evident and government efforts could usefully be directed toward arranging

[9] An exception is equipment for maintenance work, which the State performs itself.

that new procurement be limited to a much smaller number of standardized types. This would reduce maintenance costs and limit time lost waiting for repair parts. Much of the privately owned equipment is quite small and used for the present small maintenance and repair contracts; more of the larger and heavier type will be needed in the future. The mission has recommended elsewhere that duties on imported equipment be reduced, and this recommendation would apply to equipment for the construction industry.

Contractors can help in other ways to increase construction capacity and the Government would be well advised to explore with the industry ways in which this could be achieved. Work should be planned to avoid delays and interruptions that not only deny the economy the benefits accruing from the completed project but add to the cost of it; and proper phasing of different types of work on the same site can improve the utilization of men and machines, and reduce costs. Contractors would be able to execute the large volume of work in prospect more efficiently if there were more specialization among them. A specialist can do a particular job (earth-moving, paving, project-building) more quickly and cheaply; general contractors, unless they are large and well-integrated concerns, will rarely have the right equipment or skills at their disposal for all aspects of one project. But specialists must work together according to a well-ordered program and in some instances the establishment of a consortium of contractors, or at least arrangements for the pooling of equipment, may be necessary.

The Regulation of Road Transport

The rates for common carrier transport by bus and truck are subject to approval by the Government. In general rates seem to have been set at reasonable levels, and the price of highway transportation for shippers and passengers compares favorably with that in other European countries. Bus and truck services from the established companies, especially those serving regular routes, appear to be good. The improvements in the highway system resulting from the programs outlined above will make it possible to reduce costs and further improve service.

There is need to improve the efficiency of traffic moving over the highway network by better traffic administration and servicing. To the extent that taxation and administrative regulations can improve the quality of the vehicle fleet (compulsory safety inspection, for instance) and reduce the use of obsolete or unsafe vehicles (steel-tired carts and overloaded three-wheel delivery trucks), this should be carried out in gradual, but strictly enforced, fashion. Such matters as truck-weight regulations should be enforced vigorously, since over-weight trucks have been an important factor contributing to the deterioration of the main roads and to traffic delays.

To sum up, we believe that the Government has before it a vast undertaking to bring the road network into a condition which will enable road transport to satisfy the demands that will be placed upon it as the economy develops. This is the more exacting because arrears of work have to be overtaken before new tasks can safely be tackled, yet all the time the volume of traffic will be increasing. There will have to be a long and sustained effort to keep abreast. As in the case of the railways, the main concentration must be on the vital parts of the network. But, for the roads, the preservation of the basic network and the improvements in design and standards of construction will require a much greater employment of engineers, skilled personnel and mechanization than hitherto; and the availability of these resources, which are relatively scarce, particularly manpower, will determine the pace at which the program can proceed. The emphasis must therefore be on increasing capacity. As we have suggested, machines can be imported and manufactured in Spain, technicians trained at home and consultants and contractors engaged abroad. But it is no less important to make the best use of available resources, even when augmented, by careful organization and planning in the public administration, both in Madrid and in the field, and in collaboration with the construction industry. This could do much to increase productivity and make the task less formidable.

CHAPTER 12 *PORTS AND SHIPPING*

Topography and history have brought about an extensive development of ports and shipping. The Spanish peninsula, with coastal mountain ranges extending to the sea, has many natural harbors. Most of the ports are small and used primarily by the fishing fleets of nearby villages. Owing to the concentration of economic activity into a few widely-separated zones around the periphery and to the difficulties of land transportation along the mountainous coastline, coastal shipping (cabotage) has become an important activity and accounts for more than half the mercantile activity of Spanish ports (see Table 12.1). But there are a considerable number of ports equipped to handle ocean-going vessels which have been engaged in international traffic for centuries. Of the more than 300 ports, the 16 largest handle more than 1 million tons of merchandise annually (see Table 12.2) and account for some three-fourths of the more than 50 million tons handled by all Spanish ports.

Port Capacity

The economic function of a port is to handle the movement of cargo and passengers as expeditiously as possible. Time spent in the port is, from the point of view of the ship, dead time, the cost of which must be borne by the cargo or passengers. If the port works inefficiently, the time spent waiting in port is high relative to the productive period at sea, and the resultant increase in costs of transportation becomes an unnecessary burden on the economy.

The effective capacity of a port is determined by a combination of factors among which are: (a) the depth of water alongside the quays, which influences the size of ships that can use the port; (b) the length of wharves; and (c) the potential of each wharf to handle traffic, which depends in turn on the availability of labor, loading and unloading equipment (cranes), secondary transport (carriages and forklifts) and temporary storage sheds. The proper balance between wharf space on the one hand and cranes, forklifts and other equipment on the other will vary with the types of vessels and cargoes normally handled by the port. Outside the port proper, there must be sufficient storage capacity nearby so that merchandise does not pile up on the docks, and adequate transportation between the port and producing or consuming centers inland. These several factors are closely interrelated,

226

TABLE 12.1: Merchandise Traffic of Ports, 1945–1959

(million tons)

Year	Unloadings				Loadings				Total Movement of Merchandise
	Coastal Shipping	International Traffic		Total Unloadings	Coastal Shipping	International Traffic		Total Unloadings	
		Spanish Flag	Foreign Flag			Spanish Flag	Foreign Flag		
1945	8.1	1.3	.3	9.7	8.6	.2	2.1	10.9	20.6
1946	8.6	1.9	1.0	10.5	9.2	.5	3.0	12.7	24.2
1947	9.7	1.3	1.3	12.3	10.1	.3	3.3	13.7	26.0
1948	9.5	2.1	2.1	13.7	10.2	.5	3.6	14.3	28.0
1949	10.6	2.0	2.9	15.5	10.3	.6	3.9	14.8	30.3
1950	11.7	2.1	3.2	17.0	10.7	.9	3.9	16.5	33.5
1951	10.2	2.0	3.3	15.5	10.6	1.2	5.1	16.9	32.4
1952	11.4	2.3	4.8	18.8	12.7	1.1	5.8	19.5	38.0
1953	11.3	3.2	5.4	19.9	13.6	1.4	5.3	20.3	40.2
1954	12.2	3.3	5.5	21.0	12.4	1.2	4.6	18.2	39.2
1955	11.6	3.3	6.9	21.8	12.3	1.3	5.5	19.1	40.9
1956	13.7	3.9	6.3	23.9	12.6	1.7	6.7	21.0	44.9
1957	15.6	4.1	6.6	26.3	14.9	1.8	7.0	23.7	50.0
1958	15.8	6.4	8.5	30.7	15.4	1.1	6.4	22.9	53.6
1959	15.8	6.9	7.2	29.9	15.5	1.5	6.1	23.1	53.0

SOURCE: Instituto Nacional de Estadística, *Anuario Estadístico de España*.

TABLE 12.2: Merchandise Traffic of Principal Ports in 1960

(thousand tons)

Port	Total Traffic		Petroleum		Coal	
	Un-loaded	Loaded	Un-loaded	Loaded	Un-loaded	Loaded
Algeciras	118	69	–	–	2	–
Alicante	675	260	137	–	114	–
Almeria	267	892	89	–	63	–
Aviles	1,968	1,502	–	–	122	684
Barcelona	2,709	1,002	864	21	443	11
Bilbao	3,019	1,424	364	97	1,481	7
Cadiz	190	131	–	–	29	6
Cartagena	4,234	4,034	3,983	3,202	56	–
Gijon-Musel	981	3,133	93	–	96	2,673
Huelva	396	2,290	190	–	89	–
La Coruna	511	776	193	72	21	54
La Luz y Las Palmas	2,797	1,057	1,730	104	13	8
Malaga	608	312	145	35	220	–
Pasajes	1,279	531	223	–	451	1
San Esteban de Pravia	26	1,344	–	–	–	1,232
Santa Cruz de Tenerife	3,568	2,325	3,077	1,843	6	2
Santander	1,022	497	284	4	249	–
Sevilla	1,146	566	290	2	303	–
Tarragona	778	173	329	10	120	–
Valencia	1,301	641	535	18	213	–
Vigo	533	1,091	231	142	21	4

SOURCE: Based on information supplied to the mission by the Ministry of Public Works.

and an insufficiency in any one will reduce the over-all capacity of the port.

The Need for Port Investment

The central problem facing the Spanish ports is one of imbalance among the various elements of port capacity. There has been heavy investment in port infrastructure such as wharves and breakwaters. Many of the ports, spurred on in some instances by local rivalries, have developed these facilities in excess of present or foreseeable traffic needs. The existence of three large coal-exporting ports (San Esteban de Pravia, Aviles and Gijon) within a distance of 40 kms is one of a number of possible illustrations of this point. At the same time, insufficient funds and attention have been devoted to the other components of port capacity. This is particularly true of loading and unloading equipment which, it should be pointed out, was difficult to obtain during the period of foreign exchange shortages. Such ports as Tarragona, Valencia, Vigo and Santander, and most others, have too few cranes for the wharf space available and for the quantity of cargo that requires quick handling. Many of the existing cranes are overage and obsolete, and the lack of interconnecting tracks further reduces their utility. In some cases, auxiliary equipment and storage facilities are also inadequate; in others, most notably at Huelva and San Esteban de Pravia, insufficient attention has been paid to the problem of depth and the need for regular dredging. Complaints have also been voiced about the depth of the ports at Barcelona and Bilbao; on the other hand, some deep-water wharves are not being used to capacity. As a result of this imbalance, many of the ports are not being used effectively, operating capacity is well below potential and the real cost of port operations is higher than necessary.

Early in its stay in Madrid the mission was shown a *Plan for Port Development,* covering the period 1962–1969 and prepared in the Ministry of Public Works. It calls for substantial new construction of basic port facilities that cannot be justified on the basis of foreseeable traffic needs; and though port equipment is included in the plan, in some instances it is insufficient and in others the procurement is spread out over too long a period.

The mission strongly recommends that the Government re-examine its port development needs.[1] We recommend further that all new construction be halted, except in cases of obvious and urgent need or where the facilities in question are already close to completion; and that over the next two years, the Government concentrate on the procurement of all the mobile and stationary cranes, forklifts, regular and electric carriages and other equipment necessary for the efficient utilization of present port infrastructure. This will involve both an increase in the amount of such equipment relative to the 1962–1969 plan and an accelerated schedule for its procurement. In Table 12.5 (at the

---

[1] Subsequent to its return to Washington, the mission received a copy of a *Nota Sobre El Plan de Desarrollo Economico A Largo Plazo,* prepared by the Directorate General of Ports and Maritime Signals of the Ministry of Public Works. The note proposes that the 8-year plan total be reduced from 9.0 to 7.6 billion pts (5.6 billion for the principal ports and 2.0 billion for the Comision Administrativa de Obras y Servicios de Puertos a cargo directo del Estado (CAOSPE). Annual expenditures over the period 1962–1969 are set at 950 million pts instead of 1,100 million pts. It appears that greater emphasis is to be placed on equipment and less on wharves and other infrastructure than in the original plan. While these changes appear to be in the right direction, we are not in a position to comment on the revised plan in detail since we have not seen a list of the projects and equipment for each port. The mission's recommended program therefore remains as outlined in this chapter.

end of this chapter) will be found specific recommendations for each of the ports visited by members of the mission, with respect to the additional equipment to be procured and the investment projects included in present plans that should not be carried out. Table 12.5 also contains comments on some of the principal investment projects that should be carried out as part of the 1962–1969 program, including some high priority projects to be completed in 1962–1963, but it does not purport to be a full statement of the investment projects to be carried out by each port.[2]

The *Plan for Port Development* calls for expenditures approximating 9.0 billion pts over the period 1962–1969. Of this total, about 2.4 billion pts are destined for CAOSPE. About one-quarter of the CAOSPE figure is for various services such as navigation aids, coastal protection and subventions for dredges. The remainder, about 1.8 billion pts, is for very small ports, most of which we did not have an opportunity to inspect. This sum, which represents 20 percent of the investments, goes to ports which, in the aggregate, probably account for less than 10 percent of total traffic. While we are not in a position to make specific recommendations concerning individual ports in this group, we urge the Government to examine the proposed investments carefully, since some of these ports have very little prospect of earning additional revenue by expanding traffic. Many of these ports are almost exclusively used for local fishing vessels. It may be questioned whether the large number of existing ports and the high volume of proposed expenditures can be justified on economic grounds. In advance of an examination of the question of small ports by the Government, the mission proposes that, for planning purposes, the investment figure for CAOSPE be reduced to 1.8 billion pts.

The remaining 6.6 billion pts in the plan is for 29 large ports (see Table 12.3). The mission recommends two major changes in this expenditure, which are specified in detail in Table 12.5 and summarized with respect to each port in Table 12.3. These are:

a. a drastic cut in the proposed investments on port infrastructure, reducing the figure by 3.6 billion pts; and

b. an increase of 1 billion pts for expenditures on equipment and other high priority projects, all to be undertaken during 1962 and 1963.

[2] No estimate of the cost is made for certain equipment recommended in Table 12.5. This applies, in particular, to dredging material. The mission believes that the Government should first undertake an inventory of dredging material available, its capacity and the quantities to be dredged in future taking into account all other port development plans.

TABLE 12.3: Proposed Adjustments to Government's Port Investment
Plan, 1962–1969

(million pts)

Port	Original Investment Program	Proposed Reductions	Proposed Additions[a]	Adjusted Investment Program[a]
Algeciras	685	685	2	2
Alicante	70	–	–	70
Almeria	45	–	40	85
Aviles	766	500	95	361
Barcelona	831	500	250	581
Bilbao	270	145	48	173
Cadiz	194	120	20	94
Cartagena	211	35	3	179
Castellon[b]	80	p.m.	p.m.	80
Ceuta[b]	25	–	–	25
El Ferrol del Caudillo[b]	36	–	–	36
Gijon-Musel	527	381	13	159
Huelva	258	–	–	258
La Coruna	330	175	40	195
La Luz y Las Palmas	234	127	76	183
Malaga	193	26	30	197
Melilla[b]	7	–	–	7
Palma de Mallorca[b]	68	–	–	68
Pasajes	154	154	250	250
Pontevedra	113	109	9	13
San Esteban de Pravia	16	p.m.	p.m.	16
Santa Cruz de Tenerife	106	25	21	102
Puerto de Santa Maria	37	2	–	35
Santander	272	124	26	174
Sevilla	332	230	27	129
Tarragona	76	15	30	91
Valencia	308	250	53	111
Vigo	290	40	1	251
Villagarcia[b]	61	–	–	61
CAOSPE	2,394	600	–	1,794
Total	8,989	4,243	1,034	5,780

[a] These figures are subject to the qualifications expressed in the text.
[b] Ports not visited by the mission.

The revised plan would total 5.8 billion pts, arrived at as follows:

Original Investment Plan Total	9.0 billion pts
Reduction in program for small ports	–0.6 billion pts
Reduction in infrastructure program of main ports	–3.6 billion pts
Addition to port equipment program	+1.0 billion pts
Revised Plan Total	5.8 billion pts

In addition to these changes in the amount and composition of total port investment, the mission proposes a further amendment to the timing. Expenditure of 900 million pts for equipment and other high priority projects included in the original plan should, instead of being spread out over a long period, be completed in the next two years (1962–1963).

On the basis of these recommended changes, expenditures on the revised plan during 1962 and 1963, when all of the equipment program and other high priority projects would be carried out, would total 1,450 million pts. The level of annual expenditures in subsequent years would drop to 500 million pts and eventually to 450 million pts, as shown in the following table (in million pts). By way of comparison, the level of port investment expenditures in 1959 and 1960 was about 900 million pts.

	Equipment	Infrastructure	Total
1962	950	500	1,450
1963	950	500	1,450
1964	–	500	500
1965	–	500	500
1966	–	500	500
1967	–	500	500
1968	–	450	450
1969	–	450	450
	1,900	3,900	5,800

This program is designed to obtain the best use of existing port facilities and should enable the ports to handle an increased volume of traffic. At some future time, the growth of port traffic may warrant some new construction or extension of quays, wharves and breakwaters. Such construction should only be undertaken as part of a general plan embracing all of the leading ports, and after it is established that capacity cannot be increased by additional equipment or improved port organization. At that time the Government should also consider the possibility of reducing the number of ports through consolidation; ports such as Castellon, Burriana, Santa Pola and Torrevieja should receive particular attention. The problem of consolidating the three coal ports will also require attention. The problem is an important one, since large investments in equipping the ports are contemplated. In arriving at a solution the Government will wish to study a number of related questions bearing on the possibility of changing the system of marketing the coal and its transportation from the local mines to the ports.

Six of the ports visited by the mission had plans to construct dry docks. These plans should be scrutinized very closely, and a realistic appraisal made of the full costs of operation (including interest and depreciation) and the probable returns from future use. It is important to bear in mind that the Spanish merchant marine will require less use of dry docks as it becomes modernized (see the discussion later in this chapter) and that foreign shipowners generally prefer to have their ships repaired in their own country.

The same need for a careful economic appraisal of costs and expected returns applies to the proposed Sevilla-Bonanza navigation canal. Taking 2.7 billion pts as the present estimate of the cost of the project (a figure which, on the basis of past experience, is very likely to be exceeded), annual costs for operation and interest on capital will be at least 200 million pts annually. By way of comparison, dredging the river—although not carried out as often as required—amounts to only 15 million pts annually. It should be seriously questioned whether the additional revenue or savings in cost to be obtained from improved navigation and flood control will cover the increase in costs resulting from the project. The effect of irrigation projects now under way upstream on the extent of flooding and silting of the river, and the possibility of increased dredging as an alternative to the canal, should also be taken into account.

Transport to and from Spanish ports is, in general, adequate to prevent unnecessary delays or the piling up of goods at port side. Exceptions are Bilbao and Pasajes for the inward movement of cargo and Gijon for the outward movement of coal. Storage facilities in the hinterland will have to be improved; in their absence, some of the ports might be obliged to construct warehouses on space that should be used for other purposes, as has been contemplated in Bilbao. This problem should be worked out between the port management and municipalities or chambers of commerce in the areas serving or being served by the port.

Port Administration

Port management is a complicated business. The efficient operation of a port requires that the many component elements—ships, labor, wharf space, equipment, railroad wagons, trucks, storage sheds, customs, shipping agents, etc.—function properly in relation to each other.

If the proper coordination is not maintained, the capacity of the port is not fully utilized; the result is that ships wait in the harbors or even in their berths, cranes are idle, or goods are piled up on the wharves.

The responsibility for day-to-day management of each port rests with the port director. His formal title is that of Engineer Port Director. No doubt the engineering and technical aspects of the port director's work are important, but no less so, and requiring constant attention, are the commercial and economic aspects. Sometimes these seem to be given second place, to the detriment of port operations. It is highly desirable that port directors be selected in the light of the complex and varied functions that they should be expected to perform.

Each of the principal ports has a Junta de Obras y Servicios, an autonomous public body which in practice acts primarily in an advisory capacity to the port director. The typical Junta has over 20 members representing various groups and interests at the national, provincial and municipal levels, including chambers of commerce, shipowners, agriculture, labor and fishing. Because of its size and composition, the Junta generally does not play an effective part in the administration of the port. To the extent that it is not already the practice, the mission believes that a small working committee, consisting of regular port users, should be formed from within the Junta. Its task would be to maintain close and regular contact with the port director, advising him on port operating problems and investment needs; its reports should also be made available to the Ministry of Public Works.

Both the port director and the Junta are responsible to the Directorate General of Ports and Maritime Signals of the Ministry of Public Works. Most of the important decisions on port construction, and to a lesser extent port operation, appear in practice to emanate from Madrid. While it is important that the Ministry of Public Works retain over-all responsibility for reviewing port operations and investment plans, particularly in their general economic and financial aspects, the mission recommends that there be a greater decentralization of the responsibility for port management. Each port should be responsible for its own financial results and for the preparation and execution of its investment plan.

Port management would be facilitated by the collection and analysis of additional statistics. Useful statistics now exist on many aspects of port operations. They are deficient, however, with respect to the use of equipment. Data on requests for the use of cranes, on quantities handled per crane and per wharf, on the number and location of dredges and on auxiliary equipment used between the waterfront and storage sheds would make it possible to utilize existing equipment better and to anticipate future requirements.

In some of the ports, customs formalities appeared to be delaying unnecessarily the movement of goods. We recognize the important function which customs officials must perform, particularly in applying the new tariff. However, there may well be formalities and procedures that are legacies from the period of extensive licensing and controls, and could now be streamlined or removed. We suggest that port authorities work closely with the local customs representatives, supported by the competent authorities in Madrid, to reconcile the needs for customs inspection with those for a rapid movement of goods through the ports.

Payment on the basis of work performed rather than time employed is followed in some of the Spanish ports which have the best record for efficient cargo handling. We recommend that the Government consider extension of this system to other ports.

Financial Policy and Returns on Port Operations

The accounting system of the port administrations does not contain all the elements necessary for an accurate assessment of operating results. Such an assessment would reveal a financial picture significantly different from the present apparent one.

The profit and loss statement of the port includes only the receipts and expenditures from the ports' own funds. In 1958, for example, it appears that the ports as a whole earned a cash profit of 102 million pts, but if interest payments made through the state budget on port loans are included, along with certain minor adjustments, the apparent profit is converted into a loss of 108 million pts. On this basis, only the Canary Island ports, the east coast ports (except Castellon), Vigo and Aviles show a profit.

Moreover, depreciation of port equipment should be included. This would add another 100–200 million pts to the over-all deficit, with all of the ports in a deficit position. A final adjustment is to add depreciation on fixed capital installations (wharves, breakwaters, dry docks, slipways, workshops, buildings), and interest on the capital invested in the ports (other than loan capital). Both figures are difficult to estimate, but applying a conservative depreciation rate and an interest rate of 6 percent to a very conservative estimate of the present capital value would raise the aggregate port deficit in 1958 to a figure well in excess of 1 billion pts.

Since ports are a public service, we realize that decisions on port operations may not in every instance be made solely on the basis of economic costs. But it should always be possible to know what those decisions may cost the economy.

Port revenue is obtained through a direct charge for the use of tugs, cranes and other equipment and an indirect tariff on the use of port infrastructure; this tariff, which provides more than half of total receipts, is uniform for all ports in Spain, regardless of differences in the size and nature of the port facilities provided. The mission considers it desirable for each port to have a separate indirect tariff related to the cost of its own installations (provided, of course, that this cost is accurately stated in the port's accounts through the procedures recommended above). Such an individual tariff would act as a deterrent to excessive construction of wharves, dry docks and canals, etc., since the inability to recover the cost of these investments through the tariff would be reflected in the accounts of the port that made them.

The change to individual indirect tariffs for each port should be accompanied by an increase in the average level of these tariffs so that the ports as a whole are brought closer to financial equilibrium. The purpose of the mission's recommendations with respect to the priority investment program for 1962 and 1963 is to enable the ports to provide better service and facilitate the quicker dispatch of ships. This, in turn, will make economies possible in the type of ships employed, as described later in this chapter. In the aggregate, substantial savings to shipowners should be possible, and a part of these savings can reasonably be recovered by the ports through an appreciable increase in indirect tariff rates.

The financial position of the ports would also be improved by removing the subsidies they provide to various public enterprises. The mission has observed that in some ports the rates charged to some public enterprises are lower than those charged to other customers. The rental charged for port facilities may correspond to an interest rate as low as 1½ percent. These subsidies not only distort the true picture of port operations; they provide public enterprises with an unfair competitive advantage and distort the use of resources over the economy as a whole.

Shipping Needs

The merchant marine needs to be modernized. Close to half of the 1,650,000 tons of shipping are more than 25 years old and can be considered overage (see Table 12.4). The coastal shipping (cabotage) fleet, which comprises about a third of the total tonnage, has the

TABLE 12.4: Number, Age and Tonnage of Spanish Shipping in 1960

Type	Total Number	Total Tonnage ('000)	Ships 25 Years and Older	
			Number	Tonnage
1. *Tramps:*				
Continental	145	161	31	59
Intercontinental	57	283	35	189
Tankers	20	235	3	22
Subtotal	222	679	69	270
2. *International Lines (Lineas Exteriores):*				
Cargo and mixed	25	107	9	42
Fruit	27	78	7	14
Transoceanic	10	102	1	10
Subtotal	62	287	17	66
3. *Territorial Lines (Lineas de Soberania):*				
Balearic Islands	10	27	8	16
Canary Islands	11	48	6	26
North Africa	n.a.	14	n.a.	
Guinea	n.a.	29	n.a.	34
Inter-Island	n.a.	14	n.a.	
Subtotal	n.a.	132	n.a.	76
4. *Coastal Shipping (Cabotage):*				
National Tramps	256	82	95	28
Colliers	130	186	122	179
Lumber	14	52	12	44
Tankers	36	175	19	76
Regular Lines	57	64	35	57
Subtotal	493	559	283	384
GRAND TOTAL	n.a.	1,657	n.a.	796

SOURCE: Based on data supplied by the Subsecretariat de Navegacion.

highest proportion of overage vessels (68 percent). Tramps and ocean-going liners are in a somewhat better position, but even so there are some 400,000 tons that are more than 25 years old.

How rapidly the merchant marine should be modernized depends on the prospects for future traffic growth. We have not attempted to make detailed market forecasts, but consider that it would be reasonable over the next several years to program the replacement of the overage tramps and ocean liners. For reasons indicated below, some increase in the territorial service to the Balearic and Canary Islands should be provided. A possible increase in some specialized vessels might also be envisaged; more fruit ships, for example, might be economically employed, provided that the vessels are constructed to meet the standards required by the fruit growers.

The outlook for the cabotage fleet is less promising. The principal traffic is the movement of coal from the northern coast to southern and eastern ports, but the coal market has not been prospering and the ships often have no cargo on the return voyage. Coastal shipping also suffers particularly from present port conditions, since the time spent in harbor is a relatively high proportion of the total. Excess capacity, in the form of a large number of small overage vessels, has depressed freight rates. Despite this, coastal shipping has lost substantial traffic to trucking.

Modernization of the cabotage fleet is therefore dependent on the modernization of port facilities. When the ports have been equipped to provide speedier handling of cargoes, it will be possible to consider the introduction of new, larger and faster ships. The mission believes that this should be accompanied by a substantial reduction in capacity, which could be facilitated through some merging of the interests of the many individual shipowners now in the business. With efficient ports and modern vessels, a collier fleet of less than half the present dead weight tonnage might be able to handle the existing coal traffic. Reduced capacity and improved performances should make it possible to raise freight rates and improve earning prospects. Two other changes would also help to improve the prospective return of cabotage: (a) a simplification of the customs formalities to which coastal shipping is subjected at each port; and (b) removal of the requirement which, the mission understands, compels ships to remain in the coal trade once they have entered it. Although it is important to bring about these changes, they do not necessarily ensure that coastal shipping will be sufficiently profitable to provide shipowners the incentive to invest. Competition from other modes of transport is intense, and the future market demand for coal, outside the industrial complex in the north, is uncertain and will require close study.

There is one branch of shipping, on the other hand, where the present capacity and service are clearly insufficient; the "territorial" service (lineas de soberania) to the Balearic and Canary Islands. Passenger service is infrequent, capacity limited and some of the available space reserved for government employees. There are numerous complaints from travel agencies and tourists who are unable to book round trip passage in advance, and the insufficiency of ship service is undoubtedly restricting the growth of tourism. A larger number of new, faster vessels, making more frequent trips to and from the Islands, are required. The service is now provided by the Compania Transmediterranea, which has an exclusive contract that provides for low passenger rates compensated by a subsidy to cover any operating losses. The mission recommends that the Government give this problem its close attention. If the contract cannot be renegotiated to provide more adequate service, the Government should consider permitting other companies also to offer service under more suitable conditions.

Financing Ship Investment

Spanish shipowners are not, for the most part, in a position to finance ship modernization without state help. Extensive damage and loss of vessels was suffered during the Civil War. Over most of the postwar period, the merchant marine was used to transport foodstuffs for the Spanish population at low freight rates fixed by the Government as a means of keeping down the price of food. Freight rates are now subject only to more nominal control, but competition has kept them at low levels. As a result, few shipowners have been able to build up the financial reserves necessary to purchase new vessels.

The Government has been providing substantial funds for shipbuilding, in the form of loans from the Instituto de Credito Naval. These are provided at 4 percent interest, over a period of 15 years, and for up to 80 percent of the cost of the ship. In 1959 and 1960, Credito Naval was authorized to lend 1.9 billion pts and 2.4 billion pts, respectively. Ship construction which had been about 50,000–60,000 tons in 1958, rose to the sizable totals of 150,000 tons in 1959 and 157,000 tons in 1960. The Government's program calls for the provision of a total of 2.0 billion pts in loans during 1962, and of 1.6 billion pts annually thereafter.

We consider that the funds proposed for shipbuilding through the loans of Credito Naval are reasonable and recommend that the program be carried out on this basis. Over the next 3 or 4 years, while priority is given to the re-equipment of the ports, the funds should be devoted to an accelerated modernization of the tramp fleet and ocean-going liners. Except in the territorial lines, the program should aim at the replacement rather than expansion of existing capacity. The funds proposed should be sufficient to replace all of the overage capacity in these categories (some 350,000–400,000 tons) within 4 years' time, as well as to permit an expansion of service in the territorial lines.

By the time that this accelerated program for tramps and liners has been completed, the ports will have been properly equipped. It will then be possible to devote funds to modernization of the cabotage fleet, provided that it is warranted by the market prospects at the time.

Apart from the special problem of coastal shipping, this program should result in a relatively modern Spanish merchant marine within 5 years' time provided, of course, that shipowners are prepared to raise their share of the funds. It is hoped that, thereafter, shipowners will be in a position to finance the normal replacement of their vessels on a more conventional basis. It should then be possible to reduce the volume of lending by Credito Naval, which in turn should charge interest rates closer to the true market level and require shipowners to supply a higher proportion of the cost.

It can be assumed that most if not all of the ships will be produced in Spanish shipyards, but shipowners should not be required to procure exclusively in Spain as a condition of admission of the vessel to the Spanish fleet. There may be situations, for example, in which a shipowner has no prospect for operating profitably unless he can acquire a second-hand tramp abroad.

The Spanish shipyards have a capacity that has been variously estimated at between 350,000 and 500,000 gross registered tons annually. Even with the accelerated program of ship renovation, therefore, shipbuilding capacity will be in excess of foreseeable Spanish needs. The shipbuilding industry has made good progress in obtaining foreign orders. The Government should continue to encourage this development, as it has in the past, by ensuring that adequate export credit can be provided to foreign purchasers on terms competitive with those in other countries. (See the discussion of export credit in Chapter 8.) As a rough estimate, some 2 billion pts of export credit for ships may be required annually.

If there should still be excess capacity despite foreign orders, a solution should not be sought through the construction of ships by state enterprises (INI) if these have to be sold or chartered to Spanish firms at a loss. This would perpetuate excess shipyard capacity and threaten to create excess ship capacity that would depress the entire industry.

TABLE 12.5: Specific Investment Recommendations for Spanish Ports (million pts)

Port	Existing Plans to be Eliminated	Savings Through Plans Eliminated	Existing and Additional Plans to be Carried Out	Equipment to be Procured					Additional Expenses in 1962/63	Accelerated Expenses in 1962/63[b]
				Cranes[a]	Mobile Cranes	Fork-lifts	Electric Carriages	Ordinary Carriages		
Barcelona	1. Dique del Este, except for the part already started.	500	1. Muelle del Rompeolas as far as construction has proceeded, should be completed.							
	2. Dique Seco and Defensa Exterior para el Dique Seco.		2. During the time additional cranes are on order some 500,000 M2 of pavement of wharves should be thoroughly repaired and given a flat tiled surface for operation of forklifts and electric carriages.							
	3. Wharf to the eastward of the Dique Seco.		3. Oil and water supply should be provided at several points in the various basins.						100	
			4. Additional equipment.	40		25	20		150	
			5. p.m. Dredging material.							
Tarragona	1. Plan to remove varadero should be dropped.	15	1. Interconnecting crane tracks on old and new wharves.	9	p.m.				30	
	2. Dredging should be reduced when more cranes available.		2. Additional equipment.							

(continued on next page)

Table 12.5 (cont.)

Port	Existing Plans to be Eliminated	Savings Through Plans Eliminated	Existing and Additional Plans to be Carried Out	Equipment to be Procured					Additional Expenses in 1962/63	Accelerated Expenses in 1962/63[b]
				Cranes[a]	Mobile Cranes	Fork lifts	Electric Carriages	Ordinary Carriages		
Valencia	1. Plan to close existing entrance and construct new one should be eliminated.	250	1. Additional equipment.	16		4	10	28	53	
Castellon	1. p.m. It should be considered whether the amount of traffic justifies continuation of Castellon as a separate port.									
Alicante			1. Three small piers to moor tankers should be accelerated. 2. Accelerated equipment.							5 65
Cartagena	1. New road between old port and new oil port. 2. Breakwater in front of fishing port.	35	1. All other parts of the 1962–1970 plan. 2. Accelerated equipment.	6					3	15
Almeria			1. Works provided in the 1962–1970 plan. 2. Additional equipment.	12	3				40	

	Works needed		Maintenance and dredging.					
Motril	1. Extension of the Muelle de Costa.	p.m.	1. Maintenance and dredging.					
			2. Accelerated equipment.	3				9
			3. Additional equipment.	3				9
Adra	1. All new construction.	p.m.	1. Equipment when necessary.					
Malaga	1. Repairs to the left and right parts of Muelle No. 2.		1. Dredging in front of Muelle No. 2 and completion of center part.					
	2. Piers in the outer harbor for 40,000-ton tankers.	6	2. Improvement of pavement and reinforcing breakwater and speeding up of pavement repairs.				8	12
	3. Dredging of outer harbor to 12-½ meters.	20	3. Accelerated equipment (replacing electric with ordinary carriages).	8		30	22.5	27
	N.B. 2 and 3 will only become necessary after it has become certain that Puertollano oil will be shipped via Malaga, and then nautical advice as to depth required should be obtained first.		4. Additional equipment.	4	6	6		
Algeciras	1. All plans.	685	1. Additional equipment.		2		2.5	
Puerto de Santa Maria		2	1. Adjustment in price of cranes.		3			

(continued on next page)

Table 12.5 (cont.)

Port	Existing Plans to be Eliminated	Savings Through Plans Eliminated	Existing and Additional Plans to be Carried Out	Cranes[a]	Mobile Cranes	Fork-lifts	Electric Carriages	Ordinary Carriages	Additional Expenses in 1962/63	Accelerated Expenses in 1962/63[b]
Cadiz	1. Dique de Levante.	120	1. New shed on Muelle del Generalissimo and enlarged one (No. 3) on M.M. de Commillas speeded up.							10
			2. Passenger station speeded up.							25
			3. Pavement improvement speeded up and extended.						12	13
			4. Accelerated equipment and increase in price of cranes.		2	10			1	8
			5. Additional equipment, to be towed by forklifts.		2			40	7	
Huelva	1. Pavement of new fishing port should be less extensive.	p.m.								

Port	Project	Recommendations							
Sevilla	1. New Basin. [230]	1. Port improvements (four sheds, attendant provisions, pavement) speeded up.							102
		2. Accelerated equipment.	4		10		40	27	12
		3. Additional equipment.	6						
Vigo	1. Four 10-ton cranes. [16]	1. Speeding up of pavement repairs, etc.							20
	2. Tug. [24]	2. Accelerated equipment (including 2 automobile cranes) and revised cost estimate for forklifts.	12		6	10		1	39
	p.m. No slipways to build fishing vessels. Repairs to wharf to be scrutinized.								
Pontevedra-Marin	1. Two breakwaters. [109]	1. Additional equipment.	2	2				8.5	
La Coruna	1. Muelle de las Animas. [175]	1. Superstructure of breakwater extension should be completed.							
		2. Additional equipment.	12		4	8		40	
San Esteban de Pravia	p.m. If after study of the problem of excess capacity in the three coal ports this port remains open, dredging should be done.								

(continued on next page)

Table 12.5 (cont.)

Port	Existing Plans to be Eliminated	Savings Through Plans Eliminated	Existing and Additional Plans to be Carried Out	Equipment to be Procured					Additional Expenses in 1962/63	Accelerated Expenses in 1962/63[b]
				Cranes[a]	Mobile Cranes	Fork-lifts	Electric Carriages	Ordinary Carriages		
Aviles	1. New breakwater.	500	1. Speed up widening and deepening of entrance. 2. Additional equipment (3 cranes of 40–50 tons; 13 of 5 tons).	16					95	235
Gijon	1. Widening of Espigon I. 2. Espigon VI. 3. Dique W. 4. New coal conveyor.	62 210 5.5 104	1. Speed up improvement of coal conveyors. 2. Accelerated equipment. 3. Additional equipment.	13 5	6				13	8 49
Santander	1. New wharf in entrance to Darsena de Maliano. 2. Pavement of wharf above. 3. Railway to Zona Franca.	60 23 17	1. Speed up wharf of 230 meters connecting two wharves of 129 and 152.5 meters. 2. Speed up and extend repairs to rail track. 3. Speed repairs to rail track and pavement, Eastern part.						3.5	55 8.5 12

Project	Item	Cost	Recommendation					
			including substitution of one 10-ton crane for planned 3-ton crane.	11			1.5	33.5
			5. Additional equipment, including 3 cranes for the Muelle de Maliano.	5	4		21	
			6. p.m. Dredging Muelle de Albareda and Maura.					
			7. p.m. Some forklifts and other carriages may be necessary when all new cranes are functioning.					
			8. p.m. Electric current situation at Muelle de Maliano should be improved.					
Bilbao	1. Deusto Canal.[c]	127.5	1. Accelerated equipment (including cost correction).	18		14	9	49
	2. Tug and lighting.	9	2. Additional equipment.	10	4	12	39	
	3. Part of contingency funds to be cancelled.	8	3. Part of contingency funds to be used for pavement improvement.					25

(continued on next page)

Table 12.5 (cont.)

Port	Existing Plans to be Eliminated	Savings Through Plans Eliminated	Existing and Additional Plans to be Carried Out	Equipment to be Procured					Additional Expenses in 1962/63	Accelerated Expenses in 1962/63[b]
				Cranes[a]	Mobile Cranes	Fork-lifts	Electric Carriages	Ordinary Carriages		
Pasajes	1. Replace old plan with projects described in next column.	153.5	1. Completing the new wharves.	20					27	
			2. Equipment for new wharves.			20	20		74	
			3. Sheds for new wharves.						36	
			4. Cranes for Muelle Transatlantico.	6					18	
			5. Dredging of basin in front of new wharves.						48	
			6. Completely fitting out new wharves with electric lines, tractors, clam-shells, pavement.						40	
			7. Unforeseen.						7	
La Luz y Las Palmas	1. New wharf, shifting of present slipway and dredging in the present Darsena.	127	1. Additional equipment.	20		10	12	50	76	

de Tenerife										
Dique Sur.	12	equipment and sheds.	12	8	10	106	40	11	59
2. Preparations for plan Ribera III.	11	2. Unforeseen.						10	
3. Dredging for same.	2								
Total	3,642.5		273	42	105	106	228	1,043.5	896

a Unless otherwise specified, 5-ton cranes moving on fixed tracks should be procured.
b These represent expenditures for equipment and other items included in the 1962–70 plan that should be carried out in the first two years.
c Elimination is based on the assumption that completion of the canal will cost much more than the amount allocated (127.5 million pts).

CHAPTER 13 *AIR TRANSPORT*

Air transport still accounts for only a negligible proportion of total passenger and freight traffic in Spain but, as in other countries, it has been growing more rapidly than other modes; between 1951 and 1960, air freight traffic increased almost sevenfold, and air passenger traffic sixfold. Air transport has a very bright future in Spain; the difficult terrain, long distances between major centers of activity and considerable traffic to the insular provinces all favor movement by air. On the whole, public policy toward air transport has been soundly conceived, but we consider that certain changes are desirable if full advantage is to be taken of the potential for development.

The two Spanish air lines, Iberia and Aviaco, are both wholly owned by INI. Aviaco has recently been acquired, and consolidation of the operations of the two lines is now being undertaken, beginning with maintenance and overhaul. Additional savings through consolidation should be possible, provided that the quality of service is not affected. Iberia appears to be well managed and operates at low cost; the airline has shown a profit in every year but one since 1950, and has even operated profitably, unlike many other European air services, under the international tariffs set for the European and Atlantic services. Aviaco has lost money in most years, but earned a profit in 1960, the first full year of operation with newer aircraft (Convair Metropolitans).

The air fleet has heretofore been very mixed, including a number of unpressurized aircraft. With the introduction of jet-powered aircraft (DC–8's and Caravelles) in 1961–62 the situation will be much improved, as the modern piston-engined aircraft in international service can enter interior and territorial service (to the Canary Islands and the African provinces) for several more years of useful life. Unpressurized equipment will be retired from passenger service, except possibly for the Balearic Islands where the very short hauls reduce the need for altitude compensation.

Compared to other European air fares for similar services, those for the Spanish interior and territorial services appear to be quite low. It is not clear whether or not the rates require the airlines to operate at a loss, but they definitely discourage proper service. Schedules are too infrequent, and load factors are consequently too high; while Iberia operated with a load factor on interior lines of 74 percent in 1960, it is general airline experience that annual average load factors should not exceed 65 percent if passenger traffic is to be handled expeditiously,

250

particularly during peak periods. The fares on air service to the Canary Islands are among the lowest, per passenger-kilometer, in the world.

In line with the general principles of transport rate policy which we set forth in Chapter 9, the mission recommends that fares for the interior and territorial services, which are set by the Council of Ministers, be raised to cover the full costs of providing adequate service, including the costs of additional flights necessary to reduce average load factors. If the Government believes it desirable, as an exception, to maintain very low fares to the Canaries, it should grant the airlines a flat subsidy per passenger so that other services do not have to bear the burden of the artificial rates on this segment of traffic. The airlines should have the authority to adjust internal fares upward or downward within a range of 25 percent, and should be encouraged to work out the optimum combinations of fares and services by market experimentation. This policy will make it possible for the airlines to continue their expansion on a sound, self-sustaining basis.

Freight and charter services have so far not been well developed (although charter has been heavily exploited by foreign airlines) and these should be the subject of early study and actual service experimentation. Charter services will be facilitated by the changes in fleet composition now occurring, which will make additional older aircraft available.

There has been insufficient investment in airports and airways in the past, and facilities on the whole have been inadequate. However, plans already under way for modernization, which are generally well conceived, will in time remedy these deficiencies. The present stage of the program, which began in 1958 and is to extend through 1963, involves 1,400 million pts for construction of improved airport facilities at 5 cities (Madrid, Barcelona, Palma de Mallorca, Las Palmas (Gran Canarias) and Malaga) and 400 million pts for air navigation, traffic control and instrument landing facility programs. The next stage is a five-year program to begin in 1963; it includes 1,500 million pts for airport improvements at 15 locations[1] in mainland Spain, the Balearic and Canary Islands and Africa and 1,200 million pts to complete the national system of navigation and traffic control. The mission endorses this program.

[1] In the interior—Santiago de Compostela, Alicante, Sevilla, Asturias, Bilbao, Santander, San Sebastian; Balearic Islands—Ibiza and Mahon; Canary Islands—Tenerife, La Palma, Lansarote and Fuerteventura; Africa—Ceuta and Melilla.

SECTION **IV**

AGRICULTURE

CHAPTER 14 AGRICULTURE

BASIC CHARACTERISTICS

Despite the considerable development of industry and services, agriculture is still the principal source of employment in Spain, occupying over 40 percent of the total labor force in 1960. This proportion is gradually declining, but the movement out of agriculture has not been sufficient to remove the disparity in productivity and income between it and other sectors of the economy, as evidenced by the fact that gross income per person employed in agriculture was less than two-thirds of the national average in 1960. Agriculture continues to be an important source of foreign exchange earnings, accounting for about one-third of the total in 1960.

About two-thirds of the farmland is operated by the farm owner and his family. A considerable proportion of the farms are small (more than 25 percent are less than 5 hectares), and many of the smaller farmers, particularly in areas of unfavorable climate and terrain, operate under relatively primitive conditions and at close to subsistence incomes. There are perhaps one million farm workers who have no fixed employment and work only seasonally. These underemployed laborers, together with the subsistence farmers, constitute the hard core of the low-income problem in Spanish agriculture.

Natural conditions are not, for the most part, especially favorable to agriculture. Terrain is rugged and mountainous. Much of the land consists of high plateaus divided by barren mountain ranges; only about 40 percent is at an altitude of less than 500 meters. The cultivated area, now 40 percent of the total land surface, has probably reached its maximum. Rainfall is insufficient on the whole and part of the country is semi-arid; precipitation also varies sharply by season and year as well as among regions. (Map 18 shows the variations in rainfall in different parts of Spain.) A large part of the land area is subject to wide temperature fluctuations, while only a small part is free from the threat of frost. Terrain and climate have, in combination, brought about a severe problem of erosion in certain areas.

These disadvantages are real, but their importance should not be exaggerated. Given the relatively large land area of Spain and the low population density, agricultural land is sufficient for Spain to produce most of its food requirements and, indeed, to be a net exporter of farm products. And there are regions where production takes place under very favorable conditions of climate and rainfall or where irrigation is feasible. In fact, the most striking feature of Spanish agriculture is its diversity.

This diversity is perhaps most marked in its regional aspects, and all generalizations about Spanish agriculture must immediately be qualified by the wide variations among regions. There are many alternative ways of grouping regions, each of which is somewhat arbitrary and has its advantages and disadvantages. For present purposes, eight regions might briefly be distinguished. They are shown in Map 19.

Galicia[1] in the northwest is one of the most favored regions of Spain. Rainfall is sufficient, winter temperatures relatively mild and the soil is good enough to produce satisfactory yields when appropriate production practices are applied. However, population is dense and a relatively high proportion is still on the land. In addition, fragmentation of farm land into an excessive number of individual parcels—the minifundia problem of north and central Spain—reaches its extreme in this area, raising production costs. Farm income per capita is therefore low, comparable to that of the poorest part of Andalucia.

A basically similar region, which might be called *East Cantabrica*,[2] adjoins the eastern boundary of Galicia. As this region draws income from industry and tourism as well, the active population in agriculture is proportionately less than the national average and per capita agricultural income is higher. Favorable climate, fertile land and generally abundant rainfall have led to a diversified agriculture. Animal husbandry, together with the requisite facilities for meat and dairy processing, is well developed.

To the south and east lies the very large and relatively poor region of the meseta. The *North Meseta*,[3] with high altitudes, mountainous terrain, extreme winter temperatures and low rainfall, was originally occupied by forests intermixed with clear grazing spaces for cattle and sheep. The forests have gradually disappeared, and livestock has given place to grain and other crops. Yields are low, and even with subsidized prices production tends to be marginal under dry farming, with a good crop only once in several years. The *South Meseta*[4] has less mountainous terrain and milder winters, but the region is semi-arid. In Don Quixote's days it consisted mainly of very extensive pasture land. Although wheat growing shows very poor returns, dry farming is

---

[1] Provinces of La Coruna, Lugo, Orense, Pontevedra.

[2] Logrono, Pamplona, Vitoria, San Sebastian, Bilbao, Oviedo, Santander.

[3] Avila, Burgos, Palencia, Segovia, Soria, Valladolid, Huesca, Teruel, Zaragoza, Leon, Salamanca, Zamora.

[4] Ciudad Real, Cuenca, Guadalajara, Madrid, Toledo, Albacete, Badajoz, Caceres.

carried out in many parts of the region and represents over 20 percent of the total Spanish crop. Large areas are in vineyards, and sheep grazing is growing in importance. The southwest part of the region is the site of an ambitious government program of irrigation, settlement and regional development, the Badajoz Plan.

Andalucia[5] is overwhelmingly agricultural except for industrial concentrations in Cadiz, Cordoba and Sevilla. Climate is mild and the rainfall, while light, permits a variety of crops to be grown in most of the provinces. In addition to wheat, which gives adequate yields in most parts of the region, cotton, tobacco, grapes, sugar and potatoes are produced. Olives are a major crop, but while they absorb large amounts of labor the requirements are highly seasonal so that the labor calendar tends to be unbalanced in areas where olives are the principal crop; in years of poor harvest, the income of farm labor in the olive-growing area may be severely depressed. Citrus, other fruits and early vegetables can be grown very well under irrigation. Andalucia also contains the most promising underdeveloped land area in Spain: the virgin land on both banks of the lower Guadalquivir (the *marismas*) which, with dikes and drainage, could produce higher yield crops even without irrigation.

In the east, the *Levante*[6] is an unpromising region of poor and mountainous land—except along the coast and in narrow valleys—and minimal rainfall. There are too many days below freezing to classify the climate as ideal for citrus. Nevertheless, skill in using rivers for irrigation and local business proficiency have created from this hard environment one of the richest and most intensive agricultural regions in the world. As the most northern citrus-growing area of the Mediterranean basin, the Levante is well located with respect to the European markets for which it has long been the principal supplier.

Catalonia[7] in the northeast is outside of the citrus-growing region, but the climate permits diversified farming, and proximity to Barcelona and European markets has encouraged development of higher-value crops and livestock breeding, including a rapidly growing poultry industry. Techniques are relatively advanced; tractor use is proportionately the highest in Spain, undoubtedly spurred by the movement of farm labor into industry and services.

Of the *Island*[8] provinces, the Balearic Islands are not predomi-

---

[5] Cadiz, Cordoba, Huelva, Sevilla, Almeria, Granada, Jaen, Malaga.

[6] Alicante, Castellon, Murcia, Valencia.

[7] Barcelona, Gerona, Lerida, Tarragona.

[8] Consisting of the Balearic Islands and the two Canary Island provinces (Las Palmas and Santa Cruz de Tenerife).

nantly agricultural, and most of the crops are designed for local and tourist consumption. The Canary Islands are very short of water, but with intensive use of irrigation it has been possible to take advantage of the exceptionally favorable climate to produce a wide variety of crops, including bananas and early tomatoes and potatoes which are important export earners.

The foregoing description, necessarily brief, of regional diversity suggests some of the diversity of cropping and livestock situations which is also characteristic of Spanish agriculture. Roughly three-fifths of total production consists of crops and one-third of livestock products, with forestry accounting for about 5 percent (see Table 14.1). Cereals are grown in every province and, including fallow land used in

TABLE 14.1: Value of Gross Agricultural Production, 1951–60

(billion pts)

	Value	Percent
Cereal grains	42.9	19.5
Pulses (leguminosas)	5.3	2.4
Straw	3.2	1.5
Potatoes	9.0	4.1
Vegetables	13.8	6.3
Fruit	20.6	9.4
Olive oil and by-products	10.4	4.7
Wine and by-products	7.9	3.6
Industrial crops	8.1	3.7
Fodder	7.1	3.2
Grazing	4.9	2.2
Other	2.0	.9
Subtotal for agricultural crops	135.2	61.5
Meat	23.5	10.7
Milk	13.7	6.2
Eggs	7.5	3.4
Wool	1.5	.7
Products consumed on farm[a]	27.0	12.3
Subtotal livestock	73.2	33.3
Forestry products	11.3	5.2
Total	219.7[b]	100.0

[a] Manure, work performed by farm animals.
[b] Of which approximately 70 billion pts represents products consumed within agriculture.

SOURCE: Ministry of Agriculture, *El Producto Neto de la Agricultura Española en 1959–60.*

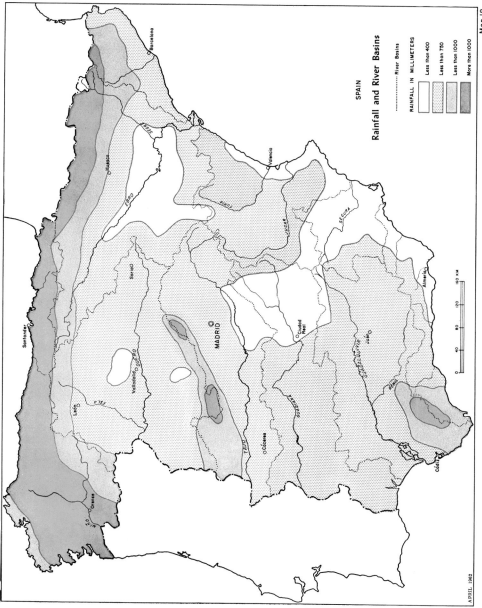

SPAIN

Rainfall and River Basins

·········· River Basins

RAINFALL IN MILLIMETERS

Less than 400
Less than 750
Less than 1000
More than 1000

APRIL 1962

Map 18

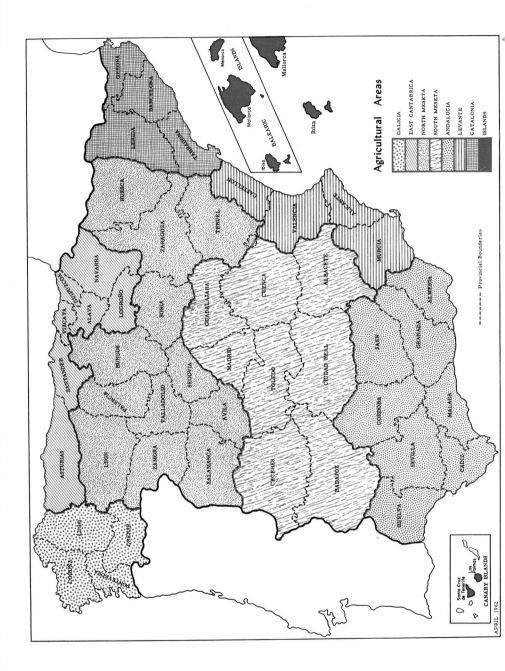

Agricultural Areas

GALICIA
EAST CANTABRICA
NORTH MESETA
SOUTH MESETA
ANDALUCIA
LEVANTE
CATALONIA
ISLANDS

------ Provincial Boundaries

APRIL 1962

cereal rotation, cover more than half of the cultivated surface. They represent only 20–25 percent of the total value of production, however. Meat, fruit and vegetables each account for 10–15 percent; the remainder is taken up by milk, olive oil, wine, eggs, cotton, tobacco and numerous others.

Agricultural production was slow to recover from the widespread dislocation of the war, and shortages of basic foodstuffs gave rise to extensive government interventions designed to encourage production, control prices at the consumer level and limit exports. According to official data, production has been increasing at a fairly rapid rate during the past decade. There are no longer any significant shortages of food products, and farm prices have been relatively stable.

THE OUTLOOK FOR FARM PRODUCTION

Now that growth of production has brought supply and demand into better balance, Spanish agriculture is entering a stage where its development will largely be determined by the future demand for farm products. Failure to take account of the outlook for market demand in orienting public policy toward agriculture could result, in some cases, in the accumulation of large and unmanageable surpluses associated with falling prices and farm incomes; in others, it could lead to supply shortages that would force prices upward and create a strong demand for imports. The result would be a serious misuse of farm resources, costly government support programs and lower farm incomes in the aggregate than would otherwise be possible.

Domestic Demand

The outlook for demand can be differentiated between the *domestic* demand for agricultural products and the *foreign* demand for Spanish exports. With respect to domestic demand, it is by now well established that there is a tendency, as incomes rise, for the demand for food also to rise, but less than proportionately. Thus, a 10 percent rise in consumer income may result in only a 2 percent or 3 percent increase in demand for food. This is because food occupies a very large proportion of the family budget in the lowest income levels; as incomes rise, an increasing proportion is spent on clothing, rent and other non-food items. There is even a point, which has already been reached in most developed countries, where the demand for certain food products (such as bread) declines in absolute amount at higher income levels.

Increased demand resulting from the growth of population acts to offset this tendency, but usually only in part.

Spanish officials have undertaken various studies of the relationship between the growth of income and population and the domestic demand for food. A major study is now under way. The most recent findings are summarized in Annex E, Table E.1. As these officials fully recognize, the present estimates, being based on fragmentary data, are subject to a wide margin of error. The mission is not in a position to evaluate the estimates or to improve upon them. In general, however, they appear to be more or less consistent with what has been observed in the case of other countries, and may be taken as broadly *illustrative* of how demand may be expected to develop with the growth of income. These estimates do not allow for the effect on demand of changes in prices; this is a point that requires further study, but in general it is believed that the effect is not likely to be very important.

From the estimates in Annex E, Table E.1 and using the rates of growth of population and income assumed in Section I of this report, it appears that the demand in 1975 for some of the principal farm products would be as follows:

Item	% Change in demand 1960–1975
Wheat	–10
Potatoes	10
Pulses (legumes)	10
Rice	15
Vegetables	25
Oils	25
Wine	35
Fruits	40
Sugar	95
Milk	80
Eggs	110
Meat	145

These figures suggest that the demand for wheat will be lower in 1975 than it is today. For potatoes, pulses and perhaps rice, the increased demand will be small enough that it can be met through expected increases in productivity without any increase, and probably with a reduction, in the land and labor devoted to their production. Increases in yields may also be sufficient to take care of the demand for vegetables. On the other hand, the demand for animal protein (meat and dairy products) is likely to be more than double and, in the absence of large imports, can only be satisfied by adding resources to their production. After some of the individual items are briefly considered, and export demand taken into account, the general implications of this demand outlook will be drawn. Table 14.2 gives background information on the acreage and production of the principal crops.

Wheat is a key problem, and we discuss it at greater length later in the chapter. More than 20 percent of the cultivated land area is in wheat, with an additional 25 percent lying fallow as part of the cereals rotation cycle. Despite shortages in some years, supply on the average is nearly sufficient to meet current demand. Spain is not in an advantageous position to compete for international wheat markets. With the probability that domestic demand in 1975 will be lower than it is today, resources will clearly have to be withdrawn from wheat production. Average yields at present are relatively low—950 kg per hectare on dry land and 2.100 kg per hectare on irrigated. With an increase in average yields of 20 percent over the 15 years, which is entirely possible through improved methods, the 1975 demand could be met on 25 percent less hectares than were required in 1959/60. If all of the reduced acreage were on dry land farming, more than one million hectares would have to be removed from wheat production if supply is to be kept in balance with demand at current price levels.

Changing food habits with rising income will probably also necessitate a withdrawal of resources from *potatoes*. If current prices prevail, 1975 consumption is unlikely to be significantly greater than today. But the expanded use of improved seed will push yields up even if no other improved practices are adopted. A similar conclusion applies to *legumes* (beans, lentils, etc.).

Sugar consumption may be expected to increase fairly sharply. Sugar beet production has been expanding rapidly over the past decade, but future demand will be sufficiently strong to require that additional land, presumably irrigated, be devoted to this purpose. In the case of *cotton* (not shown in the table on page 260), the demand for domestic output by the textile industry can be expected to expand if yields can be improved to a point where the crop is competitive at international prices. How much import substitution is possible will depend on relative price movements which are difficult to predict. A further growth of production with some increased acreage under irrigation should probably be forecast.

The most significant requirements for additional production will be brought about through the sharp increase in the consumption of

TABLE 14.2: Acreage and Production of Crops, 1959/60

Item	Dry Land Area ('000 ha.)	Dry Land Prod. ('000 tons)	Irrigation Area ('000 ha.)	Irrigation Prod. ('000 tons)	Total Area ('000 ha.)	Total Prod. ('000 tons)
Annual Crops:	8,621	–	1,461	–	10,082	–
Wheat	4,054	3,977	314	658	4,368	4,635
Other Grain Cereals	2,764	3,500	297	1,014	3,061	4,514
Pulses[a]	903	626	91	120	994	746
Potatoes	240	2,377	160	2,211	400	4,588
Sugar Beet	25	452	119	3,467	144	3,919
Vegetables[b][c]	19	331	271	4,675	290	5,006
Cotton[d]	132	73	93	118	225	190
Annual Fodder[b][f]	449	7,226	56	1,633	505	8,859
Miscellaneous	35	95	60	303	95	399
Overannual Crops:	129	–	144	–	273	–
Overannual Fodder[b][g]	56	239	139	1,109	195	1,348
Artificial Pasture[b][g]	73	373	–	–	73	373
Other	–	–	5	324	5	324
Tree Crops:	4,006	–	341	–	4,347	–
Orange[h]	–	–	90	1,442	90	1,442
Other Citrus[i]	–	–	19	222	19	222
Other Fruit[b][e]	254	826	58	820	312	1,647
Olive Trees[j]	2,156	2,051	140	177	2,296	2,228
Vineyard	1,418	2,314	34	84	1,452	2,397
Almond Trees	178	142	–	–	178	142
Total	12,756	–	1,946[k]	–	14,699[k]	–
Idle Land	976	–	–	–	976	–
Fallow	5,385	–	–	–	5,385	–
Total Arable Land	19,117	–	1,946[k]	–	21,070[k]	–

[a] Leguminosas for green, direct consumption, are tabulated under "vegetables."

[b] Distribution between dry land and irrigation is estimated.

[c] Includes (a) leguminosas for green, direct consumption and (b) melon and strawberry which the source classifies as fruit. We assumed that all hectarage is in irrigation, with the exception of the provinces of La Coruna, Vizcayo, Lugo, Santander and Guipuzcoa, where there is no irrigation.

[d] Figures refer to raw cotton (before ginning).

[e] In order to meet the figures of table 265 (pages 370–371 of the source), hectarages in dry land were forced up.

[f] Production figures refer to green weight.

[g] Production figures express hay equivalent.

[h] Hectarage includes 9,000 ha. not in production yet.

[i] Hectarage includes 2,600 ha. tangerines not in production yet.

[j] Hectarage includes 317,900 ha. olive trees associated with vineyard (274,300 in dry land, 43,600 ha. in irrigation).

[k] Including approximately 160,000 ha. which are a duplication on account of double cropping.

SOURCE: Based on the *Anuario Estadistico de la Produccion Agricola, 1959–60.*

animal protein that can be expected as consumer incomes rise. Fundamental changes in animal husbandry and the pattern of land use will be necessary if demand is to be satisfied without sharply rising prices and pressure for imports. Some of the changes involved are discussed more fully later in the chapter. How increased demand for meat, poultry and dairy products will affect, on balance, the use of land is very difficult to say, since not enough is known about the relative costs and returns for the various alternative ways of providing feeds. It appears, however, that there may be considerable room for expansion in the production of oilseed crops on some suitable farms, particularly as a means of substituting for imports which are now quite large. Perhaps the principal increases in land use and production will be in improved pasture and in the cultivation of fodder crops (alfalfa, etc.); output in those two categories might easily double. The prospect for feed grains, which now account for a large acreage, is more uncertain. Improved seed and technique can create additional production without new acreage; and in addition, international supplies of feed grains will probably be ample and available at low prices.

Export Demand

The outlook for foreign demand for Spanish agricultural products is even more difficult to predict, since more elements are involved. Exports of farm products in the past have sustained an important part of agricultural production and been the principal source of foreign exchange. The mission has not been able to investigate export prospects in detail, and the terms of Spanish access to foreign markets are undergoing change as the movement toward economic integration in Europe and elsewhere evolves.

Citrus fruit, mainly oranges, is the largest single export item. Western Europe takes the bulk of these exports, with Common Market countries alone absorbing around 70 percent of Spanish exports. Production in other countries has been expanding rapidly, and even though consumption in traditional markets may be expected to increase, export supply is likely in the future to outrun demand with a resultant drop in citrus prices. On the other hand, a decline in prices may further stimulate demand; markets in Eastern Europe are still untapped; and the market for juices and concentrates is capable of considerable further expansion, particularly at lower average prices for citrus. The cost structure of citrus growing in Spain appears to provide ample margins within which to absorb a decline in world market prices, at least in the short run. In addition, domestic demand for citrus and other fruits has been expanding rapidly, and the demand forecasts in the text and Annex Table E.1 are very likely to be excessively conservative. On balance, qualified optimism on the outlook for increased citrus demand appears reasonable. On the other hand, about one-fourth of the present area planted in citrus is not yet of bearing age, and citrus cultivation is so intensive that even a substantial increase in production can be obtained by adding only a few thousand hectares of irrigated land.

Two other of the numerous agricultural export products might be mentioned: *olive oil* and *wine*. Olive groves and vineyards each occupy over 10 percent of the arable land area, and olives, olive oil and wine are traditional and important exports. The outlook for these products cannot be forecast reliably without a market-by-market analysis, but it is unlikely that increased exports will necessitate any substantial increases in yields or in the areas devoted to olives and grapes.

Combined Outlook

We cannot do more than point very generally to the directions in which changes in demand will affect the outlook for Spanish agriculture. More information and careful analysis are required before these broad trends can be reduced to quantitative terms as, for example, in the preparation of a comparative table of land use in 1960 and 1975 through which the shifts in production could be traced in detail. Even within the limitations of present information, however, certain points are reasonably clear:

a. More than 60 percent of the present cultivated area (including part of the fallow land) is now devoted to three crops: wheat, wine and olives. For two of these (wine and olives) the prospect is that increases in demand can be met with only slight expansion, if any, of the existing acreage; in the case of wheat, the combined effect of increased yields and an eventual decline in demand will make it necessary to withdraw a substantial amount of land and labor from wheat production.

b. The need to provide feed for livestock will create an additional demand for resources, particularly in the form of more pasture land and fodder production. It is unlikely, at least over the next 15–20 years, that the amount of land and labor devoted to this purpose will equal that withdrawn from wheat production.

c. Increased resources will have to be devoted to producing more of a number of intermediate and high value crops such as cotton, sugar beet, fruits, vegetables and, if practicable, oilseeds. This additional production will take place mostly under irrigation and since cultivation is highly intensive the amounts of land involved, even under optimistic assumptions, will not have a significant effect on the pattern of land use, although it will make a significant contribution toward raising farm incomes.

These considerations indicate that the conditions facing policy makers over the next 15–25 years will be fundamentally different from those which prevailed during the past two decades. The central problem is no longer to produce more at any cost, but to produce the right amounts, and the right combination of crops, at the lowest possible cost. If farm incomes are to advance as rapidly as technical and economic conditions now make possible, public policy must be oriented toward assisting the natural forces already at work:

a. to shift resources from declining to expanding types of production;

b. to increase the productivity and returns on resources in all uses; and

c. to move excess resources out of agriculture through maximum growth elsewhere in the economy.

An approach along these lines will bring about the maximum rate of growth of farm income as a whole. If the Government wishes to provide greater assistance to certain income groups or areas, we recommend that it do so through direct measures of the type described subsequently rather than through market interventions which tend to distort the allocation of resources throughout agriculture and thus to reduce the over-all rate of growth of production and income.

How this approach might be carried out in practice is discussed in the sections that follow. They discuss, first, policies designed to increase the returns on resources in existing uses and, secondly, policies to induce shifts in resource uses.

POLICIES TO INCREASE RETURNS ON RESOURCES

The principal means employed in the past to increase agricultural yields has been irrigation. Considerable attention will be given to irrigation here because of the importance which the Government attaches to the program and of the large amounts of public funds involved.

There are other ways of increasing productivity and the return on resources used in agriculture which also deserve consideration, among them the reform of farm units which may be too large or too small, soil conservation, improved seed and livestock, better fertilizer use and increased use of farm machinery. Underlying all of these programs is the need for expanded extension services to bring improvements in technique to the farmer and greatly expanded technical education to increase the supply of farmers who are in a position to take advantage of the technological advances.

Irrigation and Colonization

The practice of irrigation in Spain is of ancient origin. Irrigated farming in the Levante is among the most highly skilled in the world and is responsible for Spain's most important export product, citrus fruit. The present area under irrigation is somewhat less than two million hectares, or about one-tenth of the cultivated area.

In recent years the Government, which has been responsible for major works, has been intensifying its efforts to extend the irrigated area in order to improve the conditions for farming in parts of the country which lack rainfall and to alleviate, in some measure, the distress which severe droughts periodically bring in their train to large sections of the rural population. Another feature of recent policy has been to combine some of the major irrigation works with colonization and regional development, whereby new communities are established on what was virtually barren land. The extent of these efforts can be gauged by the following facts: out of the 450,000 hectares that the Government has placed under irrigation in the past twenty years, most have been completed in the past decade and about 140,000 hectares in the last three years (Table 14.3).

Projects now under construction or which have been approved and initiated would provide new or improved irrigation to one million hectares. There are also projects still in the planning stage for another 1.25 million hectares. These two sets of projects would thus double the size of the irrigated area at a total cost in excess of 80 billion pts for primary works alone and not much less for secondary works.

In the face of this vast program, with its heavy forward financial commitments, the mission has done its best, with the material at its disposal, to study the needs which the program is designed to meet and its potential effect on the Government's plan for economic development. There is no doubt that irrigation can produce impressive—at times spectacular—improvements over dry-land farming by raising yields and by making possible the cultivation of a wider range of crops and of higher-value ones. But it is a relatively costly way of achieving these results, and due consideration should be given to alternative and less costly ways which may exist. In other words, in any situation investment to extend the irrigation system is not necessarily

TABLE 14.3: Extent of Land under Irrigation at Various Dates

('000 ha.)

	Constructed by the Government			Privately Constructed[a]	Total
Confederation	1940	1957	1960	1960	1960
Norte	–	3	3	92	95
Duero	15	47	67	119	186
Tajo	11	32	43	46	89
Guadiana	1	18	42	83	125
Guadalquivir	7	136	150	142	292
Sur	–	6	8	89	97
Segura	65	90	90	75	165
Jucar	89	112	134	101	235
Ebro	317	381	424	56	480
Pirineo Oriental	17	18	18	49	67
Subtotal	521	842	979	852	1,831
Canary Islands	–	–	–	28	28
Balearic Islands	–	–	–	17	17
Total	521	842	979	897	1,876

[a] Estimated by subtracting land constructed by the Government from total land under irrigation.

SOURCES: Information supplied by the Ministry of Public Works for the ten confederations; *Anuario Estadistico de la Produccion Agricola* 1959–60 for Canaries and Balearics.

the best solution. With these considerations in mind, we feel that a stage has been reached when a number of important factors have to be weighed before any new and far-reaching commitments are undertaken.

First, it is a fact that in the last 20 years over 100 irrigation projects have been undertaken at one time or another. At the present time, the Government has 71 projects under construction or initiated, 32 of which are large ones (at least 10,000 hectares remaining to be irrigated or 250 million pts remaining costs for major works). Another 79 projects are now in the planning stage. Whatever the nature and scale of the irrigation program to be adopted, the mission strongly recommends that the capital be spent on a sufficiently limited number of projects that all can be completed on a normal construction schedule. In this way, the benefits will be secured many years earlier and it will be possible to avoid the loss to the economy from locking up capital in incomplete projects.

Secondly, as we have seen, the problem in the agricultural sector is no longer simply one of producing more crops, but of producing the right crops at the lowest cost. The pattern of consumption will change and production has to be planned accordingly. Indeed, there are likely to be significant changes in the agricultural sector before the irrigation projects now under construction could be completed. Therefore, before embarking on an irrigation project, it is necessary to know, among other things, what the land to be irrigated can produce, whether there will be a market for the products and whether it is consistent with the over-all agricultural policy. This means that the need for economic criteria to determine the scale of irrigation and the suitability of the particular projects to be financed, which has always been important, is becoming increasingly important. Without a careful economic analysis, there must always be a risk that too many projects will be started or that an investment will turn out to be unproductive. We believe that the Government ought to be fully informed on the economic implications of decisions connected with the irrigation program, when such important sums are involved, and that they should be able to see at the outset whether there is any risk of locking up capital resources in a project without much prospect of return. The Centro de Estudios Hidrograficos has latterly been trying to establish a system which will enable a full economic analysis of each project to be made, but it will require more data than it now has to reach conclusions on the prospective costs and returns. We hope that, in cooperation with the experts in the Ministry of Agriculture, it will succeed in its endeavors, and that the Government will give what support is needed and ensure that these services are fully staffed and equipped for this most important work.

Thirdly, it is clearly important to obtain the maximum yield from existing investments in irrigation before deciding what new investments have to be made, and the authorities should satisfy themselves that, as land is irrigated, it is brought into full production. From information at our disposal, it seems that some of the land under irrigation could be made more productive; this could be done by providing credit for secondary or ancillary works or technical assistance for improving the cropping pattern. We have more to say on the provision of such facilities later in this chapter.

For these reasons, and because very large sums of money are at stake, the mission believes that it is opportune for the Government to undertake, as a matter of high priority, a fresh appraisal of its irrigation plans. At this juncture, when agricultural policy is being reshaped and an economic development program is being launched, it seems prudent to examine carefully how the capital works for irrigation under construction and future plans can contribute to the achievement of the Government's main objectives, and what the consequences of new expenditure will be. In the following paragraphs we suggest some of the considerations that should enter into the appraisal, as well as some ways of proceeding with the present irrigation program while it is going on.

An Economic Approach to Irrigation

In economic terms, selection of the appropriate level of investment in irrigation and of particular projects depends on a comparison of alternative costs and returns. As a general rule, the projects to be selected are those on which the prospective returns (from increased yields) exceed the additional costs of irrigation by a sufficient margin to enable a return on the invested capital at least as favorable as it would be in alternative uses. In choosing among projects, priority should, broadly speaking, be given to those which have the highest return on capital cost. This approach ensures that the scarce savings of the country will be employed so as to bring about the highest possible rate of economic growth.

There are numerous and highly complex problems in ascertaining costs and returns, only a few of which can be referred to here or in Annex D. In the case of multipurpose projects (power, urban water, etc.) the analysis should embrace all the costs and benefits involved. With respect to the irrigation component, all costs, including those of secondary works and interest and amortization of capital, should be included. If a large project consists of several separate stages, each stage should be examined separately, since it may be economical to complete one or more stages but not the remainder. Finally, in deciding how to allocate investment funds at a particular moment of time, sums already invested in projects under construction should not be taken into account; the relevant costs are the *incremental* ones necessary to complete the project.

Determination of the prospective returns is an even more difficult task, since they depend on how the land will be used, which is subject to many uncertainties. Among the factors that must be considered are the following:[9]

a. an estimate of market demand, both domestic and export, for the crops that can be grown under irrigation;

b. an estimate of the additional production required to meet the projected demand;

c. an estimate of the amount of new irrigation required to meet the production target, *taking into account* alternative possibilities of increasing production on existing dry or irrigated land by raising yields or by upgrading the cropping pattern;

d. an allocation of the demand for new irrigation among regions on the basis of climate, topography, soil and other conditions; and

e. in the light of these factors, an estimate of the most feasible cropping pattern and probable yields for each project within each region.

Once the cropping pattern and estimated yields have been determined for each project, it is possible to establish a schedule of expected annual increases in returns and costs with which individual projects can be evaluated. The process is considerably more complicated than the foregoing might suggest. Nevertheless, even with crude data it should be possible to reach some useful conclusions both as to the appropriate rate of investment in irrigation and as to individual projects that are clearly desirable or clearly undesirable.

With the limited information available, the mission has not been able to apply this approach in any detail to the existing irrigation program. Some very general impressions can be drawn however. As Table 14.4 shows, irrigated land is now used to grow a variety of crops with widely differing financial yields. The most intensive crops (Group 3) make up over 40 percent of the total value but occupy only one-sixth of the area. Conversely, the lowest valued crops (Group 1) occupy half the area but account for only one-quarter of the value. Since there is double cropping on the land used for intensive crops, the real differences are even greater.

The highest yields can be obtained in the Canaries and in the Confederations of the Jucar, Segura and Sur (approximately the east and south coastal land from Castellon to Gibraltar). At current prices,

---

[9] A number of factors relating to project management and operation of the irrigated land are also involved, but we do not discuss them here since they are generally well understood.

gross yields up to 200,000 pts a hectare annually can be obtained from bananas in the Canaries and 100,000 pts from citrus in the east and south. Capital costs are high in these areas, especially in the Canaries where the terrain is difficult and water relatively scarce, but we have little doubt that irrigation expansion need be limited only by the

TABLE 14.4: Area and Value of Irrigated Crops, 1959/60[a]

	Area ('000 ha.)	%	Value[b] (billion pts)	%	Gross Yield ('000 pts per ha.)
Group 1:					
Olives (unassociated)	95		.6		7
Forage and artificial pasture	70		.8		11
Cereals (except rice)	541		6.5		12
Vines (unassociated)	33		.4		13
Alfalfa[c]	113		1.6		15
	851	51	9.9	25	
Group 2:					
Potatoes (except early potatoes)	112		2.2		19
Cotton and other textiles	110		2.2		20
Tobacco	15		.4		25
Melons	61		1.5		25
Rice	67		1.8		26
Sugar beet	119		3.4		29
Early potatoes	48		1.5		31
	532	32	13.0	33	
Group 3:					
Vegetables/condiments	143		6.0		42
Tomatoes	50		2.9		58
Citrus (in full production)	85		6.6		77
Bananas	8		1.3		150
	287	17	16.7	42	
Subtotal	1,670		39.7		24
Unidentified and miscellaneous	116		n.a.		n.a.
Total area under irrigation May 1959	1,786	100	n.a.	100	n.a.

[a] Many small items, legumes, citrus not in full production, and some fruit trees (in all, somewhat over 200,000 hectares) have been omitted. There is some duplication due to double cropping.

[b] In general, values were derived by multiplying average national prices by irrigated output.

[c] For eleven provinces where there appears to have been duplication of green fodder and hay production in the annual statistics, only half the production has been included.

SOURCE: Based on *Anuario Estadistico de la Produccion Agricola,* 1959–60.

market, largely export, for high-value crops. As has been seen, market prospects, on the whole, are favorable. On the other hand, a considerable amount of irrigated land in these areas has not come into full production, and cultivation is very intensive (the present citrus crop, for example, is grown on only about 100,000 hectares). It is clear, therefore, that even if new irrigation takes place to the maximum extent permitted by the market, the amount of land involved will not be large.

For intermediate value crops there is likely to be more demand for irrigated land, particularly for sugar. However, we must take into account the possibility of increased yields on existing land; even assuming a very modest increase in yields (say 15 percent), it is difficult to see how the combined demand for additional irrigated land for high- and intermediate-value crops would exceed 200,000 to 300,000 hectares over the next fifteen years. To a considerable extent, it would be possible to satisfy some of this demand by upgrading irrigated land now used for grain production so that it can be used for more intermediate value crops (sugar beet and also cotton in certain areas).

Since the demand for intermediate- and high-value crops is limited, the practical effect of extending irrigated land beyond this limit must inevitably be, to a very large extent, to increase the area under low-value crops. While production of these crops is sometimes an intrinsic part of rotation with higher-valued crops, the case for additional irrigation *on a large scale* must rest primarily on the lowest-valued crops; that is, on prospects such as transferring cereal production from dry land or growing more forage crops such as alfalfa (apart from in rotation). This is so, even though the pattern of production on any individual project or farm would, in most cases, be a mixed one, including a variety of crops.

It is very difficult to say how good is the case for additional irrigation for the lower-value crops. Table 14.5 presents *very approximate* estimates of average gross yields, costs and net yields under dry and irrigated farming for five crops in Groups 1 and 2: wheat, alfalfa, potatoes, sugar beet and American cotton. Capital charges for projects costing 60,000 pts to 105,000 pts per hectare are also shown. As a general rule, the increment in net yield should exceed capital charges in order to justify irrigation. It will be noted that, on the basis of these figures, projects costing more than 90,000 pts per hectare are distinctly marginal except for sugar beet. As can be seen from Table 14.6, many of the major projects now initiated or in execution have remaining capital costs of more than 90,000 pts per hectare.

There must inevitably be doubt about these statistics, which could be resolved with better data such as may be obtained from the results of the forthcoming agricultural census. Furthermore, the figures are only averages. Yields and costs vary greatly from one part of the country to another and even from one part of a project to another. For example, the average yield per hectare for American cotton in the province of Cordoba is 18 quintals per hectare, while it is 12 quintals or less in the other three principal cotton-growing provinces (Badajoz, Caceres and Sevilla). Even within the province of Cordoba, there

TABLE 14.5: Illustrative Costs and Yields on Irrigated Land

('000 pts per ha.)

	A. Increment in Net Yields				
Crop	Gross Production (irrigated)	Current Costs (irrigated)	Net Yield (irrigated)	Net Yield (dry)	Increment in Net Yield
	(1)	(2)	(3) (Col. 1– Col. 2)	(4)	(5) (Col. 3– Col. 4)
Wheat	11.2	2.4	8.8	1.5	7.3
Alfalfa	14.7	5.7	9.0	1.5	7.5
Potatoes[a]	19.4	10.8	8.6	1.5	7.1
Sugar Beet	28.7	10.8	17.9	1.5	16.4
American Cotton	19.4	12.6	6.8	1.5	5.3

B. Equivalent Capital Charges	
Capital Costs	Annual Capital Charges
60	4.9
75	6.1
90	7.4
105	8.6

[a] Except early potatoes.

NOTES: A. Column (1) based on *Anuario Estadistico de Produccion Agricola 1959–60* except for modification to alfalfa explained in note to Table 14.4. Column (2) based on *Coste de Explotacion Agricola* (Centro de Estudios Hidrograficos). Column (4) in order to make as favorable a case for irrigation as possible, dry-land production in each case is based on:
(a) Wheat at 10 quintals per hectare, 500 pts per quintal, i.e., 5,000 pts.
(b) Costs of 2,000 pts (rough estimate).
(c) Alternate years in fallow.

B. Capital charges based on 50-year annuity at 8 percent. They do *not* include interest during construction.

C. No allowance has been made for the time lag required before full production is obtained under irrigation.

TABLE 14.6: Remaining Costs of Major Irrigation Projects, April 1961[a]

Remaining Capital Cost per Hectare[b] (in pts)	Number of Projects	Total Remaining Cost (billion pts)		Total Area (in '000 ha. equivalents[c])
		Primary Works	Total	
30,000– 45,000	1	1.2	2.0	68
45,000– 60,000	4	3.7	9.6	178
60,000– 75,000	–	–	–	–
75,000– 90,000	6	4.3	9.0	108
90,000–105,000	5	5.1	12.4	123
105,000–120,000	1	4.4	6.2	54
120,000–150,000	4	8.1	19.2	148
	21	26.8	58.4	679

[a] Major projects include those where the remaining area to be irrigated is at least 10,000 hectares *or* the remaining capital cost for primary works (Obras Hidraulicas) exceeds 250 million pts. One project which would otherwise qualify was also excluded on the grounds that there appeared to be some mistake in the costs in view of the very small area involved. This table does not include projects in Levante, Sur or Canarias.
[b] After deducting cost attributable to power or municipal water supply.
[c] One "improved" hectare is counted as 0.6 of a "new" hectare.

is greater variation, yields of 30 quintals being not unknown. Or, to take another example, the average yield for wheat is 21 quintals per hectare, but in several provinces in the northeast it is over 26 quintals, while in a number of others it is 15 quintals or less.

Because of these variations from the average, and because of the wide margin of error in the data on which they are based, the averages cannot be used for the evaluation of individual projects. Nevertheless, the relationships which they indicate raise an important question as to the appropriate scale of the future irrigation effort and point to the conclusion that a careful review of all projects, both as a whole and project by project, is necessary.

In advance of such a review, there is no *a priori* reason for supposing that some new irrigation projects could not show much better results than the average figures would indicate. But the question clearly arises whether these better results can also be obtained on existing irrigation projects, at much lower cost. One reason for variation is, of course, soil and climate. But, an equally important factor in our view is the level of production technique. Other important factors are the technical conditions of the existing irrigation works, both primary and secondary, and the reliability of water supply in some projects.

Thus, even if there is a case for new irrigation in any absolute sense, it must also be considered in a relative sense, in other words in comparison with alternatives, which include:

a. improving production techniques on existing irrigated land;

b. improving production techniques on dry land;

c. improving existing irrigation works by such means as repairing canals or increased drainage; and

d. various other alternatives such as reclamation of swamp land (e.g., on the lower Guadalquivir).

Noneconomic Considerations for Irrigation

The mission is aware that the Government's interest in irrigation is not solely an economic one. There are two principal objectives of a social nature. The first is stability of supply of staple food. The second is improvement of the welfare of the rural community. We sympathize with the Government's preoccupation with these grave problems and any comments we have to make are not concerned with the objectives themselves, but with the best ways of reaching them.

Severe droughts, which can reduce the wheat crop by as much as a quarter, cause acute fluctuations in production. But in our discussion later in this chapter on the outlook for wheat, we make some suggestions for a change in policy, which might be expected to render them less acute. As yields are increased in the present irrigated areas and on those dry lands less susceptible to drought, and as the lands most susceptible go out of production when total wheat consumption begins to fall, the pattern of production from one year to another should be more stable. Furthermore, greater stability of supply, which is a different thing from stability of production, can be assured by provision of adequate storage. Exceptionally good and bad seasons will recur, but their impact should be less, and the excess or shortfall made good by exports or imports of more manageable proportions. We therefore believe that with the prospect of a new agricultural policy, it will not be necessary to look to new irrigation as the only means of ensuring greater stability of supplies and improvement in incomes, and we hope that the less costly alternatives to which we have referred will be fully considered during the fresh appraisal of policy.

A second aspect of governmental policy is that, in the interests of the welfare of certain sections of the rural population, a number of major irrigation works have been carried out in recent years as "coordinated" projects, combining irrigation with land settlement to assist regional development. The land settlement program, which is administered by the Instituto Nacional de Colonizacion (INC), an autonomous agency under the Ministry of Agriculture, has been directed toward the important objective of raising the income of the poorer elements of the farm population by giving newly irrigated land to small dry-land farmers and farm laborers. In coordinated schemes, the Department of Obras Hidraulicas in the Ministry of Public Works builds the primary works while INC is responsible for secondary works as well as the settlement program (villages, schools, roads, aid to new farmers, etc.). In fact, an increasing proportion of irrigation expenditures is going to "coordinated" projects.

These "coordinated" projects, such as Badajoz and Jaen, have brought about remarkable transformations in the areas covered. There can be no doubt that the farmers who have had water provided for their holdings at less than full cost, or those who came as colonists, have received substantial benefits. But the capital outlay is very large and the number of persons benefiting directly is limited. Since there are plans for an extended series of such projects we feel that they ought to be reviewed in the light of the general objectives of the economic development program.

We have commented in Section 1 on investment designed to bring social benefits, and we realize that it does involve the Government in very difficult decisions, because the return on such an investment cannot be measured in numerical terms; nevertheless, the expected benefits must be viewed against the cost of the investment, and alternative methods compared. This is particularly true in the case of a coordinated project which has a mixture of economic and social objectives, but unless the irrigation works which form part of it can be justified economically, it does pose the question whether the large sums of money to be invested in them could not produce more widespread social benefits if used in other ways. Then there is the question of timing. Many of these coordinated schemes will take a considerable time to become effective; in the meantime, economic changes will mean that there will be fewer people in agriculture *in toto,* more people in intensive agriculture on irrigated land or in the rain belt of the north and, therefore, many fewer in dry farming. The dry-land farmer will be better educated, will be using better techniques and will have more land at his disposal. All of them should enjoy substantially higher incomes.

From information supplied to the mission it seems that a number of the large "coordinated" projects planned do not have a high economic rating and would be unlikely to qualify according to the standards discussed earlier in this chapter. For this reason, we suggest that when the Government is formulating its long-term program for economic development and reappraising its plans for irrigation, proposals for coordinated projects should be re-examined carefully with the foregoing consideration in mind. We do not believe that schemes for colonization and regional development should *ipso facto* require investment in irrigation works; irrigation should be included only if it can be justified on economic grounds. If the Government wishes, colonization could still be undertaken in connection with irrigation projects that are otherwise justified or with extensive dry-land farming. From what it has observed of the existing settlement program, the mission recommends:

a. that colonization only be attempted if the size of the individual farm and the cropping pattern can be such as to ensure that the farm units will be viable for a long period of time; and

b. that the facilities provided initially (farm houses, farm buildings, community buildings) be designed on a modest scale and expanded later, as needed, through the efforts of the villagers themselves.

The latter policy, which we understand is now being put into effect, should make it possible to reduce substantially the cost of colonization projects and thereby make it possible to benefit a larger number of farm families for a given expenditure, although the cost per family would still remain high.

Implications for Future Expenditure

The first priority, in our view, is to undertake a thorough review of the existing irrigation program along the lines suggested above; every effort should be made to complete this review within a year. During the interim period, the Government will undoubtedly wish to continue its irrigation effort, and we accordingly suggest that funds be concentrated on those projects which appear at present to have a high priority in any program, and that these projects be completed as rapidly as technical conditions permit.

There will be some projects or parts of projects which require only a small expenditure to complete them and obviously this should be done. Apart from these, we would expect that a major effort should be concentrated on a limited number of projects in the Confederations of the Jucar, Segura and Sur, where there are opportunities for very high yields in comparison with costs, and also in the Canaries. Outside these areas, it is difficult to generalize, but such evidence as we have suggests that the Duero valley is an area where capital costs are low and projects could support intermediate-valued or even low-valued crops. Finally, attention should be given to the promising possibilities for drainage of the *marismas* of the lower Guadalquivir.

Until the fresh appraisal by the Government is finished, it is impossible to do more than hazard a guess on the future trend of expenditure on irrigation and colonization; as we have seen, many factors—political, social and economic—have to be taken into account. But it seems reasonable to assume that there will first be a period of consolidation during which the Government will concentrate mainly on raising the level of productivity of land already irrigated and on those projects or parts of projects in the course of construction which can most readily be completed to produce a high return of marketable crops. Perhaps toward the end of this period of consolidation there should be another comprehensive survey to decide whether, and in what measure, new projects should be undertaken. The mission thinks there are grounds for suggesting that the greatly increased productivity possible during the period of consolidation, the possibilities for raising production and incomes by means other than irrigation and colonization and the market requirements then revealed, will mean that any new program then determined by the Government will be on a smaller scale than the one now underway.

Credit and Finance

State financial assistance for hydraulic works is governed by a 1911 law, with some later modifications. The law sets forth these procedures for construction:

(i) by the State with the assistance of interested parties (Articles 4–9);

(ii) by interested parties with State assistance (Articles 10 and 11); and

(iii) for the exclusive account of the State (Article 12).

Uncoordinated irrigation projects of the State normally fall in the first category. The law states that the owners of previously unirrigated land should repay a minimum of 50 percent of the cost over 25 years at an interest rate of 1.5 percent. In practice the minimum of 50 percent has also been a maximum. Furthermore, since repayment is not supposed to start until after technical completion, repayments are often delayed.

As indicated, the mission believes that, under present circumstances, irrigation projects should in general be completed or new ones undertaken only when the increment in net output exceeds the remaining capital cost[10] together with interest on that capital. If this is done, there is no reason why landowners should not repay the remaining capital cost to the State. The interest rate specified in the law bears little relation to the real cost of capital, and should be raised. However, it is probably best not to specify any rate in the law, but to determine it from time to time by executive action according to the circumstances.

On the other hand, a liberal attitude should be adopted toward the timing of repayment. A grace period may, for example, be necessary when it is contemplated that fruit trees are to be planted. Furthermore, 25 years may be too short a period for repayment compared with the life of the works involved.

The mission accordingly recommends that submissions of projects for inclusion in the budget should include an estimate of net increment in output and a financial plan for the recovery of capital costs with interest; the subsequent progress of each project should be supervised, records being kept of the capital cost, progress of repayment and current maintenance charges. We also recommend that, as in other sectors of the economy, the terms of lending should represent the "economic" cost of the capital provided: thus the rate of interest should be determined from time to time by the Council of Ministers[11] and amortization should start as soon as a portion of the land is brought into production and be sufficient to redeem the entire loan.

The second procedure, which governs projects put forward on the initiative of groups of landowners or companies, has been inoperative for a long time. Article 10 sets a limit on the loan and subsidy to be granted by the State to landowners at 257 pts and 400 pts per hectare respectively for annual and perennial crops. These figures are completely out of date; at present prices, costs are in the tens of thousands per hectare. The mission recommends that Article 10 be amended to eliminate the following:

a. the financial limitations per hectare;

b. the present subsidy and loan provisions (now limited to 50 percent and 25 percent of capital cost respectively), which would be replaced by a higher loan limitation; and

c. the specific term (25 years) and interest rate (2 percent). The same principles would be applied as in the first procedure.

---

[10] In the case of a new project, the remaining cost and the total cost are, of course, the same.

[11] The present rate is 3.5 percent. We believe is should be considerably higher.

Article 11 of the law specifies that companies which are not owners of the land may receive 99-year concessions and subsidies up to 40 percent of capital cost of hydraulic works. The mission recommends that the subsidies be replaced by loans with similar principles as the foregoing with respect to term and interest rate.

The mission believes that these changes will place the development of water for irrigation on a sounder basis. Many landowners have told the mission that they would gladly repay in full the costs of water, if they could get it. Indeed, the test of repayment would be a useful counterpart of economic analysis of projects. The changes recommended would undoubtedly involve the Government in substantial applications for loans by private parties or associations of landowners under Articles 10 and 11.

Credit for primary irrigation works is not, however, the only kind of credit required by the private sector. In a number of places old canals and other works need repair and drainage ditches should be dug. Credit is also required for secondary irrigation works, for example, where water is already available or where it will become available in uncoordinated works in the future. It will also be required for secondary works on reclaimed swamp land. Credit could also be usefully applied to finance spray equipment which, as described in Annex D, may reduce the need for water or increase the effectiveness of its use under certain conditions.

We have already stressed the importance of obtaining the maximum yield from existing investments and we believe that substantial sums will be required for these purposes, possibly of the order of 500 million pts initially and building up to 1,000 million pts subsequently. We recommend that credit on this scale be provided, as required.

Organization and Administration of Irrigation Projects

The existence of two government agencies (INC and Obras Hydraulicos) actively involved in irrigation work has led to overlapping of function and has contributed to the large number of partially completed projects. Although efforts to coordinate expenditure have recently been made through a special committee, its efforts have been devoted primarily to seeing that the relevant parts of the same project are completed by the two agencies at the same time. While this would represent some progress, a clearer definition of function as between the Ministries of Agriculture and Public Works is necessary, so long as these ministries retain their present broad responsibilities.

These functions can logically be separated into two distinct but closely related groups. The first is the design, appraisal, construction and operation of hydraulic works, including both primary and secondary works on all public irrigation projects. The second group of functions includes the provision of information on markets, farming costs and physical characteristics (such as soil surveys) required for economic analysis of projects before they are constructed; protection of headwaters through afforestation; land consolidation at the time of construction of irrigation projects and extension work after their completion; and, in cases where land settlement is part of the irrigation project, the construction works (other than hydraulic) required for the colonization program. The mission believes that this differentiation of functions could serve as the basis for a division of responsibilities between the two ministries concerned.

With water becoming increasingly scarce as industrialization and urbanization proceed, its control will become very necessary. There is a history of overexploitation of water in almost every country with a high population density and intensive use of irrigation. As Spanish agriculture is at the moment passing into this phase in certain respects, the requisite organization for recording and control of water resources should be established immediately. The mission recommends that this function be concentrated in one place and that the control of underground water be transferred from the Mines Department to the agency responsible for irrigation works.

There are two other aspects of public administration referred to elsewhere in the report that bear repetition here. First, the rather slow procedure for making progress payments to contractors has inevitably led and will, except possibly when there is recession, continue to lead to inflated bids for public works. Secondly, it is desirable that each project be separately identified in the budget, as a means of ensuring that, once approved, adequate funds are provided for its completion on the planned time schedule.

Reform of Farm Units

Among the means of increasing yields which may be alternatives to irrigation, one of the most promising is a change in the size of farm units. The size distribution of existing farms, together with the systems of land tenure and rental, impose serious obstacles to efficient resource use. Many farms are broken into units clearly too small for economical operation; at the other end of the spectrum, some farms may be underutilized because of excessive size. Rental legislation often removes the incentives to adoption of improved techniques, while common property tenure prevents the land so held from being adequately developed. A concerted attack on these problems can, over time, bring about significant increases in output and farm incomes for relatively small inputs of capital.

Large Farms. A rough indication of the relative size of farms is given in Table 14.7. The regions with largest farm units are in the southern half of Spain (Castilla la Nueva, Extremadure and Andalucia). Annex Table E.2 gives the provincial distribution of the 6.6 million hectares of farms in excess of 250 hectares. It is by no means established, however, that all farm units above a given size are too large for efficient management and should therefore be divided into smaller units. Many

TABLE 14.7: Distribution of Farms by Size and Region

Region	Average Size of Farm (hectares)[a]	Percentage Distribution of Farms by Size (ha.)				
		Less than 5	5 to 20	20 to 50	50 to 250	more than 250
Asturias and Santander	0.82	86.9	12.8	0.2	0.1	–
Galicia	1.45	80.4	12.5	4.4	2.7	–
Canarias	1.75					
Vascongadas	3.17	33.1	58.5	6.2	2.2	–
Cataluna and Baleares	3.24	25.5	35.0	19.4	20.1	–
Andalucia Oriental	3.62	28.0	20.3	10.4	25.3	16.0
Levante	3.96	46.5	14.7	9.4	22.0	7.4
Rioja and Navarra	4.50	10.5	10.1	13.3	66.1	–
Leon	5.21	34.0	28.5	11.8	18.9	6.8
Aragon	7.47	45.7	27.5	13.1	12.1	1.6
Castilla La Vieja	9.21	18.8	37.4	24.0	13.0	6.7
Castilla La Nueva	10.83	8.2	21.1	15.3	38.7	16.7
Extremadura	13.24	8.3	19.6	6.3	22.1	43.7
Andalucia Occidental	17.18	4.2	8.1	12.6	37.0	38.1

[a] Average number of hectares cultivated per farmer, including rented land.

SOURCES: Luis Garcia de Oteyza, *Los Regimenes de Explotacion del Suelo Nacional,* op. cit., page 13; Ministerio de Hacienda, *La Grande y la Pequena Propriedad,* page 5.

large farms are located in dry-farming areas of low rainfall, where large units may be necessary for extensive cultivation and pasture which alone can provide adequate returns to labor and management. Also, some of the land may be of marginal farming value. On the other hand, some farm units are undoubtedly excessive in size. In the past, inflation has encouraged investment in land for speculative purposes; the absence of up-to-date tax assessments and shortages of credit can also lead to the underutilization of large farm units.

Any major change in the large farm situation is thus closely tied to the Government's fiscal and credit policies, which are discussed elsewhere. Since December 1953 the Government has been tackling the problem directly through legislation on "farms clearly capable of improvement" which provides for expropriation, if necessary, or for forced injections of capital by the owner to bring the underutilized land into fuller use. Activity under the program has been slow. In the period 1954–1960, "under-use" studies were initiated for 216,000 hectares, with resultant investments of 43 million pts.

In view of the importance which the Government attaches to this program, the mission recommends that it pursue it more vigorously and with sufficient credit to back up its technical findings. The classification of the 10,500 farm units in excess of 250 hectares should be completed as quickly as possible, using three categories: those clearly underutilized; those effectively utilized; and those in an intermediate group needing further study. Efforts should be concentrated initially on bringing farm units in the first group into production in those areas where the potential appears highest. It should be stressed that irrigation is not a necessary feature of this program, which depends only on a determination of the optimum farm size under the prevailing conditions of terrain, climate, etc.

Small Farms. A great potential for better resource use and higher living standards exists in connection with the farms, now covering more than one-third of the cultivated area, that are composed of fragmented units, each too small for the proper application of modern technical methods. In many regions, farms under one owner or operator are made up of a large number of dispersed plots of land as a result of inheritance practices. To cite an extreme example, in Galicia, one area of 117 hectares was divided among 263 owners and broken into 2,486 plots.

Over the past decade the Government has been carrying out an admirable program of voluntary land consolidation under the Servicio de Concentracion Parcelaria. Consolidation is aimed at redistributing plots among farmers so that each management unit covers a contiguous area. The task is complex and time consuming. It involves a labyrinth of legal and agronomic considerations which are very difficult to bring to a solution acceptable to each of the several hundred owners who may be involved in a particular small area.

The consolidation effort has been carried out with a limited budget (about 100 million pts were spent in 1960) and, as can be seen from Table 14.8, the 278,000 hectares completed are a very small proportion of the land requiring consolidation. A high proportion (over 60

TABLE 14.8: Status of Land Consolidation, Mid-1961

	Area ('000 ha.)				Costs (million pts)				
						Projects in Process			
Region	Completed	In Process	Add'l Requested[a]	Add'l Required[b]	Completed Projects	Already Expended	To be Expended	Add'l Requested[a,c]	Add'l Required[d,c]
Andalucia Occidental	–	–	–	71.7	–	–	–	–	86
Andalucia Oriental	–	–	–	61.8	–	–	–	–	74
Castilla La Vieja	165.4	86.5	459.6	2,093.9	231.7	46.2	70.1	531.3	2,337
Castilla La Nueva	63.7	53.7	233.9	1,171.4	89.3	29.1	39.0	270.5	1,241
Aragon	–	23.0	6.2	330.9	–	13.6	18.5	6.7	397
Levante	1.0	2.5	–	94.2	1.4	1.2	2.4	–	100
Leonesa	35.0	50.3	77.4	1,055.7	49.0	28.3	37.8	80.3	1,302
Cataluna and Baleares	–	–	–	79.1	–	–	–	–	142
Extremadura	–	–	23.0	178.0	–	–	–	27.2	214
Logrono and Navarra	3.4	7.0	23.2	282.6	17.2	11.4	12.7	94.1	1,251
Galicia	1.39	8.5	48.4	[b]	13.9	25.0	45.9	296.4	[b]
Vascongadas	8.22	3.8	42.6	62.9	41.3	8.2	7.2	126.4	340
Canarias	–	–	–	–	–	–	–	–	–
Asturias and Santander	0.05	0.2	6.6	37.5	0.4	0.6	1.1	25.8	187
Total	278.2	235.5	920.9	5,519.7[b]	442.2	163.6	234.7	1,458.7	7,671[b]

[a] By farmers.
[b] Galicia is excluded, as no acceptable basis of estimation is now available.
[c] Including "obras de interes general."
[d] Presumably does not include "Additional Requested" by farmers. Data represent a preliminary estimate.
SOURCE: Information supplied by the Servicio de Concentracion Parcelaria, Madrid.

percent in 1960) of Servicio funds has gone into construction of bridges, roads and irrigation facilities associated with consolidation rather than into consolidation itself.

The mission recommends that the consolidation program operate subject to no budgetary restraint other than the technical capacity of the Servicio to put trained teams into the field. The sum appropriated for 1961 was 225 million pts. This should be increased as rapidly as the program can be expanded. In addition to removal of the budgetary ceiling, several steps should be taken to increase the rate at which land can be consolidated and brought into production with improved techniques and cropping patterns. These include:

a. an intensified effort to induce communal farming of dispersed land parcels on a cooperative basis so as to make concentration unnecessary;

b. temporary cooperative programs and other provisional arrangements to bring about better land use *pending* consolidation. These could be supported by special credit facilities, subsidies for machinery pools, by a Servicio guarantee that consolidation would be completed by a specified date and possibly by tax incentives; and

c. concentration of the Servicio's efforts in those regions which appear, after detailed investigation of probable yields, to offer the best prospects of high and prompt returns.

The immensity of the consolidation task also makes it desirable that proportionately less public funds and staff activity be devoted to capital works. These works should be an integral part of the over-all consolidation plan, but actual construction can often await earnings from consolidation itself. Temporary facilities can be provided through group efforts of farmers during slack seasons, and agreement to provide these facilities could be part of the original consolidation arrangement. The current subsidies to capital construction work should be discontinued.

The mission also recommends that long-term credits be provided to finance farm mortgages. Such credit would facilitate farm sales and farm enlargement as an integral part of the consolidation process, and the Servicio should work closely with the appropriate public credit institutions on this aspect of its task. Credit of this sort is also needed for the broader purpose of helping to develop a national market for land.

Farm Rentals. Improper utilization of farm land also appears to arise from existing rental arrangements. More than one-third of the cultivated area is under rental; the proportion reaches 60 percent or more in arid regions, where share rather than cash tenancy also reaches its highest proportions (see Annex Table E.3). The existing legislation has sought to provide maximum protection to the renter, by making eviction impossible for small tenants (*arrendamiento protegido*) and specifying long minimum periods for the original lease and subsequent automatic renewals. These provisions have presumably had the effect of discouraging landowners from offering their land for rent, or for rent at reasonable prices, with the result that land is underutilized.

The rental legislation also tends to hamper the introduction of capital improvements by the owner and renter. In the case of protected rentals, the owner has little interest in improvements since he has effectively lost title to the property. In nonprotected cases, there appears to be no inducement in the legislation to the use of cost-sharing arrangements that would make it easier to introduce capital improvements.

The mission considers that the Government should give a high priority to a re-examination of its rental legislation. This re-appraisal should include a study of rental arrangements adopted in other countries that have proven effective in stimulating joint renter-owner participation in capital improvements and technical advances. In view of the large land area subject to rental, even small improvements in the rental market could have far-reaching benefits.

Common Property. Another potential source of better land use is the uncultivated land[12] now held in common by the municipality or by a group of private individuals. Common property is a complex question, deeply rooted in tradition and subject to a variety of opinions. Nevertheless, the very large area held in common (7.9 million hectares in 1958) requires that it be considered on its economic merits as well. The question must be considered whether this land is always subjected to the desirable rate of improvement under a common regime. In such regions as the rain belt in the north there are large areas held in common which, it seems probable, would attract private investment and move rapidly to higher uses if individually owned. Transfer of such land to private ownership could make an important contribution to the over-all productivity of agriculture.

On the other hand, there is an even larger volume of uncultivated land (17.7 million hectares) now under private ownership, much of

[12] Uncultivated land (natural pastures, forests, etc.) in Spain totals about 26 million hectares, in comparison with the cultivated land area of about 20 million.

which cannot produce a profit however managed. Some of this land should be acquired by the State for conservation purposes, and the mission recommends that a small fund be established to this end. This two-way shift of land—from public to private and from private to public ownership—requires, as a prior step, that the economic pattern of land use be studied carefully and projected over an extended future period.

Soil Conservation

Increasing production through soil and moisture conservation appears to be another activity which affords high returns for relatively small expenditures. The Spanish terrain and climate create a serious erosion problem; the conservation authorities state that 40 percent of the agricultural land area is in a condition of "strong" or "very strong" erosion. A public soil conservation effort was organized only in 1955, and the area directly protected to date is about 85,000 hectares (see Table 14.9). Although the benefits of conservation extend to areas beyond those covered directly by the works, and the Government's

TABLE 14.9: Soil Conservation Activity, 1956–60

	1956	1957	1958	1959	1960
Area Completed ('000 ha.):					
Net[a]					
Cereals	9.2	14.7	24.5	14.4	17.8
Olives	2.0	0.2	0.02	0.4	0.2
Total[a]	19.5	19.6	33.0	27.5	29.3
Expenditures ('000 pts):					
Public					
Labor	340.6	1,259.4	1,916.2	1,843.6	5,293.7
Machine services	4,227.5	5,532.0	10,149.0	10,497.1	14,398.3
Total	4,568.1	6,791.4	12,065.2	12,340.7	19,692.0
Private	1,109.5	4,982.7	7,925.2	6,787.9	6,307.6
Completed Plans for Additional					
Projects ('000 ha.):	49.7	58.4	56.3	31.6	89.9
Farmer Requests for the					
Service ('000 ha.):	6.5	25.6	26.6	25.8	55.8

[a] "Net" applies to the area on which work was actually done and conservation directly accomplished. "Total" indicates the area indirectly conserved through work done in the "net" area.

SOURCE: Information supplied by Section 9 of the Direccion General de Agricultura.

example may stimulate farmers to undertake conservation work on their own behalf, the activity to date has reached only a negligible proportion of the area in need. From the fragmentary evidence available, it appears that conservation, when combined with improved cultivation methods, has been able to bring about substantial increases in crop yields.

Including contributions from the INC and American economic aid, the budget for this activity was about 30 million pts in 1961. A variable part of the costs of conservation are recovered from the farmers affected. There are now a substantial number of requests outstanding by farmers for the conservation work. The mission recommends that the program be expanded, with the budget increased from 50 million pts in 1962 to 200 million pts in 1966. In addition, public credit from the Servicio Nacional de Credito Agricola (discussed further below) should be made available on reasonable terms to farmers who wish to undertake conservation work on their own initiative.

Improved Seed and Livestock

There appears to be a large potential for increasing productivity through more widespread use of improved seed. Farmers planting hybrid corn have obtained yields of up to 1,500 kgs per hectare more than those using regular seed.[13] Increases in yields from improved seed potatoes are reported to range from 5 tons to 10 tons per hectare; these are significant gains over the average national yield of summer harvested potatoes in 1958/59 of 8.2 tons per hectare in dry farming and 14 tons in irrigated cultivation. Important increases in returns from better seed selection can also be obtained, it appears, for other crops. There is considerable scope for introducing these improvements. In the case of potatoes, for example, only about half of the irrigated crop in Andalucia and Levante uses selected seed material and under dry cultivation in the north the proportion is about 25 percent.

The need for a more intensive effort is indicated by the fact that the production of improved seeds has actually declined (by about 10 percent) between 1956 and 1959/60. The amount of public funds devoted annually to this purpose is not known since no figure has been seen for Government earnings from the seed market, but the total is believed to be about 60 million pts. The mission recommends that this program be expanded as rapidly as possible, without financial limita-

[13]The national average yield on corn (both hybrid and regular) in 1959–60 was 2,970 kgs per hectare, with about one-third of the land devoted to hybrid corn.

tion. A part of these funds is for the buying and selling of seed and would be used on a revolving basis. The Government should also consider expanding the role of the private sector in this field; seed distribution to farmers, for example, is handled by private firms in many countries.

Present yields from livestock, whether in the form of meat, milk, or wool, are also low and capable of substantial increases through improved stock. This problem is beginning to receive public attention, and the potential of foreign breeds of cattle is being tested on a small scale in several areas. Scattered evidence suggests that the foreign breeds tested can materially upgrade native cattle and that there may be substantial scope for improvement by better selection of native breeds. The use of improved poultry breeds is well advanced in specialized poultry areas. Some genetic improvement work on sheep is also under way. Nevertheless, the over-all effort is on a very small scale in relation to the potential return on improved livestock. The precise amount of public funds devoted to this purpose is not known to the mission, but presumably it is very small. We recommend that the appropriation be increased.

Disease and Pest Control

Little is known about the specific returns on the use of the various categories of pesticides, but there is reason to believe that small investments can result in very large yields in the case of both plants and livestock. The Servicio de Plagas Forestales has estimated that, over the period 1953–60, the treatment of 2.3 million hectares at a cost, including both public and private outlays, of 300 million pts has saved a product worth 3,650 million pts. There appears to have been little increase in the consumption of pesticides in recent years. The main effort seems to center on direct public action rather than assistance to the farmers themselves in combating plant and animal diseases.

The mission considers that the present public efforts in support of pest and disease control should be rapidly expanded, and that the private sector be enlisted in further support of this activity. The Servicio de Plagas del Campo and the Servicio de Plagas Forestales together spent about 60 million pts on disease and pest control for crops and trees in 1960. (It is possible that elements in the budget of other agencies are devoted to this purpose, but we have no knowledge of the possible amounts involved.) The mission recommends a combined figure for the two services of 150 million pts in 1962 and of 300 million pts in

1966. The efforts in behalf of animal disease and pest control should be intensified along similar lines, but at present we do not have sufficient information to suggest a specific figure.

Fertilizers

Selective increases in the use of chemical fertilizers should be able to bring about substantial increases in productivity. Fertilizer use has been growing in Spain; between 1951/52 and 1958/59, the consumption of nitrogen increased almost fourfold, that of K_2O doubled and that of P_2O_5 almost doubled. Nevertheless, the rate of fertilizer use is still below that in most other European countries with comparable agricultural conditions and there appears still to be an ample margin for profitable expansion. Little research appears to have been done on this subject, but one Spanish source has estimated that the 1959/60 use rate was at 70 percent of the economic requirement for nitrogen, 63 percent for P_2O_5 and 50 percent for K_2O. Applications at the economic rate would, according to this estimate, have increased grain output by 2.6 million tons in relation to the 1956/57 level. The value of the increased production would have been three times the cost of the additional fertilizer.

The mission is not in a position to evaluate these data, but it is clearly desirable that the Government devote the necessary research and experimental effort to determining crop responses to fertilizers under the varying conditions found in Spain. When these have been determined, the extension services should increase their assistance to farmers to adopt the optimum rate of fertilizer use. The highest returns on this activity are likely to be obtained, in the first instance, in irrigated areas and the rain belt. Dry-land farming presents a special problem, since farmers are often reluctant to invest in fertilizers when the amount of rainfall (and hence the value of the crop) is uncertain. It is difficult to remedy this situation, but further experimentation on the use of different fertilizers under varying conditions of rainfall should be undertaken. It might also be possible to establish a kind of fertilizer insurance in the form of a variable subsidy that would reduce the net price of fertilizer to the farmer in the event of a substantial shortfall in precipitation below the average for the region.

The Government should also ensure that fertilizer prices to the farmer in general are not excessive. Fertilizer prices, which were under government control until mid–1959, have been relatively stable over the past decade, but the existence of tariffs on fertilizer imports ranging from 10 percent to 20 percent suggests that there is some room for lower prices. It may be questioned whether the domestic fertilizer industry requires this protection, at the expense of the productivity of farmers.

Machinery

A gradual mechanization of farm operations has been contributing to increases in production and yields per hectare. This process can be expected to continue, and perhaps to accelerate as more equipment becomes available through domestic production and freer imports. While the Government should support this process through its credit program, it is important that support be given to the introduction of mechanization only when it is justified economically by the relative costs and returns on alternative uses of additional machinery or additional farm labor. An artificial interest rate (i.e., one below the real cost of capital) encourages the use of machinery in cases where it would not otherwise be justified and thus adds unnecessarily to the displacement of farm labor. This point will be referred to again in the discussion of agricultural credit.

The price of farm tractors and other farm machinery in Spain is high relative to international levels, which undoubtedly helps to explain why the level of mechanization of agriculture is still below that of most other countries. The price disparity results both from the high tariff on imported machinery (30 percent to 35 percent for tractors) and from the proliferation of small, high-cost tractor plants that have been able to survive because of the tariff (and the previous quotas on machinery imports). In the long run the tariff on tractors should be substantially reduced.

Technical Research and Extension Services

Technical and scientific research and extension services are specially important for improving methods and bringing them into use in the farming community. Technical research in agriculture and forestry is undertaken by the Instituto Nacional de Investigaciones Agronomicas, the Instituto Forestal de Investigaciones y Experiencias, and a number of institutes operating under the auspices of the Consejo Superior de Investigaciones Cientificas. Elsewhere the mission strongly supports the adoption of an expanded national research program, as proposed by the Comision Asesora de Investigacion Cientifica y Tecnica, which would be shaped by the needs of economic development. Included in this program are a variety of important studies on various agricultural problems, some of which are in process. Among others, we would stress the importance of research on animal husbandry, including dry-land cultivation of fodder crops and techniques for improving natural and artificial pastures. We do not know precisely how much is being spent on agricultural research, but believe it to be about 85 million pts. This important activity should be expanded, and we could envisage a threefold increase in expenditures by 1966.

The related task of speeding up, through the extension service, the rate at which new techniques and improved inputs are adopted is a more difficult one. The extension service was established as an independent agency less than ten years ago. It is currently working with an annual budget of about 60 million pts and a field staff of some 235 in about 110 offices. Like other parts of the array of public services to agriculture, its orientation is overwhelmingly technical; little attention has been paid, for example, to the economics of farm management. The service appears to be well organized and administered, and performs its tasks efficiently. The scale of its operations is gradually increasing.

In the long run, it is highly desirable that extension work be substantially expanded to reach all types of farm situations and to provide assistance increasingly oriented toward the commercialization of farm operations. There is a close association between extension and education, since technological improvements are most likely to be adopted by farmers who understand the advantages of them. Higher farm incomes also make for more effective extension work; the subsistence farmer has little margin for experimenting with new methods. Since different areas and groups have different responses to extension work, the government may wish to consider whether, in the short-term, the service should focus its limited resources on those which are most susceptible to change, and thus provide examples that would gradually spread throughout the farm system.

The rate at which the extension service can usefully expand is dependent on a reorganization of the whole of the public services to agriculture to provide for more effective coordination at all operating levels. (This reorganization is discussed later in the present chapter.) Expansion must also be phased with the increasing availability of end products from the expanded technical and economic research activities. The growth must, therefore, be gradual; the mission recommends that the budget for this service not be increased pending reorganization, and then be raised progressively to 200 million pts by 1966.

Technical Education

Education is of special importance in agriculture. Whatever influences can be brought to bear through the advisory services of the Government, the fact remains that the farmer has the final responsibility of deciding how farm resources can be organized and used. In future, there will be the need to increase productivity and to cater to changing demand for agricultural products; all this calls for adaptability, willingness to try new methods and intelligent management, while for the farm workers there will be new techniques to learn and equipment to handle. These qualities and skills can be developed through education, and the better the education of those destined to farm and work on the land, the greater will be the progress in the growth and prosperity of agriculture. Improved education will also make it easier to solve the problem of surplus labor and to move youths out of agriculture into other occupations, on which the improvement of farm incomes is generally dependent.

The planning of an expanded educational system to meet the country's economic needs is dealt with elsewhere. Our purpose in raising the subject here is to stress the need for the rural areas and the farming communities to have their proper share of the facilities. We believe that this is fully the intention of the authorities, though we realize that there are special difficulties to overcome in sparsely populated areas. The expansion of primary and elementary education which is under way will be of great benefit to the countryside; so will the extension of secondary education with some technical specialization. In the latter case, there is a need to provide not only for more peritos agricolas and peritos de montes, for more of those taking courses in Institutos Laborales (modalidad Agricola y Ganadera), but also for an increase in the output of students from Escuelas de Capataces. In the former group the number of pupils registered would be something over 10,000,[14] and though the tendency has been to increase the numbers, our view is that the present annual rate of graduation (roughly 2,000) is clearly inadequate, and, as part of the long-term program for education, there should be an expansion of these secondary schools with technical and professional specialization for agriculture and industry.

But in the latter group, the Escuelas de Capataces, which are of a lower grade, there were according to the statistics available less than 1,000 pupils registered[15] and only 350 finishing the courses in 1958/59.

[14] 7,267 at Institutos Laborales 1958–59: *Anuario Estadistico 1961;* and 3,132 at Escuelas de Peritos 1960–61: Spanish Government's report to OEEC STP/GC (61) 27.
[15] 937 at Escuelas de Capataces in 1958–59: *Anuario Estadistico, 1961.*

Here we think a special effort should be made to expand the facilities provided by this type of school. The two-year training course for youths, with primary or elementary education, who would not otherwise be likely to go on to secondary schools, seems to satisfy a real need. What is not clear is whether it is intended that the Escuelas de Capataces should come within the scope of the long-term educational program now in preparation, since they are mainly for vocational training, and we understand that the municipal authorities and sindicatos have important interests in them, in collaboration with the Ministry of Agriculture. But we suggest that the urgent need to increase the number of these schools should be considered as a part of, or as an adjunct to, the long-term program.

The mission does not have sufficient information to enable it to estimate the cost of a program for expanding the Escuelas de Capataces; but it recommends that insofar as it cannot be financed by the local authorities and sindicatos, the Government should be ready to make a substantial allocation of funds for this purpose. There will be problems similar to those connected with the extension of primary and secondary education in rural areas, and the need for the Government to discuss with the other interested authorities how rapidly the increase can be brought about and what part they are to play in financing it. Moreover, while new schools are being built, it may be possible to use existing school buildings, for special courses or even to introduce some elementary instruction in agricultural science and farm management into the final year's curriculum at elementary schools, where other alternatives are impracticable. There are many questions of this kind which could usefully be considered by the Ministries of Agriculture and National Education, and other competent authorities in order to get quick results.

Even if adequate educational facilities are provided, youths in the poorest rural areas are unlikely to attend school in the requisite numbers unless some financial assistance is provided to compensate families for the loss of their services and to cover the outlays for food, transportation, etc., necessary to attend school. As longer-term problems, we would call attention to the desirability of reducing some of the excessive specialization of professional training within the three categories of agronomist, forestry engineer and veterinarian, so that each can have a better understanding of the others' problems and a better coordination can be obtained later in the field;[16] of opening the doors of the professional schools to the larger numbers of qualified

[16] Specialization along the present lines, for example, has impeded the development of professional training in animal husbandry as such.

persons that will be available for them; of facilitating the entry of the perito agricola, who receives a high level of training, into the ranks of the agronomists; and of integrating the professional schools more closely with the universities.

POLICIES TO FACILITATE SHIFTS OF RESOURCES

The anticipated changes in demand for farm products will require significant shifts of resources within agriculture. These shifts will bring about higher incomes to farm operators and laborers, but if they are to take place promptly and with a minimum of cost and dislocation it will be necessary that the Government undertake a basic reorientation of its agricultural policies. In addition, specific measures will be necessary to facilitate some of the principal shifts; the cases of wheat, livestock and forestry are discussed below.

A multiplicity of rules and regulations have been carried over from the period of critical shortages, when public policy toward agriculture was inspired by the need to increase production of basic foodstuffs and to keep down prices to consumers. Regulations specify, for example, the proportion of land that must be kept in forage crops and summer fallow, the total weight of livestock on farms and the amount of labor to be hired. Exports of scarce farm products have been prohibited and imports monopolized by public agencies to ensure adequate supplies. Processing margins have been fixed for various products such as wheat and sugar. In the case of a few crops where overproduction was believed to be a problem, such as citrus and olives, new plantings have been prohibited without express approval. As the public interventions have increased in number and complexity, they have absorbed, in unproductive activity, a disproportionate amount of time of the personnel in the provincial Jefaturas Agronomicas. In addition, they have made it difficult for farmers, processors and distributors to react promptly and correctly to market forces.

The Government has recognized the need to reduce its interventions in the economy, and the mission believes that the time is now ripe for many of the controls and regulations, referred to above, to be withdrawn. Considerable progress along these lines has taken place recently, but sufficient publicity has not been given to the removal of controls so that many farmers are unaware of the changes. Government policy should increasingly be oriented toward creating the economic environment that will by itself induce farm resources to shift with changes in demand. This involves essentially an improvement in the functioning of the market place, both by restoring greater freedom to farmers and by ensuring that processing and distribution channels work efficiently. It also means:

a. that the policies which we have discussed above, to provide farmers with the technical and other resources necessary to achieve maximum productivity, be consistently pursued;

b. that farmers, farm workers, capital and land be free to move to their most profitable uses both within agriculture and between agriculture and other sectors of the economy; and

c. that greater reliance be placed on international trade, with exports promoted in crops for which Spain has a comparative advantage and imports relied upon when products can be obtained more cheaply abroad.

Spanish agriculture is fortunately at a stage when, through primary reliance on the market economy, it can avoid the possibility both of shortages and—of increasing importance in the future—of amassing unsalable surpluses that have been so costly in the case of other countries. This approach does not, of course, preclude direct government intervention to stabilize fluctuations in the market, to induce product uniformity and enforce sanitation measures and to remove obstacles to the functioning of the market at the processing or distributing stages. Some of these interventions are discussed below as they apply to specific commodities.

Wheat

Self-sufficiency in bread grains has been the keystone of agricultural policy. The Government's intervention to this end has been more comprehensive than in the case of any other farm commodity:

a. farmers have been required to devote a specified minimum proportion of their arable land to wheat growing (the most recent figure was 25 percent);

b. wheat prices have been fixed at a level high enough to attract resources and keep them in wheat production;

c. an autonomous agency, the Servicio Nacional del Trigo, has purchased annually the entire wheat crop and sold it at home or abroad, thus stabilizing the market and guaranteeing the farmer's income; and

d. the Servicio Nacional del Trigo has provided credit, selected seeds, fertilizers and technical assistance to wheat growers on favorable terms.

Through these measures the Government's objective is, on the average for a number of years, close to being achieved. Although there have been substantial fluctuations in output from year to year, wheat production has shown an average annual increase of slightly over 3 percent between 1951 and 1960. The abnormally bad harvests of 1960/61 and 1961/62 necessitated large wheat imports, but this should not obscure the fact that, taking good and bad years together, Spain is already approaching self-sufficiency in its wheat supply. (Additional data on wheat production, trade and yields are shown in Annex Table E.4.)

The goal of self-sufficiency is only being reached, however, at considerable cost. Wheat is now grown in every province of Spain, with close to 4.5 million hectares annually devoted to wheat production. In many dry areas a wheat crop is harvested only every other year, and a large part of the more than 5 million hectares of fallow land must also be attributed to wheat cultivation. Favorable price and marketing conditions established by the Government have placed valuable land in wheat which could have been used for the cultivation of more intensive and higher-value crops. In addition, wheat is grown to a large extent in very marginal areas and under unfavorable natural conditions which permit bare subsistence to the farmer. As a result, average yields are very low (only slightly more than 1,000 kg per hectare in 1959).

Twenty-three of the provinces of Spain, with 2.3 million hectares in wheat production, had average yields of 10 quintals (1,000 kg) or less on dry-land farming during the period of 1954–1958 (Annex Table E.5). Albacete, Zaragoza and Caceres had important acreage devoted to wheat with yields of 6.2, 7.4 and 7.5 quintals, respectively. Moreover, on most of this land a wheat crop is produced, at best, only every other year.

Now that wheat production is close to satisfying demand, and with the prospect of an appreciable reduction in future demand, the objectives of government policy should be, first, to produce wheat at the lowest possible cost (and highest return) on the lands to which it is naturally suited within the over-all pattern of crop cultivation; and, second, to reduce the magnitude of fluctuations in the wheat crop from year to year so as to stabilize farm incomes. This will require a substantial reorientation of policy in the following directions:

a. All requirements that a specified proportion of land be devoted to wheat should be removed. Even though not rigorously enforced, the present regulation is not without some effect. Its removal will enable valuable land (e.g., irrigated land or land in the rain belt) to be put to uses where the returns will be greater.

b. The Government should announce that, as a matter of policy, the price subsidy on wheat will gradually be reduced and eventually eliminated. Over time, the price advantage that has brought resources into wheat production that should be used for other purposes would gradually be eliminated, and this will bring about a set of relative farm prices that more accurately reflect consumer demand.

c. The efforts to increase wheat yields through selected seeds, fertilizers, improved methods, credit, etc., should be continued. However, these programs should be provided to farmers on the same terms and conditions as apply to other farm products, and should be concentrated on the areas which are certain to remain in wheat production.

d. Additional storage facilities should be constructed so that crops can be stored for later export or carried over to meet any shortfalls in production the following year. We recommend that 200 million pts be provided annually during 1962–1966 for additional construction of public storage facilities. The Servicio Nacional del Trigo was constructing facilities at this rate prior to 1961, when the budget appropriation for this item was cancelled.[17]

With the approach outlined above, Spain should produce sufficient wheat to meet its declining over-all needs. Spain does not have a comparative advantage in wheat growing that would justify production for export on a regular basis. Wheat would be grown on the land to which it is best suited; average yields should rise appreciably; the annual variations in the size of the crop would be reduced and improved storage would further reduce the possibility of serious shortages in any year. Imports would be necessary only to a limited extent in exceptionally bad years, which would be increasingly infrequent.

With increased yields and a smaller total production, substantially less land will be devoted to wheat production. Movement of the best land to higher-value uses will take place naturally if the market is permitted to operate. A serious problem will remain, however, in the case of the numerous farmers now growing wheat under very marginal conditions, e.g., in parts of both the North and South Mesetas. This land has limited agricultural potential. In the long run, it will have to revert to pasture land for extensive farming and grazing, with milk sheep probably providing an important source of revenue. Other parts of the

---

[17] In 1960, 200 million pts were authorized for the Red Nacional de Silos y Graneros of the Servicio Nacional del Trigo, but only 155 million pts were disbursed.

area should be reforested. The programs intended to promote this shift from wheat to livestock and forestry are discussed below. However used, the land cannot support a population of the present size, and the migration to the cities and abroad, now going on, should continue. The transition from wheat to animal husbandry and forestry is a natural one which has already been taking place, but the transition will proceed slowly and farmers will need help during it. It is important to concentrate in this region the various low-income programs described later in this chapter.

Livestock

One of the major challenges facing Spanish agriculture during the next decade or two will be to expand the supply of animal proteins (meat, milk, cheese, poultry) for human consumption. As has been seen, the output of meat in 1975 will have to be at least double that of recent years if sharp price rises and/or large imports are to be avoided. Increasing production of animal proteins will also provide the principal outlet for land, labor and capital that will no longer be required for growing wheat.[18]

A primary objective of government policy must be to bring about a closer integration of animal husbandry with agriculture. Except in the north, mixed crop and livestock farming is carried out only on a very limited scale. Widespread adoption of mixed farming will improve soil fertility, provide additional uses for farm labor and raise farm incomes; it is particularly important to introduce livestock into irrigated areas if soil adequacy is to be maintained and built up.

Livestock expansion is largely dependent on the provision of more and better pasture land. A large-scale pasture improvement program will include bringing into practical use some of the uncultivated land (desarbolados, monte bajo) now in the forestry domain. In the rainbelt alone there is a significant amount of underutilized forest land that could be used to provide forage for grazing livestock. It will also entail better crop rotation through the introduction of fodder crops into the production cycle, and better use of natural grazing land through increased transhumance. Before the latter can be accomplished, substantial modification of the Ley de Pastos, Hierbas and Rastrojeras is necessary, since the present legislation permits communities to monop-

---

[18] Another source of increased protein could be fish. The fishing industry is important in several regions, and may justify expansion through investment in modernization of the fishing fleet and in processing plants, but the mission has not been able to study this question in any detail.

olize pasture and stubble land for local use to the exclusion of migrant herds.

In addition to creating the need for more fodder crops and more and better pastures, the growing demand for animal proteins will make it possible to expand two incipient enterprises; cheese from sheep milk, and broiler and egg production. The sheep milk program is of particular interest since it might provide an alternative source of income to farmers in parts of the Meseta.

Consumption of cheese in Spain is low and very likely to increase with rising incomes; there may also be possibilities of cheese exports. Presently numbering 15 million, sheep are grown mainly for meat and wool. Milk accounted for only 12 percent of the value of the 1959 product, virtually all of it being processed for cheese. There are two good local milk breeds, the Churra and the Manchego, which account for about one-third of the sheep population, but in many areas they are not milked for commercial use due to the lack of cheese processing plants and marketing organization. Total cheese production from sheep milk is now between 15,000 tons and 20,000 tons annually, centered in the provinces of Madrid, Toledo, Guadalajara, Cuenca, Ciudad Real and Albacete. Other regions of both the North and South Mesetas have substantial areas where milk sheep are raised, but commercialization is on a smaller scale.

Expanding cheese production will require a coordinated and synchronized program at the farm and processing levels. At the farm level, several measures are necessary to increase ewe milk yields, which presently average 35 liters to 40 liters per annum. The scope for improvement is indicated by the fact that yields of up to 310 liters have been recorded in Spain. An average yield of 150 liters can be attained. Among the measures to be considered are the following:

a. Flocks should be upgraded by a careful process of selection on the basis of records of performance. Several sheep stations should be established (e.g., in Toledo and Palencia) to develop genetic improvements and multiply proven stock.

b. The major problem of feeding requires the introduction of fodder and hay crops into the rotation cycle as well as measures, some of which were noted previously, to improve the use of pasture land. Sheep farmers should be taught the advantages of arranging for an off-season feed supply.

c. Improved management practices should include the provision of shelters (which can be based on a simple, standardized design for construction with local labor and materials) and silage and hay storage facilities, as well as better parasite control.

In order for increased milk production to find commercial outlets, processing facilities must be made available concurrently. Processors will need loans to modernize plant facilities and techniques, to shift cheese production to higher-value types and to offer a milk collection service over wider areas. Secondary access roads may be necessary in some places.

In sheep areas where milk is not now being marketed, some form of capital subsidy may be required as an inducement to processors to install facilities and create a demand. (We are not in a position to estimate the amount of funds that might be required by way of credit and/or capital grant for the processing industry. Presumably such funds could be made available through the BCI.) The Government may also wish to consider granting subsidies, in the form of special credits or partial grants, for the acquisition of sheep, shelters and improved seeds, to assist farmers in the poorer regions to make the difficult conversion from wheat to sheep. We refer to this point again below.

To end the separation of animal husbandry from agriculture will require an intensification of the Government's technical services to farmers that can only succeed if a prior rapprochement among the several services (*cuerpos*) involved takes place. At present, livestock programs are the exclusive responsibility of the Direccion General de Ganaderia, whose provincial offices operate independently of the provincial Jefaturas Agronomicas. Its staff is composed primarily of veterinarians who cannot be expected to be experts in animal husbandry. Mixed farming requires an approach to the whole farm as a unit, which can only be accomplished by combining the professional skills of several services, including the Patrimonio Forestal del Estado. Some further observations on organizational matters will be found later in the chapter.

The broiler and egg industry is expanding rapidly, although the typical enterprise is still small and production costs are relatively high. Larger flocks, a measure of vertical integration by feed and processing companies and cooperatives, and more modern production and marketing methods that can readily be applied in Spain should make it possible both to increase production rapidly and to lower prices sharply in the next years. To do this, however, the industry will have to be able to count on a regular supply of feed grains and protein meals at reasonable prices (see the remarks on market stabilization below). The feed or slaughter company might be a good place at which credit to expand poultry production could be applied.

The marketing of livestock presents problems characteristic of agricultural products as a whole. Distribution of farm products now absorbs as much resources as primary production, and the proportion is bound to increase with time. Some of the problems in this field have so far received little public notice, and merit more attention from the Government. The chief difficulties appear to be high distribution costs and inefficient marketing channels that arise from a lack of competitive enterprise and from excessive intervention by municipal authorities. The municipalities control livestock slaughtering, and each municipality imposes a different system of taxes, levies and fees; taken together, they are very likely to distort the movement of meat products from producer to consumer. Fees for sanitary inspection are another source of distortion. Inspectors perform a very useful function, but they should not be expected to rely on inspection fees for part of their income. No uniform system for meat grading exists. The number of modern slaughter houses is insufficient, and credits should be provided to assist in financing a nation-wide chain. In general, the aim of government policy should be the creation of an efficient nation-wide system for marketing farm products. It may well be questioned whether the present system of local controls and levies is consistent with this aim.

Forestry

More than half of the productive land area of Spain is uncultivated and thus falls, under the present administrative organization, into the forestry domain. Spain's excellent forestry service has been directing considerable funds to the improvement of existing forests and to reforestation, with impressive results. These programs should be continued and expanded. In addition, however, there should be some important shifts of emphasis within the forestry program and between forestry and other elements of agricultural policy.

Forestry is the natural outlet for large parts of the Spanish territory, particularly since a large demand for timber products can be anticipated. Internal consumption is low but rising rapidly, and even at present Spain is a substantial net importer of timber products. The output of the national forests should therefore be increased, both to meet domestic demand and possibly to provide a surplus that could be exported at favorable prices. Forestry is also an important source of employment in rural areas, and reforestation is desirable as one of the means of protecting watersheds against erosion.

A twofold change in the direction of public forestry policy is now required:

a. some of the low-lying regions now classified in the forestry domain should be developed by the agricultural services into pasturage suitable for meeting the increasing need for livestock grazing land; and

b. the forestry service should shift the geographical center of its reforestation effort from the north (e.g., Cantabrica) where it has naturally been attracted by high returns to areas such as the Meseta and parts of Andalucia (Cordoba, Jaen, Granada) where the yields are lower but the need for public assistance greater to facilitate the shift from over-cropping with wheat into forestry. Private enterprise should be relied upon to develop the more profitable forest lands in the north and in Sevilla and Huelva, as it is now doing to an increasing extent. A more specific program along these lines should be worked out on the basis of the detailed land-use projection referred to earlier.

Two organizations of the Ministry of Agriculture have the principal roles in public forestry work: the Patrimonio Forestal del Estado (PFE), which works primarily (but not exclusively) on the reforestation of state-owned land, and the Subdireccion de Montes ÿ Politica Forestal, which works primarily on forestry management on commercial land of public interest held by municipalities.[19] The PFE had budget expenditures of close to 800 million pts in 1961, of which 500 million pts came from a 4 percent Treasury loan. We recommend that the total size of this budget be increased only gradually during the period that the shift in geographical and functional emphasis is taking place. Yields will be lower in the south, and with conservation work in connection with irrigation projects assuming increasing importance it remains to be seen whether the Patrimonio Forestal del Estado will be able to continue to earn and pay 4 percent interest on a large proportion of its funds. We do not consider that PFE should be expected to earn a direct return of 4 percent or more on all its projects, since many of the benefits of forestry work are indirect and accrue to other activities (such as irrigation and conservation).

Budgetary expenditures on forestry management (primarily through the Subdireccion de Montes) totaled about 200 million pts in 1960, part of which was financed from the retention of 10 percent of the revenues from the sale of forestry products by the Subdireccion on behalf of the municipalities. The mission suggests that the total be increased to 300 million pts by 1966, working toward the objective of bringing all publicly owned forestry land under management plans

---

[19] Forestry management (*ordenacion*) is designed to protect existing forests against degradation and destruction by misuse; it is also undertaken by the Patrimonio Forestal on state-owned land.

and to a sustained yield status. Part of the increase can be covered by raising the share of forestry revenues which the Direccion is permitted to retain and reinvest, provided that the Direccion is free to put these revenues to their most productive uses.

A large proportion of the forestry land is in private hands and outside of any public program. While much of this land has little potential for further development except for conservation purposes, considerable reforestation of private land could be expected to take place if credit (and technical advice) were made available. We propose that a small fund be provided for this purpose.

Realization of this program will require a closer integration and better division of tasks between the forestry agencies and other agricultural departments. Thus, the land capability and use projection, including that for land now classified as forests, must be performed on an inter-cuerpo basis. Transfer of forest land into pasturage, and vice versa, should be undertaken by the competent parts of the Ministry of Agriculture. The PFE must work closely with the Ministry of Public Works in associating reforestation with the protection of irrigation projects.

Market Stabilization

The programs described above are the principal ones involving an important shift of resources within agriculture. There is, however, an additional function that the Government may be called upon to perform to an increasing extent and which requires some comment—market stabilization. In the past, farm surpluses have not been a serious problem, and adjustments in imports have made it possible to maintain stable prices without market intervention except in the case of wheat and a few other products. As production expands, market intervention by the Government to stabilize prices may become necessary for some other farm products.

The primary purpose of market stabilization should be to iron out seasonal fluctuations in prices within the crop year, although some inter-year stabilization may be required. This involves two elements: first, the fixing of a support price by the Cabinet, upon the advice of the Ministry of Agriculture, for a selected number of farm products and in advance of the growing season; and, second, market intervention by the Government in the form of buying, storing, selling and such other activities as may be necessary to sustain the announced prices. This system would enable farmers to make investment and planting decisions on the basis of firm expectations as to future minimum price levels for the products in question. Once the system is functioning, the Government can withdraw from its present processing and distributing operations, which can be conducted by private enterprise. The first crops for which it is likely to be necessary are the remainder of the cereals and pulses.

The great danger in any system of market stabilization or price support is that prices will be set too high. Surpluses then accumulate which can only be disposed of at considerable cost, and uneconomic resource use is imbedded in agriculture. A second and related danger is that pressures will accumulate to extend the stabilization program to more and more crops, whether or not they are in need of it.

In view of these problems, it is important: first, that the price supported by the Government be considered as a floor, to be fixed at some point *below* the equilibrium level that would clear the market without surpluses and deficits; and, second, that the stabilization program be confined to the minimum number of commodities for which it is essential in order to avoid sharp fluctuations in prices as a result of wide variations in output. These can only be accomplished by a close and continuing study of the outlook for supply and demand in the case of each of the important farm products, a study that would be the responsibility of the proposed unit dealing with statistics, economic analysis and planning referred to subsequently. Such concepts as "cost of production" or "parity" of income or purchasing power have no place in the determination of the support price, since the purpose of the program is to reduce price instability but not to ensure a particular level of income to the farmer.

The agency best equipped to assume responsibility for administering the market stabilization program as a whole is the Servicio Nacional del Trigo. Wheat production no longer requires special promotional efforts *different* from those provided for other crops, and the Servicio has an excellent record of efficient service. Personnel from the Comisaria de Abastecimiento y Transporte, whose functions for the most part are no longer required under present day conditions, might be absorbed into the new operation. The funds necessary to provide working capital for the market stabilization operations are very difficult to estimate in advance. Adequate storage capacity, public or private, will have to be available to support the stabilization effort. For the time being, however, no additional appropriation is recommended; the funds already at the disposal of the Servicio Nacional del Trigo should be adequate for some time since, if the price is fixed properly, market stabilization need not and should not extend to purchasing more than a portion of the annual crops covered by the program.

POLICIES FOR DISTRESSED AREAS
AND LOW-INCOME GROUPS

As stated at the outset, the mission's approach is to encourage the most efficient use of resources within agriculture, and between agriculture and other sectors of the economy, as a means of increasing the over-all growth of production, employment and income as rapidly as possible. We believe that in this way all groups in the population will, in the long run, achieve the greatest gain. It must be recognized, however, that even the highest attainable rate of economic development may result in only a slow and gradual improvement in the situation of some of the lowest-income groups. No other approach is likely to bring about a lasting improvement in this situation more rapidly. But there are a number of specific measures, consistent with this general approach, that can provide additional relief to poverty in the rural areas while development is taking place.

Two groups are of primary concern—the landless laborers with only casual employment, estimated to number about one million males, and the small-scale subsistence farmers, of which there are perhaps twice this number. Both groups stand to benefit from the rise in farm productivity and income, but it would be illusory to imagine that any dramatic change can take place rapidly. The benefit to farm laborers is more likely to take the form of higher remuneration and possibly a longer period of employment each year than an increase in the number employed. Farm employment will be subject to divergent forces. On the one hand, the demand for farm labor will increase with the increased cultivation of higher-value and more labor-intensive crops (cotton, sugar beets, vegetables, oilseeds); on the other hand, labor will be released by the drop in wheat production and gradual mechanization of farm operations.

The Government has been attacking the problem of rural poverty primarily through the programs of INC. These programs are commendable and have achieved some important results. Execution of the programs appears, on the whole, to be of a high standard. However, by combining the settlement of propertyless workers on the land with major irrigation or reclamation schemes, including the construction of villages, schools, etc., the INC has spent large sums of money to improve the position of a relatively small number of rural families. In addition, the program has tended to fix agricultural resources in areas where their returns are relatively low. The Government may well wish to consider whether it would not be desirable to shift the emphasis to programs which, at less cost, will be able to reach and assist a larger number of beneficiaries.

The first step in considering a new approach is to identify the areas and types of families in greatest need of assistance, so that government programs can be geared most effectively to the needs and potentialities of the individual farms and families. The subsequent task has several component elements: education, relocation, credit and concentration of other government programs. These elements might best be conferred upon a single government agency, which would carry out some of them itself and ensure that those programs which are the primary responsibility of other government agencies have their maximum incidence in those rural areas where they are most needed. INC, which has the experience most adaptable to this task, might be used for this purpose.

The educational program described in this chapter and elsewhere would develop the rural educational system through the secondary level and provide additional schools for technical training. It would make two major contributions toward alleviating the problem of rural poverty: first, farm youths would receive the training necessary for employment *outside* of agriculture, thus relieving the pressure of excess farm population; and, second, youths returning to the farms would have the background necessary to carry out technical improvement programs. The danger, however, is that in some areas where the need is greatest the fewest farm youths will attend schools. To remedy this, the mission proposes that two subsidies be provided to families in the low income groups: a grant to the parents, to compensate for the loss of earnings while the youths are in school; and subsidies in kind (food, clothing) to the children to ensure that they have the requisites for regular attendance and effective effort.

A second major task is to facilitate by all possible means the movement of excess farm population into more remunerative employment elsewhere in Spain or abroad. There is also considerable scope within agriculture itself for raising farm incomes by moving farm labor from surplus to deficit areas. To this end, the agency should work closely with the labor exchanges to bring suitable job opportunities to the attention of rural families. Subsidies could also be provided to needy families to cover the costs of transportation and relocation in new areas.[20]

The agency would have a similar task of ensuring that the various credit facilities available to agriculture were brought to bear with maximum effectiveness in support of the development of the areas of greatest need. Special programs might also be devised, as for example,

[20] See the discussion of labor exchanges and relocation subsidies in Chapter 15 (Industry).

farm machinery pools and the provision of machine services on terms that farmers in the distressed areas could afford.

A number of the other government programs discussed elsewhere in this chapter could, without distorting the desirable pattern of resource use, be concentrated in low-income areas. Reforestation and conservation, both of which create a substantial demand for labor, are cases in point. Similarly, the long-term credit program to facilitate land transfers, described previously, could be pursued actively in these areas. As previously suggested, some financial assistance might be provided to farms to facilitate the transfer from wheat cropping to sheep grazing on the poorer regions of the Meseta. Standby programs for secondary road construction and rural housing can also be used to provide seasonal employment and additional incomes where necessary.

The amount of funds to be devoted to these programs is a question which the Spanish Government alone can decide. Initially, at least, the resources that can be used effectively will be limited by the administrative and organizational problems involved in mounting the new programs. We suggest, as an indication of one possible order of magnitude, that the budget allocation be set at 300 million pts in 1962. This sum would be used to pay the two educational subsidies and any special credit facilities or subsidies not provided by other institutions. It would be in addition to the funds provided for use by INC for the settlement program described previously.

ORGANIZING FOR DEVELOPMENT

The large tasks ahead in the field of agriculture will, in the mission's view, require that some important changes in organization and administration be considered on a priority basis. Briefly stated, the central problem at present appears to be inadequate coordination, both in Madrid and in the field, among the various elements necessary to formulate and carry out a development policy. This has arisen essentially from two causes:

a. the establishment of a large number of autonomous and semi-autonomous agencies to deal with problems that could not be handled by the ordinary services because of the burden of their regulatory work; and

b. the tripartite division of professional personnel, following the pattern of the higher educational system, into the fields of forestry, veterinary medicine and agronomy, each concerned exclusively with its own specialty even though the problems with which they deal are largely interdependent.

Coordination among these numerous agencies and services takes place, at best, on an *ad hoc* basis or through the office of the Minister. In the field, all of the principal services[21] are to be found in any provincial capital where they are likely to be needed. But formally they work independently of each other as separate units, communicating with their own headquarters in the department of the ministry or autonomous agency concerned, and not necessarily with each other. For example, the extension service should be linked with the agricultural and livestock services upon which it is, in practice, largely dependent; animal husbandry should involve the whole gamut of agricultural services instead of being the exclusive responsibility of the veterinarian; other groups than the forestry service should be concerned with the development of pasture land. This would enable the provincial services to operate nearer their potential effectiveness, which in view of the general excellence of the individual staff members, is high.

It is difficult to see how the kind of program envisaged here, which calls for an intensification of the Government's work with the farmer at many levels and for many purposes, can be carried out unless the services in each provincial capital are concentrated into a single Jefatura. It should be possible for a farmer, whose interests will seldom be confined to one particular aspect of agriculture, to obtain the advice he needs in one place and from one authority, based on the coordinated view of all the competent services. Therefore, it should be the aim to concentrate under one chief and, as soon as possible, under one roof all the elements (soil conservation, extension, research, irrigation, pest control, etc.) necessary to construct and execute a viable agricultural program for the province.

In view of the extent of field operations and the variety of regional problems encountered, it may be worth considering whether a certain number of regional offices should be established. Their number would scarcely be less than six, and they might conveniently be organized on the same geographical basis as the 12 Confederaciones Hidrograficas.[22] These offices would not deal directly with farmers; their function

[21] Jefaturas Agronomicas, Jefaturas de Montes, Jefaturas de Ganaderia, Distritos Forestales, Patrimonio Forestal del Estado, Servicio Nacional del Trigo, Extension Agricola, Servicio de Concentracion Parcelaria, Instituto Nacional de Colonizacion, and the like.

[22] Including the Balearic and Canary Islands.

would be to remove from the center a part of the work load of co-ordinating the 50 provincial offices and to assist in intra-regional and inter-regional planning of investment and resource use.

The official channel of communication to and from Madrid for the single Jefatura in each province should be through the regional office to a Department of Field Operations which the mission considers it advantageous to establish in the Ministry of Agriculture. The newly constituted Department would be responsible for managing the operations of the field offices. It would not be a policy-making body, but would be responsible for conveying to the various operating departments of the Ministry the questions of program or policy arising in the fields that lie within their respective jurisdictions. This arrangement would not preclude other lines of communication on technical matters between ministerial departments and the provincial offices, but would constitute the official and formal chain of command.

These changes raise the more general question of the distribution of functions within the Ministry. This must, of course, be determined by the Minister and the competent Spanish authorities and there are a variety of ways in which it can be done. But we draw attention to the importance of an early and careful study of the organizational structure of the Ministry because we doubt whether the present arrangements will prove adequate for the requirements of the new program for agriculture, and there is always a risk that rigidity in organization will have an undue influence on policy. In seeking a unified approach that is based on the coordinated views of all the competent services and agencies, there are several points that the Government may wish to bear in mind.

a. Some means must be found of ensuring that the skills of the highly qualified staffs of agronomists, veterinarians and forestry specialists are integrated to form a cohesive agricultural program. It will also be necessary to integrate the autonomous agencies into the organizational structure of the Ministry as rapidly as possible. One of the several possible approaches to these two problems would be to organize the departments (direcciones) of the Ministry so that such matters as production, marketing, technical development (research, technical education, extension) and land and water development could be dealt with in one place over the whole range of agriculture; each department would be formed from the staff of the three cuerpos as well as staff of the presently autonomous agencies.

b. It will in any event be desirable to bring about a coordinated approach to the highly important problems in the field of land

and water use and development. One way of doing this would be to establish a department that would embrace the activities of soil conservation, reforestation, irrigation, land consolidation, land settlement and the problems of large farms.

c. Quasi-commercial organizations that operate in the market place (such as the agricultural credit service) might be separate from the internal hierarchy and report directly to the Minister.

d. As a longer-range problem, the system of higher education for professional personnel will have to be re-examined and made consistent with the organizational and administrative arrangements that are adopted. As indicated previously, it may be necessary to give more emphasis to general agricultural education and interdisciplinary studies to make sure that professional specialization does not begin too soon and is not carried too far.

Special mention should be made of the need for a new unit of statistics, economic analysis and planning to carry out these activities on a much larger scale than is now possible. If the operating services are to provide the farmer with sound advice on resource use, a large amount of important data and information must be collected and analyzed concerning such matters as the returns or yields on alternative techniques, the economics of pasture improvement, the income potential of farms of various size under varying crop, water and climate conditions, and so forth. Work of this kind is highly important. The proposed unit would also be responsible for planning the agricultural investment program and for the budgetary process within the Ministry.

FINANCING AGRICULTURAL DEVELOPMENT

Private and Public Credit

To bring about the desired shifts in the use of farm resources and improvements in farm organization and technology, it will be necessary to provide additional capital to agriculture, in the form both of increased injections of private and public credit and of expanded budgetary appropriations. There will also have to be concurrent changes in the organization and direction of credit policy.

While substantial credits have been made available to finance private agricultural investment in the past, the supply has been limited relative to the need, particularly with respect to long-term capital.

The principal sources of credit to farmers are private or quasi-public

—the commercial banks and the savings associations (Cajas Generales de Ahorro)—as can be seen from Table 14.10. Commercial banks provide the bulk of credit used by farmers, in the form of short-term credit (generally less than one year) at commercial rates of interest ranging between 7 percent and 9 percent. The credit may frequently be renewed, but there is no prior assurance that it will be. Although the Cajas, with a network of more than 1,700 outlets, presumably receive a large part of their resources from farmers, loans to farmers account for only a small proportion of their assets. This is undoubtedly due to the fact, described elsewhere in this report, that the Cajas are required to place 65 percent of the increases in their deposits in government securities (recently in INI paper) and a further 10 percent in housing. Thus, at a recent date 60 percent of their assets were in government securities, as against 28 percent for loans to the entire private sector.

TABLE 14.10: Estimated Amount of Agricultural Credit Outstanding

(million pts)

Type and Source	End of Year				
	1955	1956	1957	1958	1959
Commercial Banks	n.a.	n.a.	15,011	15,698	17,989
Cajas Generales de Ahorro[a]	n.a.	n.a.	1,905	2,445	2,820
Servicio Nacional del Trigo[b]	466	663	749	927	984[c]
Instituto Nacional de Colonizacion	302	410	692	785	1,421
Banco Hipotecario	2,341	2,680	2,792	3,031	3,326
Servicio Nacional de Credito Agricola	2,410	3,602	3,995	4,167	4,185
Total	n.a.	n.a.	25,144	27,053	30,725

[a] The figures for the Cajas are believed to be substantially underestimated.
[b] Credit granted in the course of the year without subtracting payment of credit in previous years.
[c] Estimate based on first half of year.
SOURCE: Information supplied by the Bank of Spain.

Cajas loans are both short and medium term, primarily the former, and at a variety of interest rates; even in the agricultural sector, their lending policy appears to be very conservative.

Among the wholly public credit agencies, the Servicio Nacional del Trigo provides short-term credit for seeds, fertilizers, etc., while the Instituto Nacional de Colonizacion lends on a longer-term basis, both at low interest rates and interest free, in connection with its own projects, and also acts as a distribution agent for the Servicio Nacional de Credito Agricola. The Banco Hipotecario, although primarily engaged in urban housing, has some 3.3 billion pts of agricultural loans outstanding. These are used for permanent improvements and for operating capital, are all secured by first mortgages on rural property and are made at interest rates of about 7 per cent for periods of 15 years or less.

The principal public credit agency for agriculture, the Servicio Nacional de Credito Agricola, occupies a relatively minor status in the organizational hierarchy of the Ministry of Agriculture. In the past, a large part of its resources has been provided by the commercial banks and savings associations, which have been required to lend specified amounts of funds to the Servicio at a 2 percent rate of interest. These organizations have discounted most of their Servicio paper at the Bank of Spain, which has been, *de facto,* the principal source of funds. In 1961, financing of the Servicio was for the first time transferred directly to the Treasury. The Servicio has no lending outlets of its own in the field, but utilizes those of the Cajas or other collaborating institutions. It also makes loans directly to farmer groups (cooperatives, communidades de regantes, etc.) or individual farmers. Loans are made at subsidized rates such as 2.75 percent, 3.25 percent, or 3.75 percent; as a result, the Servicio is always fully loaned up, and must arbitrarily ration its credits. The Servicio operates under various limits, such as those on the size of individual loans to farmers (150,000 pts) and on the proportion of its loans that may be in the long-term or 6–15 year category (20 percent).

We believe that four steps are essential to enable private and public credit to flow into agricultural uses at the rate and in the directions needed for development.

a. As we have recommended earlier,[23] the Cajas Generales should be freed from the present restrictions on their investments. There seems to be little doubt that this would substantially increase the volume of lending to agriculture if suitable adjustments are made in the lending policy of the Cajas.

b. The commercial banks and savings associations should no longer be required to lend funds to the Servicio Nacional de Credito Agricola (SNCA). The additional financing required by the SNCA should be provided by the Government.

c. To an increasing extent, credits now provided by the Servicio Nacional del Trigo and Instituto Nacional de Colonizacion should be extended either by the banks and savings associations or by the SNCA.

[23] See Chapter 7.

d. The activities of the SNCA, as the principal public lending agency, should be expanded. At the same time, lending policies should be re-examined with the following changes in view:

i. the interest rates charged should approximate the cost of money in alternative uses. An interest rate of 5 percent or 6 percent would appear to be the minimum from this point of view. As stated elsewhere, if farmers are to be subsidized, it is preferable to do so through measures other than low interest rates which artificially stimulate the demand for capital at the expense of labor;

ii. the ceilings on individual loans should be raised, to reflect the need for larger individual credits as agriculture becomes more advanced technically and commercially; and

iii. the SNCA should organize a loan appraisal service, based insofar as possible on a plan for the development of the individual farms as a whole unit.

It is difficult to estimate what the demand for public credit would be if lending policies were reoriented along these lines. Since the deposits of the Cajas increased by more than 15 billion pts a year in 1960 and 1961, it seems likely that they, together with the commercial banks, could provide the expanding needs for short-term capital plus a substantial part of those for medium-term funds. This would leave the public credit agencies, notably the SNCA, responsible for providing most long-term capital as well as shorter-term funds for specialized purposes that do not readily fit into private lending operations.

Table 14.11 gives our present estimates of the need for additional resources by the SNCA to support the new or expanded activities described in this chapter. These are shown in lines 1 to 9. In addition, allowance is made in line 10 for SNCA's existing operations in the medium- and long-term field, insofar as they are not covered under previous headings. We have assumed that the need for loans for these other purposes will expand, but that a substantial part will be taken over by the Cajas. Moreover, the continuing need for new funds in the future will be reduced by reimbursements. We have estimated the average net requirement, very roughly, at 300 million pts a year. The total figure on line 11 of Table 14.11 is our best estimate of the additional funds to be provided to the SNCA by the Treasury in 1962 and 1966. The situation will have to be watched carefully, and the figures adjusted as necessary in order to enable the SNCA, at each moment of time, to have sufficient resources to meet the demands for agricultural credit placed upon it. We should emphasize that we have assumed that the financing of a key item—agricultural processing plants (slaughter-houses, canneries, etc.)—will be handled through the Banco de Credito Industrial.

TABLE 14.11: Projected Need for Funds by Servicio Nacional de Credito Agricola for Selected Credit Items, 1962 and 1966

(million pts)

	1962	1966
Short to Intermediate Term:		
1. Pasture, livestock and poultry developments[a] [b]		
2. Farm buildings and machinery[a]	300	700
3. Demonstration farms		
Intermediate to Long Term:		
4. Irrigation (existing and new)	500	1,000
5. Reforestation		
6. Land sales		
7. Soil conservation	200	800
8. Activation of large farms		
9. Agricultural processing plants	p.m.	p.m.
10. Other purposes	300	300
11. Total	1,300	2,800

[a] These elements of the livestock improvement program should be financed initially by the SNCA. After they have become soundly established, they may be transferred to private financing (by commercial banks or savings associations).

[b] This program should be financed on a revolving funds basis, so that the need for new capital will decline after the fourth year.

Direct Public Expenditures

In addition to this increase in public credit provided to finance agricultural development, it will also be necessary to increase the direct public outlays (from the budget, Treasury accounts, or autonomous agencies' own resources) in support of the various programs described in this section.

For a number of reasons, it is difficult to suggest a precise figure for the amount of direct public expenditures that will be required. There is some uncertainty as to what amounts were actually spent by the Ministry of Agriculture or autonomous agencies on specific programs in recent years (e.g., 1960 or 1961). With respect to forward projections, in some instances (such as irrigation) we have recommended that studies be undertaken, and reliable estimates cannot be made in advance of their completion. In addition, where new funds or programs are to be established, or existing ones expanded as rapidly as technical conditions permit, it is difficult at this time to predict the sums that may be required in the future.

We have therefore considered it preferable not to project the need for public funds for specified agricultural uses in any detail. It is possible, however, to give an approximate idea of the orders of magnitude involved. In 1960, public expenditures on the various programs described in this section totaled about 7,500 million pts.[24] The two largest items in this total are irrigation, where we have recommended a fresh appraisal, and colonization, where we have recommended that a shift of emphasis be considered. Since these adjustments will take time to accomplish, we have assumed that total public outlays in 1962 will be the same as in 1960. By 1966, however, we would anticipate that public funds devoted to agricultural purposes would rise to nearly 10,000 million pts. Of the increase of 2,500 million pts, 1,500 million pts represents the net increase in credit for various purposes. (The remaining 1,000 million pts is an estimate of the net effect of the various adjustments in expenditure described in the text.)

We should like to stress, however, that the crucial question, for agriculture as well as other sectors of the economy, is not how *much* should be spent, but *how* it should be spent. Within the totals mentioned above, the mission has proposed important shifts of emphasis to accelerate the pace of agricultural development and to spread its benefits as widely as possible: greater emphasis on technical developments (research, extension, improved stock), on better land use (consolidation, conservation, division of large farms, rental legislation) and on the education of the farmer; more emphasis on completing high-priority irrigation projects and on bringing existing irrigation works into full production while an appraisal of the needs as a whole is going on; special programs to facilitate the shift of resources to meet the changing pattern of demand; and, as an alternative to land settlement, consideration of other programs designed to reach and assist a larger number of families in low-income groups and distressed areas.

[24] We have included in this figure, and in the estimates for 1962 and 1966, a figure for the *net* increase in public credit to agriculture (line 11 of Table 14.11).

ANNEX D *IRRIGATION*

Problems of Economic Analysis

Before any individual project can be analyzed, it is necessary to have an idea of the purpose it is to serve. For intensive crops in particular it is necessary to have an estimate of the relation between the market for crops grown and the capacity in terms of land to grow them.

One way of determining the relation between market and capacity is to keep a careful check on the way in which land use patterns change. Upgrading of land from low-value to high-value crops is going on continuously in Spain. It is when land in an area partially devoted to intensive crops approaches the point where it is wholly devoted to intensive crops that the need for new irrigation works emerges.

Therefore, in the first place, it would be desirable to have an inventory of land use for irrigated land. The inventory should specify the amount of land, district by district, devoted to different kinds of crops, together with an estimate of the gross yield (per hectare) with due allowance for double or triple cropping. In order to obtain net yields, cost estimates will be necessary, including those of the farmer's own labor.

The size of the district to be surveyed would have to be determined pragmatically. A confederation will in some cases be too large a unit, since there may be considerable differences within it, either in climate (e.g., the Guadalquivir) or market conditions (e.g., the Tajo).

Once the land-use pattern is determined, an annual check should be made on the trend in crop pattern, for example, by sample surveys. In this way the need for new irrigated land for specific purposes can be foreseen. It will of course be necessary to check the consistency of local estimates of the growth of demand by a general market analysis on a regional, national or international scale according to the crop.

Given this information, the various alternative ways of meeting the demand for new production via new hectarage in irrigation can be assessed. In comparing projects certain principles should be observed. The first is complete definition of the project. Since irrigation projects are often multipurpose, all parts including ancillary works should be included in estimates of capital costs and of benefits to be received. For example, capital costs should include the cost of high dams, electric power installations, afforestation to prevent silting of reservoirs and

317

so forth. They should also include secondary works such as land levelling, terracing, etc. Benefits should include power produced and water for municipal supplies as well as expected agricultural benefits.

In order to assess agricultural benefits, not only must the market be assessed, but also production conditions must be ascertained. Various information would be required for this purpose, among which that obtained from soil surveys would figure prominently.

A key point to be borne in mind is that, in considering how best to allocate funds at a particular point in time (e.g., in preparing the biannual budget), the relevant costs are the incremental costs required to complete the projects. In determining how best to apportion funds in the future in order to obtain the highest return from the new funds to be invested, past expenditures should be disregarded. This means that it may be desirable to complete some projects which perhaps should never have been started in the first place, in cases where the additional sums required for completion are less than the additional returns that the completed project will bring. Conversely, it may be better to discontinue some projects even though substantial sums have been invested in the past, since further expenditures on them would provide relatively small returns and the money could be put to better use elsewhere.

In comparing alternative projects, a convenient measure is the rate of return at which future benefits, when discounted, equal capital costs. All benefits should, therefore, be set out on a realistic *annual schedule*. If power is not likely to be used immediately, the benefits will not accrue until after the lapse of several years and will therefore be less valuable.

It is often the case that there are alternative versions of the same project. For example, it may be possible to complete a project by stages. In certain areas, drainage without irrigation and drainage with irrigation may be alternatives (as in the lower Guadalquivir valley). In this event, the alternative versions should be assessed as though they were alternative projects and the version with the best prospects selected.

Information on land use, markets and project potentialities hardly exists at present. This lack is not due to a shortage of qualified people. At least a preliminary estimate of land use in irrigated areas could be undertaken immediately, using the resources of the Confederaciones Hidrograficas, some of which have already done good planning studies, in cooperation with INC and the Ministry of Agriculture's statistical service, which is very well qualified but understaffed.

A good opportunity for a more comprehensive (at least in some respects) survey of irrigated land will present itself with the coming agricultural census. Provision should, if possible, be made for obtaining any information of special interest for irrigation purposes as a part of this census. For example, areas which form part of irrigation projects in hand or being studied could be so coded.

Soil surveys should be undertaken as rapidly as possible. The mission recommends that the very small allocation of money necessary for this purpose be made forthwith.

Most of the information available to the mission was methodically compiled by the Centro de Estudios Hidrograficos (CEH). In spite of all the careful work that has gone into its compilation, the Centro de Estudios Hidrograficos has been the first to acknowledge the serious lack of information about the characteristics of each project. Soil and climate are not the same everywhere in Spain, so that some projects would undoubtedly rate lower or higher on that account. Nor is it possible to assume, except as a first approximation, that the cost of dry-land crops foregone is the same everywhere. Undoubtedly they are higher in the north than on the south coast, for example.

The only information on yields for judging individual projects at present available is the average dry and irrigated yield of all crops by provinces. However, it is not reasonable to expect that large additions to irrigation areas in Madrid province, for example, will be devoted to the kind of high-value crops now destined for the Madrid market. In fact the area presently devoted to vegetables, melon, watermelon and strawberries is only about 5,000 hectares (even if there is no duplication), so that the 8,000 hectares now under cereals could, through upgrading, take care of very sizable increases in production, unless there are adverse characteristics in this area that are at present unknown.

Another point in the analysis of projects is the need to include the capital costs of secondary works. In compiling the figures in Table 14.6, for example, the mission used INC accounts for coordinated projects and various field observations by the mission. However, there is obviously a considerable margin of error in these estimates and efforts should be made to improve them. Similarly, in Table 14.6, the mission made the arbitrary assumption (also adopted by the CEH) that one "improved" hectare is equivalent to 0.6 "new" hectares. This assumption does not affect many projects, but it does affect some greatly.

Finally, the remaining capital costs (*inversiones pendientes*) are open to considerable error. The mission understands that they do not actually represent costs of completion, but payments still to be made, since the Government is in arrears in payments for contract work performed. Allowance has, however, apparently been made for probable increases in costs because of changes in design and so forth. In any future analysis, these points will require attention.

Irrigation Technique

In general, irrigation technique in Spain is of a high order, so that the mission has little comment to make in this respect. There are, however, a few suggestions to be made.

Sprinkler irrigation is already used in a number of parts of Spain, but it could be more widely used with advantage under appropriate conditions, especially in the south, the Levante and the Canaries, where water is expensive. Sprinkler irrigation is economical in the use of water, because use can be controlled more accurately and adapted to the requirements of soil and crops. While the capital costs of equipment are high, there may be considerable savings in land preparation, leveling being less necessary, field works such as furrows and ridges unnecessary and drainage less important (because less water is used).

The mission recommends that further research be undertaken by OH in association with the Ministry of Agriculture for experimentation and demonstration purposes to ascertain the precise conditions under which sprinkler irrigation could be economically employed. This should first be done in the areas most likely to be adaptable to the practice, namely the Confederaciones of the Jucar, Segura and Sur, and in the Canary Islands.

The mission was also struck with the preference for the open channel system both in major canals and secondary and tertiary works. In some cases, capital costs for piped supply will be higher than for the open channel system, but maintenance charges and water losses lower; in others there may be a saving in both respects.

The most likely areas for piped supply are the mountainous areas of the Jucar, Segura, Sur and the Canaries, where much tunneling, bridging and land leveling might be avoided. It is a fortunate coincidence that these are the areas most suited to sprinkler irrigation, since piped supply under pressure has obvious advantages in sprinkler application.

The mission recommends that future designs of projects should include piped supply as one alternative in the estimates of capital and operating costs.

In addition, the mission considers that salinity deserves more investigation than it has so far received. There are a number of coastal areas where soil salinity exists and where successful techniques for dealing with it might make the land more productive. Furthermore, samples of ground water should be taken periodically and records of salinity kept.

ANNEX E AGRICULTURAL STATISTICS

TABLE E.1: Estimated Income Elasticities of Demand for Major Food Products, 1961–1975

Item	1961–65	1966–70	1971–75
Vegetable Products:			
Wheat	–0.2	–0.25	–0.4
Potatoes	0.1	–	–0.1
Pulses	0.1	–	–0.1
Rice	0.2	0.1	–
Sugar	1.0	0.9	0.6
Fruit	0.5	0.3	0.2
Vegetables	0.3	0.25	0.1
Oil	0.3	0.25	0.1
Wine	0.5	0.35	0.1
Animal Products:			
Meat	1.2	1.1	1.0
Milk	0.8	0.7	0.6
Eggs	1.0	0.9	0.8

SOURCE: A. Camilleri, *Modernizacion de la Agricultura,* I Congreso Sindical, Comision de Trabajo: Agricultura y Pesca, Cuaderno No. 3, Madrid, 1961, page 59.

TABLE E.2: Provincial Distribution of Farms in Excess of 250 Hectares in 1954[a]

Province	Number of Farms	Total Area ('000 ha.)	Area in Farms in excess of 250 ha. as percent of total area of province
Albacete	544	391	26
Badajoz	1,622	978	45
Caceres	1,336	841	42
Cadiz	533	307	42
Ciudad Real	428	274	14
Cordoba	771	349	32
Granada	363	234	19
Huelva	496	366	19
Jaen	374	243	18
Salamanca	397	218	18
Sevilla	970	610	43
Toledo	567	419	27
Other[b]	1,406		
Spain	10,548	6,635	

[a] Parts of the north and northeast are included in the total but not in the breakdown. This omission is not believed to be of significance.
[b] Provinces in which "large" farms occupy a total of less than 200,000 hectares.
SOURCE: *Proyecto de Desarrollo de la Region Mediterranea—Espana.* pp. 122–123.

321

TABLE E.3: Percentage Distribution of Cultivated Area, by Type of Tenure

Region	Farmed by Owner	On Shares	Rented Cash or non-Share Pro-tected	Non-Pro-tected	Total	Totals[a]	Total ha. Under Rental
Andalucia Occidental	66	9	7	19	26	35	810
Andalucia Oriental	62	9	9	20	29	38	761
Castilla La Vieja	71	4	16	9	25	29	741
Castilla La Nueva	70	8	9	14	23	31	1,072
Aragon	75	13	5	8	13	26	361
Levante	46	39	5	11	16	55	1,351
Leonesa	71	1	10	18	28	29	441
Cataluna and Baleares	54	32	8	6	14	46	602
Extremadura	55	21	2	22	24	45	972
Rioja and Navarra	66	10	14	10	24	34	190
Galicia	67	11	21	b	22	33	198
Vascongadas	61	b	36	2	38	38	58
Canarias	66	24	3	6	9	35	55
Asturias and Santander	60	2	38	b	38	40	51
Spain	64	14	9	14	23	37	7,663

[a] Discrepancies due to rounding.
[b] Less than one.

SOURCE: Luis Garcia de Oteyza, *Los Regimenes de Explotacion del Suelo Nacional,* Revista de Estudios Agro-Sociales, October–December 1952, Tables 1 and 2.

TABLE E.4: Basic Data on Wheat, 1952/53–1960/61

	A. Output and Trade ('000 metric tons)				
Crop Year	Produc-tion	Imports	Exports	Change in Stocks	Apparent Consumption
1952/53	4,098	111	–	–250	4,459
1953/54	3,026	968	–	–102	4,096
1954/55	4,773	306	38	+868	4,173
1955/56	3,991	90	69	–133	4,145
1956/57	4,196	34	24	–414	4,620
1957/58	4,900	–	130	+552	4,218
1958/59	4,540	–	565	–397	4,372
1959/60	4,635	33	91	–76	4,653
1960/61	3,522	–	–	n.a.	n.a.

Table E.4 *(cont.)*

	B. *Acreage and Yield*			
	Hectares (thousand)		Yield per ha. (kilograms)	
Crop Year	Dry	Irrigated	Dry	Irrigated
1952/53	4,038	224	920	1,710
1953/54	4,026	230	660	1,580
1954/55	4,021	239	1,057	2,189
1955/56	3,996	292	849	2,052
1956/57	4,005	300	893	3,068
1957/58	4,059	318	1,040	2,124
1958/59	4,041	324	958	2,062
1959/60	4,054	314	981	2,098
1960/61	3,950	284	760	1,830

SOURCE: Based on *Anuario Estadistico de Espana,* 1954 to 1960.

TABLE E.5: Average Yields per Hectare of Wheat by Province in Dry Farming, 1954–1958

Province	Wheat Area ('000 hectares)	Yields (quintals per hectare)					1954–1958 Average
		1954	1955	1956	1957	1958	
I. *"Cereal Provinces":*							
Logrono	33.4	18.0	15.4	23.5	15.7	14.0	17.3
Alava	23.1	13.7	14.8	15.9	15.0	12.5	14.4
Gerona	29.5	14.5	12.5	13.5	15.7	14.1	14.1
Cordoba	134.2	13.3	12.4	13.2	13.7	16.0	13.7
Navarra	106.3	15.6	11.7	15.2	11.8	11.0	13.1
Segovia	87.2	13.8	12.2	11.8	14.2	13.0	13.0
Barcelona	32.1	16.9	12.2	9.1	11.9	11.0	12.2
Soria	72.2	12.2	11.2	9.2	12.8	10.5	11.2
Jaen	94.3	10.0	11.2	10.1	12.4	11.0	10.9
Sevilla	151.7	10.1	8.9	9.8	11.3	14.5	10.9
Cadiz	84.0	13.9	6.7	8.0	12.3	13.6	10.9
Burgos	189.9	11.2	10.7	9.5	12.5	9.5	10.7
Badajos	205.0	9.7	8.1	9.6	14.2	11.5	10.6
Salamanca	150.6	10.1	9.9	9.1	12.1	11.5	10.5
Lerida	66.9	16.5	5.3	11.2	11.6	7.5	10.4
Palencia	142.9	10.8	12.7	7.8	10.2	10.0	10.3
Avila	65.2	9.8	9.7	9.6	11.1	10.0	10.0
Madrid	67.4	10.5	9.2	8.5	12.4	9.5	10.0
Zamora	128.4	9.3	10.2	9.2	9.1	10.8	9.7
Tarragona	21.1	12.1	8.1	10.6	7.7	8.7	9.4
Toledo	194.6	9.1	8.6	8.0	11.5	9.8	9.4
Malaga	63.0	8.8	8.6	9.5	10.6	9.5	9.2
Guadalajara	102.8	10.3	7.6	7.0	12.3	8.5	9.1
Valladolid	203.0	9.9	9.2	7.6	9.0	9.0	8.9
Ciudad Real	196.8	8.3	7.9	8.9	10.1	9.2	8.9

(table continues)

Table E.5 (cont.)

Province	Wheat Area ('000 hectares)	Yields (quintals per hectare) 1954	1955	1956	1957	1958	1954–1958 Average
Leon	88.3	9.4	10.2	7.5	8.5	7.7	8.7
Huelva	40.6	7.9	6.6	7.4	10.3	8.5	8.1
Huesca	96.4	13.7	6.2	9.5	5.9	5.0	8.1
Cuenca	209.9	9.8	7.1	5.9	9.5	7.8	8.0
Granada	104.4	8.5	6.2	7.1	9.3	8.5	7.9
Valencia	19.6	7.8	5.1	12.6	6.1	7.0	7.7
Caceres	158.5	8.3	5.3	6.5	9.6	8.5	7.6
Zaragoza	162.4	13.9	4.7	8.0	6.1	4.6	7.5
Teruel	70.6	8.5	5.6	7.9	8.6	6.5	7.4
Castellon	31.9	8.5	3.7	6.8	6.1	7.0	6.4
Albacete	181.1	7.7	4.0	5.4	7.9	5.9	6.2
Murcia	36.0	8.4	2.3	5.5	5.1	4.5	5.2
Alicante	12.3	6.0	2.5	5.3	5.3	4.0	4.6
Almeria	28.1	3.9	1.1	3.5	3.1	3.6	3.0
Total	3,885.7	10.6	8.4	8.8	10.4	9.6	9.6
II. "Non Cereal Provinces":							
Orense	1.0	16.7	14.4	18.0	17.2	18.0	16.8
Lugo	12.0	13.8	16.3	19.3	16.2	17.5	16.6
Coruna	27.8	17.9	15.8	19.3	15.2	14.0	16.4
Guipuzcoa	4.1	13.3	13.3	15.4	15.8	14.0	14.4
Pontevedra	–	13.9	12.7	12.5	15.2	12.0	13.3
Vizcaya	6.3	8.9	10.2	14.0	19.8	11.5	12.9
Oviedo	7.8	10.8	13.2	12.6	9.4	11.0	11.4
Santander	4.6	7.0	6.8	7.2	8.1	7.2	7.3
Baleares	45.0	7.6	5.5	6.8	6.3	8.0	6.8
Santa Cruz de Tenerife	10.0	6.9	5.5	6.5	3.6	5.5	5.6
Las Palmas	6.5	3.5	4.0	3.7	–	3.5	3.7
Total	126.0	10.6	9.8	11.6	10.2	10.5	10.5
GRAND TOTAL	4,011.7	10.6	8.5	8.9	10.8	9.6	9.7

SOURCE: Servicio Nacional Del Trigo, *La Produccion Triguera Nacional y Rendimientos por Hectarea del Secano, por Provincias, Durante el Quinquenio de Intensificacion de la Produccion 1954–58.*

SECTION **V**

INDUSTRY AND POWER

CHAPTER 15 *INDUSTRY*

Further industrial development is essential, not only for the rapid growth of the Spanish economy as a whole, but also for significant progress toward increasing employment and promoting regional development. The industrial sector is already quite extensive; manufacturing, mining, construction and power together account for close to one-third of the national product. The prospects for further industrial expansion are very good, provided that public policies can be oriented to create an economic climate in which Spanish enterprises, both private and public, can operate with maximum efficiency.

The closer association of Spain with the economies of Western Europe and other areas that has been taking place since 1959, and Spain's recent decision to seek association with the Common Market, present industry with a new opportunity and a new challenge: the opportunity, to gain access to vast new markets on which a broader expansion can be based; the challenge, to meet the competition, both in these markets and within Spain itself, of European industries which are more advanced technically than those of Spain. With these developments, increasing the productivity and lowering the unit costs of Spanish enterprises have now become of overriding importance.

Resource Base and the Growth of Industry

Spanish industry, like agriculture, is striking for its diversity. In part this diversity can be attributed to the broad base of domestic raw materials and sources of energy, abundant manpower and skilled management that has made possible the development of a wide variety of industries.

Iron ore and coking coal, while not of the highest grades, are available at reasonable cost and in sufficient quantities to support a growing steel industry over a substantial period of further development. There are additional deposits of high phosphorous ores which at present are used exclusively for export. There is also ample coal for thermal power although, as indicated in the next chapter, primary reliance is placed on hydroelectric energy, in which there also appears to be a substantial margin for future expansion. Crude oil is the only source of energy which must be supplied entirely from abroad. While this is an important deficiency, and constitutes a significant drain on the balance of payments, prospecting for oil is now taking place on the mainland

327

and in the Spanish Sahara. With respect to other industrial raw materials, Spain's endowments are modest but not inconsiderable. Moreover, its resources have still not been fully explored. It has the world's largest deposits of sulphur pyrites; mercury, zinc, copper, lead, tin, wolfram and manganese are also mined, although some in relatively small amounts. Spain is also fairly well supplied with textile raw materials, but prices are generally above world market levels.

Perhaps Spain's most important developmental asset, however, is an abundant supply of industrious and easily trained manpower. The qualities of Spanish workers have gained wide recognition in other European countries, and there has been increased migration of workers to these countries under agreements with the Spanish Government. To take advantage of this asset, Spain has an able managerial class and an established financial community.

Over the past 20 years the Government has made vigorous efforts to stimulate the development of industry. Production was at first slow to respond, in large part due to pervasive shortages of raw materials, equipment and power. Industrial growth entered a new phase in the 1950's, particularly after 1953 when economic aid from the United States became available and the more serious shortages were relieved. As shown in Table 15.1, industrial production increased at a rate of 8–10 percent a year between 1951 and 1958; the comparative stagnation in 1959 and 1960 reduced the average for the period as a whole to about 6 percent. This growth has been led by the rapid expansion of the metal product and chemical industries, particularly in some of their newer branches (automobiles, fertilizers, petrochemicals, tractors). The traditional consumer goods industries—food, drink and textiles—lagged behind, as did mining as a result of the exhaustion of some deposits and intensified competition in the world sulphur markets.

Apart from mining, the great bulk of industrial output has been for the domestic market. The proportion of industrial products in total exports has never been high, but in the 1950's it was lower than previously.

Table 15.1 also suggests something of the wide range of activities within the industrial sector. Spanish industry contains most if not all of the branches of activity associated with a modern industrial economy, including heavy metallurgy, shipbuilding, oil refining and petrochemicals, a steel industry currently producing in excess of 2 million tons annually and consumer durable industries producing such goods as television sets and refrigerators. In most cases, of course, the output of individual firms is still on a small scale since it has mostly been confined to the dimensions of the Spanish market and even this market is generally shared by many producers. Despite the diversity of industries, activity has been concentrated, for the most part, into a relatively few regions of intensive development. The north coast (where most of the steel and heavy industry is located), the Barcelona area (textiles, leather, mechanical industries)

TABLE 15.1: Indices of Industrial Production, 1951–1960

(1958=100)

Item	1951	1952	1953	1954	1955	1956	1957	1958	1959	1960
Mining	72.3	79.9	80.1	81.3	85.6	89.7	97.0	100.0	91.0	94.0
Food	77.1	86.9	86.6	84.1	85.7	95.9	96.9	100.0	110.5	111.1
Drink	66.3	70.4	86.7	79.4	76.8	83.0	86.1	100.0	91.8	98.3
Tobacco	56.5	68.8	61.2	68.7	73.7	81.4	85.3	100.0	99.2	98.2
Wood and Cork	60.6	60.2	59.0	63.9	75.8	76.6	88.4	100.0	95.0	78.8
Paper	59.6	63.2	61.7	72.2	77.2	84.3	90.9	100.0	102.6	104.8
Textiles	63.2	77.5	82.8	82.7	88.3	93.4	98.0	100.0	93.1	90.2
Leather and Shoes	81.4	85.9	83.7	85.7	90.2	92.0	98.1	100.0	93.9	96.4
Chemicals	38.6	43.8	44.4	51.4	56.8	62.8	89.5	100.0	109.5	118.1
Basic Metals	52.6	56.7	59.2	66.8	74.5	78.5	84.2	100.0	113.5	110.4
Metal Products	44.7	49.3	54.2	58.5	64.0	73.4	85.2	100.0	86.5	74.6
Transport Equipment	28.0	37.1	37.2	42.9	49.9	67.6	83.6	100.0	94.8	108.4
Petrochemicals	34.3	41.0	55.4	55.8	61.3	71.6	82.2	100.0	105.4	106.0
Nonmetallic Minerals	59.7	63.0	66.7	72.1	78.4	83.7	91.4	100.0	101.2	95.4
Electricity	50.8	57.7	59.5	65.8	73.1	84.1	89.5	100.0	105.8	112.7
Building and Construction	64.4	68.7	72.2	82.7	94.0	98.5	96.1	100.0	103.4	95.9
General Index	56.9	63.3	65.9	70.4	76.9	83.7	91.4	100.0	100.1	98.6

SOURCE: Ministry of Commerce.

and Madrid are the three main centers of industrial activity. While there has been an encouraging growth of some secondary centers such as Seville, many regions, particularly in the center and south, have experienced little industrial development. Except where irrigation is possible, these regions tend to be the poorest in Spain; without local industry to create a demand for farm products and to draw off surplus farm labor, rural employment and income remain very low.

The growth of industry has been accompanied by a corresponding growth in industrial employment. Although employment statistics are incomplete, it appears that the industrial labor force was slightly in excess of 3 million people in 1958, thus comprising about 28 percent of the total labor force.[1] According to the same data, the industrial labor

[1] Data from the *Consejo de Economia Nacional*.

force expanded on the order of 2 percent a year during the years 1950–1958, when output was growing in excess of 8 percent a year. These statistics are open to question, however, and it is possible that industrial employment has in fact been increasing at a faster rate than they would indicate.

Structural Problems

Despite this background of an adequate resource base and an impressive rate of past industrial growth, it would be misleading to conclude that the future development of industry will be an easy task. There are a number of serious flaws in the structure of Spanish industry, some of which were created by the particular circumstances under which industrial growth took place and the specific patterns which it followed.

One of the principal problems facing Spanish industry is that, in many branches, firms are too small to operate efficiently. The economies of large-scale operation vary, of course, according to the nature of the industry, but there can be no question that many Spanish firms are well below the optimum size for efficient production. This is in part attributable to the tradition of small-scale family enterprise, which has been maintained longer in Spain than in most other European countries. The cotton textile industry of Catalonia is an example of the extreme fragmentation resulting *inter alia* from family enterprises. The inefficiencies resulting from this structure are pointed out in the report of a special commission set up to study the industry's problems, a report which recommended a major reorganization of the industry.[2] Even in relatively new industries, such as those producing motor vehicles and tractors, there are a surprisingly large number of firms; given the limited size of the Spanish market which they serve, few of them are able to attain the size necessary to take advantage of the economies of large-scale production.

It is difficult to measure statistically the incidence of small firms. Such evidence as exists suggests that there is not only a proliferation of very small enterprises, but also a relative lack of medium-sized ones (with 100–500 personnel); there appears to have been some tendency toward polarization at the two extremes.

Often accompanying the problem of size is that of obsolete or insufficient equipment. Many Spanish firms are not sufficiently mechanized, or else equipped with old machines considerably less efficient than

---

[2] *Plan de Reorganizacion de la Industria Algodonera Espanola.*

their modern counterparts. It is not uncommon to find in a single factory, and even in a single assembly line or production process, machines of very different conditions, ages and countries of manufacture. The precise extent of the equipment problem is not clear, but on the basis of the scattered data available, the opinions of industrialists and the mission's observations, the problem appears to be a serious one. Again to take the textile industry as an example (because more is known about it as a result of recent studies) it is estimated that only 15 percent to 20 percent of the equipment is modern.[3] In the heavy mechanical industry, it is estimated that only about one-fourth of the equipment is modern,[4] and the situation is similar though somewhat less serious in other sectors. Moreover, in a situation where the equipment problem is so widespread, the modern and well-equipped plants are likely to be handicapped by their dependence on components and materials from less efficient suppliers.

Even allowing for the fact that the most modern equipment is not necessarily the most efficient in an economy of skillful and low-cost labor, there can be no doubt that the state of its equipment is a severe handicap to Spanish industry. It has resulted not only in low productivity but also in poor quality of consumer goods and intermediate products.

Under these conditions, it is readily understandable that large segments of Spanish industry are characterized by low productivity and, as a consequence, high costs and selling prices that make their products uncompetitive. Precise measurement is again impossible, but in the textile industry, for example, output per spindle and per loom in Spain is substantially lower than in other Mediterranean countries as well as the more industrialized countries of Europe.[5] Spain's Central Siderurgical Association has estimated that production per worker in integrated steel plants in Spain in 1959 was little more than one-third of that in Italy, Belgium, or France. As a very general rule, the less competitive industries appear to be those producing the more complicated manufactured products, such as trucks and motor vehicles, which are dependent on the development of a number of ancillary industries to supply component parts. In branches of industry based on local raw materials which do not require extensive processing or fabrication, or in which low labor costs are of particular advantage and the economies of scale are not of dominant importance, Spanish industry has shown that it can produce at competitive prices.

[3] *Industria de Algodon,* I Congreso Sindical, 1961, p. 64.
[4] *Estudios Sobre la Unidad de Europa,* 1959, Tomo VIII, p. 365.
[5] E.C.E., *Economic Survey of Europe, 1959,* Ch. VII.

There are, of course, exceptions to this general pattern, reflecting once more the varied face of Spanish industry. Within a single branch of industry can usually be found a mixture of the old and the new, the large and the small, the efficient and the inefficient. Impressive modern plants exist side by side with ones that have hardly changed since the 19th century, and within branches of industry requiring wholesale reorganization there are individual enterprises competing successfully in world markets.

How to deal with these structural problems in order to establish a more efficient and competitive industrial economy can best be considered in the light of some of the special conditions that brought them about. These conditions include:

a. the period of economic isolation, which led to the adoption of extensive controls;

b. the shortage of foreign exchange that persisted during this period;

c. a shortage of capital for investment in industry; and

d. business uncertainty as to the future course of economic policy, the role of public enterprises, the effects of taxation and other matters.

We will mention these factors only briefly here, since they will be discussed at greater length in subsequent parts of this chapter.

Import restrictions and other controls, however necessary they may have been, have protected Spanish industry from foreign competition, thus enabling enterprises to develop or survive even though high cost. As a consequence Spain has been insulated from the effects of industrial developments in other parts of the world, making it difficult for new products and technologies to enter from abroad; and, the growth of industries designed to serve only the Spanish market has led to the establishment of firms that were too small for economical production. The controls, to some extent, tended to inhibit or distort production and investment patterns; by reducing the scope for internal competition, they have also reduced the pressures that would have revealed weaknesses in the structure of industry and forced remedial action.

Despite these controls—and in part, because of them—the period of economic isolation was also one of inflation. Inflationary pressures tended to reinforce the isolation of industry by making the domestic market more attractive to Spanish producers and reducing the incentive to export. As in other countries that have experienced prolonged inflation, prospects of quick and easy profits also encouraged speculative investment and reduced the consciousness of costs, and the responsiveness to market competition, that are necessary if investment decisions are to be soundly based.

The period we have been describing was also one of a continual and serious shortage of foreign exchange. With scarce foreign currencies allocated on a priority basis for imports of essential foodstuffs and raw materials, licenses for the purchases of foreign machinery and equipment were particularly difficult to obtain. This difficulty has been a serious handicap to the modernization of industry. The fact that some enterprises were more successful than others in obtaining import licenses for equipment accounts for some of the variations in the extent of mechanization that can be observed. More generally, owing to the shortage of foreign exchange and the consequent encouragement of national production, industries were etablished without particular regard to their international competitive position.

Accompanying the shortage of foreign exchange has been a shortage of funds for investment in industry. The rate at which an economy grows is, of course, closely dependent on the level of its savings, and the extent to which funds for investment are in short supply is one way of measuring the extent of its development. The more serious the shortage of investment capital, however, the more important it is that this capital be used as productively as possible. In this regard, the structure of banking, public credit policy, tax regulations and other factors can and have had a significant influence. Some of their less favorable effects have been to make it difficult for firms to obtain through normal credit channels the medium- and long-term capital required for expansion, particularly in the case of small, family-owned enterprises and of new enterprises. In addition, the expansion of some public enterprises has substantially reduced the flow of savings to finance private undertakings.

The rate at which private investment in fact takes place is also dependent on how businessmen visualize the future. The stabilization plan, by decisively halting the inflation and removing some of the protective covering of external and internal controls, faced Spanish businessmen with a changed economic environment. Many of them responded with courage and initiative, but the hesitancy of some others, although easy to understand, has acted as a brake on the subsequent recovery of private investment. Other factors have added to the climate of uncertainty. Now that the primary objectives of stabilization have been achieved, the business community has been awaiting an indication of the future course of government economic policy and the rate and direction of growth of the economy. Foremost among their preoccupations is the question of the future role of state-owned enterprises in fields in which they compete with private industry. Investment decisions are also handicapped by the dearth of useful statistics and economic studies on industrial subjects; by the lack of accounting standards that would make it possible to ascertain the true value of business enterprises; and by the complexity of the tax system which makes its burden and effect difficult to anticipate.

Objectives of Government Policy

The structural problems we have been describing were due in large part to the exceptional conditions of the period of economic isolation. These conditions no longer obtain. The central objective of government policy today is to modernize Spanish industry and make it more dynamic and competitive, so that it may have an expanded role in international trade and be prepared to play its part in Western Europe under conditions of economic integration. Broadly speaking, there are five ways in which public policy can be exercised to help bring this about. These are:

a. creating an environment in which private industry grows not only rapidly, as it has at times in the past, but also along lines that will ensure its efficiency and competitiveness;

b. defining the role of public enterprises with respect to private industry;

c. increasing the availability of public funds to finance private industrial expansion, and improving the access of firms to these funds;

d. providing special assistance as necessary in connection with specific problems such as regional development; and

e. improving the flow of statistics and economic studies on which informed business decisions can be based.

Each of these policies is important to industrial growth, but what happens with respect to the economic climate in which private industry develops is likely to be the most decisive. What is needed is a further change in the industrial environment, insofar as this can be effected by public policy, to give greater freedom and greater incentive for the private sector to turn its resources to the most productive uses. Such an environment would also be the one best calculated to attract the capital and technical assistance from abroad which Spanish industry needs for its development. The principal action on the part of the Government should be to remove the remaining interventions and controls. So long as these controls continue, they will impede businessmen from making the large-scale adjustments that will be necessary if development is to proceed along the right directions including, in particular, the growth of export industries. There are also some positive measures that can be taken to enhance the flexibility and adaptability of resources, especially with respect to labor.

This approach is, in our view, the one best calculated to provide, in the long run, for the growth of the industrial sector along efficient lines that will increase its competitive strength. It must be recognized, however, that in the short run there may be some situations in which efficiency and growth are not wholly compatible objectives; where this may be so, as in the case of tariffs or labor controls, we have recommended that programs be adopted gradually so that industry has time to adjust to their impact without disrupting the rate of growth. It is also true that the removal of controls will not, by itself, ensure the competitiveness of Spanish industry. The greater scope given to market forces will tend in the direction of increased competition, but where serious monopoly conditions persist it may be necessary to take direct action, e.g., through adjustments of tariff or import policy to introduce more competition from abroad.

The environment in which private industry operates is also substantially influenced by the role which the Government assigns to public enterprises. The mission considers that the time has come to define this role in the light of the developing situation. In particular, it is desirable both to limit the intervention of public firms in fields which can be left to private enterprise and to eliminate the special advantages enjoyed by public enterprises. We also think it very desirable to improve the accountability of the public sector, in its economic as well as financial sense; this entails not only fuller dissemination of financial reports but also ensuring that INI firms, insofar as possible, are under the same disciplines that private firms encounter in the market place.

An improved environment will help to allocate the private resources available for investment in industry to their most productive uses. In the long run, by augmenting the return on capital investment, it is also likely to increase the amount of funds available from savings within Spain and from abroad. Even so, the need for funds to finance the reequipment, modernization and expansion of Spanish industry is potentially so large that it will also be necessary to increase the funds provided from public sources. At the same time, some changes in administrative procedures and lending criteria should be considered to ensure that the funds provided make an effective contribution.

As in other sectors, the primary objective of government policy toward industry should be, in our view, to attain the highest possible rate of growth. Any major diversion of resources from this objective in an effort to increase employment or to promote the development of more backward regions is likely, on the whole, to result not only in a lower rate of growth but also in less progress toward these other objectives. There are nevertheless some measures compatible with the goal of efficient industrial growth that will help to reduce regional disparities in income and employment.

An essential element of an industrial environment conducive to growth is the availability of statistics and economic studies on which informed business decisions can be based. Improvements in this field both through the systematic provision of data and projections to private groups as part of the planning process and through an increase in the regular output of statistical materials should help to remove some of the uncertainty that has impeded investment decisions in the past.

In the subsequent parts of this chapter we have attempted to spell out in more detail how these policies might be implemented in specific circumstances. A gradual relaxation of labor controls is an integral part of the process of creating a new industrial environment, but we have found it convenient to discuss this subject separately. In making specific recommendations, we have borne in mind that the adjustments which are required are extensive, that they will not be easy and that time will be required to accomplish them. For this as well as other reasons, we have not attempted to draw up a detailed blueprint of the necessary actions in each field, but rather to point to the general lines along which the problems should be approached. With additional time, experience and information, more detailed policies can be evolved.

Improving the Industrial Climate

As we stated previously, the principal measure that the Government can take to establish an environment that is conducive to rapid industrial growth is to remove the controls which continue to hamper the free working of the economy. These controls were designed, by and large, to deal with problems and conditions that have since been successfully overcome or overtaken by events. Although considerable progress has been made in dismantling the complicated machinery of interventions and controls to take account of the changed circumstances, much remains to be done.

A very rough but useful distinction can be drawn between two kinds of controls that have been employed in the past: what might be called conjunctural or equilibrium controls, on the one hand, and structural controls on the other. The terms are not precise, and the two categories overlap, but the former covers the internal and external controls (on prices, wages, imports, etc.) designed to contain inflation and limit the balance of payments deficit, while the latter refers to controls on investment, procurement and other business decisions for the purpose of encouraging or protecting certain types of activities and discouraging others. Some of the controls in the first category have, in practice, also had important effects upon the direction of investment and the protection of individual firms, but this presumably was not their primary intent.

Equilibrium Controls. During the early postwar period most industrial products were subject to individual price controls, raw materials in short supply were allocated by the Government as was power and strict controls were placed on imports in order to ration scarce foreign exchange. As supplies increased and inflationary pressures eased somewhat, controls on prices and raw materials were gradually relaxed; a further relaxation took place as part of the stabilization plan, which also introduced the first significant liberalization of import controls and terminated the multiple exchange rate system which had had various distorting effects.

Except for a few products, the allocation of rationing of industrial materials has now been virtually eliminated. The number of products whose prices are fixed by the Government is also relatively small, but it includes some important items as can be seen from the following list: coal, cement, iron pyrites, certain paper, lubricating oils, lead, superphosphates, industrial alcohol, uranium, sugar, antibiotics and some iron and steel products. In addition, the prices of a large number of products are subject to a system of "supervised freedom" which requires that price increases be submitted to the Government which may oppose them *ex post*.

The mission has not examined in detail the situation with respect to each of the products subject to direct price control, but we are persuaded that general economic conditions are now such that these controls can be removed. Price controls are, at best, a short-term (and often self-defeating) means of dealing with shortages or imbalances in individual products markets, and they tend to introduce distortions of their own. If there are supply problems, or if it is desired to subsidize the users of some product, there are better ways of dealing with these matters. In cases where prices have been fixed over a long period of time and the equilibrium price is likely to differ substantially from the present one, it may be desirable to lift the price control in stages. The system of "supervised freedom" does not, in practice, appear to have led to many interventions by the Government and therefore has not presented any serious problems, but it has potentially the same kinds of disadvantages as direct price controls.

Removal of the remaining quantitative controls on imports of industrial raw materials and equipment is no less vital to the healthy growth of Spanish industry. We have dealt with this subject in an earlier chapter, but would again like to stress how important it is that business enterprises be able to obtain the materials and machinery that are needed for modernization and expansion from the best sources and on the most favorable terms.

Structural Controls. The principal controls that we have called "structural" are three in number and were adopted in 1939 as part of the Law for the Protection of National Industry. They are: the prior authorization by the Government of industrial investments; the establishment of a preferential category of industries "of national interest"; and the requirement that government agencies and public enterprises procure all of their supplies and equipment in Spain. These regulations, it will be noted, were adopted shortly after the Civil War and immediately after the outbreak of the Second World War. Accordingly, they were inspired by the need to direct very limited investment funds to accomplish a number of particular and urgent tasks: to reconstruct devastated sectors of the economy; to promote industries required for national defense; and to promote industries that would give the economy greater self-sufficiency. However necessary they may have been for these purposes, it is evident that the progress which the economy has made in the intervening period of more than 20 years, the improved trade conditions that now exist and the need for Spain to assimilate its policies to those of other European countries, require that these controls be re-examined.

Under the 1939 law, investments in new industrial plants, or for the expansion of relocation of existing plants, must be approved in advance by the Ministry of Industry (either in Madrid or through its provincial offices). The procedure varies according to the size of the investment, the number of employees in the firm and the extent to which imports of machinery or materials are involved, but in general all investments of any consequence have required the approval of the Ministry of Industry. In 1960, the law was amended to raise from 50,000 pts to 2 million pts the figure below which investments not requiring imports of materials and machinery were exempted from the prior authorization. Certain types of cement plants under designated conditions were also exempted. The criteria to be followed in reviewing the requests for authorization have not, to our knowledge, been published.[6] No time limit is fixed for the authorization process. One important feature is the publication of the application in the *Official Gazette* in advance of its approval, so that interested parties may have the opportunity to comment upon it. There is no procedure for administrative appeal from the decision of the Ministry of Industry.

The Ministry of Industry has advised the mission that a large majority of the requests for authorization have been approved in recent years. Industrialists have informed us that, for the most part, the authorization process is a minor harassment rather than a major hindrance to private investment. Despite the fact that it is generally not difficult to obtain the authorization permit, the requirement stands as a significant obstacle to the healthy growth of industry. This is so for a number of reasons:

a. The criteria apparently followed in practice in approving or denying applications have been unclear and, to some extent, inconsistent; from what has been observed earlier, it is evident that they have not prevented unsound investments from taking place.

b. In the absence of criteria that are self-administering, the authorization process has left much too broad an area for administrative discretion.

c. The procedure is time consuming, and although most applications have been processed expeditiously, some have taken months or years to be decided; this has introduced an element of uncertainty.

d. The procedure of advance publication has made it possible for established firms to block the entry or expansion of competitors.

e. For both practical and psychological reasons, the requirement has been a deterrent to foreign firms considering investment in Spain.

The mission believes that Spain's economic development has reached a point where the investment authorization process no longer

---

[6] One criterion, which still appears to carry weight, is the extent to which the product can be manufactured without importing parts from abroad. This criterion, which can lead to uneconomic production and damage the export prospects of an industry, appears to us to be out of date.

serves a useful purpose. We see no reason why it could not be discontinued forthwith. If private investment resources are to be utilized as productively as possible, investment should be left to the decision of individual businessmen facing the discipline of the market place. Except in very special cases where national defense or some socially harmful investment is involved, the Government should not have the negative role of preventing investments from taking place; rather, it should adopt the positive one of creating an environment in which private investment contributes most effectively to the growth of the economy. To the extent that certain types or regions of industrial activity need to be encouraged, this should be done by direct measures to which we refer subsequently.

The 1939 legislation also established a category of "industry of national interest" for the purpose of stimulating the introduction of industries needed for national defense or self-sufficiency. The benefits, which are provided for a minimum period of 15 years, include: authority to expropriate land; tax reductions up to 50 percent; a guaranteed minimum annual return on capital of 4 percent; and reductions in customs duties. Some or all of these benefits may be granted in any particular case; in return, the enterprise must accept State designation of a controller and delegate director. Industries receiving these benefits are required to use only articles of Spanish manufacture, unless exceptions are specifically authorized.

The criteria of "national interest" specified in the law are so broad that it is difficult to find any industry to which they could not be applied. As a result, the burden of interpreting them has been placed at the administrative level. As in the case of investments permits, the mission did not find that any well-defined economic criteria were being used. Although the qualification as of "national interest" is generally granted in principle to a whole branch of industry, in practice each enterprise must apply separately for qualification and to receive some or all of the benefits as the Government may decide in each case. This qualification procedure has made it difficult to administer the law equitably. Also, INI enterprises are automatically defined as of national interest, even in branches of industry in which at least some of the private firms are not so classified.

As a minimum, we would recommend that the procedure be modified so that all the firms in a particular branch of industry to be designated as of "national interest" would automatically qualify and receive identical benefits. The benefits provided also seem unduly generous —15 years, for example, is an excessive period of tax relief for most industries. Government participation in the direction of the companies is also undesirable, since it can readily conflict with their conduct as private enterprises. Beyond this, however, we question whether, even on an industry-wide basis and with modifications to meet these other objections, the concept of "national interest" is useful for development. In an economy in which resources are relatively flexible and mobile and there are no major barriers to international trade, it is not necessary to establish priorities among sectors. Resources will tend to move into the activities in which their productivity to the economy is highest and government controls are more likely to distort than to facilitate the adjustment process. There is still a role for special incentives to overcome short-term or institutional obstacles to the introduction of new industries or to the necessary adjustments in existing sectors faced with a particular difficulty, but the role must be defined and administered very carefully.

The third of the controls established in 1939 was the requirement that a wide variety of public bodies use articles exclusively of Spanish manufacture. The law applies to state, provincial and municipal bodies (including RENFE and INI firms), organisms of the National Movement, public monopolies, suppliers of public services, industries of national interest and companies "enjoying benefit or protection in any administrative, economic, or financial form." Imports may be authorized by the Ministry of Industry through special orders and for designated reasons, which include the absence of Spanish production, differences in quality and urgency of timing.

This "Buy Spanish" provision, like the other controls that we have been considering, leaves a broad area for administrative discretion with respect to interpreting differences in quality and timing as between Spanish and foreign manufacture. The law appears to have been applied very strictly during most of the period that it has been in force; some tendency to relax it is apparent now that the balance of payments situation has improved.

There appears to be no question that the requirement to procure exclusively in Spain has obliged public firms (such as RENFE) to equip themselves under disadvantageous conditions with respect to price, quality and time of delivery that have added materially to their costs and lowered the efficiency of their operations. While this requirement has no doubt encouraged the growth of supplier industries in Spain, the protection of these industries from foreign competition is one of the factors contributing to their development along high-cost lines. Moreover, the supplier industries themselves have been handicapped in obtaining materials or equipment from abroad, and this has made it difficult for them to produce the quality of goods required.

In our view, this requirement should also be reconsidered in the light of the changes in circumstances since its adoption. It is very important to the productivity of the public sector—which the law defines very broadly—that it be able to obtain equipment and supplies of the desired quality and at a reasonable price. To the extent that protection of national producers is necessary and justifiable, the tariff is the appropriate instrument, and the new tariff rates for most industrial items are more than adequate for this purpose. On the other hand, we recognize that many governments have a similar type of requirement (although many of them have much lower tariffs than does Spain). If the Government wishes to maintain the law, we would suggest that it be modified along the following lines:

a. The provisions permitting procurement abroad for reasons of quality or time of delivery should be interpreted in a liberal fashion.

b. Provision should be made for procurement abroad for reasons of price. Given the high tariff levels, a price differential of more than 10 percent (including the tariff) should be sufficient reason for an exemption.

c. Insofar as possible, the Government should publish a list of the items to which the policy of national procurement would apply, such as equipment related to national defense or to the development of new (infant) industries. For items not on the list, the public sector would be able to procure on the same conditions as private enterprises.

Other Controls (Tariffs and Taxation). In considering the various controls that influence the climate of industry, we should also mention two of the most traditional forms of government intervention; tariffs and taxation. Both of these have been discussed in earlier chapters and we will not go into them in detail here. On the former subject, many branches of Spanish industry will require some degree of tariff protection during the period that modernization and re-adaptation are taking place; it is most desirable that such protection be kept to the minimum necessary for this purpose, that it be applied flexibly and removed as soon as possible and that imports of material and equipment needed for development take place at the lowest possible cost.

Taxation impinges on industry in a variety of ways, and the goal of a tax system that is conducive to growth and does not introduce distortions or inequalities is still to be attained. To some extent, this is a universal complaint against tax systems, but the Spanish system has some special problems of its own. The most important industrial tax, on business profits, is applied in such a way as to make its economic effects impossible to judge. While it marks an improvement in some respects over the tax formerly employed, it does not appear to be sufficiently closely related to profits or to provide the industrialist with the requisite degree of certainty as to his future tax burden. The multiplicity of other taxes paid by business enterprises, and their lack of clarity and certainty, add to the problem. The mission understands that income from securities is, *de facto* if not *de jure,* more heavily taxed than that from other sources, in part because the tax is easier to collect; if so, this undoubtedly helps to explain why many investors seem to prefer real property to business securities. Another matter is the rebate of indirect taxes on exports (*desgravacion fiscal*) which has not yet been extended as thoroughly as it should or administered with sufficient flexibility. On a more positive note, the recent law providing special tax arrangements for the revaluation of assets to reflect current values will make it easier for renewal and replacement of equipment to take place.

Labor Flexibility, Mobility and Training

The expansion and modernization of industry will involve not only a significant increase in the over-all level of employment but also shifts in the structure of employment among industries and changes in the requirements for particular skills within industries. The labor requirements in some industries may decline, and even in expanding industries the reorganization of particular enterprises may involve temporary reductions in labor requirements; on the other hand, there will be firms and branches of industry whose demand for labor will increase rapidly. Shifts in technology will, at the same time, change the proportion of skilled to unskilled workers in various fields, and in general greatly increase the need for highly trained technical personnel.

These changes are a natural part of the development process. To adjust to these changes and to assist in bringing them about, however, a considerable degree of flexibility is required of the labor force.

Under the existing regulations governing industrial employment, workers can be dismissed for "economic" (as distinct from "disciplinary") reasons only through a procedure involving the permission of the Ministry of Labor. This provides a considerable measure of job security; at the same time, there is a legal prohibition of strikes. In addition, the Government establishes, through extensive regulations and in considerable detail, the minimum wage rates, supplementary salary and overtime pay rates and other wage and employment conditions both on a national basis and for individual branches of industry.

In economic terms, this system must be considered in the light of its effect on the needs of the developing economy. Replacement of old and inefficient equipment may be inhibited to the extent that the gains from the use of new machinery are dissipated through the need to retain labor made superfluous by its introduction. Also entrepreneurs may be hesitant to engage in new ventures that involve an increase in their labor force if the force must be maintained in full even if it should later prove to be excessive.[7] Furthermore, inflexibility in the wage structure makes it difficult to adapt the remuneration of employees to differences in, or to changes in, their productivity.

Undue rigidity in the pattern of employment and compensation can impede the rationalization and growth of the industrial sector. If old equipment is to be replaced, small firms consolidated and industries reconverted at a pace that will appreciably improve the competitive position of Spanish industry, the labor market must have a reasonable degree of flexibility. As one element, this will entail some modification of the regulations regarding dismissal. On the other hand, it must be recognized that economic efficiency may, in the short run, sometimes conflict with the workers' interest in job security. Although a growing and more efficient economy is strongly in the interest of labor, means must be found of handling the transitional problems that arise.

The mission is aware that this is a difficult area, and that some elements of the problem transcend our terms of reference. However, the Government has in the last several years initiated several important steps toward greater flexibility, and these point in the direction to be followed by subsequent measures.

A necessary condition to any increased flexibility in the use of labor is an adequate system of unemployment insurance. The new legislation on this subject (adopted late in 1961) provides unemployment compensation of 75 percent of the basic wage, plus family allowance and two bonuses, for a period of up to six months. Although it is too early to evaluate the new system, its terms appear reasonable and we would urge that it be put in force as quickly as possible and that it be administered expeditiously. Beyond this, the transfer of workers from individual plants or branches of industry in which there is an excess to those where workers are in short supply would be greatly facilitated by:

a. a nationwide employment exchange to provide up-to-date

---

[7] The prohibition against dismissal only applies to "permanent" employees. A measure of flexibility can sometimes be gained by hiring employees on a temporary basis.

information on the demand for and supply of workers by region, city, occupation and type of training; and

b. a fund to assist in the movement of industrial labor from surplus to deficit areas, in Spain or abroad, including a subsidy to cover costs of transportation and resettlement in a new location.

Some progress has already been made in these two directions, and we understand that the Government has further measures under active consideration.

Another recent development in the direction of greater flexibility is the widespread use of collective bargaining agreements. These make it increasingly possible to relate wages to productivity at the plant level and also provide a framework for considering how the interests of job security can be reconciled with management's need for greater adaptability in the size and structure of the labor force.

Now that these programs are being developed, the Government is in a position to consider what additional steps are possible to relax the regulations governing the dismissal of workers. It might, for example, be possible to relax the procedures so as not to require government authorization for dismissal involving only a small proportion of the labor force employed and also to expedite those requests for dismissal requiring government approval and to approve them more readily when they are related to the development needs of the enterprise.

How rapidly progress can be made along these lines will depend, more than anything else, on the rate at which industry and the economy in general expand. The Government has properly recognized the need to proceed with caution during the recent period of readjustment to the effects of the stabilization plan. Further adjustments will be easier and less costly to make under conditions of rising production and employment; with the favorable prospects for industrial expansion both in the immediate future and over the longer run, it should now be possible to consider a further relaxation of the regulations.

Greater flexibility and mobility of the labor force will help to increase its productivity. In addition, there is a need to raise the level of skills and productivity by more intensive vocational training. There are already shortages of some skills, and more will become apparent as industrial growth proceeds unless the pace of vocational training is stepped up. As the demand for skilled labor at home increases, the emigration of trained personnel for employment elsewhere in Europe is less likely to continue, and this is desirable, since loss of such personnel in the future could handicap the growth of Spanish industry. The expansion of vocational training schools should be based on a careful study of requirements by industry, type of occupation and area. Special consideration should be given to the rapid retraining of workers who are seeking new employment after having been displaced.

Role of Public Enterprises

How rapidly industrial development takes place will depend on the relationship that exists between public and private enterprises, and in particular on the role that is assigned to the Instituto Nacional de Industria (INI) and how this role is carried out.

Direct participation of the Government in industry is clearly a matter which countries in different stages of development have treated differently. Whatever the extent of this participation, three principles have to be borne in mind. First, the Government should direct its efforts to those situations where the need for public initiative is clearly evident. Secondly, the Government must exercise adequate control over the public enterprises to ensure that they carry out effectively their assigned role. Third, since private enterprise also has a role to play, the activities of the public enterprises should assist rather than discourage private initiative.

INI was established in 1941, when the need to reconstruct the economy was paramount and wartime conditions isolated Spain from foreign markets and suppliers. It played a vital part in reactivating the economy and overcoming shortages that had developed in critical areas. Over the succeeding years, its activities have resulted in the creation of substantial new productive capacity and modern industry.

The legislation establishing INI stated that its primary purpose was to promote the revival of industry in fields related to national defense and economic self-sufficiency. It was also stated that INI would enter fields which, because of the size of the investments required or the low expectations of profits, were not attractive to the private economy. This statement indicates that it was not intended that INI replace or substitute for private capital; this is further confirmed by references in the legislation to encouraging private initiative and stimulating private enterprise as well as by the requirement that state industries not compete unfairly with private individuals in the manufacture of articles not connected with national defense.

The industrial complex of INI has reached large proportions. Table 15.2 lists 61 of the principal industrial enterprises in which INI has a majority or minority participation. It does not include smaller companies (with less than 10 million pts of capital) or those in which INI's interest has taken the form of loans or the purchase of bonds.

TABLE 15.2: List of Principal INI Enterprises as of February 1961

(million pts)

Sector and Name of INI Company	Nominal Capital	Nominal Capital Subscribed by INI
Iron and Steel:		
E.N. Siderurgica	12,600	11,270
Siderurgica Asturiana	120	40
Mining:		
Potasas de Navarra	754	746
Minas de Almagrera	235	220
E.N. Adaro	80	80
Minas de Hierro del Conjuro	32	24
Minera Industrial Pirenaica	30	30
E.N. Petroleos de Aragon	10	5
E.N. Petroleos de Navarra	10	5
Mechanical Industry:		
E.N. del Aluminio	720	540
Maquina Terrestre y Maritima	450	124
General Electrica Espanola	335	42
E.N. Santa Barbara de Industrias Militares	300	300
Marconi Espanola	250	86
S.A. de Construcciones Agricolas	168	146
Boetticher y Navarro	140	112
Ferroaleaciones y Electrometales	104	54
E.N. de Optica	80	80
Experiencias Industriales	75	45
E.N. de Rodamientos	70	42
Rodamientos A. Bolas SKF	12	4
Empresa Auxiliar de la Industria Pesada	10	10
Electric Power:		
E.N. Hidroelectrica del Ribagorzana	3,000	2,816
E.N. de Electricidad	2,250	2,240
Hidroelectrica Moncabril	1,500	912
Gas y Electricidad	450	448
Cia Hidroelectrica de Galicia	419	369
Transportation:		
Iberia Lineas Aereas de Espana	490	490
Aviacion y Comercio	150	25
Autotransporte Turistico Espanol	50	42
Cia Auxiliar Maritima de Escombreras[a]	20	–
Aircraft and Automotive:		
E.N. de Autocamiones	2,100	1,923
Sociedad Espanol de Automoviles de Turismo	900	459
E.N. de Motores de Aviacion	200	188
Construcciones Aeronauticas	150	50
E.N. de Helices Para Aeronaves	80	80
Aeronautica Industrial	42	14
La Hispano Aviacion	30	10

(*table continues*)

Table 15.2 *(cont.)*

(million pts)

Sector and Name of INI Company	Nominal Capital	Nominal Capital Subscribed by INI
Shipbuilding:		
E.N. Elcano de la Marina Mercante	2,075	2,075
E.N. Bazan de Construcciones Navales Militares	700	700
Estilleros de Cadiz	575	547
Heavy Chemical:		
E.N. Calvo Sotelo	4,993	4,981
Refineria de Petroleos de Escombreras	1,539	489
Sociedad Iberica del Nitrogeno	350	23
Textiles, Cellulose, Paper and Artificial Fibers:		
E.N. de Celulosas de Pontevedra	486	486
Fabricacion Espanola de Fibras Textiles Artificiales	455	198
E.N. de Celulosas de Huelva	410	410
E.N. de Celulosas de Motril	384	384
Industrias Quimicas Textiles	200	92
Industrias Textiles del Guadalhorce	146	146
Agriculture and Food Processing:		
E.N. de Industrializacion de Residuos Agricolas	750	750
Frigorificos Industriales de Galicia	300	258
Industrias Frigorificas Extremenas	225	130
Industrias Gaditanas de Frio Industrial	45	34
Industrias Pesqueras Africanas	25	15
Telecommunications:		
Empresa Torres Quevedo	229	229
E.N. Radio Maritima[a]	100	–
Telefonica de Tanger[a]	40	–
Transradio Espanola[a]	25	–
Cire[a]	15	–
Banking:		
Banco Exterior de Espana	400	40
Total	42,883	36,058

[a] INI participates in these firms through shares held by other INI firms.

The widespread nature of INI's activities, covering almost the whole gamut of industry, is apparent from the list. The total value of INI's shareholdings was placed at 60 billion pts in 1961.

INI has made important contributions to expanding production in the various fields that it has entered. With very different conditions now facing Spanish industry, however, a definition of the role of public enterprises is a matter of priority.

We have considered this definition under three main headings:

a. the scope of INI's operations;

b. equality of competition between public and private enterprise; and

c. accountability and control.

The first question is what should be the scope of operations of public enterprises. We are not concerned with past activities as such, but with considering what is their cumulative effect on the situation today and what would be the effect on the growth of private industry if they were continued. The mission has been informed that INI has entered fields in which private industry was already well established, and although there are some instances in which this entry may have served to stimulate the private firms to greater activity, there are other instances in which the reverse must have been the case. Moreover, INI has in some cases acquired a majority or minority interest in existing private firms, even though these firms were not in financial distress; and we understand that it has sought to reserve for itself fields of activity in which private interests were prepared to operate. We recognize that the number of cases where INI has interpreted its functions so widely are comparatively few. But while any such cases exist, and there is a possibility that they will recur, there are bound to be doubts as to the future intentions of INI with respect to the scope of its activities.

We believe that the more broadly the mandate of INI is interpreted, the more uncertainty it creates. Businessmen have been reluctant to make new investments in view of the uncertainty as to the future intentions of INI. Spanish and foreign firms have encountered long delays when seeking authorization to set up plants in fields that INI also wished to enter. Continued uncertainty of this kind can only retard the growth of private industry and the inflow of foreign capital.

Although the original legislation provides, in most respects, a reasonable definition of the role of public enterprises, it is clear that its successful application in present circumstances is dependent on the administrative interpretation given to it. The mission considers that the best way of approaching this question would be for the Government to determine in the light of the needs of the development program what specific new activities, if any, INI would be expected to undertake. Some flexibility is necessary, however, since INI's role should change from time to time as old problems are solved and new ones emerge. The determination should therefore be made at periodic intervals, such as three years; and it should also be announced publicly to take care of the problem of uncertainty. Over the next five to ten years, when a new relationship with the private sector is being worked out, caution should be exercised in assigning any new activities to INI.

There may indeed be some cases where the Government may decide that INI intervention is necessary because private capital and initiative are clearly deficient—perhaps because the amount of capital required or the risks involved are too great—or where there are serious imperfections in the market (e.g., a monopoly situation) and all other means of dealing with these problems have been exhausted. Such cases are, however, exceptional. In general, we are of the view that INI should not go into any field in which private enterprise has active plans for entering. Similarly, INI should not expand by the acquisition of existing private firms or by the establishment of its own firms in fields where private firms can profitably operate. In marginal cases, the benefit of doubt should be given to the private sector. The new activities of INI in the future should be essentially those of an industrial pioneer, opening up new fields and developing them to the stage where private enterprise could then take over. A particularly important feature of this pioneering and supporting role arises in connection with regional development, which is discussed later in the chapter.

The original legislation contemplated the gradual liquidation of INI's participation in some of its activities. The mission believes that this principle is sound. Some sales have in fact taken place and the mission recommends that the process should be continued. Increased participation of the general public in INI companies should be made possible by selling in the market parts of INI holdings. The program of sales should be determined in conjunction with the Ministry of Finance, special emphasis being given to selling shares of companies in which INI has only a minority interest. The amount and timing of sales should be such as to avoid any significant diversion of market funds from the financing of private industry. Proceeds of sales should be taken into account in considering the annual financial plan of INI. These actions would help to define the boundaries of INI's activities and to direct these activities to the fields of greatest need.

The second point to be considered is the need for equality in the competitive position of INI with respect to the private sector. In part by virtue of the fact that they are public firms but also for other reasons, INI companies have enjoyed important advantages over their private competitors. Some of these are financial. Until 1957, INI firms were able to finance their expansion by direct recourse to the public budget. Following two years when INI was financed, in practice, by borrowing from the Bank of Spain, it has been required to meet its external capital needs in the market. This is a welcome development, but INI firms still have an advantage over private firms seeking capital in the market since their securities are among the public paper in which the Cajas de Ahorro must invest part of their funds. This advantage is further enhanced by the fact that the principal and interest on INI securities are not only guaranteed by the Government, but the interest on INI securities is tax exempt as well.

Other advantages of INI firms include their automatic inclusion in the category of "national interest" (with attendant taxation and other benefits) even though private firms in the same activity may not be so classified. Some INI enterprises have received indirect subsidies when other public enterprises have allowed them higher prices than are paid for the same products when purchased from private firms.

We believe it desirable that INI enterprises should operate, insofar as possible, under the same conditions as private firms. In particular, each INI company should be treated as a financially autonomous unit responsible for its own financial management. Those companies which are profitable should be expected to obtain their external capital financing on the same basis as private firms; on the capital market they should borrow under their own names (without the automatic government guarantee of their bonds) and without the requirement that certain public institutions acquire their shares. The recommendations that we have made elsewhere with respect to broadening or eliminating the category of "national interest," to the removal of the prior authorization of investments and to the gradual elimination of import controls will work to remove any possibility of preferential treatment of INI in these fields.

New INI firms, and some of the existing companies, may not be in a position to earn a profit for some time. Furthermore, there may be some INI activities which, by their nature (e.g., in defense or pioneering fields) should not be expected to be profitable. Financial assistance to such enterprises should be provided directly through the state budget, and be clearly identified as such; it should be based on a careful budgetary review by the Government of the financial plans and requirements of the enterprises. In some cases it may be desirable to write off the relevant part of the past capital costs of unprofitable enterprises so that future operations are not handicapped by them. On the other hand, dividends from profitable INI firms should be paid into the general treasury in the same way as income received from other enterprises wholly or partly owned by the State.

The third question to be considered is the accountability and control of INI enterprises. Even if INI is exposed to a greater extent to the disciplines of the market and to more effective competition from the private sector, the Government must be in a position to exercise effective control over the operations of INI as a public enterprise. This requires both that adequate information be supplied by INI on its operations and that this information be subject to careful review by the appropriate government authorities. Considerable information appears to be available to the Government but we believe it would serve a useful purpose to disseminate it as widely as possible outside the administration, perhaps placing it before the legislature in addition to distributing it to other interested groups. INI has recently begun to publish more financial material, a movement which we strongly commend. Since INI is a large and important organism in the public sector, it is important to avoid the impression of secrecy. It must be made clear to the public at large that INI's constituent enterprises operate without deriving any special advantages, either from each other or from other state enterprises, that might not be available to competing private firms.

Another important question for the Government's consideration is whether the lack of effective competition or of adequate public accountability is conducive to cost-consciousness on the part of these public enterprises. Some of the investments are obviously well-conceived and executed, but there may be others that are not. There should be some means of ensuring that all funds invested are producing a sound return, even after due allowance is made for the broader considerations that have also entered into INI's mandate. For this reason as well as those referred to above, the Government should require each of the INI companies to publish a comprehensive annual report and analysis of the results of its activities, including a statement of its future plans and a detailed financial account of its operations (to be independently audited). INI could thus provide an important service to the entire industrial sector by setting examples of the use of improved accounting practices and financial reporting.

Finance for Industry

The rapid pace of industrial modernization and expansion necessary to achieve Spain's development goals will require an increasing volume of investment resources. At present, these resources are provided to private industry through a variety of channels, but several broad types of situations can be distinguished.

Self-financing of industrial investment through depreciation reserves and retained earnings appears to take place on a considerable scale, but no reliable figures exist on its magnitude. For small, family-owned firms this is likely to be the principal source of finance for new investments. Short-term credit from the commercial banks, usually for renewable periods of not more than 18 months, has also been an important source of funds particularly for firms with good banking connections who could generally count on rolling them over. The effective cost of such borrowing has been around 8 percent to 9 percent. The volume of short-term credit has been augmented in recent years through special 18-month "pre-financing" loans, authorized by the Medium- and Long-Term Credit Committee, provided by the commercial banks and discountable at the Bank of Spain.

With the exception of a brief period in 1959–60, short-term credit has generally been in plentiful supply. The most serious financing need has been and is for medium- and long-term capital. The larger private enterprises have satisfied a substantial part of their long-term financing needs through the capital market, by issuing shares and, to a lesser extent, long-term obligations usually convertible into shares. These shares and debentures are customarily underwritten by one or more of the large mixed (commercial and investment) banks which, in the past, have retained substantial quantities of the securities of the companies for which they raised capital. The volume of private and public issues placed on the capital market in recent years is shown in Table 15.3.

TABLE 15.3:   Issues of Private and Public Securities, 1950–1960

(million pts)

Year	Private				Public	Total
	Stock Assessments[a]	Stock Issues	Debentures	Sub-total		
1950	1,424	992	1,123	3,540	8,180	11,719
1951	895	3,017	531	4,443	5,953	10,397
1952	1,799	1,861	191	3,850	10,425	14,275
1953	1,231	2,524	2,245	6,001	9,825	15,827
1954	1,050	3,899	2,430	7,379	10,125	17,504
1955	1,148	5,120	2,584	8,853	16,725	25,578
1956	1,641	9,369	2,334	13,345	19,994	33,339
1957	2,571	14,767	2,215	19,553	11,466	31,019
1958	4,217	11,372	2,930	18,519	8,098	26,617
1959	4,705	11,411	2,873	18,989	7,947	26,936
1960	1,911	11,628	4,687	18,227	11,131	29,359

[a] "Dividendos pasivos."

SOURCES: Annual Reports of the Bank of Spain.

Firms not large enough to borrow on the capital market, and newer firms without established banking connections, have had the most difficulties in finding long-term capital. The Banco de Credito Industrial (BCI), an official credit institution, has been the principal source of funds for these groups but, as we indicate below, its lending has met only a portion of the needs.

Broadly speaking, there are two principal ways in which the Government can assist in financing private industrial development. The first is to improve the various conditions under which the financing of private capital investment takes place. This involves many elements, and the recommendations contained in this and other chapters with respect to the climate of private investment, reforms of the credit system and other ways of improving the allocation of resources within the economy all have a bearing. One additional point that we might briefly mention here concerns accounting. More complete and more reliable financial information and reports, verified through a system of independent professional audit, would not only assist business management in its decision-making process but would also make investment in Spanish firms more attractive, particularly to foreign investors. The legislation recently adopted by the Government to permit the revaluation of fixed assets at current peseta values marks an important step in this direction. Improvement in accounting methods is closely related to reform of the tax system to which we have referred previously, including the standards of tax enforcement that are applied in practice.

The second way in which the Government can assist in the financing of private industrial investment is through the direct provision of public funds. The primary instrument for this purpose is the Banco de Credito Industrial, and the mission recommends both that more funds be allocated to it and that steps be taken to widen the scope of its lending operations.

The Banco de Credito Industrial was organized in 1920 under private ownership, but the Government has provided the great majority of its loanable funds and the BCI may properly be regarded as a "public" lending institution. Any ambiguity on this score has been removed by the recent Banking Reform Law which provides for the nationalization of the BCI. BCI lending has taken a variety of forms. Short-term advances are made to government contractors by discounting certificates. Medium- and long-term loans to industry from the Bank's resources are the typical function of the BCI; these loans consist of a Treasury component (90 percent) and funds provided from the private capital subscription of the Bank (10 percent). In addition, special industrial loans have been made since 1958 with the BCI acting as agent for the Medium- and Long-Term Credit Committee, which has provided 100 percent of the funds. The BCI also administers on behalf of the Government the Hotel Credit Fund (Credito Hotelero)[8] and, since very recently, funds for the development of the motion picture and cotton textile industries. At the end of 1960 it was given the task of consolidating, in the form of medium-term loans, some of the pre-financing credits extended to industry by the private banking system.

The "typical" BCI loans have been directed toward small- and medium-size industries, particularly the latter. The ceiling on individual loans has generally been placed at 40 million pts and most loans are under 20 million pts in amount; loans are not granted to firms with a capital in excess of 100 million pts, that have been in business for less than three years or that are listed on the stock exchange. In principle, BCI lends for periods of 5 years to 15 years, but the longer-term loans have been greatly reduced in number and the normal maturity is about 8 years. A real estate mortgage is generally required as collateral. Interest rates are $5\frac{1}{2}$ percent on loans of up to 6 years' duration, and $5\frac{3}{4}$ percent on longer-term loans.

The volume of BCI lending for these various purposes has generally been increasing in recent years, as can be seen from the figures in Table 15.4, but there have been marked fluctuations from year to year, in part due to shifts in the importance of the various funds administered by the BCI. The large increase in 1960 is a result of the expansion both in regular lending and in the special loans through the Medium- and Long-Term Credit Committee. On the other hand, very few hotel loans were made in the year. Table 15.5 gives the distribution by industry of BCI loans, including those of Credito Hotelero; although most branches of industry have been recipients, the bulk of the loans have gone to the mechanical and textile industries.

The sharp changes in the volume of BCI lending of different kinds in the recent past make it particularly difficult to establish a base from which to project the Bank's need for funds over the next years.[9] The volume of medium- and long-term loans outstanding at the end of 1960, including special loans, was about 6 billion pts, and we have assumed that this figure reached about 8 billion pts at the end of 1961. If the BCI is to expand the scope of its lending activities along the lines

[8] The operations of this fund are described at greater length in Chapter 17.

[9] We do not propose to take into account the short-term lending of BCI, which is dependent on the Government's policy with respect to the payment of contractors and is unrelated to the developmental functions of the Bank.

TABLE 15.4: Volume of Loans and Reimbursements of the Banco de Credito Industrial

(million pts)

Year	Increase in Medium- and Long-Term Loans Outstanding			Loans Granted		
				Medium- and Long-Term Loans		
	Net In-crease	Reim-burse-ments	Gross Dis-burse-ments	From Own Re-sources[a]	Special	Short-Term Loans[d]
1950	156	76	232	252		237
1951	135	78	213	232		293
1952	148	103	250	323		315
1953	270	146	416	520		540
1954	313	128	441	675		685
1955	601	159	760	932		693
1956	571	188	759	1,107	n.a.	761
1957	1,002	223	1,225	747	78[b]	1,677
1958	631	313	944	1,261	n.a.	1,711
1959	720	357	1,076	841	n.a.	1,689
1960	769	403	1,172	1,609	495[e]	1,538

[a] Including loans of Credito Hotelero.
[b] This is a partial figure for loans to basic industries financed by the counterpart of U.S. economic aid, on which the BCI has acted as an agent for the Ministry of Industry.
[e] Loans authorized and financed by the Medium- and Long-Term Credit Committee, and for which the BCI acts as disbursing agent.
[d] These loans or advances to government contractors are typically of three to four months' duration and the large majority are liquidated in the same year that they are incurred.
SOURCE: Information supplied by the Banco de Credito Industrial.

which we describe below, the mission estimates very roughly that some 16 billion pts of new medium- and long-term loans should be extended for all purposes during the years 1962–66 inclusive; this would involve an average annual rate of lending of 3.2 billion pts, including special loans for tourism and the textile industry, and the special loans for which the BCI acts as agent for the Medium- and Long-Term Credit Committee. (The comparable figure in 1960, a record year for the BCI, was 2.5 billion pts.) Reimbursements, which have been running at about 400 million pts annually in recent years, are likely to rise sharply as a result of two factors: the recent increase in the volume of lending; and the shortening of the average term of the loans. Allowance should also be made for an increase in the pipeline of undisbursed funds. We calculate, therefore, that the need for *new* funds to carry out the various

TABLE 15.5: Distribution by Industry of Loans Extended by the Industrial Credit Bank, 1955–60

(million pts)

	1955 Value	1955 %	1956 Value	1956 %	1957 Value	1957 %	1958 Value	1958 %	1959 Value	1959 %	1960 Value	1960 %	Total %
Aeronautics	–	–	10.6	1.0	–	–	–	–	–	–	16.0	1.0	0.3
Food	17.0	1.8	28.5	2.6	39.7	5.3	19.8	1.6	–	–	51.9	3.2	2.5
Graphic Arts	3.0	0.3	1.5	0.1	6.5	0.9	2.0	0.2	3.0	0.3	28.0	1.7	0.5
Mechanical Constructions and Foundries	218.3	23.4	297.7	26.9	233.0	31.2	250.4	19.8	192.5	22.9	309.6	19.3	21.8
Shipbuilding	86.0	9.2	–	–	1.2	0.2	7.5	0.6	–	–	0.6	0.1	1.4
Cork	–	–	–	–	–	–	–	–	–	–	–	–	0.2
Hotel Credit	81.0	8.7	132.6	12.0	95.7	12.8	183.2	14.5	132.4	15.7	18.3	1.1	9.4
Leather	–	–	10.0	0.9	–	–	–	–	–	–	–	–	0.1
Electric Utilities	47.9	5.1	77.4	7.0	46.5	6.2	107.0	8.5	35.8	4.3	67.4	4.2	7.1
Electrical Goods	–	–	–	–	–	–	123.4	9.8	71.5	8.5	112.5	7.0	3.1
Refrigeration	7.5	0.8	2.4	0.2	11.8	1.6	7.5	0.6	11.4	1.4	33.0	2.0	0.9
Flour and Bread	–	–	3.0	0.3	–	–	–	–	–	–	–	–	0.1
Lumber Yards	7.5	0.8	2.3	0.2	27.0	3.6	–	–	–	–	–	–	0.9
Construction Materials	55.9	6.0	126.6	11.4	29.5	3.9	71.5	5.7	80.4	9.6	150.4	9.4	8.1
Non-ferrous Metals	–	–	–	–	–	–	–	–	7.0	0.8	137.9	8.6	1.2
Mines	41.5	4.5	47.2	4.3	71.0	9.5	104.4	8.3	59.0	7.0	93.3	5.8	5.5
Paper	16.3	1.8	36.5	3.3	33.9	4.5	21.5	1.7	66.0	7.8	14.0	0.9	2.9
Plastics	2.6	0.3	46.7	4.2	2.2	0.3	10.8	0.8	10.8	1.3	25.0	1.6	1.2
Chemicals and Pharmaceuticals	92.5	9.9	52.2	4.7	29.4	3.9	97.3	7.7	51.1	6.1	239.4	14.9	7.7
Irrigation	–	–	–	–	2.1	0.3	–	–	–	–	–	–	0.6
Steel	–	–	–	–	–	–	–	–	43.0	5.1	20.0	1.2	0.8
Textiles	205.9	22.1	111.0	10.0	103.4	13.9	204.5	16.2	76.6	9.1	179.2	11.1	18.6
Transport	1.4	0.2	52.5	4.7	–	–	–	–	–	–	–	–	0.6
Glass	5.0	0.5	27.0	2.4	8.1	1.1	5.0	0.4	–	–	76.0	4.7	1.3
Wines and Alcohols	1.2	0.1	4.0	0.4	–	–	0.7	0.1	–	–	–	–	0.1
Other	41.9	4.5	37.6	3.4	6.1	0.8	44.6	3.5	0.5	0.1	36.2	2.2	3.1
Total	932.3	100.0	1,107.3	100.0	747.2	100.0	1,261.1	100.0	841.2	100.0	1,608.6	100.0	100.0

SOURCE: Information supplied by the Banco de Credito Industrial.

lending functions of the BCI over the next five years can be placed in the approximate order of 10 billion pts, or 2 billion pts annually.

This expansion in the funds provided to the BCI should be made attendant upon a number of important changes in its operations, which are designed to enable it to perform a more vital role in assisting industrial development. The principal recommendations that the mission offers for consideration by the Government in this regard are as follows:

a. The function of the BCI has, in our view, been properly defined as that of providing developmental credit to enterprises not in a position to obtain it from conventional sources. However, it appears that smaller firms, newly established businesses, and those lacking the customary forms of collateral security have difficulty in qualifying under the present BCI standards and criteria of lending. It is necessary, therefore, that the BCI modify its approach so that it can better satisfy the financing needs of these types of firms, for which the availability of public funds may be particularly important. It may be desirable, for example, to establish special conditions for lending to small firms, perhaps through a special department for this purpose which could use the results of the industrial studies referred to in para. c. below.

b. By the same token, the BCI should adopt a more venturesome approach to the problem of risk. While the Bank is justifiably proud of its record of extremely low losses (6 million pts on a total of 7,600 million pts of medium- and long-term loans), greater risk-taking should be inherent in the nature of an industrial development bank; the first criterion of lending should be the prospects for success of the business venture, and undue weight should not be given to guarantees that the funds loaned could be recovered if the investment were a failure. It goes without saying that a willingness to assume somewhat greater risks should in no way imply a relaxation of the BCI's standards of careful project appraisal. An enlargement of the Bank's statutes to permit equity investments might make it easier for the institution to provide assistance in some instances, as in the case of firms requiring external financing for longer periods than the conventional terms of BCI loans.

c. The BCI should enlarge the scope of its technical assistance to borrowers. A close and continuing relationship should be established with the client firms, which could greatly profit by the Bank's advice and assistance in confronting the problems of rationalization, development of new export outlets, or adjustment to the impact of tariff reductions and increased competition. In this connection, the BCI should take an active role in helping to organize industry-wide studies of developmental problems, which could serve as a basis for subsequent loans to individual firms or groups of firms in the process of reorganization. Through its project appraisals and lending operations the BCI could also assist its clients with their accounting procedures and financial management.

d. If the BCI is to exercise properly these new or expanded functions, it will be desirable to establish branches in the principal industrial centers, such as Barcelona, Bilbao and Sevilla. These branches should have the power to make loans without consulting Madrid on all the details, particularly as the BCI will, if our recommendations are adopted, be directing more of its effort toward smaller firms.

e. We have some doubts whether the consolidation of short-term (i.e., "prefinancing") credits granted originally by private banks is consistent with BCI's functions as a development bank. Such consolidation could be undertaken by the private banks themselves which, as we have indicated earlier, should be encouraged to extend the term of their loans. Moreover, it is questionable whether the BCI should have its funds tied up in loans for which it has had no responsibility in the first instance. We have made no allowance for any such consolidation operations in estimating the BCI's need for funds over the 1962–66 period.

Regional Development of Industry

The geographical pattern of development, as well as the rate of that development, is determined by such factors as the location of raw materials, sources of energy, population centers and foreign markets. These locational factors invariably bring about a pattern of industrial development that is spread unevenly over the territory of a country, with resulting disparities in the level of incomes in different areas or provinces. As we indicated in the first chapter of this report, these disparities may widen during the early stages of development; at later stages migration from the poorer areas and the increased demand for the products of these areas tend to arrest, and perhaps eventually to reverse, the process.

Governments have understandably been concerned about sharp regional differences in the levels of wealth and incomes, and have attempted to deal with them in a variety of ways. In Spain, one of the notable developments has been the establishment of such regional programs as the Badajoz and Jaen Plans, which have involved a concerted attack on regional poverty through the dual development of agriculture (with irrigation) and of processing industries and auxiliary services related to agriculture. Special inducements, such as classification in the category of "national interest," have been given to industries that located in these regions. These programs show what can be accomplished by taking maximum advantage of the resources of an area. On the whole, they have been well conceived, and have made a notable contribution toward raising the incomes of the persons affected. The costs have been high, however, and with many of the Spanish provinces now preparing individual development programs it is important that these efforts be viewed in the proper perspective if the desired results are to be attained.

The problem of accelerating the development of poorer regions is a very difficult one. Unless the economic potential of a region is considerable and a certain amount of development is already under way, the expenditure of modest sums for this purpose has little chance of succeeding. In order to make a substantial contribution to income and employment, massive use of public funds would be required, and even then the outcome might well be in doubt. Moreover, as we have shown throughout this report, there are many highly-productive uses to which these funds can be put that will increase the rate of growth of the economy as a whole. Beyond a certain point, therefore, there may be a conflict between raising the average level of income of the country and spreading income more evenly throughout it. The Government has stated that its primary objective is the maximum rate of growth of the economy as a whole, and that regional development should be pushed only when it will not interfere to a significant degree with the achievement of that objective. The mission considers that, in the long run, this approach will provide the maximum of benefit to the Spanish people as a whole.

This should not be taken to mean that nothing can be done to encourage regional development and to lessen regional disparities in income. A very considerable expansion of industry will be taking place in the next two decades, and while the Government cannot successfully reverse the factors leading toward uneven geographical development it can, through judicious policies, influence these factors marginally so as to spread the pattern of development somewhat more evenly. Properly conceived, investments in the less developed areas can make a contribution to over-all growth that is justified in economic terms as well as in social terms.

The essential elements of a regional development policy are two-fold: first, careful selection of a limited number of regions with the best prospects for development; and second, adoption of measures that will accelerate development of these regions without interfering with growth elsewhere in the economy.

Selection of the limited number of regions should be based on their potential for future development. This involves a detailed examination of their resource potential including such elements as the costs of providing water for irrigation, the availability of untapped mineral or energy resources, touristic assets, location relative to markets, etc. In general, it is desirable that some development already be under way, or else the costs may prove to be prohibitive. In regions distant from large cities or industrial complexes, the availability of under-utilized local resources is likely to provide the principal basis for development; closer to the large centers of population and industry some new and smaller centers might be developed as part of the decentralization of areas that are already overcongested. The region to be developed should be delineated as precisely as possible; normally it will be a zone much smaller in size, for example, than a province. In the areas that have little foreseeable potential for development, the Government's goal should be to maintain a tolerable level of life while expediting the movement of population to other regions, and expenditures for this purpose would be primarily social in nature.

Having selected the appropriate areas or zones for development, it will generally be necessary to give special inducements to attract industries to them. This arises from the natural tendency for industries to group themselves around established industrial centers, where they can take advantage of the external economies provided by the existence of basic utilities, roads, access to markets, etc. However, it is important that the inducements do not tend to create distortions of their own and thus lead to investments that can be of only small value to the areas in relation to their costs to the economy. For example, inducements which take the form of subsidizing the cost of capital (e.g., through low interest rates) tend to attract the more capital-intensive industries, whereas the main problem is to create productive employment for the local population. Except where an important new industrial resource is being developed, the types of industries that are most appropriate for these areas are those that:

a. have a high level of employment per unit of investment either in the initial plant or together with the auxiliary operations induced by it in the same vicinity; and

b. operate at minimum of cost disadvantage as a result of location vis-a-vis markets and suppliers (i.e., industries producing products in which transportation is not an important element of the total cost). The disadvantage of untrained labor should be considered as temporary and consequently not taken into account.

The subsidies or inducements most appropriate to such industries are likely to be those based on the use of labor. Appropriate forms of assistance, for example, might be for the Government to assume the social security costs of personnel for a defined period of time, or else a subsidy based on the number of personnel employed. If special credit assistance is required, it should be provided by ensuring that funds are available to suitable industries rather than by subsidized interest rates.

One important way in which the Government, and INI in particular, can assist in this process of selective regional development is through the establishment of industrial estates. These industrial estates, which are being utilized in an increasing number of countries, are designed to provide new industries in selected areas with the external economies that they would otherwise find in large centers, and thus to offset the attraction of more plants to areas that are already becoming overcrowded. The task of INI would be to acquire the necessary land for a series of industrial estates in the regions or zones selected for development and, within each estate, to plan the layout of facilities, prepare factory plots and construct those factory buildings which are to be rented to prospective industries. INI should also provide the necessary community buildings, and coordinate the activities of other government departments to ensure that the necessary roads, electricity, water, sewerage, other utilities and housing were provided on schedule. Industries that settle in the estates would be privately owned and managed, and would either rent the land and buildings from INI (with option to purchase) or construct their own buildings.

Through these industrial estates, new industries would be provided with the facilities necessary for them to operate from the start under most of the conditions enjoyed by industries already operating in highly developed centers. The possibility of reducing the initial capital costs by renting land and factory buildings should make the estates attractive to small and medium-size enterprises, for which the estates should be primarily designed. It is very important that the estates be planned on a modest scale, and that they be developed in stages in accordance with the expressed demand of industries to locate in them. The first estates should be considered as experimental, and placed near towns of considerable size in zones that appear to have the highest development potential. Further expansion should be based on the results of experience.

An important service of INI in connection with these industrial estates would be to provide entrepreneurs with technical assistance on such matters as design of machinery, production methods, quality control and marketing techniques (especially in the case of export industries). This would help materially to accelerate the process of industrial rationalization through the introduction of new equipment and techniques. Vocational training of labor should also be an integral part of the program, so that local labor can be employed to perform the various skills that are required. Such training would also help to attract the labor-intensive industries best suited to the development of these regions.

Economic Studies and Statistics

As we have stressed repeatedly in this report, the effectiveness of economic policies and decisions depends in large part on the adequacy of the statistics on which they are based. The public and private sectors of industry are no exception to this rule. In many areas where important decisions must be made, industry and the Government now operate at a considerable disadvantage as a result of the poor state of industrial statistics. These deficiencies are becoming better known, in part as a result of the Government's decision to seek the advice of the OECD and others in this field. Significant progress has been made in the past several years by the Sindicatos, OCYPE and other groups in overcoming some of the difficulties, but we would urge the Government not to underestimate the importance of a reform in the organization, collection and analysis of industrial data.

The problems in this area can be grouped under three headings: deficiencies in the basic data; problems of coordination; and the need for more economic studies and analyses. Each of these is important, but improvement of the first is perhaps a prior condition to progress on the others. The work of the mission was handicapped by the absence of such fundamental data as a census of industries and a census of occupations. We understand that both of these deficiencies are in the process of being remedied. Wage statistics, data on the sources of investment financing and data on consumption by products or areas are among those in greatest need of improvement. It is somewhat anomalous that highly refined techniques of mathematical and economic analysis are currently being applied to basic data the reliability of which is open to question. Use of these techniques is to be encouraged, but the collection of more complete and accurate data should be the matter of first concern.

In some fields, the basic data are being collected by more than one department or organization. This is not undesirable in itself, but sufficient attention has not been paid to the importance of coordination of the various groups involved. As a result, in some instances there is unnecessary duplication, while in others one set of data cannot be compared or integrated with other series because of differences or inconsistencies in the coverage or in the categories and classifications that are employed. The different ways in which Spanish industry is grouped into sectors by various organizations presenting statistics on employment, production, or wages is a case in point. We have made some general observations on the problem of coordination of statistics in Section I of this report.

The third problem, a dearth of useful economic studies and analyses dealing with matters of interest to Spanish industry, is undoubtedly related to the other two. For the most part, present industry studies are little more than collections of partial statistics, with few attempts at analysis, diagnosis or projection. The study of the cotton textile industry is an exception, and illustrates how an analysis of the situation and problems of an industry can help in formulating national policy and in guiding the decisions of individual businessmen. The BCI and INI are both in an excellent position to encourage the development of more studies of this kind, and with more experience it should be possible to carry them out in greater depth and detail. Consideration should be given to the establishment of regular publications in which the results of industrial research undertaken by the Government, the universities and private groups could be made generally available.

Another important means of providing better information to private industry will arise out of the planning process. The projections of demand in major sectors of the economy will be prepared in the first instance by governmental planning committees on which the private sector will be represented; subsequent refinement and revision of the projections as the economy develops and as better data become available will necessitate continued collaboration between the Government and the private sector. Widespread dissemination of the market forecasts and expected trends in the basic sectors (steel, cement, energy) will be of great assistance to individual entrepreneurs in making their production and investment decisions. In this way, the close participation of private industry in the planning process itself will make for more rapid industrial growth.

CHAPTER 16 *ELECTRIC POWER*

Power has been one of the most dynamic industries in Spain, as is to be expected in a country that is industrializing rapidly. Net generation of electricity increased threefold between 1949 and 1959 (see Table 16.1). Even an increase of this magnitude could not keep pace with demand during the early postwar years, and there was considerable rationing of power until the mid–1950's.

Initially, hydroelectric power was utilized almost exclusively, but the need to increase production rapidly and with a minimum investment of capital led to the stimulation of thermal electric production. Nevertheless, at the end of 1959, about 70 percent of the installed capacity, and a slightly higher proportion of generation, was still hydro-

TABLE 16.1: Electricity Generation and Consumption in Spain, 1949–1959

(billion kwh)

Year	Net Genera- tion	Net Import	Total Availa- bility	Losses	Con- sump- tion	Esti- mated Restric- tions[a]
1949	5.35	+0.05	5.40	−1.22	4.18	1.70
1950	6.60	+0.06	6.66	−1.51	5.15	0.65
1951	7.98	+0.08	8.06	−1.80	6.26	0.10
1952	9.07	+0.07	9.14	−1.98	7.16	−
1953	9.31	+0.08	9.39	−2.11	7.28	0.50
1954	9.71	+0.14	9.85	−1.93	7.92	0.47
1955	11.46	+0.13	11.59	−2.31	9.28	0.03
1956	13.31	−0.11	13.20	−2.62	10.58	0.01
1957	14.01	+0.02	14.03	−2.74	11.29	0.25
1958	15.84	+0.01	15.85	−3.06	12.79	0.03
1959	16.93	−0.17	16.76	−3.26	13.50	−

[a] Potential effective demand unsatisfied.

electric. It is difficult to ascertain the extent of water power reserves with any degree of accuracy, and estimates have varied widely over time; very roughly, however, it appears that perhaps less than half of the hydroelectric potential has been brought into use to date.

Despite the active role that INI has played in helping to develop thermal electric power since the war, most of the generation, transmission and distribution of electric power is still in the hands of private enterprise. For example, more than 88 percent of all power generated

365

in 1959 was produced by private companies, the remainder being produced by companies either wholly owned by INI or in which INI has a majority interest. While there are in fact about 3,200 different companies engaged in the various aspects of electricity supply, the degree of concentration is much greater than this figure would indicate: the 25 largest private companies generated 77 percent of all the power produced while all the other private companies only produced 11.5 percent. Furthermore, those 25 private companies, together with two mixed companies with a majority INI interest, are shareholders in Unidad Electrica, S.A. (UNESA) which coordinates the development and operating plans of its constituent companies by means of a central planning mechanism.

Since the electric power industry is mainly private, the principal functions of the Government are regulatory and rate-setting. However, as will be seen, this role can be crucial, particularly as it has an important bearing on the amount of funds devoted to new investment and the distribution of these funds within the industry.

Administrative Control

Because public waters belong to the State, a concession is required to exploit them. Concessions for hydroelectric plants are granted by the Direccion General de Obras Hidraulicas of the Ministerio de Obras Publicas on the basis of the technical and economic merits of the designs submitted. After the concession has been granted, the design has to be submitted to the Direccion General de Industria of the Ministerio de Industria for authorization to construct. This double examination can cause delay, but the mission understands that a decree has recently been adopted providing for a better coordination of functions between the ministries concerned.

Water concessions are normally granted for 75 years and are free of charge. When the electric plant takes advantage of works (e.g., a dam) built by the Ministerio de Obras Publicas primarily for other purposes (e.g., irrigation), a fee must be paid to the State either in the form of a capital sum or at a certain rate per kwh produced and 25 percent of the energy must be reserved at a concessionary price (0.12 to 0.20 pesetas per kwh) for uses of public interest. The practice of reserving to the State 25 percent of the power produced by power stations taking advantage of a reservoir built by the Ministry of Public Works began in 1939. At present the total quantity reserved to the State is about 185 million kwh (1.3 percent of water power produced in 1960) but only 42 million kwh were used by the State in 1960. The main purposes for which this energy is reserved are railway electrification, water pumping for water supply and irrigation.

From the point of view of the power company, the fee and the price concessions are in essence a combined payment for advantages obtained from works constructed by the Ministry, and are on that account justified. However, it should be recognized that the concessionary price, if it is passed on to a third party, is a subsidy even though it does not appear as such in the accounts of the beneficiary. As we have pointed out earlier, hidden subsidies are apt to introduce undesirable distortions. We cannot say, in this particular instance, what effect the distortion has had or will have but, as a general principle, we consider that all payments, implicit or explicit, by power companies should go directly to the Treasury and should not be used to provide concessionary rates to certain categories of users.

UNESA and Electricity Distribution

One of the principal functions of UNESA is to regulate the dispatching of electricity within Spain. It performs this service on behalf of the Ministry of Industry and its rules apply to all companies, INI as well as private, whether or not they are members of UNESA. The main rules that have been established for the exploitation of power plants are as follows:

a. power has to be generated first from run-of-river hydro plants;

b. reservoirs whose level is above normal come into service before other reservoirs;

c. after run-of-river plants and reservoirs with above-normal water levels, those thermal power stations come into service whose operation is critical for the coal mines;

d. the other thermal power stations are brought into service according to their generating costs, the last being those using imported fuel; and

e. unless there is a strong countervailing economic advantage, priority is given to power stations belonging to the company that needs the power.

These regulations present two problems. First, the low priority given to thermal production based on imported fuel may have been necessary during the time of critical foreign exchange shortages, but it is no longer justified on this basis and, since it may discourage production which would otherwise be economical, the mission recommends that it be discontinued. Secondly, the favorable priority given to production from distressed coal mines is, in effect, a subsidy to these mines. Without denying the importance of establishing a program to deal with the problems of such mines, we question whether a subsidy from the power industry is an appropriate form of assistance for this purpose.

Power Rates

One of the most important functions of the Government is the fixing of maximum prices charged to consumers for electricity supply. Enterprises are free to set lower prices, but practically all companies set their charges at the legally established maximum and, because these rates are the same throughout the country for each class of user (*tarifa tope unificada*), all consumers within a particular class in effect pay the same rates irrespective of local cost conditions. The regulations distinguish six different kinds of users, four of which cover domestic consumers, the others being rural electrification and industrial users.

The mission is not in a position to evaluate all the effects of this unified price system, especially as such an evaluation would have to take into account the rather complicated and uncertain effects of the OFILE system of compensation to power producers which we describe subsequently. To the extent that unified prices destroy in practice the incentive to large consumers with a choice of location to go to areas where costs of power production are relatively low, the effect would be uneconomic. It would make little sense, for example, to use unified rates to attract industries that are power-intensive and use relatively little labor away from areas with low-cost electricity; to do so adds to the real costs of production for the economy as a whole without there being a significant social gain in additional employment.

We realize that the reason behind the unified rates may in part have been social, to secure equal benefits to consumers in different areas. But it may be questioned whether, under this system, it is always the consumer who benefits. We recommend, therefore, that consideration be given to some method of pricing under which there would be effective differentiation between large consumers according to area.

The Recargo and Its Impact on Investment

In addition to the prices fixed by the tariffs, each final consumer has to pay a *recargo,* which is an extra amount determined as a percentage of the basic price. While the power distributing companies collect from the final consumer all payments due, including both the regular tariff and the *recargo,* the total amount accruing by reason of the latter charge is subsequently credited to a central agency, the Oficina Liquidadora de Energia Electrica (OFILE). The amount of funds involved in the *recargo* is very substantial; at present, about 57 percent of the total amount paid by final consumers is retained by the distributing companies and 43 percent is credited to OFILE on account of the *recargo.*

The funds received by OFILE are redistributed to the power companies as contributions to the capital and operating costs of new generating plants. Although OFILE is also empowered to compensate for higher costs of imported power, where such imports have been judged necessary, and also to contribute to the construction and operating costs of those transmission lines and substations regarded as in the public interest even though under-utilized, these latter powers have rarely been exercised and OFILE disbursements have been considered primarily as a mechanism for stimulating additions to total generating capacity.

The method of calculating the amount to be paid annually by OFILE to each new power station varies according to the type of station. In the case of a hydroelectric plant, the payment is based on an established amount per installed kw, the total amount then being adjusted according to the annual hours of utilization. (The established amount per installed kw in each case depends on the year of construction and the whole range of payments is periodically reviewed and often amended.) Payments thus take into account only installed capacity and degree of utilization. This of course favors companies fortunate enough to be located where sites are physically cheaper to exploit, but it does also mean that, where a company has a choice of sites, the method by which OFILE contributions are calculated will result in an indirect incentive to exploit the cheapest sites first. Because the initial capital costs per installed kw vary according to circumstances, as does the degree of utilization, the annual contribution of OFILE represents a varying proportion of the initial investment in each case. It is clear, however, that the contribution represents a substantial part of the financial charges on capital account.

In the case of thermal power stations, the method of calculating the annual OFILE contribution is somewhat different. One of two formulae is adopted. Under Formula A, an annual contribution per kw installed is also paid (60 percent of the basic contribution to hydro plants in the case of steam plants and 50 percent in the case of thermal plants other than steam). In addition, the company receives 90 percent of the cost of fuel per kwh actually produced. On the other hand, there is a Formula B, whereby the contribution covers the difference between total annual expenditures (including interest, depreciation and a 6 percent return on capital) and total revenues.

On paper, the use of either formula is optional. In practice, only INI companies have obtained agreement from OFILE for the use of Formula B. Under certain circumstances, the latter formula can be the more favorable from the point of view of the company because it assures it of a 6 percent return on capital irrespective of the demand for, and therefore utilization of, its generating capacity. On the other hand, when utilization is particularly high, Formula A might be just as remunerative—or even more so—than Formula B. Thus, in the early 1950's, when installed capacity was lagging behind potential effective demand for electric power, Formula A probably produced at least as attractive a remuneration for generating companies as Formula B would have, while the offer of Formula B could at the same time stimulate investment in thermal stations in situations where the risk of low utilization was greater but where any reasonable increment to total generating capacity was regarded as in the public interest. We will suggest below that the period of such shortages as to justify this line of argument is now past. Here, we would simply argue that, in any event, Formula B has the disadvantage that it lessens the incentive on the part of the company to maintain tight control on expenditures because the OFILE contribution guarantees a minimum return on capital.[1] Furthermore, when a company is engaged in other activities besides thermal power generation—as indeed most companies benefiting from Formula B are—it is very difficult to isolate those costs properly chargeable to such generation from those to be ascribed to other activities.

Later in this chapter we recommend that the *recargo* system be eliminated altogether. But as we recognize that certain difficulties may make it impossible to do this immediately, we recommend, as an interim measure, that Formula A and Formula B be unified in such a way that, first, a premium would in effect be offered for increased efficiency and second, that incentives be offered that would give priority to investment in areas where high utilization is likely. This recommendation would entail the suppression of Formula B, but at the same time some modification of Formula A. As it now stands, Formula A could act as an incentive to build thermal power stations with the lowest possible initial investment but without regard to the total amount

---

[1] Formula B does not entirely remove this incentive, since the guaranteed rate of return is based on an average of the costs of three thermal plants, rather than the actual capacity costs of each plant.

of fuel consumption required. Such a power station might be most profitable to the company, but less economic to the country than alternative plants might be. Accordingly, any adjustment of the formula should be in the direction of striking a balance between initial costs and a high level of efficiency in terms of fuel consumption.

Even if the formula by which companies are remunerated for building and operating thermal power stations is appropriately adjusted, and even if it is possible, which is doubtful, to establish a relationship between that formula and the method by which companies are aided with respect to hydro plants so that there is no incentive to make uneconomic choices as between the two types of stations, the question still remains as to whether in general the policy of subsidization as a stimulus to additions in generating capacity will continue to be justified in the coming years as it has been in the past.

We calculate that consumption requirements will continue to rise in the coming five years, probably at an annual rate of increase for the period as a whole of about 8.5 percent (the average rate experienced during the period 1949–59) with the expected rate of increase being somewhat higher in the earlier years and somewhat lower in the later years (see Table 16.2). Allowing for some decline in transmission losses (which are still rather high compared with other European countries and which could be reduced) net generation would have to increase at a slightly slower rate, as would the peak load capacity. According to the best information available to the mission, investment plans already

TABLE 16.2: Estimated Power Consumption and Net Power Generation, 1960–1965

(billion kwh)

Years	Consumption	Losses	Net Generation Required	Peak Load (thousands of kw)
1960	14.5	3.5	18.0	3,360
1961	16.0	3.7	19.7	3,680
1962	17.5	3.9	21.4	4,000
1963	19.1	4.1	23.2	4,360
1964	20.7	4.4	25.1	4,720
1965	22.4	4.6	27.0	5,000

decided by the companies concerned will assure that this generating capacity is on hand, even during a dry year and making a generous allowance for transmission losses. In fact, in certain areas there is likely to develop an excess capacity. For example, one of the companies of the

INI group, Empresa Nacional Hidroelectrica del Noguera Ribagorzana, S.A. (ENHER), has contracted to export to France two billion kwh a year between 1963 and 1974 with a peak load capacity of 600,000 kw, agreeing to a severe penalty for any shortfall in the contracted supply. The company must also go to the expense of building a special transmission line to the French border. The question therefore arises whether, as a result of the incentives provided by OFILE, capacity is now being created which is not of the highest priority to the Spanish economy.

In view of the expectation that supply will at least keep up with demand—and in some areas perhaps exceed it—the mission believes that the time has come to reshape the whole structure of incentives for new investment in the electricity supply industry. We recommend that OFILE contributions to *new* generating plants—hydro and thermal —be eliminated (possibly by stages) and that part of the *recargo* be transferred to, and incorporated in, the basic rates. The effect would be to compensate power companies not for building capacity but for providing and distributing more power. This would mean that power companies would be free to make investments either in new capacity or in reducing transmission losses, whichever would appear more economical, and would eliminate a bias toward generation that no longer has any rationale and that could, if continued, readily result in the construction of excess capacity.

One of the difficulties that might be encountered in putting into effect the foregoing recommendation is that some companies are concerned only with generation or have very few distribution functions. This is true of most of the INI companies, which came into being during the 1950's when the shortage of generating capacity was acute. Most of the private companies are integrated and distribute as well as generate. Under our recommendation, a non-integrated generating company would suffer financially unless it took steps to integrate. However, integration is usually desirable technically and economically. In certain cases, private companies have offered to buy existing INI generating facilities, and this would be in conformity with the INI statute and with the recommendations that we have made in the preceding chapter. In other cases, there is the possibility of joint ventures between INI companies and private companies, such as a proposed venture between the Compania Sevillana de Electricidad, S.A. and an INI company to operate a thermal station based on the mines at Penarroya. Furthermore, a certain measure of integration could be achieved by a suitable rearrangement of the pattern of distribution. For example, Saltos del Nansa, S.A. was previously concerned only with generation, selling the power it produced to other companies for distribution; when difficulties arose in pricing arrangements, it was agreed that certain classes of industrial consumers would deal directly with Saltos del Nansa which now sells directly all the power it produces. Saltos del Sil, S.A. is another private company without its own distribution outlets and other private companies are now suggesting the allocation of some of their previous customers to Saltos del Sil as a *quid pro quo* for possible reductions in the OFILE contribution.

Thus, it seems to us that these difficulties, while not to be dismissed lightly, can be overcome. With the proposed modification in the OFILE arrangements, the incentive toward particular types of investments that might prove to be excessive in this sector of industry would be reduced and funds released for other purposes. The problem of investment priorities within the power industry would be determined more closely by market factors and incentives in favor of generating plants, beneficial in the past but now detrimental, would be removed.

SECTION VI

OTHER SECTORS

CHAPTER 17 *THE INTERNATIONAL TOURIST TRADE*

The Importance of Tourism

Spain's international tourist trade has registered notable gains in each of recent years. The Spanish Government is making efforts to maintain—and if possible to accelerate—this momentum. Tourism is a sector of dynamic growth, and its continued expansion can bring considerable benefits to the economy. Tourism has become a major source of foreign exchange; earnings were about $300 million in 1960 and, from preliminary indications, a substantially larger amount in 1961. Such earnings have contributed significantly to the favorable balance of payments and have thus made possible the purchase of an increasing quantity of imports needed for economic development. Tourism is, of course, also an important industry in itself and generates income and employment. Furthermore, many popular holiday resorts are located in areas where, apart from tourism, few other economic activities have yet been developed.

During the 1950's, the number of tourists increased at a rate of about 15–20 percent each year. The number of tourists took a spectacular jump in 1960 of some 45 percent over the previous year. Thus by 1960 the total number of tourists arriving in Spain from abroad had surpassed six million—nearly a fivefold increase in a decade (see Table 17.1)—and it appears that the numbers are still increasing at an impressive rate, although perhaps somewhat below the extraordinary one of 1959–60.

Official foreign exchange earnings did not reflect the rise in the number of tourists visiting Spain in the 1950's (see Table 17.1). This can only be ascribed to the fact that until the introduction of the stabilization program, part of the foreign exchange receipts did not find their way into official channels. But since mid-1959, the increase in the international tourist trade has been fully reflected in foreign exchange earnings going through official channels and henceforth there is no reason why this should not continue under conditions of financial stability.

Factors in the Growth of the Tourist Trade

The factors in Spain's recent successes and bright prospects in the tourist trade are not difficult to discern. Spain is blessed with a sunny,

377

pleasant climate and many attractive beaches. The appeal of the Spanish coast, particularly along the Mediterranean and on the Balearic and Canary Islands, is backed by a wide range of other attractions. Inland, against a background of varied scenic beauty, there is a rich selection of historical and cultural attractions: cathedrals, old cities and museums. And the natural charm of the Spanish people, their traditions, customs and folklore, have a wide appeal.

TABLE 17.1: Number of Tourists Visiting Spain and Tourist Receipts, 1951–1960

Year	Number of Tourists[a] (thousands)	Official Receipts from Tourism ($ million)
1951	1,263	n.a.
1952	1,485	n.a.
1953	1,710	94.1
1954	1,952	90.0
1955	2,522	96.7
1956	2,728	94.8
1957	3,187	76.9
1958	3,594	71.6
1959	4,195	158.9
1960	6,113	296.5

[a] In accordance with usual United Nations practice, the tourist is defined as any person traveling for a period of twenty-four hours or more in a country other than that in which he usually resides. Persons who stay there for more than 12 months should be considered as immigrants and not as tourists. However, visitors ashore from a sea cruise or a cruise by land are considered as tourists, even when they stay less than twenty-four hours.

Thus it is easy to understand why the foreign tourist is drawn to Spain. Furthermore, in recent years general conditions elsewhere in Europe—whence the majority of Spain's visitors come—have favored international travel. Economic prosperity in other countries has boosted the total travel market as, with social progress, leisure and travel have been accorded a higher priority among middle- and lower-income groups. The spread in automobile ownership and the development of cheap and efficient air transport have facilitated long-distance travel. The liberalization of exchange controls has made foreign travel more feasible and the simplification of travel regulations and customs formalities in many countries has made it less burdensome. Spain, for its part, has also made notable progress in easing its formalities and we would suggest that the Government take the few remaining steps to bring its requirements into line with those of other European countries, thereby enhancing the attractiveness of Spain to the potential foreign visitor.

Given the upward trend in international tourism and the inherent attractions of Spain, the comparatively cheap prices of most tourist goods and services have been decisive in inducing many foreign travelers to select Spain for their vacations. Furthermore, Spain has generally been able to offer the tourist a high standard of comfort and service. Because the major expansion in the Spanish tourist trade—particularly on the Costa Brava, the Costa del Sol and the Islands—has been relatively recent, most hotel accommodations have been built to modern standards of comfort. In addition, service is generally excellent because of the abundance of manpower in the tourist areas where there is usually little competition for labor from other industries.

Despite all these favorable factors, there is no cause for complacency. A continued expansion of the Spanish tourist trade will not take place automatically. Other Mediterranean countries are making highly competitive efforts and are opening up new attractions all the time. Fashions in travel are highly volatile and it cannot be assumed that consumer preferences for Spain will continue indefinitely. Thus, in order to maintain—and, if possible, increase—Spain's share in the total international travel market, vigorous action will have to be taken.

First of all, the appropriate amount of hotel accommodation will have to be constructed to meet future demand. Shortage of accommodation not only limits total tourist capacity directly at the time of the shortage, but has a harmful forward effect in discouraging prospective tourists, even if additional accommodation may subsequently be constructed. In any event, the existing accommodation could be better utilized if the seasonability of the market were successfully combated. If additional tourists could be encouraged to visit Spain off-season, the total number of tourist/days could be expanded. Improvements in transport and communications are another essential pre-condition to continued expansion. Finally, the maintenance or increase in Spain's share of the international travel market will depend on price stability; all the other advantages could be seriously vitiated if the advantage of Spain's comparatively low prices were impaired or eliminated.

The Role of the Government

To meet all the requirements of continued expansion, vigorous action both by the Government and by the tourist trade will, as we have stated, be necessary. We believe that, since tourism is by its nature a service industry requiring sensitive responses to changing consumer demand by a large number of individuals, it is best handled for the most part within the framework of private enterprise. Though limited to certain clearly defined areas of activity, the role of the Government, nevertheless, remains crucial. Its major task is to provide the appropriate structure within which private initiative can operate most effectively. To do so, the Government must concern itself with such collective needs as providing national publicity and tourist information and with the reasonable regulation of the industry in such fields as tourist prices. It should encourage investment in hotels and other tourist facilities but should only intervene directly where private initiative and capital are not forthcoming. It should provide the necessary infrastructure of transportation and public utilities and services. It should organize the collection of adequate statistics on which future planning must necessarily be based. And to accomplish all these tasks it should look for improvement in its own administrative organization and encourage improvement in local organization so that tourist development can be decentralized in a way that gives maximum expression to local needs.

Hotel Investment

A good example of the delicate balance between public and private initiative can be found in the provision of hotel accommodation and other forms of tourist investment. While there are a number of state-owned establishments along various much-traveled highways (albergues de carretera) and at historic sites (paradores), the majority of Spanish hotels have been privately built and are privately operated. The market outlook is such that additional accommodation can be built for the most part with private funds; hotel operations have been sufficiently successful to generate funds for further investment and to attract new capital from within Spain and abroad. But, if the amount of expansion in hotel accommodation which we envisage (see below) is to take place, it is clear that private investment will need stimulus and assistance from the Government.

Direct public financial support for hotel investment is provided by the Credito Hotelero, a revolving fund established in 1942 and administered by the Banco de Credito Industrial. Loans are granted for a period of 10 years to 25 years. On loans made from the original funds, a rate of interest of 4.5 percent was—and continues to be—charged, a rate which has always been below the market level. The Credito Hotelero has been very active and has financed the construction of nearly 7,000 hotel rooms since its inception. The 700 million pts that had been allocated to the fund over the years were virtually exhausted at the end of the 1950's because the increase in the volume of new loans out-ran repayments. After a period of inactivity, the fund was revitalized in 1960 and 1961 by the allocation first of an additional 250 million pts and then of a further 500 million pts. With the allocation of the latter amount, the method of operating the fund was slightly changed and the rate of interest on loans from these funds raised to $5\frac{1}{4}$ percent, a rate still appreciably below the market.

In the absence of recent or adequate statistics, it is difficult to estimate future hotel accommodation needs and, therefore, to estimate the financial requirements of the Credito Hotelero. It is clear that there are already shortages in certain resort areas where applicants for hotel reservations are often turned away, particularly at peak season. Furthermore, as we have suggested, total demand is likely to increase appreciably in the future.

With improvement in the collection of tourist statistics, which we recommend, and with detailed studies of such factors as seasonality and peak requirements, the Government will be in a better position to estimate future requirements. However, even on the basis of present evidence and assuming very conservative projections of future tourist demand, it is clear that total hotel investment will have to increase to such an extent that additional funds will have to be allocated to the Credito Hotelero.

To arrive at an approximate idea of the orders of magnitude involved, we have estimated that there were about 100,000 hotel rooms in 1961.[1] Assuming an increase in the number of tourists and in the demand for hotel accommodations of 10 percent annually, a total of about 60,000 additional rooms would be needed during the five-year period 1962–66. At an average cost of 400,000 pts a room, the total investment would amount to some 24,000 million pts or an annual average of 4,800 million pts. The Credito Hotelero has in the past financed some 10 percent of all new hotel construction. At about this latter rate, some 500 million pts of loans would be granted annually by Credito Hotelero.[2] We should emphasize, however, that with present information such calculations must be very rough and are designed primarily for illustrative purposes. The need for funds on the part of Credito Hotelero should be re-examined at periodic intervals and, pro-

---

[1] The hotel census for 1959 shows 82,698 rooms and we have assumed for this illustration a 10 percent increase in 1960 and 1961.

[2] This figure has been taken into account in estimating the total requirement of the Banco de Credito Industrial for new funds during the period 1962–1966 (see Chapter 15).

vided that lending policies are oriented along the lines that we indicate below, the organization should be given sufficient funds that it is able to meet expeditiously the legitimate demands that are placed upon it.

In administering the new allocations, we suggest that the policy on interest charged by the Credito Hotelero be reconsidered. We do not believe that there is any justification for rates of as wide a concessionary margin as hitherto charged. As we have stated, the outlook for the hotel business is bright and there is therefore no need to offer incentives to this degree. Furthermore, if the rates charged by the Credito Hotelero are too far below those charged by other public and private lending institutions, excessive and uneconomical building of hotels will be encouraged. The primary importance of the Credito Hotelero should lie not in its interest rate, but in its channeling of public funds into the industry, thereby augmenting the total volume of hotel investment.

By a judicious use of public funds, the public authorities can ensure that the expansion of hotel accommodation takes place where it is most needed. In this connection, we would stress that funds for tourist expansion should first be concentrated in existing areas of tourist activity, where consumer preferences have already been demonstrated and where basic facilities exist. In these areas, relatively small investments will yield immediate and high returns. If such funds were spread around the country irrespective of the previous performance of each area as a tourist attraction and the facilities that are already available, much of the additional accommodation would be under-utilized while in the popular areas the contribution to meeting the hotel shortage would be proportionately reduced. This does not mean that, in the longer run, new tourist regions might not be opened up if their potential profitability is reasonably clear; we are simply urging that public money for tourism, like all public funds, should go first to the areas of greatest return.

Another way in which the Government can influence the amount of hotel investment is by altering its policy on price controls. There is strong evidence that present officially regulated prices are too low to cover current operating costs. As a result, price controls are more often honored in the breach than in the observance. This is bad for customer relations and in the long run discourages tourism; potential clients ought to have reliable information about the costs they may be expected to incur. Moreover, the existence of price controls—even though they may frequently not be observed in practice—tends to discourage further hotel expansion by creating an additional uncertainty as to level of expected return on new investment.

While we recommend abolishing official price controls, we do not advocate that all price discipline be removed. Hoteliers should be allowed to fix their own prices on an annual basis. Different rates could be established for various seasons of the year, in accordance with the recommended policy of attempting to reduce the seasonality of the tourist trade and to extend the peak season. However, once the hotelier had established his schedule of prices for the full year, this schedule should be communicated to the Direccion General de Turismo and published in all official documents, such as the Guia de Hoteles de Espana, well in advance of the season. Hotels would then be compelled to maintain the published rates during the year and would be liable to severe sanctions for exceeding indicated prices. Under this system, the Direccion General de Turismo would continue its controlling function.

We do not believe that the abolition of price controls would lead to an excessive rise in hotel prices. Militating against such a rise would be the intensified competition between hotels as increasing numbers were built, in part as a result of the stimulus to new hotel construction that removal of the price controls itself would provide. In addition, the competition of other Mediterranean countries would induce hotel operators to maintain comparatively low prices.

Yet another source of funds for hotel investment could be found abroad. There is every indication that foreign capital would be available, provided official encouragement is forthcoming. The Government has already made significant progress in liberalizing Spanish laws concerning foreign investment and we have made recommendations concerning further liberalization in Section II. The Government has also recently removed the requirement of prior authorization for the foreign purchase of land, and this is of particular significance for the hotel business. Furthermore, the abolition of price control, as suggested above, would encourage not only domestic investors but also those from abroad.

Finally, investment in the hotel industry—as indeed in other industries—would be assisted by further liberalization of imports. Many items of hotel equipment can only be obtained abroad and it would be helpful to the hotel business if such items were added to the free list. For example, the supply of plumbing equipment is virtually limited to one Spanish company which apparently cannot furnish the full range of modern designs, and not all the furnishings and equipment are available in Spain in appropriate quantities, qualities, or form.

The motels and wayside restaurants operated directly by the Government have been intended to provide tourist accommodation at places where private facilities did not exist, such as at strategic crossroads remote from urban areas and in certain inland historic towns. They have also been conceived as models for price, comfort and personal service which, it is hoped, private operators will emulate. There were 38 establishments controlled by the Administracion Turistica Espanola in 1960 and their operating budget was approximately in balance. However, these establishments pay neither taxes nor interest charges on capital; there is also no allowance for depreciation since all new investment is financed directly by the Government through the budget of the Direccion General de Turismo. If these costs had to be met, there is no doubt that these operations would show a loss. We believe that in the future these costs should be shown in the accounts since, although they are not charged directly to the establishments concerned, they are a cost to the Government which in turn owns the establishments. We accept the fact that these establishments offer a public service, but good business administration nevertheless requires that total real costs be ascertained, particularly since in some places the government facilities are now in competition with private hotels that must cover full costs.

The object of the state-owned chain should be to supply tourist facilities where private initiative is not likely to supply them; it should not be to compete with private facilities on unequal terms. There are probably still some locations where, on this basis, additional state-owned establishments could be operated usefully, but we urge the Government to concentrate on relatively modest facilities in order to avoid a heavy capitalization from which it would be difficult to retrieve an economic return. We also recommend the sale to private interests of state-owned establishments in areas where private capital can now readily take over. Conceived in these policy terms, the state-owned establishments, while performing a vital function, are likely to have only a marginal effect on the total supply of hotel accommodation over the next few years.

Infrastructure

It is clear that there is an intimate relationship between investment in hotel and other tourist facilities and investment in the infrastructure which serves tourism and the rest of the economy. Tourist development makes additional demands on transport, water supply, posts and telecommunications and the like. There is therefore a great need to coordinate plans in all these fields and we comment on the administrative implications of this need below.

We have already discussed in Section III our recommendations with respect to transport. Here it should be noted that improvement in transport will be of great benefit to the tourist trade, particularly if the needs of the latter are borne in mind when considering the former.

It is particularly important to improve the roads: 75 percent of all tourists arriving in Spain come by road, either by private car or by bus. Many of the roads included in our suggested program in Section III serve tourism, some almost exclusively but most in combination with other purposes; a good example of the latter is the proposed East Coast autopista. However, it should be noted in this connection that there is a two-way relationship between the road program and tourism. We have recommended that priorities in the road program be related in large measure to current and prospective traffic densities. So far as roads serving resort areas are concerned, the tourist authorities are often in the best position to project likely future demand. Consequently, they should supply such projections on a regular basis to those responsible for road works so that these tourist requirements are systematically taken into account.

The less hardy motorists would come to Spain if the roads were improved. Improvements in passenger rail services along the lines recommended in the chapter on railways would help to attract more nonmotorists. Increased air transport, both internally and externally, on the appropriate routes and with suitable schedules, will also be a future necessity. Particularly important for tourist travel to the Balearic and Canary Islands is an increase in the capacity and frequency of service of the shipping lines connecting with the mainland. We have stressed this point earlier, but it deserves to be mentioned again.

Foreign tourists also expect other public services, such as water supply, the mails and telecommunications to be in good working order. Hotel accommodations have grown very rapidly in some resort areas without adequate parallel development of these public services. Investment in the latter is essential to the long-term prosperity of the tourist trade and should be considered by the Government on a priority basis.

Transportation and the other components of the infrastructure necessary to support tourist development should be provided on the basis of careful planning of resort areas to take advantage of the important opportunities for external economies. For example, the cost of bringing water supplies to a relatively large, intensively-developed resort is proportionately likely to be very much less per unit of service than to a small resort. In this connection, it is clear that numerous scattered developments, each with one or two hotels, are usually uneconomic when the cost of providing infrastructure is taken into account. Accordingly, public authority should review applications for

Credito Hotelero loans for such construction with particular care and advise prospective investors that the provision of public services to such hotels will customarily be accorded low priority.

Hotel Training

While there is no general shortage of manpower, well-trained hotel employees, speaking foreign languages, are relatively scarce. Staff training deserves the full attention of the industry and the Government. As the most urgent measure, we recommend the extension of existing hotel schools, operated by the sindicatos, especially of the well-equipped school in Madrid and of the smaller ones in Barcelona and Sevilla. Similar training centers should be opened on the north coast as well as in Mallorca and the Canaries. Likewise, training of guides and interpreters, which is already being well done, should continue on a larger scale. Some young hotel employees could be trained abroad. Owing to the shortage of labor, most traditional tourist countries in Europe would be glad to utilize Spanish personnel. Thus given an opportunity to study hotel techniques in other countries, having been trained in foreign languages and having become acquainted with international tourism, such trainees would be particularly valuable on their return.

Administrative Organization

The Ministry of Information and Tourism is responsible for tourism within the central administration, and one of its five departments, the Direccion General de Turismo (DGT), specializes in it. The Secretaria General Tecnica, among its many tasks, also concerns itself with some aspects of policy, such as planning the development of tourism. Furthermore, as we have already mentioned there are many matters of vital concern to tourism, such as roads, railways, aviation, postal services and customs and frontier formalities, which fall within the competence of other ministries and certain parastatal bodies such as RENFE and INI (Iberia, Aviaco, Atesa), as well as the sindicatos. Because of the numerous interests involved, a forward-looking policy to expand tourism can only succeed if there are specific arrangements for taking a comprehensive view of its problems, and if there is close coordination among the various authorities concerned.

An Interministerial Committee for Tourism was created in 1954, with 23 agencies represented, but it seems that it has never flourished, and in recent years it has been inactive. A committee of such a size could scarcely be expected to do more than hold periodic reviews. There have probably been informal meetings of those most interested, but something more than this is needed if the problems of tourism are to be given the attention they require.

Accordingly, we recommend the establishment of a small permanent interdepartmental committee, which by regular and frequent meetings could keep all the main problems of tourism under systematic review. Its regular members should be limited to those most intimately concerned with tourism; in addition to the representative of the Ministry of Tourism as such, members would presumably be drawn from such ministries as those of Commerce, Finance and Public Works, and from the Sindicato de Hosteleria. Whatever its permanent composition, other agencies would be consulted on an *ad hoc* basis according to the agenda. One of the functions of the committee would be to ensure coordinated action by making all agencies aware of those developments in the tourist trade which impinged on their particular interests so that all the agencies concerned could act in a coordinated fashion. For example, the ministries involved would need to know of projections in tourist trade in planning road and water supply and, by the same token, the tourist interests would need to know of road and water supply programs, in planning policy emphasis for the location of new tourist developments.

The mission suggests that the Government also consider how tourism can be given a more prominent and assured place within the administration, and its affairs brought fully within the purview of economic discussions. In any case, we think that the interdepartmental committee, to which we have referred, should be part of the permanent organization on which the Comisario del Plan will rely, so that the results of the committee's work and its submissions on policy can be reviewed in the context of economic development and, when necessary, considered by the Delegate Committee. An industry which contributes so much to the country's foreign exchange resources will be of special interest to them.

In addition, the procedure for obtaining budget allocations for the promotion of tourism should ensure that its needs are considered as a separate issue and on their own merits, so that there is no risk that they will be subordinated to the other needs of a ministry mainly concerned with different questions. A separate sub-secretariat might be worth considering on this and other grounds. Deficiencies in budgetary allocations have, for example, probably inhibited Spain's tourist pub- licity efforts abroad. Spain spends proportionately much less in this field than her main European competitors and, if Spain is to hold her own, much more attention should be given to improving this type of publicity. While increasing funds for this purpose does not guarantee such improvement, an augmented budgetary allocation is clearly a necessary pre-condition.

To implement tourist policy, more complete statistics should be obtained. At present tourism is measured only by a frontier check of the number of foreign visitors, which is in itself an inadequate guide to the demand for various types of tourist services. At least, an effort should be made to obtain hotel occupancy rates. The data could be obtained by instituting a system of hotel records giving length of stay (number of tourist nights) and geographical distribution of tourists. Use could be made of the registration card each tourist has to fill in after arrival at a hotel. Moreover, regular cooperation with the sindicatos would facilitate the more widespread use of statistics on the hotel industry. Sample surveys of travel movements in Spain should also be introduced. More complete and accurate statistics are not only needed for evaluation of tourist earnings but could guide tourist policy, especially in directing publicity abroad and in attracting foreign investors.

Local and regional initiative in tourism should be encouraged. While the Ministry of Information and Tourism has a Delegation in every Province (Junta Provincial de Informacion Turismo y Educacion Popular), delegates are also occupied with the other tasks of the Ministry and are, as a rule, not in a position to give enough encouragement to local tourism by adequate publicity. The creation of local and regional Centros de Iniciativa y Turismo, financed and backed by local authorities, industry and trade, should therefore be generalized. There is a strong case for transferring the proceeds of the tourist tax (the *poliza del turismo*) to local authorities for the promotion of tourism. In this process of encouraging local initiative, it is important to obtain the collaboration of the local business communities, through chambers of commerce or retail trade associations, in order to promote the sale of Spanish goods to foreign businesses and to improve methods of packaging and delivery abroad.

In conclusion, it should not be thought that in making the foregoing recommendations and suggestions we are unmindful of the remarkable progress shown in recent years in the development of the tourist industry in Spain. Our concern is to see that it is consolidated, and even extended, in the years ahead, when competition will be severe, because it has a vital contribution to make to the economic development of the country.

CHAPTER 18 *EDUCATION AND SCIENTIFIC RESEARCH*

Although the mission was not asked to make a detailed study of investment in education, beyond an appraisal of its cost, the connection between education and economic development is so important that the report would be incomplete without some reference to it.

In order to expand and modernize the economy, the Spanish Government is expecting substantial sums to be devoted to fixed investment. However, such expectations will not produce the desired results unless proper attention is also given to investment in human resources, since the supply of skilled manpower will be an important factor in determining the rate of economic growth. If foreign trade is to be expanded, and Spanish products are to be competitive, Spanish producers must be able to match the skills of their competitors. Rising output with modern techniques will increase the demand for skilled manpower at all levels—a demand which can only be met if the output of the educational system is planned accordingly.

Fortunately, by virtue of its participation in the Mediterranean Regional Project organized by OEEC (now OECD), the Spanish Government has already agreed to undertake studies of its educational requirements for the next fifteen years. The Government is preparing a manpower study to be related to general plans for economic development and has promised to establish priorities in educational planning. In the preparation of this long-term program, the Government will be guided by the methodology developed by OECD and will be in regular consultation with that organization.

The mission welcomes the decision of the Government to participate in the project and hopes that it will press on with these important studies so that the balanced development of the educational system may proceed with the minimum delay. Because the outcome of these studies must be awaited and because the mission itself did not make a detailed study of Spanish education, we will content ourselves with commenting on certain aspects of the educational system which we believe should be accorded some priority in the formulation of a long-term program.

Among the probable objectives of such a program, we believe two stand out as worthy of particular attention. First, there is the need to ensure that all children within the present compulsory school ages (6–11) receive an education; secondly, there is a need to provide a basis for

389

professional and technical training for those who continue with their education. In the process of modernizing the economy and increasing productivity, techniques will be constantly changing, and flexibility of mind and adaptability in the use of skills are important. In particular, the prosperity of the rural community in many parts of Spain, where natural conditions are difficult, will largely depend on a readiness to try new patterns of production and to discard old methods. A sound general education is indispensable for all this.

The second objective is to increase the numbers receiving scientific and technical education, both at secondary school and university levels, and especially the former, since demands for skilled manpower will grow sharply with the expansion of the economy.

Until recently the educational system in Spain did not dispose of sufficient means to keep pace with present-day needs, but since 1956 there has been a considerable effort to expand it. However, much remains to be done. In planning for the future, there will be a need for much more statistical information and other data required to establish a model of projected educational patterns, including the flow of students and teachers and the concomitant needs for facilities and equipment; there will also be a need for the interchange of information between the Ministry of Education and the Comisariado del Plan.

Primary Education

Primary education in Spain is designed to cover eight years of studies, normally starting at the age of 6 and continuing up to and including the age of 13; in some schools, facilities are also provided for pre-school activities for children between 3 years and 5 years of age. School attendance is legally compulsory from the age of 6 up to and including the age of 11. In essence, then, six years of primary education are currently regarded as terminal for those not proceeding to higher studies, but an additional two years of elementary education is required of those who do.

Although school attendance is legally compulsory from 6 until 11, there are still a number of children who do not in fact attend school during these ages, particularly in the more remote areas. This is largely because of lack of school facilities and teachers.

The Spanish Government has made considerable effort to close this gap. In 1957 a building program was initiated and by October 1, 1961, about 15,000 new classrooms had been completed and a further 9,000 were under construction and expected to be completed by the end of 1962. Of this combined total of 24,000 classrooms, 13,500 were net additions to the total classroom capacity and the remaining 10,500 were replacements for existing inadequate premises. Thus, allowing a national average of 40 pupils a classroom and assuming that the 9,000 classrooms under construction on October 1, 1961, are in fact all completed by the end of 1962, total net capacity will have been augmented by more than 540,000 pupil-places by the latter date as compared with 1957.

Despite this remarkable achievement, the Ministry of Education calculates that at the end of 1962, there will still be some 180,000[1] children aged 6–11 for which accommodation will still not exist and a further 220,000 such children attending school in very inadequate buildings. Accordingly, the Ministry believes that it will be necessary to complete the construction program after 1962 by building 10,000 more classrooms, 4,500 for additional classroom capacity and 5,500 for replacement classrooms.

The mission fully endorses the objective of providing accommodation for all children aged 6–11 with the minimum possible delay. But we are not in a position to judge whether or not the above *aggregate* figures for the country as a whole are an appropriate reflection of the *net* needs taking a number of factors into account. Trends in internal migration must be considered both in locating the areas of greatest construction needs and in assessing aggregate requirements. Since internal migration is so closely affected by economic developments, it is most important that there should be consultation between the Ministry of Education and the Comisariado del Plan in devising future school expansion programs.

It is not only important to provide for an increase in the quantity of primary education but also for an improvement in its *quality*. Many schools are woefully short of instructional equipment and books; more money must be allocated for these purposes. In many remote areas, education is available only in one- or two-room schools. In increasing classroom capacity, care must be taken to phase construction so that the necessary equipment can be provided on completion and so that teachers will be available to man them.

There is at present no shortage of new recruits to the primary teaching staff. In 1961 there were 18,400 applicants, all graduates of teacher training schools, for 7,000 available teacher posts. The problem is to retain entrants into the teaching profession throughout their careers. Salary scales are low: a single teacher starts at 16,920 pts a year, and the national average would be about 25,000 pts a year, to which a small

---

[1] Exclusive of population increase in the interim.

housing allowance is added if no living quarters are provided. Such scales are not conducive to teachers giving their undivided attention to their work or to attracting and retaining the best qualified, particularly now that economic expansion is under way. There is already a drain to more lucrative posts. The mission therefore hopes that the Spanish Government will give careful consideration to the question of improving the terms of employment of teachers.

We understand that the Spanish Government is actively considering raising the legal school-leaving age to 14. If so, the question of what and how the children, who would have otherwise left school two years previously, should be taught becomes critical. At present, the seventh and eighth year primary studies are designed as preparatory to further education because, being voluntary, they are usually taken by pupils who are going on with higher studies. Once the seventh and eighth years of study become compulsory for all children, the proportion will rise of pupils for which this stage of education will be terminal; accordingly, thought will have to be given to modifications of curricula and other policy adjustments.

In considering raising the legal school-leaving age, the problem of "wastage" would also have to be considered. A number of children repeat grades and then drop out of school before reaching the terminal grade. There are of course many variables involved in wastage, but until the problem has been more clearly understood and steps have been taken to reduce it, it would be very difficult to institute a meaningful extended system of compulsory education. The decision as to the appropriate timing of such a move will obviously take into account the outcome of the studies now being taken in conjunction with OECD and which undoubtedly will provide specific data on some of the factors to which we refer.

So far as pre-school enrollments for the 3–5 group are concerned, only a relatively small proportion of these children can be accommodated at present. To fill this gap would be very expensive. We believe that the problem is less urgent than meeting the needs of children 6 to 11 and, possibly, to 13, particularly since nonofficial agencies often meet the demand for pre-schooling where it is felt. Consequently, we recommend that expenditures for these purposes from public sources not be accorded a high priority in the coming few years.

The Emphasis on Technical Education at the Secondary Level

The expansion of scientific and technical education will have to be planned with some care, particularly below university level, where the need seems to be greatest. In recent years there has been a welcome increase in secondary education in general, but we calculate that only about 15 percent of the children of secondary school age are currently in school; this is a low proportion and we believe steps ought to be taken at once to make it possible to increase it. There also have been some increases in the numbers specializing in scientific and technical subjects. But the latter only represents a small proportion of the total. In 1958/59, for example, there were, apart from those in teacher training and art schools, 554,000 pupils in secondary schools, of which only 133,000 were in diversified courses (see Table 18.1).

TABLE 18.1: Secondary School Enrollments in Spain, 1958/59ª

(thousands)

Course	Pupils
Diversified:	
Bachillerato Laboral	13.1
Universidades Laborales^b	3.1
Formacion Profesional Industrial^c	61.2
Escuelas de Comercio	31.4
Technical Schools (medium grade)^d	24.2
Subtotal	133.0
General:	
Bachillerato General^e	421.4
Total	554.4

ª The last year for which statistics were available for *all* comparable courses.
b This course is part general high school and part specializing in sciences and administration (age 10–16).
c Two-three years elementary education followed by two-three years specializing in industrial technology and craftsmanship (age 12–16).
d Technical schools for Peritos (up to 19).
e General High School (age 10–16).

SOURCE: *Datos y Cifras de la Ensenanza en Espana, 1960,* Ministerio de Educacion Nacional, Secretaria General Tecnica.

Although estimates of the deficiency in technically trained personnel vary considerably, all seem to agree that it is substantial, and this must be a matter of concern to the Spanish authorities. The training of highly skilled workmen and the middle range of technicians (such as assistant engineers, farm and works managers, draftsmen, experts in market research, accountants and the like) requires a good general secondary education, probably of longer duration for the latter category, supplemented by specialized training.

While good progress continues to be made in expanding specialized secondary training, scarcely 30,000 students can yet be successfully completing these courses in any one year. Such manpower studies as have been made indicate that demand far exceeds such supply,[2] particularly for certain specialisms. There are only some 3,000–4,000 students of agriculture and forestry in the Escuelas Tecnicas de Grado Medio, so that in five years' time the annual output could not be much more than 600; in view of the urgent agricultural problems (see Section IV), this number will obviously be insufficient to man the appropriate programs. The same is true in other fields of specialization.

It is thus clear that the supply of trained specialists at the secondary level needs to be expanded, probably in all categories. We hope that, in the current studies on the long-term educational program, priority could be given to reaching some agreement, even though provisional, on the estimated numbers of technically trained manpower below university level, who will be required each year to augment, and improve, the quality of the labor force, both in industry and agriculture, according to the trends foreseen in the economic development program, so that no time is lost in taking action to fill the gaps. Before any large-scale investment is undertaken there should be a clearer plan of the kind of specialization required, what types of training establishments would be most useful and where they should be located. As an interim measure, while these plans are being formulated, existing plans could proceed and further expansion be undertaken in this part of the educational system, without much risk that the output would exceed requirements in any sector.

Attention will also have to be paid to the problems of wastage, particularly in technical and specialized secondary education. There is some evidence that the attrition rate between the first year of a course of studies and the final year is considerable. We do not have information on dropout rates, but they must be relatively high. Because these forms of education occur at an age level above that of compulsory attendance the problem of retention can be acute. A number of solutions are possible: improved pre-selection of candidates, augmented vocational guidance, curricula revision, guaranteed posts for qualified students, bursaries and the like. The Government will undoubtedly wish to consider all these questions. It would, after all, be extremely wasteful to invest in an expansion of first-year intakes without a commensurate increase in the output of fully qualified students completing the entire course.

[2] The Ministry of National Education has estimated probable annual demand by industry for young people with specialized training at 45,000, and the sindicatos expect this demand to rise to 75,000.

Scientific and Technical Education at the University Level

With expansion of the economy, there will also be an increasing demand for the top grades, not only managers and administrators, but engineers and scientific and technological research workers, graduating from the higher technical schools and universities. The former have made rapid strides: in 1954/55 there were 3,573 students registered, in 1958/59, 7,908 and in 1960/61, 14,068. It was expected that there would be about 1,000 graduates in 1961/62 rising to 2,500 in 1963/64. In the universities there has also been a small increase proportionately in the number of students in the science faculties, but not enough to change the balance in favor of the traditional schools. Between 1954/55 and 1958/59, the number of students registered in the science faculties rose from 11,993 to 15,063 but, since there was also a rise in total university enrollment, the proportion in these faculties only moved from 20 percent to 23 percent. This mission would once again draw attention to the problem of wastage. In the period 1952/53 to 1954/55, the average number of students registered in faculties of science was 12,600; but the numbers graduating in 1957/58 and 1958/59 were only 475 and 565 respectively. The Spanish authorities should be chary about investing in new capacity before this problem is solved.

Among the questions to be considered in the current studies on the future of the educational system will be the extension of facilities in the higher technical institutes, for example, more opportunities for specializing in the various branches of engineering, better laboratories, workshops and so on. But it also seems a matter of urgency to deal with the question whether existing facilities are being used to the full, and if not, why not. There seems to be some evidence that the system of admissions remains restrictive: the standards of selectivity applied have undoubtedly limited the number of students registered in the higher technical institutes. Once the rate of admissions can be increased, new institutes will have to be established, and we suggest that a better geographical distribution of such facilities should be obtained by locating new institutes in parts of Spain other than Madrid.

Vocational Training for Adults

Education is a long process and the reforms now being considered will not turn out the finished products for many years to come; nor will they solve the problem of the present surplus labor from the land which, for the most part, will be unskilled. This gives added importance, particularly over the coming years, to the purposeful use of adult education programs geared directly to immediate economic aims. These programs should be on a coordinated basis, relating literacy and other general courses for adults to specific vocational and adaptation courses.

One interesting program is the Formacion Profesional Acelerada run by the sindicatos, under which adult unskilled workers received intensive training for six months to make them skilled in one of a number of trades. There were four centers at the end of 1960, but it was planned to have 21 centers by 1965 through which some 10,000 skilled workers would pass annually. The objectives of such a program are clearly well-chosen, provided there is sufficient flexibility to organize training for the skills most in demand as technical processes change or new industries develop.

There are obviously many ways in which such types of programs can be fostered. The mission therefore suggests that the Government arrange, in collaboration with the sindicatos, State industry and private industry, for a comprehensive inquiry into this urgent and important question, which would be complementary to the inquiries on the long-term needs of the educational system for economic development. The training programs for adult workers, designed to provide them with the new skills demanded by modern industry and agriculture, should be considered in conjunction with other educational programs such as those designed to provide vocational training for youths who have terminated their general education at the elementary level.[3] It is necessary to make an assessment of existing facilities, public and private, and how they can best be augmented to turn out annually an agreed number of trainees; and how the responsibility and finance will be shared by the State, by municipalities, by sindicatos, or by industry.

One important question to be examined before extending such programs is cost. For example, it is estimated that, after allowing for amortization of buildings and machinery, the 21 centers comprising the Formacion Profesional Acelerada would cost 311 million pts a year, or 30,000 pts for each trainee (of which 15,000 pts is required for his subsistence allowance). It must be recognized that the courses and the type of trainee require installations and instruction which differ from those to be found in other technical educational centers, but the cost of one of these centers (buildings and installations) is put at 38 million pts, or nearly double an education establishment for a Formacion Profesional Industrial which would cater to 500 full-time pupils. It might

[3] See also Chapter 14 for suggestions on Escuelas de Capataces and training for agriculture.

be worth considering whether the buildings are too elaborate, or whether there is any possibility of having more specialization in the different centers. The mission believes that, while facilities must be adequate, priority should be given to providing some sort of training to the largest number of adults in as short a time as possible and that, accordingly, careful cost control at each center is vital.

Scientific Research

Scientific research in Spain is mainly carried on in institutions established under the auspices of the Consejo Superior de Investigaciones Cientificas (CSIC). This body, which is responsible to the Minister of National Education, was legally constituted in 1939 to develop and organize research in Spain and, within the limits of its resources, it has succeeded in doing this. It has organized research in the various branches of science under the administration of eight Patronatos. It has also concerned itself with encouraging research in the universities, training scientists, awarding fellowships, promoting international exchanges of students and publishing. But, though it had this wide jurisdiction and there are comparatively few private institutions in Spain, research was also undertaken in several other institutes established by various ministries; and this, among other things, led to the creation of the Comision Asesora de Investigacion Cientifica y Tecnica (Advisory Committee) on February 7, 1958, to advise the Government how to formulate a national research program. The committee submitted its recommendations, but during the stabilization period action to implement them was deferred.

If Spain is to undertake industrial expansion under competitive conditions and raise productivity, in an age when such rapid advances are being made in science and technology, the country cannot afford to lag behind many of her closest trading partners who are giving considerable emphasis to scientific research.

The mission believes that the formulation of a national policy for scientific research should be pressed. The Government clearly had this in mind when the Advisory Committee was set up, and it seems desirable and opportune to proceed forthwith to agree upon the program, and to provide funds and facilities for implementing it. The mission believes that, in establishing such a program, the following points are important.

The work of all institutes and other centers of research, whether under the auspices of CSIC, ministries, or other patrons, should be coordinated to ensure that they undertake the most urgent and useful kinds of research which would be consistent with the economic development program and an aid to the industrial and agricultural expansion foreseen therein. For instance, the need to increase productivity on the land would call for coordination between the institutes of the Ministry of Agriculture[4] and those of the CSIC, like Alonso de Herrera, who would be specially interested.

The need to stimulate the interest of private industry in research should be given close attention.[5] If industries do not organize research on their own account, they should be made aware of the services and facilities provided by the Patronatos and their institutes, and they should be encouraged to use them to the full. This will entail new efforts to organize the dissemination of information by CSIC, and to establish close working relations with individual enterprises or representatives of industries. The CSIC and INI group have already been collaborating effectively through "coordinated institutes."[6]

There are two questions affecting the institutes themselves. It appears that some of them either lack equipment or possess obsolescent equipment. This is bound to stultify research work. One of the first tasks should be to make good the deficiencies, and provide the institutes with up-to-date equipment, from abroad if necessary, since foreign exchange is no longer a problem. Secondly, it is said that the emoluments are no longer sufficient to enable highly qualified scientists to undertake research work on a full-time basis, though this need was fully recognized in the decree of June 13, 1951, describing the requirements for their career. This could have serious consequences. Continuity and concentration are needed for this work, but this is not possible if research workers have to find other means of support. Furthermore, there is a risk that they will be tempted to take remunerative posts in other countries, where there is a great demand for trained scientists. If these difficulties are to be overcome and the economy is to benefit from research, it does seem to be a matter of some urgency to review the present conditions of service for research workers and their assistants. Their remuneration should be determined at a level which will enable them to devote full time to research work and provide the institutes with the permanent staff they need, both now and in the future.

[4] Instituto Nacional de Investigaciones Agronomos and Instituto Forestal de Investigaciones y Experiencia.

[5] In this connection, the Government has recently authorized the setting up of Asociaciones de Investigacion for groups of enterprises under the supervision of the Comision Asesora (decree 22 Sept. 1961).

[6] e.g., Calvo Sotelo and Piritas Espanolas.

There must clearly be many centers of research throughout the country, but the maintenance of nearly two hundred may involve too great a dispersal of resources. The mission is unable to judge of this, but it may be opportune, when the needs for re-equipping them are reviewed, to consider whether some concentration would be practicable and lead to a greater economy of effort and better coordination.

There seems no doubt that scientific research in Spain has been hampered by lack of funds. Apart from some grants from private sources and earnings from contracts with private industry, the bulk of the funds come directly or indirectly from budget allocations. The mission has not seen any detailed statements since 1958, but it was estimated that the total funds available for research in that year from all sources were some 460 million pts, or one-tenth of one percent of the national income. If the scientific and technical resources of the country are to be mobilized under a national program for research and in the interest of economic development, and if the importance of continuity is recognized, a substantial increase in budget allocations must be foreseen, even allowing for the possibility of higher receipts from private sources. In our view, such an investment will be well worthwhile.

CHAPTER 19 *HOUSING*

Housing is an important sector of the Spanish economy, absorbing a substantial proportion of both public and private investment funds. It is also a field of considerable complexity. The mission reviewed the housing and urban development scene in Spain, the relationships between the various organizations and instrumentalities involved, the forms of financing provided and the results obtained in some detail. However, it feels that the outstanding need is for further study of the demand for housing of various kinds by different income groups or regions. This should be facilitated by the results of the 1960 census. In this summary, we have confined our comments to a few general matters concerning the Government's approach to housing conditions.

Government Policy

Housing has been in short supply in Spain for many years. In the 1920's and the 1930's, private investment in housing slowed perceptibly, mainly because of distortions in the market brought about by the imposition of rent controls. The devastation during the war greatly aggravated the housing shortage, and it was well into the 1940's before reconstruction efforts made appreciable headway. Although a ten-year housing program was adopted in 1944, construction was on a modest scale until the 1950's. With the institution of a five-year plan for 1955–60, housing construction picked up markedly, particularly toward the end of the period (see Table 19.1).

The Government has assumed major responsibility for housing finance and construction. Encouragement is given to private builders, but they depend on the public authorities for important financial benefits, in the form of grants or subsidies, loans, or tax exemptions. In addition, the Government itself, or one of its chosen instrumentalities, directly provides much new housing construction.

Given the shortage situation of crisis proportions during the 1950's, the heavy direct involvement of the Government in housing construction is readily understandable. But now that there has been an impressive increase in housing construction, the mission believes that the Government can turn away from a policy of indiscriminate stimulation of housing starts to one which is more selective. The Government should concentrate its direct action on those needs which are both urgent and unlikely to be met in the private market, leaving the rest of

400

the task to that market, in which its own role would be limited to special financial supports.

A first step in the reorientation of Government policy along these lines would be to reduce the number of public and quasi-public agencies operating in the housing field and to encourage more coordination and more specialization in the functions of the agencies that remain. These functions include making loans, granting subsidies, building houses for sale and renting houses. We feel that the Government would

TABLE 19.1: Dwelling Units Completed in Spain, 1951–1960[a]

Year	Number of Units
1951	30,985
1952	34,497
1953	36,502
1954	47,467
1955	57,898
1956	73,141
1957	75,203
1958	77,064
1959	111,838
1960	127,842

[a] Excluding private building unaided by State legislation, estimated at an additional 10–15 percent.

have a clearer view of the housing program and of its cost, if a sharper distinction were made between these functions as between agencies and, certainly, within agencies where more than one function is combined. There are a number of ways in which this could be accomplished, and while selection of the appropriate one is a matter for the Government to determine, we would stress the importance of prompt attention to this problem.

The need for coordination applies also to the actual construction of housing. At present, hundreds of thousands of buildings have been started but many remain incomplete because of lack of coordination in the flow of credit, the failure to provide essential public services (e.g., water, sewerage, access roads) to accompany the projects and the often deficient organization in the contracting and building industry. The number of dwelling units under construction in the first half of 1961 was said to total 450,000, with almost 100,000 of these in Madrid alone.

While the completion of those units with an immediate prospect of occupancy should be a matter of high priority, some already completed projects are unoccupied because their location has been poorly selected with reference to trends in economic growth or because they have been built to cost standards so high as to encounter a deficiency in effective demand. At the same time, the housing needs of large sectors of the Spanish population have scarcely been met, especially in rural areas where thousands of families still live in primitive caves and shacks. The Direccion General de Vivienda estimates that there are more than 400,-000 families living in units unfit for habitation. There are also more than 600,000 families sharing dwellings with other families and many of such dwellings must be overcrowded to the point of creating health hazards. Population increase and new family formation are creating additional housing needs.

Low-Income Housing

It is because of this paradox of unoccupied dwellings of certain types in certain places side by side with serious shortages elsewhere that the mission suggests that the Government be highly selective in its future policies. The principal deficiency now appears to be in housing for the very low-income groups, and a significant improvement in housing conditions and living standards could ensue if the Government were to concentrate its financial and construction efforts on alleviating this deficiency.

A public housing program directed towards meeting the housing needs of the lower income groups would inevitably involve a substantial subsidy, in one form or another, from the Government. Thus, in determining which housing should be constructed and operated by the public authorities directly, the criterion should be the degree to which public financial assistance is needed. The Government's obligation to supervise the disposition of public funds is such that, if those funds become predominant, it may be more efficient for the public authority to take direct responsibility without the interposition of intermediaries. The system whereby subsidies, such as those for "viviendas subvencionadas," are paid to builders does not appear to have led to the requisite concentration of building on the most acute needs.

Even with a redirection of public assistance along these lines, it will be many years before all low-income families are provided with housing that meets minimum standards. But only by concentrating public effort on these needs is there likelihood of making appreciable headway. As the economy develops, conditions will change and so will the definition of minimum standards. Future programing ought, therefore, to concentrate on medium-term (five or six years) and to be cast in more specific terms as part of the national development program.

Rural Self-Help Program

A large proportion of the low-income groups can be found in rural areas. To date these areas have been less benefited than urban areas by the various forms of public assistance for housing construction. The dispersion of rural population makes it difficult to provide assistance effectively through conventional types of programs, and if the needs of these rural areas are to be met with reasonable speed and within reasonable cost limits, new techniques for providing shelter will have to be considered.

One of the most hopeful possibilities is for the public authorities to supply minimum housing which can then be improved through self-help programs. Under such programs, plots are laid out, foundations put in place, access roads built and water, sewerage and power connected—and often rudimentary structure is supplied. The occupants are then expected to improve their units by their own labor with technical assistance from a central organization. Financial assistance, in the form of subsidized materials and special credits, is also provided. Cooperatives and other non-profit groups can usefully assist in such programs.

There are many examples of self-help projects in Spain, the experience of which should be studied. A notable one is the Constructora Benefica "San Vicente de Paul" of Murcia. Several are under way in the Madrid and Barcelona areas which appear to be producing results by reducing construction costs through the collaboration, organization and self-help efforts of the people themselves. This experience, as with that of the housing cooperatives, remains to be generalized and supported by an adequate organizational structure. It should be possible to apply such techniques, with some modifications, in rural areas also.

To produce best results, aided self-help projects need sound technical assistance and orientation. The mission suggests that the Instituto Nacional de Vivienda should establish a special new section to accumulate experience and devise techniques for application in this important field.

Support for the Private Sector

Apart from constructing or aiding the construction of low-income housing, the Government's principal role in housing should be, as we have indicated, one of stimulating and supporting private investment. With the development of the Spanish economy and the growth of personal incomes, the proportion of public financing of housing should decrease, while the proportion of resources from the private sector increases. We realize of course that this must be a gradual process, but with the establishment of an appropriate institutional structure and the requisite facilities it should be possible to encourage greater activity on the part of private capital.

The principal forms of public support for increased private activity in the housing sector would be twofold: first, the establishment of a national system of insurance for private mortgages, and secondly, the provision of supplementary credit, in the form of second mortgages. First mortgages would continue to be obtained in the private sector, from banks, insurance companies and other financial institutions. It is to be hoped that the Cajas Generales de Ahorro, once they are released from the obligation to invest part of their assets in government securities (see Section II), would take a more active role in housing finance. The Government can help to stimulate this development of private credit through the establishment of a mortgage insurance system, now in use in a number of countries, which would guarantee repayment of the first mortgages.

Credit provided by the Government for private housing construction should, in our view, be in the form of a system of second mortgages, limited to a designated proportion of the total cost of the housing unit or development. At present a high proportion of government credit in the housing field is interest free or at artificially low rates of interest. We see no justification for this; such loans are in effect a subsidy and represent a real cost to the economy, and we believe that any subsidy burden assumed should be concentrated on low-income housing, in accordance with our recommendations above. The objective of government action should be to inject public capital into the private market where it can be most effective as a supplement to private initiative, *not* to subsidize the consumer.

The public credit mechanism can be made to serve social purposes in other ways. For example, the period of amortization can be stretched in the case of those less able to make quick repayments.

Private investment in housing is often discouraged by the existence of rent controls which tend to inhibit an adequate return on capital. Rent controls have led to serious undermaintenance of dwellings, a problem of particular importance in Spain where, according to the 1950 census, 75 percent of the housing units had been built before 1900. In addition, the controls have often resulted in inefficient use of existing dwelling space.

Many authorities are agreed that the time has come gradually to eliminate rent control, in part because of the large volume of housing construction of the last several years. The removal of rent control should be a gradual process over a period of years, with areas selected for decontrol as their housing shortgages ease. The first candidates would appear to be Bilbao and Madrid. The precedent now exists of using the cost of living index to revise rents annually, fixed on a square meter basis, for dwelling units built under the subsidy legislation. This precedent should be extended on an interim basis to ease the transition to rent decontrol by applying such a formula. Another principle should be to lift rent control progressively with prior attention to the larger, luxury dwellings. Also, the removal of rent controls should be linked with some obligation by the landlord to make needed repairs and establish good maintenance practices.

The Construction Industry

The construction industry in Spain, as in most countries, accounts for a sizable proportion of national employment, and therefore merits particularly careful attention. Housing and urbanization provide the major share of employment within the construction industry on a continuing basis. Of the 650,000 to 675,000 estimated to be employed in the industry as a whole, more than 330,000 were engaged in housing and urbanization activities in 1960. The construction industry suffers from fragmentation—there are more than 6,000 general contractors—and a lack of capital for modernization and expansion of operations. There is no longer a shortage of building materials as in the past; rather the problem is one of providing greater opportunities to employ profitably the materials that are increasingly available from national industries.

While the construction industry has done a good job of keeping down most costs, it has so far had only minor success in reducing overall construction time for completion of its projects. Such delays add to costs which are otherwise reasonable.

The mission considers that the contracting process within the building industry should be reviewed, to put more of a premium on compliance in all respects, especially construction schedules. The successful experience of large projects, such as Ochoargoa in Bilbao, with 3,660 dwelling units completed in record time with excellent results, should be analyzed to arrive at general conclusions and new recommended procedures for construction supported by public aids. Better credit facilities should be available to contractors to enable them to acquire modern equipment and machinery for improving their operations. Public lending agencies, particularly the Instituto Nacional de

Vivienda, the Instituto para la Reconstruccion Nacional and the Banco Hipotecario, should make greater efforts to speed up their certifications and payments for works, once completed. Otherwise, many contractors find themselves increasingly victims of private lenders who charge high rates of interest for funds advanced on a short-term basis.

Research and Training

Spain has had some useful if limited experience with housing research and training, but for the most part this field of activity has been neglected. In addition, what little body of organized and continuing research is in progress is not brought to bear effectively on decisions for particular programs. Experience is not being accumulated in a systematic way, nor are sufficient basic surveys being conducted to aid in the formulation and evaluation of policies and programs. Considering the size of public and private investment in housing, basic and applied research efforts should be greatly intensified. Again, we do not wish to prescribe the particular institutional arrangements that might be most suitable, but it is clear that the Government has an important responsibility in ensuring that such arrangements come into being. Some of this research could yield immediate benefits in the maintenance, design and construction of building units, but it should also be addressed to broader social and economic aspects of housing. To this end, research should bring to bear the combined efforts of economists, engineers, architects, sociologists and others toward the solution of housing problems.

Urban Development

Housing needs must be considered within a framework of broader urbanization trends, and construction of housing must be closely related to other aspects of urban development. Because migration from rural to urban areas is taking place at a rapid rate in Spain, it is particularly important that adequate investment be allocated to provide the improved land and the structure of public services necessary to accommodate this inflow. At the same time, it is recognized that existing local public services, especially water and sewer systems, urban transport, markets, streets, etc., in many municipalities are deteriorated or outmoded, and need replacement, as part of the urban renewal process.

In the view of the mission, Spain's efforts to attend to these needs, at present focused at the national level through the land development agency of the Ministry of Housing (Gerencia de Urbanizacion), the

Bank for Local Credit (Banco de Credito Local) and the Office of Provincial Plans of the Presidency (Planes Provinciales), should be complemented by further measures to strengthen and invigorate local governments more directly, as has been done in the case of Barcelona, so that they will be better able to attend to their needs through added resources provided by more flexible revenue sources, as well as improved local planning and administration. Local governments should also be encouraged to join together, as has been done in the Bilbao area, for planning purposes and the provision of services on a metropolitan basis. The Office of Urban Planning (Direccion de Urbanismo) of the Ministry of Housing should complement its broader regional physical planning studies by fostering more detailed programing and budgeting among the agencies concerned with the execution of local public works and services.

As a step toward clarifying the general criteria which should be applied toward these objectives, the mission believes it important that the planning and programing for the lending and grant-in-aid activities of the Government be based on more specific surveys of investment requirements for local services than appear to be available at the present time.